Heritage and Tourism

Place, encounter, engagement

Edited by Russell Staiff,
Robyn Bushell and Steve Watson

Routledge
Taylor & Francis Group

LONDON AND NEW YORK

First published 2013
by Routledge
2 Park Square, Milton Park, Abingdon, Oxon OX14 4RN

Simultaneously published in the USA and Canada
by Routledge
711 Third Avenue, New York, NY 10017

Routledge is an imprint of the Taylor & Francis Group, an informa business

British Library Cataloguing in Publication Data
A catalogue record for this book is available from the British Library

Library of Congress Cataloging in Publication Data
A catalog record for this book has been requested

ISBN: 978-0-415-53264-8 (hbk)
ISBN: 978-0-415-53265-5 (pbk)
ISBN: 978-0-203-07461-9 (ebk)

Typeset in Baskerville
by FiSH Books Ltd, Enfield

Printed and bound in Great Britain by the MPG Books Group

He ritage and Tourism

The complex relationship between heritage places and people, in the broadest sense, can be considered dialogic, a communicative act that has implications for both sides of the 'conversation'. This is the starting point for *Heritage and Tourism*. However, the 'dialogue' between visitors and heritage sites is complex. 'Visitors' have, for many decades, become synonymous with 'tourists' and the tourism industry and so the dialogic relationship between heritage places and tourists has produced a powerful critique of this often-contested relationship.

Further, at the heart of the dialogic relationship between heritage places and people is the individual experience of heritage where generalities give way to particularities of geography, place and culture, where anxieties about the past and the future mark heritage places as sites of contestation, sites of silences, sites rendered political and ideological, sites powerfully intertwined with representation, sites of the imaginary and the imagined.

Under the aegis of the term 'dialogues' the heritage/tourism interaction is reconsidered in ways that encourage reflection about the various communicative acts between heritage places and their visitors and the ways these are currently theorised, so as to either step beyond – where possible – the ontological distinctions between heritage places and tourists or to re-imagine the dialogue or both. *Heritage and Tourism* is thus an important contribution to understanding the complex relationship between heritage and tourism.

Russell Staiff is a Senior Lecturer in Cultural Heritage at the Institute for Culture and Society and the School of Social Science and Psychology, University of Western Sydney, Australia.

Robyn Bushell is an Associate Professor at the Institute for Culture and Society and the School of Social Science and Psychology, University of Western Sydney, Australia.

Steve Watson is Principal Lecturer at the Business School, York St John University, UK and Book Reviews Editor on the *International Journal of Heritage Studies*.

Key Issues in Cultural Heritage
Series Editors: William S. Logan and Laurajane Smith

Contents

List of illustrations

List of tables

List of contributors

María de los Ángeles Plaza-Mejía, PhD, is Senior Lecturer of Managerial Skills and Strategic Management at the University of Huelva, where she is responsible for its Business Internationalization Programme. She is an active member of the research group on 'Innovation and Development Strategies in Tourist Firms' (GEIDETUR). Her research is mainly focused on industrial tourism.

Robyn Bushell, PhD, is Associate Professor at the Institute for Culture and Society, Director of Academic Programs in the School of Social Science at the University of Western Sydney. Her work focuses on the values underpinning everyday life, quality of life, sustainable development and heritage management. She works closely with a range of national and international bodies related to heritage conservation (including UNESCO World Heritage Centre, International Union for Conservation of Nature [IUCN], UN-World Tourism Organization) in formulation policies and planning frameworks, in particular community development strategies involving tourism. Her current research interests examine the entangled relationships between the local and global and between conservation and development in heritage places.

Denis Byrne, PhD, leads the cultural heritage research programme at the Office of Environment and Heritage NSW and is an Adjunct Professor at the University of Technology, Sydney. His interests centre on the heritage of human engagements with nature in Australia. His research in Asia has concerned the manner in which popular religion and belief in the supernatural manifest in practices of restoration and renovation which conflict with the West's conservation ethic. His book *Surface Collection: Archaeological Travels in Southeast Asia* (AltaMira 2007) explores new approaches to the writing of archaeology and heritage.

Fiona Cameron, PhD, is a Senior Research Fellow at the Institute for Culture and Society, University of Western Sydney. She has researched and published widely on museums and their agency in contemporary societies around 'hot' topics of societal importance and the digital, materiality and museum collections. Fiona has been a chief investigator on seven ARC grants on topics ranging from the agencies of the museum in climate change interventions to material culture, collections, documentation and complexity. Recent books include three co-edited collections, *Theorizing Digital Cultural Heritage: A Critical Discourse* (MIT Press 2007) and *Hot Topics, Public Culture, Museums* (Cambridge Scholars 2010); *Climate Change Museum Futures* (Routledge, forthcoming) and a co-authored monograph, *Theorizing Digital Cultural Heritage for a Complex, Entangled World* (MIT Press, forthcoming). Recent articles have been published in the *Journal of Material Culture* and *Journal of Heritage Studies*.

Georgina Lloyd, PhD, is currently the Siem Reap Project Officer of the Angkor Heritage Management Framework Project and the Co-director of the University of Sydney Robert Christie Research Centre in Siem Reap. She has conducted both doctoral and postdoctoral research on intangible cultural heritage at Angkor. During her Endeavour Postdoctoral Research Fellowship she collaborated with the Authority for the Protection and Management of Angkor and the Region of Siem Reap (APSARA) to develop a safeguarding policy for intangible cultural heritage. Her doctoral research examined legal and policy approaches for the safeguarding of intangible cultural heritage across Asia and particularly in Cambodia. Georgina has spent the last five years living in Siem Reap and during this time has also been the recipient of an Endeavour Doctoral Research Fellowship and UNESCO Research Fellowship.

Sarah Mengler is a PhD student in Art History at the University of Cambridge. Her doctoral research is focused on developing new vocabularies for interpreting Indigenous material culture. Sarah was a Research Officer at the University of Western Sydney on the 'Reconceptualising Heritage Collections' project and has also previously worked in the Department of Anthropology, University College London. Recent publications include articles in the *Journal of Material Culture* and *International Journal of Heritage Studies*.

Fred Nelson has worked on natural resource governance, rural development, land tenure and payments for ecosystem services in eastern Africa since 1998. From 2000 to 2005 he served as the first Tanzania Programme Director for the Sand County Foundation, working with local pastoralist communities in northern Tanzania and facilitating the creation of the Tanzania Natural Resource Forum. From 2007 to 2010, he worked as an independent consultant on rural development and natural resource management concerns, with clients such as the International Institute for Environment and Development, the Finnish Embassy, Wildlife Conservation Society, CARE-International and the International Union for Conservation of Nature (IUCN). Since the beginning of 2011 he has been the Executive Director of Maliasili

Initiatives, an organisation established to support leading local organisations in Africa working at the interface of natural resource conservation, social justice and rural development. He is a member of the IUCN Commission on Environmental, Economic and Social Policy and World Commission on Protected Areas. He is the Editor of *Community Rights, Conservation, and Contested Lands: The Politics of Natural Resource Governance in Africa* (Earthscan 2010).

Nuria Porras-Bueno, PhD, is Senior Lecturer of Business Administration at the University of Huelva, where she is an active member of the research group on 'Innovation and Development Strategies in Tourist Firms' (GEIDETUR). She is the author of many papers in this field and is committed to a programme of research in tourism and destination development.

Juan Francisco Salazar, PhD, is a member of the Institute for Culture and Society and Senior Lecturer in Communication and Media Studies at the School of Humanities and Communication Arts, University of Western Sydney. He has published widely on Indigenous media and communication rights in Latin America, where he has also collaborated with several Indigenous media organisations. He has also provided consultancy to international cultural agencies and foundations on Indigenous media issues. His current research focuses on environmental communication, documentary cinema and cultural studies of Antarctica.

Neil Asher Silberman is President of the International Council on Monuments and Sites (ICOMOS) International Scientific Committee on Interpretation and Presentation (ICIP). His books and edited volumes on Heritage, Archaeology, and their impact on contemporary society include *Archaeology and Society in the 21st Century* (Israel Exploration Society 2001), *The Bible Unearthed* (Free Press 2001), *Invisible America* (Henry Holt & Co 1995), *Between Past and Present* (Doubleday 1989) and *Digging for God and Country* (Knopf 1982). From 2004 to 2007, he served as Director of the Ename Center for Public Archaeology and Heritage Presentation in Belgium. He is now a Fellow of the Center for Heritage and Society of the University of Massachusetts Amherst.

Helaine Silverman, PhD, is Professor in the Department of Anthropology at the University of Illinois and the Director of the university's Collaborative for Cultural Heritage Management and Policy (CHAMP). She is an Expert Member of the International Scientific Committee on Archaeological Heritage Management (ICAHM) of the International Council on Monuments and Sites (ICOMOS) and a member of Forum-UNESCO. Her research focuses on the cooperative and conflictual production of archaeological monuments as cultural heritage sites as undertaken by global agencies, national governments, regional authorities, local administrations, community stakeholders and the tourism industry. In addition to her own publications, she is the editor of two book series dealing with cultural heritage, archaeological heritage management, tourism and communities.

Im Sokrithy is a Khmer archaeologist and researcher. He is the Vice-Director of the Department of Land and Habitat Management of the Authority for the Protection and Management of Angkor and the Region of Siem Reap (APSARA). Im has conducted extensive social research on traditional livelihoods and intangible heritage in villages around Angkor and was formally the research team leader of the Department of Culture and Research, APSARA. He is a lecturer at the Royal University of Fine Arts Phnom Penh, member of the Advisory Board of the Friends of Khmer Culture and a senior member of the technical committee for the Intangible Heritage Research Project of Angkor.

Anna Spenceley, PhD, is a tourism specialist based in South Africa. She is the founder of STAND cc (Spenceley Tourism and Development) consultancy. Her clients include the World Bank, USAID, the Commonwealth Secretariat, the Netherlands Development Agency (SNV), the International Trade Centre of the United Nations Conference on Trade and Development (UNCTAD) and the UN-World Tourism Organization. She chairs the Tourism and Protected Areas Specialist Group for the International Union for Conservation of Nature (IUCN) World Commission on Protected Areas.

Russell Staiff holds a PhD in Art History from the University of Melbourne where he was the Foundation Lecturer in the Postgraduate Visual Arts and Tourism programme. He began his life in heritage and tourism as a tour guide in Italy. Currently, he teaches in the heritage and tourism programme at the University of Western Sydney where he is also a member of the Institute of Culture and Society. He researches the various intersections between cultural heritage, communities and tourism, particularly in Southeast Asia. He is completing a book *Re-Imagining Heritage Interpretation: Enchanting the Past/Future*.

Alfonso Vargas-Sánchez, PhD, is Professor of Strategic Management at the University of Huelva, where he heads a research group on 'Innovation and Development Strategies in Tourist Firms' (GEIDETUR). He is the author of papers published in journals such as *Journal of International Food and Agribusiness Marketing, European Journal of Information Systems, Human IT, Journal of High Technology Management Research, Technology Analysis & Strategic Management, International Journal of Case Method Research & Application, Tourism & Management Studies, Journal of Tourism and Development, International Journal of Business Environment, Journal of Travel Research, Journal of Sustainable Tourism* and *Tourism Management*, among others.

Emma Waterton, PhD, is based at the University of Western Sydney in the Institute for Culture and Society. Her interests include unpacking the discursive constructions of 'heritage', explorations of tourism, heritage and affect, visuality and explorations of innovative methodologies. Publications include *Politics, Policy and the Discourses of Heritage in Britain* (Palgrave Macmillan 2010), the co-authored volume (with Laurajane Smith) *Heritage, Communities and Archaeology* (Duckworth 2009) and the co-edited volumes (with Steve Watson) *Culture, Heritage and Representations* (Ashgate 2010), *Heritage and Community Engagement* (Routledge 2010), (with Laurajane Smith) *Taking Archaeology Out of Heritage* (Cambridge Scholars Press 2009) and (with Steve Watson and Laurajane Smith) *The Cultural Moment in Tourism* (Routledge 2012).

Steve Watson, PhD, is Principal Lecturer in the Business School at York St John University in the UK. His professional background encompasses the operational aspects of tourism management in local government. His research focuses on the representational practices of heritage tourism and the ways in which these relate to a variety of discursive formations and the application of theories of performativity and affect in heritage tourism. Recent publications include (with Emma Waterton) *Culture, Heritage and Representation* (Ashgate 2010) and (with Emma Waterton and Laurajane Smith) *The Cultural Moment in Tourism* (Routledge 2012).

Tim Winter, PhD, is Senior Research Fellow at the Institute for Culture and Society, University of Western Sydney. His interests centre on cultural sustainability and the matters surrounding cultural heritage in developing economy countries. He has published widely on heritage, development, modernity, urban sustainability and tourism in Asia. His recent books include *Routledge Handbook of Heritage in Asia* and *Shanghai Expo: An International Forum on the Future of Cities* (Routledge 2012). Tim has consulted for the World Bank and World Monuments Fund and held Visiting Scholar positions at Cambridge University and Getty Conservation Institute.

Andrea Witcomb, PhD, is Associate Professor in Cultural Heritage at Deakin University, where she directs the Cultural Heritage Centre for Asia and the Pacific. She is the author of *Re-Imagining the Museum: Beyond the Mausoleum* (Routledge 2003), Editor (with Chris Healy) of *South Pacific Museums: Experiments in Culture* (Monash University ePress 2006) and co-author (with Kate Gregory) of *From the Barracks to the Burrup: the National Trust in Western Australia* (UNSW Press 2010). Her interests range from the impact of multimedia on exhibition practices to relations between museums and communities. She is particularly interested in interactive and cross-cultural interpretative practices.

Series Editors' foreword

The interdisciplinary field of heritage studies is now well established in many parts of the world. It differs from earlier scholarly and professional activities that focused narrowly on the architectural or archaeological preservation of monuments and sites. Such activities remain important, especially as modernisation and globalisation lead to new developments that threaten natural environments, archaeological sites, traditional buildings and arts and crafts. But they are subsumed within the new field that sees 'heritage' as a social and political construct encompassing all those places, artefacts and cultural expressions inherited from the past that, because they are seen to reflect and validate our identity as nations, communities, families and even individuals, are worthy of some form of respect and protection.

Heritage results from a selection process, often government-initiated and supported by official regulation; it is not the same as history, although this, too, has its own elements of selectivity. Heritage can be used in positive ways to give a sense of community to disparate groups and individuals or to create jobs on the basis of cultural tourism. It can be actively used by governments and communities to foster respect for cultural and social diversity, and to challenge prejudice and misrecognition. But it can also be used by governments in less benign ways, to reshape public attitudes in line with undemocratic political agendas or even to rally people against their neighbours in civil and international wars, ethnic cleansing and genocide. In this way there is a real connection between heritage and human rights.

This is time for a new and unique series of books canvassing the key matters dealt with in the new heritage studies. The series seeks to address the deficiency facing the field identified by the Smithsonian in 2005 – that it is 'vastly under-theorized'. It is time to look again at the contestation that inevitably surrounds the identification and evaluation of heritage and to find new ways to elucidate the many layers of meaning that heritage places and intangible cultural expressions have acquired. Heritage conservation and safeguarding in such circumstances can only be understood as a form of cultural politics and that this needs to be reflected in heritage practice, be that in educational institutions or in the field.

It is time, too, to recognise more fully that heritage protection does not depend alone on top-down interventions by governments or the expert actions of heritage industry professionals, but must involve local communities and communities of interest. It is critical that the values and practices of communities, together with traditional management systems where such exist, are understood, respected and incorporated in heritage management plans and policy documents so that communities feel a sense of 'ownership' of their heritage and take a leading role in sustaining it into the future. This series of books aims then to identify interdisciplinary debates within heritage studies and to explore how they impact on the practices not only of heritage management and conservation, but also the processes of production, consumption and engagement with heritage in its many and varied forms.

William S. Logan
Laurajane Smith

Chapter 1

Introduction – place, encounter, engagement
Context and themes

Russell Staiff, Steve Watson and Robyn Bushell

A prologue, a reflection, a flavour

Taking a very broad historical perspective, the relationship between travel and visiting special places is neither recent nor unusual, nor bound to particular geographies or cultures. Pausanias, in the second century CE, travelled to Greece and recorded his visits to religious sanctuaries. The Indigenous nations of Australia, prior to colonisation and today, in some places continue to mark their movements with a deep awareness of journeying and spirituality conjoined inseparably. Buddhist pilgrims criss-crossed Asia throughout the time of the Common Era. Medieval pilgrimages to the Holy Land and to places such as Santiago de Compostela, in northwest Spain, are well documented, as are the travels of young British male aristocrats on the Grand Tour in the eighteenth century. In these cases space, time and distance were thought to be governed by something profoundly significant and in each instance there existed a reciprocal relationship between the traveller and the place to which they journeyed, a relationship that resulted in a transaction of some kind.

Of course, the historical and cultural circumstances of these various travels to places considered special is vastly different, and any easy historicism is fraught. However, it highlights a degree of ordinariness about the quest to go to places considered out of the ordinary. It also points to the communicative nature of such journeying: conversations with the deities – symbolic, material, spiritual and knowledge interactions and engagements that intensify the sanctity of the place (whether sacred or secular). For the traveller, such engagements produce benefits: spiritual, aesthetic, educative, a sense of mental health or personal wellness, conversations with fellow travellers, encounters with those met along the way. The communicative act between special places, people and fellow travellers is invariably potent with representations. It's always deeply an experience of the body and all its capacities for meaning making (intellectual, imaginative, somatic, sensual, emotional) and movement. Communication is often performed (or enacted), and the media used for transmission is about connectivity (not just the immediate connectivity of being in place but that

that have helped us to conceptualise both tourisms and tourists such that we could unpick tourist motivations, for example, and appreciate (to some extent) the statistical techniques that might be used to attempt to factor-analyse such abstract concepts as 'destination image'. And, on a higher plane, we could be guided by the explanatory strength of the big theories: the completeness offered by structuralism with its analysis of power and authority and its discursive corollaries, the transparency of social process afforded by constructivism, the justice of postcolonial theory, the disruptions of postmodernism; each one of these leaving essences of thought and reflection that might in some sense (though not always clearly) be applied to what we do and teach.

In recent years new perspectives have emerged: non-representational theories, affect, mobilities, actor-network theory. Yet in the face of all of these theoretical developments, from the momentous to the prosaic, there seemed to be something missing. It was still not entirely clear what was happening around those ragged intersections of heritage, tourism and tourists that really interested us, nor what each of the theoretical movements outlined above could contribute to an understanding of them. In creating that moment of reflection we have had to dissolve some certainties, to revel in doubt and to fill the resulting space with a variety of thoughts and analysis, new directions and meanings, and that is the purpose of this book.

Our reflections have led us to a concern with context and the relationship between concepts of place, encounter and engagement, and with the way that theory works in supporting this structure. With this in mind we have turned to the discussions that took place during the planning of the book and the idea of situating it within the emerging and developing theoretical and conceptual influences that have appeared over the last decade and which have begun to underpin and position research in both heritage and tourism. Since the book itself is located at the intersection of heritage and tourism we agreed that it was worthwhile reflecting on how these developments might relate to the book as a whole and to the individual contributions of each chapter. In doing so it has become apparent to us that there is a duality in the emerging literature in heritage. As such, we have identified theories and conceptual approaches that are *contingent* on the way that both heritage and tourism are structured by representational narratives and that are *negotiated* in more open, non-representational and performative situations.

There is no attempt here to comparatively evaluate these distinct perspectives. We merely suggest that they exist, and that an understanding of them and their differences may help to circumscribe our debate and elucidate it in ways that provide insights that are theoretically informed. Our *contingent* approach, then, is based on conventional structuralist themes that identify sources of power and authority in the touristic nexus and examine the ways in which these are implicated in representational and discursive practices. Representation is a key cultural practice in the 'giving and taking of meaning' through discourse in the context of a circuit of cultural production and consumption (Hall 1997) and has found its clearest expression in heritage in the work of Smith (2006). Representation has also been discussed in the context of visual culture as a vital means of processing cultural production and recognised for heightening significance in touristic practices (Crouch and Lübbren 2003; Waterton and Watson 2010).

Studies may, therefore, be concerned with the politics of such practices or with the operational modalities to which they give rise. They provide opportunities for the deconstruction of practice and representation and the analysis of powerful discourses. They identify the deterministic aspects of power relations and seek to situate heritage tourism in wider debates about power, social structure and their sustaining narratives. They account for the political economy of heritage tourism, its national and touristic contexts, and its role as a resource bounded by a need for economic development precariously balanced by concerns for limits and sustainability.

Our *negotiated* approach is an attempt to capture meaning in different ways – methods that have come to be distinguished by a concern with the performative locus of tourism, the mobilities and fluidities that define moments of encounter and engagement, the nature of meaning as emergent in practice and embodied non- or pre-cognitive responses to experience. Broadly defined as non-representational theory and derived from recent thinking in cultural geography (Dewsbury 2003; Thrift 2007), it might be considered in opposition to representational theory or perhaps more usefully in contradistinction to it and more-than-representational in its effect (Lorimer 2005). We are inspired by Crouch's (2002: 207) provocation: 'Tourism is a practice and is made in the process. In making these claims I challenge familiar representations of tourism as product, destination, consumption'.

Table 1.1 is indicative of these relationships and recognises that the duality as it is presented here has emerged or 'moved on' from conventional analyses that have sought (fruitlessly, we believe) to taxonomise heritage, tourism and tourists and to represent them as passive recipients of tourism as it is constituted in its operational modalities.

While the purpose of this framework is to facilitate some theoretical coherence in moving the debates forwards in ways that respond to the concerns of the book, it is also recognised that such a variety of subject matter and approaches presents a considerable challenge in terms of developing common themes and perspectives. It is perhaps sufficient for the framework to provide an indicative range of theoretical bases from which our debate might be advanced. With this in mind the following considers in more detail the contexts and themes that frame our discussion.

processes of representation, signification and consumption. The role of place in this melange is therefore more fully surveyed in tourism and 'place myth' (Shields 1991), performance of place (Bærenholdt *et al.* 2004) and 'sense of place' (Schofield and Szymanski 2011) have ensured that 'place' has become an important concept in tourism and heritage, where it resonates with a significance in the wider economy. In this context, the 'global paradox' is apparent, where a newly globalised, time-space compressed and networked world would appear to imply standardisation (Coleman and Crang 2002: 1–2), universal values and appearances in the 'global high street'. Yet, in this network the local is given greater significance as a source of distinction and difference. Place thus endows values that mean something only, paradoxically, in a global context (Coleman and Crang 2002: 3; Meethan 2001). Lucy Lippard (1997) explores such a vision in relation to the role of place in a global society that is effectively multi-centred. Again the paradox is revealed in that places become more important at a time when apparently they are less so: 'A multi-centred population is more often forced to consider places than a mono-centred one: choice alone, the forks in the road, demands it'. (Lippard 1997: 44). Place may also provide the imaginative, literal and physical contexts for an engagement with the past that is not historical in any formal scholarly sense but which resonates more with the notions and practices of heritage through the gathering together of residues, memories, local artefacts, traditions and individual pastness in genealogy. Linkage with place is thus achieved through a concept of its past, and time linkage with the past is achieved through place and its continuities – and yet these relationships are conditioned by interplays of power, politics and professional roles (Waterton 2005, 2010).

The notion of place can also be subject to scalar interpretations: destination, attraction, object – a kind of touristic calibration that defines and organises activity in ways that are appropriate, predictable and knowable in advance. At each level, tourism is made viable and the tourist is facilitated through the semiotics of prepared space and representational practices. In this sense tourism can be seen as a mode of spatial organisation that in turning its attention to places transforms them into the means of its own systemic practice. The destination is thus an important context for encounter and engagement, sustained by an 'autonomous discourse of tourist consumption'. (Hughes 1998: 20). Tourism is thus spatially circumscribed and necessarily enclavic, not just in purpose-built resorts where 'real life' might be permeated with risk (or poor services) but also around significant attractions (Edensor 1998, 2001). It is around these performed sites of tourism that people construct their own performance as tourists and, of course, as sightseers, where subjectivities and inter-subjectivities emerge and combine with place and with personal experience:

> Places [...] only emerge as 'tourist places' when they are appropriated, used and made part of the living memory and accumulated life narratives of people performing tourism, and these performances include embodied and social practices and traces of anticipated memories. Tourist places produce particular temporalities. They are inscribed in circles of anticipation, performance and remembrance.
>
> (Bærenholdt *et al.* 2004: 3)

How we perform as such is provoked by representations, both external and subjective, and by embodied and sometimes non-cognitive responses to place. Representations include not just those which press upon us in our here and now, but those that we have accumulated over time and which are internalised forms of knowledge and knowing. Our second context, therefore, is the performative encounter between tourists and place.

Places beget encounters and touristic encounters are heavily mediated by the modalities of organised 'industrial' tourism. These encounters are also anticipated: expectations are formulated and encounters are modulated by marketing imperatives and the cultural constructs that make important in some way places, attractions and objects. While encounters are prepared by representations, nothing can fully prepare us for the 'encounter in place' – the moment when a place or an object is encountered for the first time and where, throughout subsequent occasions, subjectivities are shared and memories add to anticipations. Encounters experienced by tourists are heavily mediated by representations but not entirely glossed by them. There is something held back, something reserved, which connects with what is expressed perhaps more purposefully by travellers – something of the self, something of the imagination. How do representations interact with imaginations? Is there a linear correspondence between what is represented about a place or an object and what is imagined? Are representations forms of shared imagination provided, as it were, off the shelf, to passersby and visitors? If this is the case then we might regard representational practices not just as informative but as formative and even manipulative. Either way, they are powerful, especially when combined with the essential visuality of tourism in general and heritage in particular (Waterton and Watson 2010).

Heritage produces imaginaries and we encounter them willingly enough even if we reject them passionately. We allow the encounter to take place, perhaps without the conscious exercise of choice. Our encounters may, however, be the result of choices made, of interests and passions, of seekings and findings, as tourists or as travellers (where the distinction can be or is asserted). Heritage, more often than not, is encountered as part of a place and only sought in its own right when it has iconic qualities. A cathedral may be sought, but the streets around it are also part of the main attraction and often prepared for tourist encounters with appropriate services together with discourses of identity, nationality and selected pasts, presented and displayed.

Distinctiveness and the 'production of difference', as Barbara Kirshenblatt-Gimblett calls it (1998: 152), are the main values here – the keynotes of Spanish*ness*, English*ness*, Balinese*ness* and any number of essences and essentialisms. An encounter with difference is therefore an encounter with the perceived essence of place, its myth and its imaginaries, to which heritage contributes its validating materialisms, its physical evidence of 'hereness' (Kirshenblatt-Gimblett 1998: 153) and its tokens of 'authenticity'.

The sheer multiplicity of touristic encounters at destinations, at attractions and with objects, is almost a denial of its ontological status. How can shopping in Las Vegas be equated in any sense – ever – with a wander through the ruins of an ancient temple? Yet both are prepared for and expecting tourists, and in significant numbers. It is not only the variety of encounters that at once excites our imagination and diminishes our understanding, it is the pervasiveness of such encounters that does so. Destinations and attractions are found everywhere. They sprout up (whether wanted or not) in places that might formerly be out of bounds or dedicated to some other purpose, but which to postmodern sensibilities follow the logic of eclectic commodifications and re-commodifications. Lippard has drawn attention rather graphically to this trend:

> Bizarre local straws are grasped at as attractions, and where there are none to grasp, no history, no theme parks, no beaches, no mountains, no luxury, no picturesque poverty, straw attractions are created. Where will it all end?
>
> (1999: x–xi)

The transformations are well rehearsed – from harbours to marinas, factories and mines to museums, from urban decay to gentrification – with culture and heritage providing the physical anchors by which places are linked to global networks and mobilities (Sheller and Urry 2004; Zukin 1991, 1995).

The encounter has thus become ubiquitous. It might be considered that encounters with prepared heritage places and attractions are almost inevitable, unavoidable, but what is it that makes such encounters meaningful, especially when there are so many of them and they exhibit such an eclectic presence in our lives? The term 'public realm' has even been coined and freely deployed to describe the places that merit attention and facilitate encounters, places that are often described in terms of a need for enhancement. Heritage is one of the values that is sought to realise such enhancements. We are left with the problem of meaning in such places and spaces and in respect of the calibration of destination, attraction and object. How do people engage with these things?

For encounters to become engagements some other, additional element is required. Tourist motivations are well researched from an operational point of view, but to theorise them effectively something more than conventional notions of motivation is implied. The notion of performativity has provided a helpful framework within which to understand engagement and its corollaries (in terms of the emergence of meaning in action) have helped to develop understandings of engagements with heritage, especially where the goal is to understand engagement beyond the simple coming together of an equation between attraction and motivation. Smith has set the scene for such reflections:

> The interconnection between heritage and tourism does not only reside in the macro or institutional scale with the interchange between the creation of economic resources and marketable cultural meanings. Rather, it also exists at the level of individual visits. Each visit is constitutive of the meaning of a heritage site. Heritage sites are not simply 'found', nor do they simply 'exist', but rather they are constituted at one level by the management and conservation processes that occur at and around them and, at another level, by the acts of visiting and engagement that people perform at them.
>
> (2012: 213)

Such constitutive moments have now become a major focus of attention and a locus of research in heritage studies (Smith, Waterton and Watson 2012), particularly in relation to processes of unpicking the nature of engagement in context, in place, encounter and engagement, as meaning that emerges *in situ* (Crouch 2010). The journey to this point could be seen as a triumph of tourism theory, and milestone publications such as Coleman and Crang (2002) and Bærenholdt *et al.* (2004) have blazed a significant trail in tourism, however, we believe there is much more to pursue and much more that remains to be done in our own field, both theoretically and in terms of applied theory and the implications for practitioners. With that in mind, what does this book add to the understanding of the contexts outlined above? Cutting across these contexts and instances are a series of themes that are picked up and examined by our contributors.

Themes

The original brief to the contributing authors focused on the dialogic relationship between, first, heritage places and tourists and, second, heritage places and the tourist industry more widely, especially the power of tourism (however conceptualised, but including government agencies as well as the private sphere) to represent heritage in its promotional campaigns, its itineraries, its use of guides and in the production of travel paraphernalia (whether guidebooks, websites, souvenirs and so forth). Partly, this was in response to the prevailing conceptualisation of the heritage place/tourist encounter as being dialogic and partly because we believe, as Buzinde and Santos have argued in their studies of slave heritage tourism:

> Within heritage tourism studies, the dialogic meaning making relationship between producers and consumers has remained relatively under researched as scholars have predominantly focused on management attributes.
>
> (2009: 440–1)

Also, as our prologue and introduction to this chapter intimates, we did not want our authors to be hemmed in by the distinctions that normally erupt from the words 'heritage tourism', especially as 'heritage' (without the added word of the appellation) already deeply configures the visitor into itself. Laurajane Smith (2006), in her study of heritage as a cultural process, powerfully illustrates that 'what goes on at the site' is the critically important dimension. Without place/people interaction, on whatever level and including tourists, there cannot be a practice or a discourse we call 'heritage'. So the dialogic, in its widest sense, became the way authors were asked to respond to place, encounter and engagement. So what themes have emerged?

The intimacy of heritage encounters

When Robert Dessaix (2008), an Australian writer, is sitting on a step near the top of the casbah in Algiers, he imagines not the Phoenicians or the Romans or even the French, but an encounter between Oscar Wilde and André Gide. It is an idiosyncratic personal response to a place where highly significant European men of letters had intensely experienced something of themselves in a heady atmosphere of Orientalism, colonialism and taboo sexuality. Dessaix's travels and reveries in Algiers fuse him with his literary discoveries as an adolescent when, then and now, memories and desires are reconfigured in place, where sensuous geographies provoke deep reflection.

For travel writers the intimate encounter of place, however described, is fundamental to their art. But such intimacy is also at the heart of the heritage experience by travellers. Denis Byrne, following on from his ground-breaking work in *Surface Collection: Archaeological Travels in Southeast Asia* (2007), broaches the subject of intimacy on many levels. The notion of critical proximity, rather than critical distance, is considered in order to explore and achieve empathy through a precarious personal journey in place that involves a re-imagining, an uncanny reading of places where embodiment is a kind of collision of deep feelings (whether sinister, exhilarating, disturbing or joyful). And these intense intimacies with place decentre manufactured and heterodox (heritage) communications with place, landscape, objects, buildings and so forth because the material and the natural (never separate entities) have agency. Byrne's own meditations, despite being personal, imprint upon the landscape a knowledge that can be shared through the act of 'writing places and people' and where the immediacy of past events, forever lost, is conjured as a powerful act of the imagination and of empathy, both always much more than the usual ways places are intellectually and politically marked as heritage. Byrne asks us to ponder two important and evocative questions: what is it, exactly, that tourists are in dialogue with, and can we distinguish 'the projection of our own desires and what is projected towards us by a place and its people'?

The emotional negotiation and re-negotiation of place and object is theorised by Fiona Cameron and Sarah Mengler. Here the traveller is the author of their own narratives that are powerfully enmeshed with the materiality of things in spheres of intimacy that are personal and political, which deeply connect with questions of identity, gender, ethnicity, religion and mobility (of people and heritage objects). By assuming, and then illustrating, the permeable, open-ended and dynamic relationship between heritage places, objects and the 'everyday', a dense description of 'interaction, translation and negotiation' is mapped so that there is no longer any discernible or defensible segregation of authorised encounters and engagements from those that are unauthorised. In this way, tourist experiences of heritage occur within 'non-linear, dynamical and fluid spaces', and as such they are open to globalised flows and political appropriations that are intensely and intimately personal. Like Byrne, Cameron and Mengler conceive of the heritage and traveller interaction as one full of all sorts of enmeshed desires and potentialities, and where the human/non-human is inescapably entangled with the visitor's subjectivities.

Heritage, tourism and the work of representation

A constant and enduring way of understanding and interpreting the dialogic relationship between the people/place entwinement has been through representation theory (Hall 1997) and the recognition of the co-dependency of the material with its representations in the quest for meaning, knowledge, power and world-making (Cosgrove 1984; Duncan and Ley 1993; Tuan 1974). Within cultural heritage conservation praxis, representation is crucial as places are mapped, described, photographed, filmed, drawn, measured (and so forth) and turned into digital models, illustrations and diagrams. Dynamic environmental processes are, paradoxically, provisionally fixed in representations so that all manner of conservation actions can be undertaken (e.g. Stubbs 2009). Heritage representations are, of course, more than conservation practices and form a web of signifying activities that have powerful effects (Smith 2006; Waterton and Watson 2010). Tourism,

Heritage is, on one level, a scopic regime (see Crary 1990). Indeed, the whole heritage enterprise depends on forms of visualisation that, in turn, produce knowledge/power effects. There is the mapping and pictorial documentation (images, diagrams and models) of sites and the ways these representations are analysed and become producers of knowledge (whether archaeologists, architects or conservators). There is the history of these visual records so that, for example, today's Egyptologists facing increasing environmental and human degradation of sites refer back to earlier drawings, paintings, photographs, maps and diagrams in their work, especially the records of those who came with and just after Napoleon Bonaparte, and they note discrepancies and varying interpretations (e.g. Fletcher 2004). To this archive is added the results of newer imaging techniques such as satellite photography, digital scanning and computer-generated images. Visualisation is, therefore, a way of knowing (the monuments of ancient Egypt) and also recording (these monuments). In turn, the various visual representations create a 'visual ecology' within which material culture is given a particular visibility and visual identity. The term visual ecology we have borrowed from the perception psychologist and theorist James Gibson (1986), but it is used here very differently. When we stand amongst the enormous columns of the Temple of Karnak, for example, our looking is a process informed and produced by our visual environment – pictures in our guidebook, the maps and diagrams we may have accessed, even perhaps the film *Death on the Nile* (1978) (with Peter Ustinov, Maggie Smith, David Niven and Bette Davis), the procession of images in tourism brochures and magazines and the countless television documentaries over the years. Karnak has visibility: it is far from an unintelligible visual experience but, instead, is a highly mediated ocular encounter.

In complementary ways Russell Staiff, Emma Waterton and Steve Watson explore the 'double helix' configuration of mediated seeing, vision bound to representation in a continuous and spiralling non-hierarchical and non-cause and effect relationship – or, as several art theorists have described it – 'pictured vision' – whereby the seeing is informed by pictorial knowledge (e.g. Alpers 1983; Bryson 1983). For Waterton it is the dominant images of British heritage, for Watson it is to be found in the imagery of the rural–historic in England, and for Staiff it is in the Hollywood cinematic constructions of 'ancient Rome'. Vision and visuality are two of the critical axes in the processes described by Helaine Silverman and Andrea Witcomb in their respective chapters on Cuzco and immersive technologies.

The performative and/or the embodied

The theoretical dimensions of place/tourism/performance have already been discussed introduction (see above). Here, we are concerned with those created performances that resuscitate the past in an overt and highly orchestrated action, often political, which fuse history and both cultural and intangible heritage in an attempt to produce a variety of embodied responses: empathy, nostalgia, nationalist fervour, pride, a sense of belonging, of being there and so forth. These are the concerns of Helaine Silverman and Andrea Witcomb.

The relationship between heritage places, tourism and performance has a long history. The imperial exhibitions of the nineteenth century CE in metropolitan Europe, and in the various colonial domains, provide one of the antecedents to the highly manufactured performances that evolved in the twentieth century CE. Minted to express imperial power, these elaborate concoctions synthesised modernity, science and technology, industrial enterprise, colonial cultural traditions, archaeology and the Western historical project where material culture and performances were essential ingredients for visitor consumption (Greenhalgh 1988; Hoffenberg 2001).

By the end of the twentieth century CE, performances at heritage places had morphed into a variety of productions. There were the grand spectacles like those at Ayutthaya in Thailand where parts of the great Hindu epic, the *Ramayana*, were lavishly performed within the archaeological remains of the historic city for the Thai royal family. There were performances of Verdi's opera *Aida* at the pyramids of Giza and Puccini's *Turandot* in the Forbidden City, Beijing. Concerts have been regularly performed at various locations in Angkor. At Sacsayhuamán, Incan plays are produced in Incan ruins. On a different scale, local festivals and other types of performances at less grand heritage places are regularly advertised by the tourism industry. Helaine Silverman's study of the re-invention of the Incan festival of *Inti Raymi* in Cuzco illustrates a complex interplay between place, identity politics and tourism. A cultural performance of self to self also plays to national and international spectators where tourism is an essential component of the ritual. Tourism is not just a purveyor of economic benefits in Cuzco, but provides the necessary dialogic vehicle that communicates the political/postcolonial rhetoric of the occasion to a much wider audience.

In every example, from the Crystal Palace in the nineteenth century CE to contemporary performances, technology has been a crucial attribute of the experience – sometimes overtly so and at other times less so – and not just the technology of the production, but also the integration of these performances with the media. It was newspapers and the telegraph 125 years ago; today, it is the digital capacities of the tourist/visitor. YouTube and Google Images abound with videos and photographs audiences have posted to record their participation.

Various immersive technologies are the subject of the essay by Andrea Witcomb, but the writer raises serious ethical concerns about such approaches designed to stimulate empathy and interest in the encounter of heritage places/objects/memorials. Witcomb poses very significant questions about performance/immersion as an interpretive experience: what happens when the performance circumnavigates content or theatrically reproduces power relations that cannot be critiqued by the audience in the moment, or when critical engagement is seemingly closed off altogether? The rapid convergence in the field of technologically mediated experiences (drawing together advances in video games, cinema, theatrical spectaculars, theme parks) is increasingly applied to museum and heritage sites (see Cameron and Mengler this volume). The powerful utilisation of technology keeps alive concerns that have an extensive recent history: what are the effects of a 'society of the spectacle'? (to use Debord's [1994] phrase, with its spectre of degraded knowledge); what are the implications when affect is designed to circuit break critique?; and, are there ethical implications in the heritage encounter, and if so, whose ethical positions are we considering?

Political narratives

The publication of *Routledge Handbook of Heritage in Asia* (Daly and Winter 2012) is testament to the idea that all heritage is political. What the chapters in this collection reveal (as with many chapters in the *Routledge Key Issues in Cultural Heritage* series) is that heritage, however conceived, exists within the political economy matrix. Whenever a variety of values are at stake, when different perceptions are entangled, when different imaginaries overlap, when a multitude of stakeholders compete, when the local is in tension with the global, when heritage is put to different uses, when ideological positions are jostling for ascendency, when the state is in conflict with its citizens or international bodies and so on, power and politics is at the heart of heritage contestations. Consequently, the dialogic function of both heritage and tourism cannot be immune from these contestations.

Helaine Silverman describes the politics of the revival of 'ancient' and 'lost' Incan 'traditions' in Cuzco. The performances she recounts are, crucially, about the politics of survival and the politics of cultural renaissance, about the recalibration of an imagined Incan past, projected onto the present/future and integrated into the festival calendar of the Catholic church, particularly the Feast of Corpus Christi. The process of *indigenismo* cultural recuperation attempts to engage national agendas, national politics and national identity. Juan Salazar and Robyn Bushell present a companion narrative about Indigenous tourism in San Pedro de Atacama, northern Chile, where heritage and tourism by the Atacameño or Lickanantay Indigenous peoples is contextualised by the emergence of a radical Indigenous politics, but at the very time they are losing control over their cultural heritage. The dialogic relationship between heritage, Indigenous people and tourism is one marked by advocacy, legitimacy, visibility and resistance.

Tim Winter's study of tourism at Angkor is presented as a type of 'clash of cultures' within which heritage and tourism create contrapuntal discourses and narratives that, in turn, affect the way they engage with each other. These contradistinctions can be characterised as sets of simultaneous divergences: Eurocentric post-Enlightenment thinking and other knowledge practices; contrasting views about conservation (top up, bottom down; universalist principles, local praxis); the traffic between local authorities and global bodies; tourists as homogenous outsiders versus tourists as mobile subjects marked by ethnicity, gender, sexuality, class, religion, geography and so forth; and dissimilar conceptions of modernity, leisure, history, travel and material culture.

Georgina Lloyd and Im Sokrithy's study of Angkor has a different, but nonetheless related, focus to that of Winter's chapter. In Therevada Buddhist cultures intangible heritage is central to any notion of material conservation and is deemed central to the way Angkor is encountered by visitors. However, in this encounter, visitors engage with modified forms of intangible heritage, forms that reveal varying degrees of standardisation, homogenisation, commodification and a freezing of material heritage into a fossilised past of Khmer glory, 'rediscovered' by the nineteenth century CE French explorer, Henri Mouhot. It is another tale of the exclusion, the silencing and the invisibility of contemporary Khmer culture and, in turn, it reveals something of the politics of global and national heritage played out in the tourist encounter.

The problems that ensue from the heritage–tourism engagement

One of the enduring conceptions of the heritage–tourism encounter has been that which characterises it as being a 'fraught relationship'. While we would argue the binary of threat/benefactor is no longer adequate (Bushell and Staiff 2012), this is not the same thing as suggesting tourism in heritage places is benign or without significant dangers and problems. Indeed, the world's media has delighted in portraying tourism to heritage places as toxic (see, for example, articles in *The Guardian*, 6 September, 2009 and *The New York Times*, 6 January, 2012). One of the factors at the centre of this 'crisis' description of the heritage–tourism engagement has been a conceptual one: how should the relationship be represented so that it is possible to think outside of the uncritically repeated polarities endemic in the 'danger' stories?

Possible approaches include challenging certain widespread narratives, another is to focus on sustainability more generally, and yet another is to focus on the motivations of tourists. Neil Silberman challenges, and deconstructs, the narrative that suggests regional economic woes can be vanquished by developing heritage sites as tourist attractions that aspire to large-scale visitation because treating heritage as an economic resource downplays the dialogic significance and agency of local communities and their desire to narrate their own stories to visitors. In the case of Africa, Anna Spenceley and Fred Nelson emphasise sustainability in the context of managing contestation over land tenure, rights over resources, local community power to conserve cultural and natural resources and to develop locally owned tourism enterprises and regard the larger framework of sustainability as a vital mode for managing competing needs, desires and claims.

Alfonso Vargas-Sánchez, Nuria Porras-Bueno and Ángeles Plaza-Mejía explore visitor motivations and the levels of satisfaction expressed in surveys of tourists at historical mining sites in Huelva Province, Spain. The inquiry offers insights into the reasons for tourist visitation at an early stage in the evolution of a heritage destination. The research illustrates the strengths and weaknesses of aggregate studies and what they can, and cannot, reveal about tourists engaging with heritage places. To this end, this analysis is at the very opposite end of the spectrum to the contributors to this volume who collectively reflect upon the place/encounter/engagement: Denis Byrne's chapter is at one end and the account of tourism and heritage mining sites at the other.

Conclusion

Overall, the essays in this volume provide a contemporary 'snapshot' of the dialogic relationship between heritage places and the encounter/engagement of tourists (and the tourist industry), but it is also a necessarily partial view because, as we have suggested, globally there are myriad encounters between people and special places all marked, in their diversity, by significant attributes worthy of investigation, but not possible here. There are also divergent cultural perspectives involved and the essays, formulated within Western knowledge practices, only provide a glimpse of alternative epistemological traditions. These are also requiring voice. And hovering over everything we have discussed are the global processes that are fundamentally changing heritage place/visitor relationships: the advent of social media combined with G3/G4 telecommunication networks and increasingly sophisticated, and ever more powerful, devices such as iPads.

Because the heritage place/tourist engagement is in a time of technological transition, we are mindful of the fact that the contributors in this volume entertain the new forms of technologically mediated communications as either background or as foreground in their analyses. This is suggestive in itself. Uncertain about the dialogic futures of the heritage/tourist enterprise, many questions and concerns remain unresolved and open ended. However, to return to our opening reflection, irrespective of the nature of the dialogic relationship between heritage places and tourist encounters we can be sure that the desire to travel to places that are special will not diminish, and the means to do so (both economic and technological) will enable ever more people to undertake an activity that, in our times, is the greatest peaceful movement of people, other than migration, in the human history of the planet.

References

Alpers, S. (1983) *The Art of Describing*, Chicago: University of Chicago Press.

Bærenholdt, J., Haldrup, M., Larsen, J. and Urry, J. (2004) *Performing Tourist Places*, Aldershot and Burlington: Ashgate.

Bryson, N. (1983) *Vision and Painting: The Logic of the Gaze*, New Haven: Yale University Press.

Burnett, R. (2005) *How Images Think*, Cambridge MA and London: MIT Press.

Bushell, R. and Staiff, R. (2012) 'Rethinking relationships: World Heritage, communities and tourism', in P. Daly and T. Winter (eds) *Routledge Handbook of Heritage in Asia*, Abingdon, Oxfordshire and New York: Routledge.

Buzinde, C. and Santos, C. (2009) 'Interpreting slavery tourism', *Annals of Tourism Research*, 36(3): 439–58.

Byrne, D. (2007) *Surface Collection: Archaeological Travels in Southeast Asia*, Lanham MD: AltaMira Press.

Chen, J. (1998) 'Travel motivation of heritage tourists', *Tourism Analysis* 2: 213–5.

Coleman, S. and Crang, M. (eds) (2002) *Tourism: Between Place and Performance*, Oxford: Berghahn Books.

Cosgrove, D. (1984) *Social Formation and Symbolic Landscape*, Madison: University of Wisconsin Press.

Crary, J. (1990) *The Techniques of the Observer*, Cambridge MA and London: MIT Press.

Crouch, D. (2002) 'Surrounded by place, embodies encounters', in S. Coleman and M. Crang (eds) *Tourism: Between Place and Performance*, Oxford: Berghahn Books.

Crouch, D. (2010) 'The perpetual performance and emergence of heritage', in E. Waterton and S. Watson (eds) *Culture, Heritage and Representation. Perspectives on Visuality and the Past*, Farnham, Surrey: Ashgate.

Crouch, D. and Lübbren, N. (eds) (2003) *Visual Culture and Tourism*, Oxford: Berg.

Daly, P. and Winter T. (eds) (2012) *Routledge Handbook of Heritage in Asia*, London and New York: Routledge.

Dann, G.M.S. (1981) 'Tourist motivation: an appraisal', *Annals of Tourism Research* 8(2): 187–219.

Dessaix, R. (2008) *Arabesques: A Tale of Double Lives*, Sydney: Pan Macmillan.

Dewsbury, J.D. (2003) 'Witnessing space: knowledge without contemplation', *Environment and Planning A* 35: 1907–32.

Debord, G. (1994) *The Society of the Spectacle*, Cambridge, MA: Zone Books/MIT Press.

Duncan, J. and Ley, D (1993) *Place/Culture/Representation*, London and New York: Routledge.

Edensor, T. (1998) *Tourists and the Taj: Performance and Meaning at a Symbolic Site*, Routledge: London.

Edensor, T. (2001) 'Performing tourism, staging tourism: (re)producing tourist space and practice, *Tourist Studies* 1(1): 59–81.

Part I

The intimacy of encounters

Chapter 2

Gateway and garden
A kind of tourism in Bali

Denis Byrne

Generally speaking, the heritage places encountered by tourists are clearly defined spaces featuring architectural or archaeological remains, these remains being the central focus of the visitor's attention. This is the case at places like Angkor Wat, the Taj Mahal and the Forbidden City. Even where heritage comes in the form of cultural landscapes – the Banawe rice terraces, Chinatown in Malacca, the ruins of the former Thai capital, Ayutthaya – these are spatially circumscribed and clearly distinguished physically from what surrounds them. Framed in terms of heritage tourism, heritage places often take the form of what Tim Edensor (1998, 2001) has described as 'enclavic' spaces, meaning they are 'single-purpose' places carefully managed to focus the visitor's attention on the heritage items and 'minimize underlying ambiguity and contradiction' (Edensor 2001: 63). Such places are eminently visitable.

The subject of the first part of this chapter is a kind of heritage not so easily visitable and not enclavic in Edensor's terms. It comprises the physical traces of events that occurred during the Cold War in Asia, events which in the decades after they occurred were subject to censorship and sanctions against public acts of remembering, amounting to an imposed forgetfulness. The events saw the violent mass death of civilians at the hands of the state during circumstances of political polarisation in which other fractions of the civilian population were either complicit in the suffering and death of the victims or unsympathetic to their fate. This was the case with the massacre of civilians in Bali in late-1965 and early-1966, which took place as part of the Indonesian army's purge of communists. Unlike some other instances of the mass killing of civilians (the Jewish Holocaust obviously comes to mind) the violence in Bali was not spatially concentrated at nodal sites. There were no centralised death camps. The killings were dispersed at numerous sites across the island and there was no dedicated infrastructure created to facilitate them. The heritage of the events of 1965–66 is not, then, 'visitable' at particular sites. Not merely is it not visitable, for the most part it is not even *visible* – it exists 'below the thresholds at which visibility begins' (de Certeau 1984: 93). It seems unlikely that even an interested and historically informed tourist would succeed in finding any physical traces of these events.

And yet, insofar as the whole island in 1965–66 was gripped by a violence that directly or indirectly extended everywhere, there is a sense in which millions of us today, by going to Bali as tourists, do unconsciously visit the 'heritage' of the killings. Many of the older Balinese we as tourists see on the island today, working in the fields, walking to the temples or sitting on the beach, experienced the events of 1965–66 or even participated in them.

With an eye to the theme of the present volume, I pose the question of what potential there exists for a tourist to communicate with the human dimension of this history. By this I mean communication in the form of empathy, distinct from or in addition to any effort that might be made to achieve a political or intellectual understanding of the events. I am aware that governments and non-governmental institutions sometimes mount determined campaigns to encourage people to empathise with those in the past who experienced traumatic events. Graham Carr (2003: 65–8), for instance, describes various efforts to encourage Canadian students to empathise with the D-Day experience of Canadian soldiers on the Normandy beaches in June 1944, efforts which extend to staging pilgrimages to those beaches. While places and physical traces certainly also play a central role in my discussion, I am more interested in the possibilities of an empathy that is voluntary rather than encouraged or coerced. Meaghan Morris (2006: 5) has urged scholars in the humanities to develop a 'critical proximity' to their subject matter, as distinct from the usual *critical distance* that 'objective', instrumentalist academic writing usually strives for (see also Simon 2010). I am interested in the potential of heritage tourism to put people in situations of critical proximity to past events and perhaps precipitate them into moments of empathy with past others.

The problem with being there – Bali in the early 1990s

I should mention at the outset that my approach will be personal and auto-biographical. To begin, I will briefly recapitulate a previously written account of an experience I had in Bali in the early 1990s while attempting to find archaeological traces of the 1965–66 killings (see Byrne 1999, 2007).

The early 1990s were to be the last years of General Soeharto's military dictatorship in Indonesia which, by that time, had endured almost 30 years. In Bali, though, as a tourist–sojourner enjoying the sun and the sea, the verdant rice fields and the charming people, that side of Indonesia (the politics of oppression) seemed a long way off. My idyll was interrupted one day when I stumbled upon a copy of a black-covered book edited by the historian Robert Cribb (1990), which described what had occurred in Indonesia in late 1965 after the military seized power in Jakarta. For the first time, and to my shock, I learned that an estimated 100,000 communists and supposed communists were killed on the island of Bali alone. Over the following months I tracked down and read other historical accounts and gained a fuller picture of what had happened (Crouch 1973; Hughes 1968; Van der Kroef 1972; Vickers 1989). Sitting in my bungalow, by the light of low-voltage lamps, I read, for instance, of people in 1965–66 sitting in their house compounds at night listening for the sound of trucks that might have been coming to take them away; of how it was enough for some people just to hear the roar of a truck for their hearts to beat wildly with fear (Robinson 1995: 298). The island I thought I knew now began to take on a shadowy, sinister aspect. I read of riverbeds choked with bodies and of mass graves near the beaches, of 'blackened areas where entire villages had been burnt to the ground' (Vickers 1989: 170).

What I wish to convey here is the sense of there having opened up in front of me a deeply disturbing, previously unguessed-at dimension of a place I thought I already *knew*. I cannot say this previously unsuspected history 'materialised' in front of me because part of the strangeness of the experience was that the material reality surrounding me remained unchanged. The rice fields and villages I passed on my motor scooter during afternoon rides along the back roads looked just the same as before. The warm wind ruffled the palm fronds the same way, the waves rolled onto the beach just as always and the faces of the people I passed in the streets and laneways were as gracefully composed as they were previously. And it was not simply that life continued on around me just as before. It was as if the landscape around me silently refuted the truth of what I had been reading, a situation that made me want to read more.

Reading is important in all this. For most of us it is through the act of reading that historical events of this kind enter our consciousness. There was certainly nothing about the 1965–66 killings on Indonesian television in the early 1990s (not that we had a television, or a phone for that matter), and the internet had yet to make its appearance in popular culture. Indonesians could not read the history of the killings in their own language and even to possess publications on them in English or other foreign languages would pose a risk. A generation of Indonesians who had witnessed the events of 1965–66 were silenced by fear while a subsequent generation, in the words of Ann Stoler (2002: 646), was 'schooled with purged history books and with access only to book-stores immaculately emptied of ways of making sense of the world into which they were born'. We might expect this excision to have created a glaring gap, but the government ensured that an extraordinary amount of classroom time was devoted to learning an alternative version of national history (McGregor 2005; Reid 2005: 173). If in the early 1990s there were no visitable heritage sites attesting to the events of 1965–66 or monuments commemorating the victims, and if this was still the case ten years later in the early post-Soeharto era

(Santikarma 2005), then that is partly attributable to the success of this educative effort.

In Malcolm Caldwell's (1975) volume, *Ten Years of Military Terror in Indonesia*, I came upon an unprovenanced black and white photograph that crystallised for me the horror of the killings, making them real and some-how personal in a way which text could not.[1] It shows a young man standing with his back to the soldier who is bayoneting a figure on the ground. The young man is roped around the neck and wrists to this fallen figure behind him. The rope is pulling him backwards towards what is being done to that person. He cannot see what is happening but he must be able to hear it and must know that the same thing is about to happen to him. Perhaps the most chilling thing about this photograph is that we also know. The mere act of looking at this image, 27 years after the event, somehow made me feel complicit and ashamed. Writing this in 2012 I still remember that feeling, but it is only recently that I have been able to put a name to it, thanks to an essay by Elspeth Probyn (2010: 82) in which she writes of how 'shame arises from a collision of bodies, ideas, history, and place'. There are things that humans have done to other humans that shame us all. Shame is an embod-ied state or experience which in my case arose from my eyes 'colliding' with a photographic image of something happening to other bodies 30 years earlier. This embodied capacity we have to experience shame annuls the supposedly protective distances of geography and time.

Around the time I first saw the photograph, and as I began writing about my quest for archaeological traces of the killings, the wet season arrived in Bali and the low ceiling of grey cloud that hung over the island became an element of the gloom that now permeated my view of things. The sensory environment of the season – the aroma of decaying vegetation and of steam rising off wet roads, the feel of books whose paper swells and warps and smells of mildew – now seemed to speak to the events of 1965–66. Vegetation became a signifier of catastrophe. In the part of the island where I lived I began to notice abandoned houses and other ruined build-ings covered in tropical vegetation, their concrete shells blackened with damp, their roofs fallen in. These were recent ruins, nothing to do with the mid-1960s, but I had never given them much attention before. Now they were suggestive of ruined lives and lost futures. In its tropical luxuriance and the rapidity of its growth, vegetation now appeared in the guise of a censoring agent: it colluded in covering things over; it softened what was jagged and abject. I now had photographs of these modern ruins pinned to the woven bamboo wall panel over my desk in the bungalow.

My archaeological training made it impossible for me to believe in the possibility of an event without a footprint. As it happened, I never managed to find actual physical traces of the 1965–66 killings: no trace of former burnt villages, no trace of the mass graves mentioned in the literature, though rumour pointed to a luxury hotel having been constructed in 1972

In the immediate aftermath of the events of 1965–66, state censorship and other mechanisms of suppression meant that public mention of the killings, let alone commemoration of the dead, was impossible. In such conditions we can understand how the survivors of state terror could come to be 'incarcerated' within the space of their own memories; how landscapes might come to be encoded or 'encrypted' with signs of past events that people register and read silently (Mueggler 1998).[4] These were the conditions that produced the situation in which there are now no visitable sites of 1965–66 in Bali. Having considered how a gateway might serve as a mediating site for an empathetic experience on the part of a tourist I turn briefly to consider the role it might have played in the life of a Balinese in the aftermath of 1965–66.

There is a sense in which the immediate force that a site has for a survivor cannot be passed on because it 'works' via first-hand memory.[5] A mother, for instance, could explain to her children that the last time she saw their father was as he was being taken away through the gateway, but the gateway can hardly carry the same charge for the children because they cannot *see* him in the gateway in that final moment the way their mother can. What might stay with the children, then, would be the knowledge that their mother, in the years after 1965–66, often 'saw' their father in the gateway. Their experience of seeing–feeling how she was affected might equally stay with them. And they, in turn, might pass this on to their own children.

But often it seems that those with the primary, first-hand experience of dark events choose not to relate it to their children at all. It may simply be too painful, too difficult to put into words. We also need to remember that many of the casualties of Cold War violence in Asia were regarded as enemies of the state. This was certainly the case in Indonesia where in the years after the killings people with close links to victims were automatically under suspicion themselves. Extended family members of victims had special marks on their identity cards which, among other things, disqualified them from ever holding jobs in the public service, a situation which endured until Soeharto's overthrow in 1998. Parents may thus have kept things from their children in order to protect them. The children, after all, would have to make their way through life under the new political conditions: perhaps the less they knew, the better. This has been advanced to explain why few families in Taiwan came forward in the 1990s to claim government compensation for deaths or imprisonment suffered by family members under the so-called White Terror (1947–1987) of the Kuomintang.[6] In Indonesia the fact that in the post-Soeharto (post-1998) era there has been comparatively little public 'remembering' of the 1965–66 atrocities has been attributed to the spectre of the communist threat having been by no means entirely put to rest, to the power of the military still being largely intact, and to a 'diffidence' that exists about dealing openly with events that were disruptive to so many families and communities (Zurbuchen 2005: 14–5).

There is, of course, no simple equation between history and heritage. Not all history is represented as heritage. The visitable heritage landscape of a country rarely represents more than a very selective sample of its history: a combination of particular circumstances has to be in place for traces of past events to make it into the heritage record. In the first place, as has become clear, there must be surviving physical traces 'in place' (I am not concerned with museum collections of 'moveable heritage' in this chapter). There then needs to be a willingness by those in authority to permit these traces to be the subject of attention. But beyond all this, many of us (e.g. Byrne 2009; Smith 2006; Smith and Waterton 2009) consider that 'heritage' is best understood as a discourse which constructs the material past in particular ways. Smith (2006: 4) theorises a form of this discourse which has developed principally in the West and which 'authorises' a way of looking at the material past which lays emphasis on monumentality and aesthetics and which conflates it with the idea of the nation.

The heritage sites we visit as tourists are, as it were, expecting us. They are arranged and rearranged to cater to our expectations and these expectations are part of a complex cultural and bodily 'training' in how to *be* tourists (e.g. Urry 1990). However, the emphasis on the constructedness of the tourism experience may have been overdone. We tourists are not to be thought of as passive consumers of whatever roles might have been scripted for us. David Crouch (2005: 23) argues that tourists do not just visit places, rather 'people as human subjects practice and perform places'. He and others (e.g. Edensor 2001) point to the tourist's capacity to be reflexive and experimental and in various ways to defy expectations. It seems best to think of the tourist experience as relational.

Looking back on my early 1990s attempt to find the events of 1965–66 in the landscape of contemporary Bali I am inclined to think in terms of such relationality. On my side, and in Crouch's terms, I was engaged in a certain performance of place. Whatever feelings were involved in that performance, in that 'archaeology of feeling', they were my own. I am aware that I could never really know how a Balinese would have felt in 1965–66 or in the years after. This understanding seems critical to the empathetic potential of heritage mentioned at the outset of this chapter – the potential I see for heritage places to trigger feelings of empathy for past others. These feelings are our business. They do not put us inside the minds or bodies of others and they may (let's face it) be very wide of the mark. But surely this is no more than the limitation inherent in all human communication. It is the willingness to communicate, the preparedness to imagine the situation of others, which establishes the possibility of community.

My 'performance of place' in Bali might also be described as one that was enacted *against* place, by which I mean that everything I saw in the landscape around me seemed to say that the events of 1965–66 could never have occurred there. Against this denial and armed with my reading, with some photographs and with my imagination, I tried to will these events back into place. But it would be untrue to say my surroundings were simply an obstacle to this project of recuperation, and this is where the other side of relationality comes in: I realise now that I cannot but have been using my surroundings as a cue. It was the gateway in my own garden, after all, that first suggested to me the role gateways might have played in 1965–66. On a broader scale, the whole landscape of early 1990s Bali vibrated with possibilities for conjuring up 1965–66 once my mind was open to this. Chris Tilley (2008: 271) draws on phenomenology to assure us that we cannot experience our surroundings in just any way we might like; we cannot be immune to the cues they give out.

I would not want to end the first part of this essay leaving the impression that 'Bali the paradise island' entirely receded into the background in the face of my new knowledge of the island's dark past. This would be to underestimate the power of that exoticist construct and my susceptibility to it.

Fashioning a paradise island

In the 1920s and 1930s the Dutch colonial government and certain European sojourners put a great deal of effort into fabricating an image of Bali as a peaceful, cultured, beautiful place standing apart from the rest of the world. The first tourists began arriving on the island in 1914, lured by the Dutch steamship company, the KMP, which issued brochures and books extolling the attractions of a place unspoilt by modernity and populated by charming, half-naked people of an artistic bent (Vickers 1989: 91–92). And yet, as Adrian Vickers points out, the tourists began arriving less than a decade after the Badung *puputan*, an event in which 1,000 men, women and children of the court of Badung, in south Bali, were shot down by the Dutch army when they marched out of their besieged *puri* (palace) shortly after the Dutch invaded the island.

Right from the beginning of the island's tourism era, darkness thus lay just below the surface of the paradise veneer. The physical landscape has always been a major element of this veneer and is central to what is regarded as the island's visitable heritage. A great deal of effort has gone into honing a certain representation of this landscape, not least by European artists resident in it from the 1920s onward. The first of these was the German, Walter Spies (1895–1942), who arrived in 1927 and built a house on the edge of a deep ravine at Campuan, an area of rice farms just north of the village of Ubud, on land lent to him by the aristocratic Sukawati family. He began to support himself by the sale of his paintings and drawings and over the next 13 years he became the leading interpreter to the Western world of Balinese culture and landscape.

Writing about Spies' paintings, the anthropologist James Boon (1986:

237) says that 'Everything in his canvasses projects sensuality, idealized Balinese youths included. The pervasive eroticism stems from interplays of the elements, of hillscape/waterscape/skyscape.' The sensuous, sinuous bodies of the Balinese, as depicted, are continuous with the sensuous curves of the contoured rice terraces and of a tropical vegetation which itself has always been a Western metaphor for the languorous and sensual East.[7] Margaret Mead (1977: 155) added her own sense of wonder at the sensuousness of the Balinese which she saw as continuous with the landscape. Ensconced in her field-base higher up in the foothills from Campuan, she describes a boy hanging washing on a clothes line: 'Their movements seem to have no beginning and no end, but flow from any point to any point.'

I do not mean to question here the sensuousness of Balinese bodies in the 1930s – bodies by definition are sensuous – or to quibble over whether these bodies did or did not flow from point to point. But we need to understand that this construction of Bali was blind to certain other realities. Much of 1930s Bali under the Dutch was, for instance, quite impoverished.[8] Almost invariably the Balinese were depicted by European artists as slender and lithe, and undoubtedly many of them were, but many of their bodies were wasted from the effects of hunger and rampant tuberculosis (Pollman 1990: 12; Vickers 1989: 134).

Walter Spies collaborated closely with particular Dutch administrators and scholars on what was referred to as the *Baliniseering* (Balinisation) programme. What this sought to do was keep Balinese culture unspoilt, while at the same time exerting colonial control via the old royal families. Unlike in Java and Sumatra, there were to be no missionaries permitted on the island and no Dutch plantations: the landscape would remain one of rice fields, temples and quaint villages where the Balinese would live as it was supposed they had lived since time immemorial. For their own good, the Balinese were to be denied access to modernity. The proponents of Balinisation (the so-called 'Bali lobby') were against the Balinese having trade unions or watching movies; they were against them wearing shorts and trousers instead of sarongs and they were opposed, needless to say, to their involvement in the nationalist movement (Pollman 1990: 13). There were few schools – the Balinese were not to be spoiled by modern education. The surface image of a cultured, genteel people living in verdant paradise was not merely at odds with the grinding poverty many actually lived in and with the island's history of violence, it also ignored a growing, self-consciously modern young intelligentsia who were interested in nationalism and the reform of the caste system (Nordholt 2000).

The conservation of what we would now label as the island's 'built heritage' was part of this larger, comprehensive programme. The Dutch paid for the rebuilding of temples in the traditional style after the earthquake of 1917 as one element of an associated programme of restoring the old aristocracy, now loyal to the Dutch (Vickers 1989: 135) and also in order to prevent the villagers rebuilding the temples in some innovative new style (Pollman 1990: 14). Walter Spies was director of the public museum in Denpasar and collaborated with Dutch archaeologists. What the Bali lobby attempted, in a sense, was to render an entire culture archaeological. As is typical of a certain kind of cultural conservationism in our own times, the protagonists saw lack of change as only natural to Balinese culture while at the same time their conservation programme sprang precisely from their apprehension of the culture's amenability to change.

In the postcolonial era the work of maintaining and elaborating Bali's image has been taken on by the national and provincial governments and by private tourism operators, many of whom are Balinese. Degung Santikarma (2005: 317), who contrasts the attention received by the October 2002 bombings in Bali and the urge to build monuments to commemorate the victims with the enduring silence about the 1965–66 atrocities, also points to the way the bombings ruptured the carefully culti-vated 'image of Bali as an isle of peace, invulnerable to its own history of violence'. Enormous efforts were made by the government, the media and Balinese reliant on the tourism industry to quickly repair this rupture.

This goes to the question of just what, in a place like Bali, we tourists are in dialogue *with*. Can we engage in a dialogue with a heritage place unmediated by heritage discourse? Can our touristic experience of a place like Bali ever circumvent Orientalist and colonialist renderings of Asia that have long been embedded in our own culture and which can be enor-mously seductive? I would think not, but David Crouch (2005: 27–31) encourages us to see that while tourists are seduced by places and repre-sentations of place they also flirt with places (see also Crouch 2010). Thinking back on my own involvement with Bali I can see myself flirting with the place even as I was being seduced by it, and I believe it would require an unweaning confidence to know where one began and the other ended.

The Campuan Hotel: flirting with Walter

Walter Spies fell victim in 1939 to an anti-homosexual witch-hunt carried out by the Dutch authorities, part of a wider morality campaign sweeping colonial Asia around that time. He was imprisoned in 1942 and he drowned at sea while being transported to Ceylon as a German internee.[9] His house and garden were subsequently turned into the Campuan Hotel where upmarket thatched bungalows are now sequestered among luxuriant trees and shrubs on narrow bands of flat ground that step down the side of the ravine. These terraces are all that remain of the 1920s rice terraces Spies would have seen when he first visited the site. If you walk through the small, open-sided lobby of the Campuan Hotel, which is level with the road from Ubud, and climb down the pathways and stairs through the garden, you enter another world. It may also occur to you that you are descending, like an archaeologist, down through the strata of Bali's tourism history.

Figure 2.1 Walter Spies' bungalow, Campuan Hotel, 2011
    Photo: Denis Byrne

Halfway down you come to a rectangular lotus pond (an echo of a flooded terrace?) at one end of which is the bungalow Spies built for himself in the 1930s.[10] There is a photograph of him sitting on the veranda holding a monkey, a parrot perched on the back of his chair and a Balinese boy walking up the side of the house behind him.[11] Moving on, down a narrow stone stairway flanked by stone images of demons green with moss you pass a pedestal shrine in a small stone-walled enclosure that is partly overrun with creeping plants. A thread of incense smoke meanders through the still air. Across another narrow terrace and down more fern-shrouded stairs you come to a swimming pool set discreetly into the last terrace, invisible from the garden above. On the far side of the pool is a stone paved ledged just wide enough to lie on and beyond this is the final plunge down into the bottom of the ravine where, invisible through the leaves, a small river runs. Here around the swimming pool you might imagine you hear the voices of some of the visitors Walter entertained at

It could be tempting to think of the Campuan garden as pure seduction, there being nothing 'real' there beyond what Walter Spies, and subsequently the hotel owners, fabricated as a paradise set within the larger construct of Paradise Bali. And yet this was the reality Walter lived. Could he have distinguished what was a projection of his own desires from what was being projected towards him by the place and its people? He observed the wild plants and insects in his garden (Spruit 1997: 65) and made exquisite drawings of them. If he was projecting a paradise mythology onto his surroundings his environment was also coming at him with its own specificity. Even in his own garden, he could not experience Bali in just any way he might like (Tilley 2008: 271).

Nor, I suggest, can we now experience his garden in any way *we* might choose. The garden is 'sticky' (Ahmed 2010: 35) with affects deriving from Walter's former presence there. He spent years in the garden and in a real sense it was an extension of him. We can imagine that the present-day paved pathways might originally have been the tracks made by his own feet, that his habitual trajectories through the garden eventually solidified into formal paths and steps. Our feet now 'follow' his – they have no choice, there is no other way through the garden but via these paths that are a sedimentation of his repetitious bodily movements. In following his paths, our bodies are thus 'in touch' with his, an entailment about which some hotel guests might have mixed feelings if they knew Walter was queer.

Figure 2.3 A pathway in the garden at the Campuan Hotel, 2011
Photo: Denis Byrne

For the tourist in Bali, 'reality' can seem like something always withheld. Whole areas of the island's recent history are hidden from us. Equally, the reality of contemporary Balinese social life is veiled in layers of mythology developed to seduce us into believing we are present in a kind of paradise. Yet I suggest we can think of tourism, including heritage tourism, in terms of exploration. Exploration, of course, is a trope as old as Orientalism and the two are not unrelated, but I am thinking of the kind of everyday exploring we do with our senses and imaginations in addition to that which our feet might do when they deviate off the beaten track. This kind of exploration can feed off those physical objects put in place precisely to deceive us. How often, for instance, do we find ourselves at some heritage site where the sheer labour expended on restoration, instead of leaving us convinced, leaves us wondering why. 'Who is behind this?' we find ourselves asking. '*What* is behind it?' In a similar way, for those visitors to Bali who happen to learn of the events of 1965–66 (a possibility made increasing likely with the internet) the absence of traces, rather than stifling their interest might actually excite it. And similarly, although what is specifically queer about Walter's presence in the Campuan garden is withheld from us in the sense that his sexuality is stifled in the brochures and signage, we can choose to reinstate it.

Notes

1   This photograph appeared above the caption: 'As two men await certain death, a soldier bayonets those at his feet' (October 1965). The photograph is more likely to have been taken in Java than Bali but the circumstances of death in both places were similar.
2   Santikarma (2005: 312–3) describes visiting a mass grave in the post-Soeharto era in the company of a Balinese man who had witnessed the killing and burial of around 220 people at that site in 1965. The grave appears to have been on the north coast of the island but Santikarma does not give its location.
3   More recently, at a workshop on fictocritical writing at the University of New South Wales (Oct 2010), Muecke referred to it as 'digging for affect'.
4   Mueggler's particular use of the word 'encrypted' in his 1998 article suggests it can stand for the crypt as a burial site while simultaneously referencing the hidden meaning of an encoded message.
5   Marianne Hirsch's work (e.g. 2001) on the Jewish Holocaust is relevant here. She makes the point that the experience of actual recollection is available only to the survivors of the Holocaust. For those who come after, including the 'second generation', the Holocaust can only be available via acts of representation, projection and creation.
6   I heard this explanation offered by speakers at a human rights symposium in Taiwan in November 2010.
7   David Spurr (1993: 22) tells us: 'the body is that which is most proper to the primitive, the sign by which the primitive is represented. The body, rather than speech, law, or history, is the essential defining characteristic of primitive peoples. They live, according to this view, in their bodies and in natural space, but not in a body politic worthy of the name'.

representing violence in Bali', in M.S. Zurbuchen (ed.) *Beginning to Remember: The Past in the Indonesian Present*, Singapore: National University of Singapore Press and Seattle: University of Washington Press.

Simon, J. (2010) 'Critical distance', *Cultural Studies Review* 16(2): 4–23.

Smith, L. (2006) *Uses of Heritage*, London: Routledge.

Smith, L. and Waterton, E. (2009) *Heritage Communities and Archaeology*, London: Duckworth.

Spruit, R. (1997) *Artists on Bali*, Amsterdam: Pepin Press.

Spurr, D. (1993) *The Rhetoric of Empire*, Durham NC: Duke University Press.

Stoler, A. L. (2002) 'On the uses and abuses of the past in Indonesia', *Asia Survey* 42(4): 642–50.

Tilley, C. (2008) 'Phenomenological approaches to landscape archaeology', in B. David and J. Thomas (eds) *Handbook of Landscape Archaeology*, Walnut Creek, CA: Left Coast Press.

Urry, J. (1990) *The Tourist Gaze*, London: Sage.

Van der Kroef, J. (1972) 'Origin of the 1965 coup in Indonesia: probabilities and alternatives', *Journal of Southeast Asian Studies* 3: 277–98.

Vickers, A. (1989) *Bali, a Paradise Created*, Ringwood, Victoria: Penguin.

Zurbuchen, M. S. (2005) 'Historical memory in contemporary Indonesia', in M.S. Zurbuchen (ed.) *Beginning to Remember: The Past in the Indonesian Present*, Singapore: National University of Singapore Press and Seattle: University of Washington Press.

Chapter 3

Authorising the unauthorised

Liquidity, complexity and the heritage-tourist in the era of social media

Fiona Cameron and Sarah Mengler

Introduction

The borders between heritage institutions and everyday life are increasingly porous. Authorised heritage interpretations, values and attributed significance endowed by the institution when inducted into a networked environment are increasingly subject to a more complex field of relations, values and interpretations. These ideas were explored in the Australian Research Council Linkage project Reconceptualising Heritage Collections (University of Western Sydney and Powerhouse Museum). With a focus on the Powerhouse Museum's Palestinian collections and on dialogues through wikis and focus groups with five main stakeholder groups in Australia, Israel and Palestine (curators from the Powerhouse Museum, Palestinian Cultural Centre staff, Palestinian nationals, Palestinian Australian people and Israeli curators), we illustrate how the heritage institution can act as an open and dynamical space for the interaction and ongoing translation and negotiation of the heritage object, thereby confronting any artificial conceptions of authorised/unauthorised engagements.

The Reconceptualising Heritage Collections project, for which the authors were the lead investigators (Cameron as chief investigator and Mengler as researcher), studied the object within the context of the Powerhouse Museum's collections. The Powerhouse Museum in Sydney is the New South Wales Government's prominent state museum, with over 385,000 objects in its collection, covering decorative arts and design, Australian history and society, engineering and design, sciences, koori (Indigenous) history and culture and transport. The institution's foundation can be traced to the 1879 Sydney International Exhibition, with the current institution located in a power station in Ultimo, a result of a major redevelopment in 1988 (as part of the nation's bicentennial celebrations). Like many cultural and heritage institutions, only a small percentage of works (around 20 per cent at the Powerhouse Museum) can be displayed at any one time in exhibitions.

The online database therefore occupies an important role in offering access to museum collections. The online projects of the Powerhouse Museum are ambitious, intriguing and simultaneously verify and challenge both notions of the role of the museum and relations between collections and knowledge production. This, coupled with the museum's focus on community, creativity, design and its relation to society and everyday life, made the museum an interesting partner for the project. With the advent of Google-enabled searches in June 2006, the museum's collections were more directly embedded into mobile global flows and fluids thus allowing objects to play a greater role in the 'unauthorised' interpretation of collections.

The Reconceptualising Heritage Collections project comprised three components:

- Google-enabled searches and the induction of the museum's collections directly into public culture via the OPAC 2.0 collections database;
- Collections wiki, which focused on two Powerhouse Museum objects: a British Mandate coin (c. 1927) and a *thob abu qutbeh* (wedding dress), and dialogic interactions between Powerhouse Museum curators, Israeli curators from Jerusalem, and four Palestinian curators from cultural centres in Ramallah during a three-week period in January 2008 and subsequent focus group discussions in February 2008. One focus group involved museum curatorial staff (with 12 participants) and the other, a mixed group, comprising five Powerhouse Museum curators, nine Palestinian Australians, and three Palestinian curators based in Ramallah; and
- The conceptual development of new transdisciplinary interfaces for collections documentation.

Participatory media, Web 2.0 and congregational spaces such as YouTube, Flickr, MySpace, Facebook and Twitter enable the engagement of individuals in discussions on current matters and the broadcasting of their personal thoughts and opinions to a global audience. Museum collections, such as the Powerhouse Museum objects, are being inducted into this hyper-complex world not only through Google-enabled initiatives but also through links to the social media listed above. Interactions with such collections – both planned and serendipitous – are being conducted through these multiple and extended networks and flows of people, ideas and objects that transcend national boundaries. These interactions can be enacted anywhere and at anytime by anyone thereby highlighting the extension of museum experience to one embedded in public culture highlighting the potential advent and consequent commonality of the seemingly unauthorised. Institutional trustworthiness in these debates (including via the internet) is based on the idea of authorised expertise, credibility and transparency of sources. On the net, users face the problem of deciphering reliable sources, while at once recognising the advantage of having access to a range of sources, ideological positions, values and approaches to build up a better picture of the object (see Cameron and Mengler 2009). Museums are experiencing this complexity as objects enter the online environment and engage with practices, such as folksonomies, which enable 'unauthorised' interpretative practices to flourish. All this poses a new set of challenges for engaging with heritage collections, highlighting the complexities of cultural exchanges and interactions that are both complex, entangled and, at times conflictual, contesting the nature of institutionally attributed significance and interpretation. These initiatives enabled the researchers to observe and interpret the dynamical interactions of heritage objects and actors within the public domain.

An initial example that demonstrates the porosity of the boundaries between authorised and unauthorised interpretations of heritage objects and the emergence of a greater requirement to engage a non-linear, dynamical and fluid space for negotiating these relations occurred in 2007. Angered over the Hollywood movie *300* and the way Persians were represented (in the battle of Thermopylae) Iranian nationals mobilised collections from the British Museum through Google to counter negative representations of their culture in an attempt to perpetrate a positive image of their people and culture (Cameron 2008; Jones 2007). In observing how Google searches changed object significance we noted that the popularity of collection objects fluctuated depending on social, political and economic events. The popularity of the 'Speedo swimsuit' increased on its anniversary, in the lead-up to and during an important international swimming event. These observations highlight the fluidity and complexity of object circulations in global flows, the potential to mobilise collections to support political projects; how competing ideologies, values and systems of meaning are able to assemble in cyberspace; and how museum culture and public culture are increasingly more entangled.

Heritage institutions can no longer limit or determine in advance the shape, heterogeneity and combination of associations, values and meaning that cluster around objects. Nor are they able to limit actors to a singular imposed, authorised curatorial order. Rather, the complexity of expertise and resultant heritage exchanges (both intended and unintended) can be conceptualised through a transdisciplinary practice framework. Greater emphasis needs to be placed on an object's broader field of relations and material configurations, and how these evolving values and meanings might be linked between disparate actors, actants and the collections record (Cameron and Mengler 2009).To this end, a broader conception of the object is required that more clearly articulates these interactions. Political theorist Jane Bennett (2010a: para. 24) argues that 'when humans act they do not exercise exclusively human powers, but express and engage a variety of other actants, including food, micro-organisms, minerals, artefacts, sounds, bio- and other technologies, and so on'. Bennett's work argues that the insertion of the non-human as an actant, as having agency-adding vitality to this communion of interactions around collections, thereby closes the museological gap between the separate domains of life (the social and the non-human; organic and inorganic matter) and the complex object. Rather than thinking of objects as dead things, collections instead become enlivened as vibrant heterogeneous assemblages, as mixtures of different types of content comprising human and non-human elements and organic and non-organic matter such as metal, stone, cotton, threads, people, digital codes, ideological, religious and spiritual phenomena, aesthetic values, heritage values, laws, social practices, technologies, political views and the environment (Cameron 2012). Each of these components are themselves composites of things that have their own properties and expressive forms, agencies and capacities to affect and be affected in the context of dynamical relations, as they come together in various combinations, and interact, compete, emerge and dissipate (Cameron 2010) according to differentiated movements of speed, direction and intensity. Dynamical relationships of functional flow – as well as more volatile relationships of friction conflict (Bennett 2010b: 23; Harrison, Byrne and Clarke forthcoming) and turbulence – act as creative and productive forces. The notion of friction, as heritage scholars Rodney Harrison, Sarah Byrne and Annie Clarke (2012: 17) argue, 'acknowledges the fundamentally awkward, unequal, contingent nature of cross-cultural engagements and as generative processes, as collaborations in which things are made despite the presence of consensus or common goals, where things coalesce are maintained and things are kept in motion'.

Bruno Latour and Peter Weibel's (2005) 'object-oriented democracy' and Latour's (2005) 'parliament of things' as congregations of humans, intentionality, non-human things and forces act as an imaginary to conceptualise the nature of this distributed agency, the compossibility of heritage objects and these entangled relations and interactions as pluri-modal heritage representational systems and as non-representational dynamical processes (Cameron 2012). Most importantly such representational and non-linear dynamical processes can no longer been seen as something to be necessarily predicted, controlled, minimised and accordingly eliminated (Cameron 2008, 2012). In turn, such a formation articulates the heritage tourist and the lay person as valued actors having valued opinions, experience and expertise. When configuring heritage objects as 'compossibilites' of content and as things that are fluid, mobile, are made and remade, reconfigured and recomposed through these dynamical interactions, such an imaginary gives rise to many refashioned interpretative frames and renderings of the complex object. Expert systems are reframed such that many actors exhibit different agencies and capacities to affect the way objects are known and valued, and in turn are affected by others (for questions of agency, see Latour 2005; Bennett 2010b).

Interpretations previously regarded as unauthorised – operating outside a closed collections-documentation system – now have validity within a fluid, open and mobile collections-documentation system. To this end, a more complex imaginary develops for the heritage object as a composite of different types of content, using notions of liquid museums (Cameron 2010), the attractor and transdisciplinarity.

The object, the audience–tourist and their historical legacies

In order to further interrogate these ideas, it was necessary to look at the way the heritage institution has been conceptualised. This history affects both the way the heritage object and the audience (or tourist) is framed. Induced into a fever of knowledge accumulation and intelligence gathering, the Victorian archival industry began a process whereby information concerning the known world was synchronised and unified. The process of archival synchronisation and unification was accomplished by reconciling specific forms of discrete and quantifiable knowledge into universal principles of aggregated data. The museum system of expertise and knowledge is underpinned by an eighteenth century notion of classification and materiality based around concepts of objectivity and classificatory completeness. This system, 'locked in' during the nineteenth century following the advent of disciplinary hierarchies, acts as a frame endowing collections with a descriptive schema and significance (Bennett 1995: 2). These concepts have been augmented more recently through the development of social history and museum practice with the inclusion of cultural and social descriptors. Even so, the opportunity to actually discover and highlight the object or artwork's agency is foregone. Objects become either Latour's (1987) 'black boxes', used as evidence to securitise social and symbolic meaning, or Gell's (1998) time–space stoppages (see Cameron and Mengler 2009).

This conception of the museum also has implications for the way the audience or tourist is conceptualised. Cultural theorists Zygmunt Bauman (1987) and Michel Foucault (1991) illustrate how a state system operates as a distinctly modern means for shaping and governing social conditions through particular apparatus and intellectual strategies. Accordingly, museums as knowledge institutions act as sites for exercising a specific form of power and knowledge through education (see Bennett 1995), and as moralising and reforming lessons (Cameron 2007). From this vision of modernity, education is equated with disciplining populations, enforcing conformity to a particular elitist moral order, consequently accompanied by the rejection of localised and other knowledge systems. These knowledge practices therefore reduced an individual's capacity to exercise their own moral dispositions (Cameron 2011). Or, to frame this notion from the macro perspective, the paradox of the museum is that it is on one hand a public space comprised of a cosmopolitan society, on the other, a space in which diverse groups are deemed to belong to a single global community, sharing a singular morality. Accordingly, the museum is deemed to operate as a venue to promote a shared humanity. That is, one that assumes that the world can operate as an orderly and harmonious system according to a common cosmos (Cameron and Mengler 2011).

Our initial study of the Thermopylae incident seemed to indicate an alternative reality. In the Thermopylae case the object was the very medium through which values, ideas and social distinctions and concepts of the non-human (such as land and territory) are constantly reproduced, legitimised or transformed. The object was used as a medium to reproduce and assert certain contemporary representations of Iranian identity. In the American Association of Museums' report *Demographic Transformation and the Future of Museums*, Elizabeth E. Merritt summarised this dynamic noting: '[The] major take-away from this research is that diversity is fractal – when you take a closer look at categories, they break down into subgroups that *contain just as much complexity*'. (2010: 30) Terms such as 'diversity' have different meanings for different audiences. Divisions such as race, ethnicity, income, education and geography are no longer adequate because they are too simplistic. The complexities and dynamics enabled through modes of participation and consequent location of institutions in social networks are increasingly relevant.

As a starting point in conceptualising a new cosmopolitical collections space, Dant (2006: 299) argues for a pluralist system of objects' significance, stating that the value of material objects does not derive solely from their origins in production, their meanings in consumption, their practical use in everyday life, nor from the networks associated with their emergence as technical entities. For Dant, the value actually derives from all of these factors. Dant's musings however precede the advent of social media. In considering Dant's observations and our own, no definitive categorisations can capture all that can be known about where constituent parts come from, how objects are interconnected, how they can be traced, where objects belong or how they are consumed. Therefore the language of categorisation is not (yet) completely known or available, but rather operates as an emergent process.

Moving from the idea of pluralism as a means of complicating the object, French author André Malraux (1965[1947]), in his book *Le Musée Imaginaire*, formulates an alternative view, suggesting that synergies between humanity and materiality offer up one interface. Within museums, objects are physically and conceptually separated from society and from nature, used as metaphorical stand-ins for socially and culturally constituted meanings. In this context they are conceived as extra-material in their origin and thereby subordinated to culture and history (Pinney

2005). Malraux (1965[1947]) suggests connecting materiality and humanity more deeply in order to link, in this instance, art to the social and to richer, more temporally situated forms of experience (Hetherington 2006). This allows objects to be seen as in translation, thereby unlocking agency in multifarious ways. These positions challenge the basis of the museum metaphorical tradition as primarily symbolic and static.

Cultural theorist Bruno Latour (2005) also rejects any division between the material and the social world, technology and society to which the museum system upholds. In considering Latour's argument in the context of heritage institutions, the different dimensions of an object cannot be separated from the technical object in any straightforward way because they constitute the precondition of its existence in the first place. Rather, Latour's focus is on making an object's activity as a trail of associations easily visible. More importantly, Jane Bennett's formulation of assemblages as confederations of human and non-human elements and its application in this instance to the re-theorisation of heritage collections as assemblages (Cameron 2011, 2012) opens a space to consider the dynamical relational connections and interactions not only with the social and/or the human but also the non-human. It is within this dynamical field of relations that collections now circulate beyond the confines of the authoritative heritage institution and from which the heritage object emerges as plural–modal composite of things.

Therefore conventional understandings of the so-called 'gap' between serious researchers and serendipitous visitors via online collections oversimplify the situation. The emergent contested status of the complex object produces uncertainty on the side of museums and of society. Consequently there is also the potential for knowledge domains to clash on what has become regarded as a shared interface. On one side, the heritage institution is a source of expertise and authority, possessing trusted information, certain knowledge, leading to specific future possibilities. As one participant in the Powerhouse Museum Curatorial Focus Group stated: 'My concern is if we are authoritative then we have to see our records as sacrosanct even though we recognise that they are not necessarily fixed... it is open to public correction but not negotiation.' (Powerhouse Museum Curatorial Focus Group 2008). On the other hand, the participatory forces of the internet potentially enable members of society to become content producers, able to assert their own identity, to disrupt power relationships and re-constitute their own lives and futures (Fraser 1997; Young 2000; Rodriguez 2004).

The objects: *thob abu qutbeh* and the British mandate coin

In order to further investigate this notion of the complex object and to interrogate heritage collections as vital assemblages of composite things (both human and non-human) operating within dynamical processes, an in-depth study around two objects was established by the Reconceptualising Heritage Collections team. These objects were a Palestinian *thob abu qutbeh* (wedding dress) and a British Mandate coin. Networks were established with museums and cultural centres in Ramallah in Palestine and in Israel and conversations between curators and community groups were activated through a collections wiki. These participants were invited to comment on the Powerhouse Museum record through a blog and construct their own documentation record. Additional source material was also provided in the wiki. The focus group discussions centred on the two objects and their multifarious interpretations formulated through dialogic processes in the wiki. While the contributions of Israeli curators were captured on the wiki, it was decided that due to the highly sensitive nature of the Palestinian–Israeli situation and our desire to promote further one-on-one discussions, the focus group participants would be restricted to Powerhouse Museum curators, Palestinian curators and Palestinian community members. Specific questions were asked about museums and their role in assigning value, meaning and significance to Palestinian heritage items; the validity of other types of expertise in documentation and the potential for collaborative documentation practices using social media involving a range of actors as well as the limitations of these approaches.

The aim of this exercise was to establish a conceptual framework for a transdisciplinary interface that could acknowledge and capture disparate, complex and at times contentious cosmopolitical interpretive formulations. Through these research methods the required ubiquitous interactions in global space and time could be instituted and observed. The objects were chosen because of their highly political nature as embodiments of ongoing geopolitical conflicts and border disputes. The collection items also exhibited significant production differences, with the coin being produced by a colonial power and the dress by Palestinian women. Borders as a concept and method (see Mezzadra and Neilson 2010) were used to conceptualise the objects, documentation systems and the discussions as multiplicitous penetrations into the collections-documentation space. Here, objects acted as a mobilising force by acting as a meeting place and as points of contact for multifarious dialogic interactions, as polysemic – having multiple histories and narratives thereby meaning different things to the various stakeholders and conversely a place where validations, disruptions of cultural representations could be undertaken and where the non-human can be factored into collections documentation. Both objects link to borders as a political problem and directly to disputes over land and sovereignty in the Israeli–Palestinian conflict.

The *thob abu qutbeh*

The *thob abu qutbeh* is a silk 'special occasion dress' made in Palestine in about 1940 (maker unknown). The Powerhouse Museum curatorial narrative of the *thob* in the object record operated as a bordered container speaking as a symbolic stand-in and expression of Palestinian women and culture. Here the object operated as an isolated static entity, frozen in place and time through the description of its physicality and production as representative of a wedding dress and to its use as a kaftan at hippy parties during the 1960s. A curator described this approach, stating that 'the Palestinian traditional dress is representative of Palestinian women and culture that represents more than the object. The dress becomes a symbol to discuss this relationship'. (Palestinian focus group 2008: participant C3).

Palestinian curatorial readings of the same object talked of the *thob* as a living tradition worn by women in villages and refugee camps. It stood as a national symbol and a marker of identity, social class, marital status and origin. According to one Palestinian cultural centre worker it was 'part of a living tradition worn by many women in villages and refugee camps... a tradition that keeps transforming – a national symbol as a representation of place, lost to Palestinians, that maps the landscape and locations'. (Palestinian focus group 2008: participant PC1). A Jewish reading, on the other hand, sought to challenge the use of material culture and the *thob* as a statement of resistance and occupation and the deployment of collections data as a political tool. Rather, participants in the wiki asserted that the *thob* has a Judeo–Christian origin (*RC* wiki project 2008: participants J1–6). For Palestinian nationals the *thob abu qutbeh* operated as a regional and national symbol and marker of identity. The *thob* was seen as a statement of resistance against the Israeli occupation and as a politicalised map of the landscape. As one focus group participant stated: 'After the occupation the *thob* becomes a flag – while the flag cannot be displayed, you could be imprisoned for it, the dress takes its place'. (Palestinian focus group 2008: participant P2). The Palestinian cultural centre curators also saw the style and colour of each *thob* speaking of its specific location and to land lost in the occupied territories: 'The journey began with celebration – a thread to show happiness until occupation. The colours of the thob are bright and reflect the area where a woman came from, embroidered flora/fauna symbolise the region'. (Palestinian focus group 2008: participant P5). The motifs symbolise flora and fauna, cypress trees, the cotton, silk threads and dyes as organic elements originate from the land, the soil, insects, silk worms and cotton plants each having their own agencies as entangled social and material worlds. The diasporic readings (those of Palestinian Australians) of the *thob abu qutbeh* also spoke of the *thob* as a symbol of identity. In this context, their focus was less on the *thob* as a political tool, instead the object spoke more directly to the emotional links to homeland,

that make up heritage objects. Here the attractor concept and transdisciplinarity offer a means to further explain and explore the concept of the 'unauthorised' in heritage.

Redefining and repositioning the heritage object

Chaos theory is a discourse that has previously been used primarily in mathematics, the stock market and science (Gleick 1988). In art, the chaos theory has been deployed to explore the visual components of popular works such as the smile of the *Mona Lisa* and Pollock's 'drips' (Taylor 2007: 28). Similarly Pinney (2005: 266) uses non-linearity a concept central to chaos theory – when discussing images, advocating their treatment as 'compressed performances', caught up in recursive trajectories of repetition and pastiche whose dense complexity makes them resistant to any particular moment. That is, images are not simply always a reflection of something happening elsewhere.

Chaos theory enables the conceptualisation of a museum system and curatorial practice as complexity (as relational, as fluid, as systems, networks and assemblages). Here documentation systems become a border zone, that is, being both permeable – allowing non-linear interactions and contributions of communities – and, conversely, resistant – creating a boundary or barrier that enables the expertise of museum staff to be retained as the collection continues to be exposed to the online environment (Cameron and Mengler 2011). It is this dynamic between the internal 'authorised' heritage interpretation and the 'unauthorised', termed within chaos theory as 'exogenous' and 'endogenous' variables, which creates what is called an 'attractor' in chaos theory. The interactions of these two variables ultimately create feedback loops, setting the dynamic for interactions throughout the space. Latour's early work is useful here in helping to unpack the relationship between exogenous and endogenous variables. Latour's work explored the relationship between the daily activities of scientists in this context termed endogenous variables and the results they produced as exogenous variables. Latour found a disjunction between science's account of its own praxis and the ethnographic data he collected. Consequently Latour's ethnographical work challenged a certain vision of the sciences as unmediated expressions of objective facts. This related to the organisational nature of scientific work – both in a restricted sense of the operations of a given social institution and in the more general sense of an ordering or classification of the material world.

The attractor concept describes how a system develops its own a sense of self-organisation over a period of time rather than as a centralised hierarchical direction based on a linear trajectory (Castells 2004). Trajectories that get close enough to the attractor must remain close even if slightly disturbed or if points from the basin of an attractor converge towards the attractor. Most of the chaotic behaviour occurs within the attractor and initial conditions will lead activity to converge on this particular space (Smith and Jenks 2005). It is the heritage object – in the Reconceptualising Heritage Collections project example, the *thob* and coin – which is the attractor. The heritage object achieves this attractor status first by its composition as an assemblage of different types of content through which dynamical interactions occur, and second through its placement within the liquid museum (Cameron 2010).

According to Bauman's (1991) pluralist power theory, different interest groups have a stake in different matters and propose different govern- mental strategies, each exhibiting variable powers to act (Cameron 2011: 2). To deploy Bauman's (1991, 2000) pluralist power theory and the notion liquid modernity here, heritage interpretation now entails plural models of order where power is dispersed across multiple actors and dispersed sites, legitimising the pluralisation of authoritative opinion, expertise, multiple rationalities, different technologies and techniques for acting (Cameron 2011: 2). The dynamical interactions that characterise contemporary life, along with the notion of dispersed agency, restructure the heritage institu- tion and site as a *liquid institution* (Cameron 2010, 2011). Deleuze and Guattari's (1987) and DeLanda's (2006) assemblages provide the concep- tual tools to conceive of institutional forms as dispersed, interconnected, mobile and emergent. By using the concepts liquidity and assemblage, the heritage institution can be conceptualised more readily as processual and machinic operating within the plural governmental arrangements and rationalities and deploying different technologies and techniques for acting. Institutions or heritage sites are no longer solely conceived as hier- archical, closed or fixed to a physical location. As assemblages, institutions and heritage sites can be thought of as made up of components of material (buildings; people; computers; exhibitions, collections; geographical loca- tion, environment; funding, etc.) and expressive forms (practices and capacities such as mission; expressions of legitimacy; expertise; trust; authority; networks; dispositions; aspirations; contracts; brand; authorised heritage interpretations, etc.) operating as, and in dynamic gathering or assembling and dispersing or disassembling processes, which transcend national boundaries. Each of these components within institutional assem- blages operate as a mobile configuration that is at once diverse, distributed, at times uncoordinated and exhibiting varying capacities.

In a liquid modern frame, knowledge production and education are no longer bound to specific apparatus (such as the school or the museum). Questions of agency can no longer be formulated along one line. Pluralised governmental possibilities emerge (Cameron 2011). Interpreting Bauman's ideas in the context of this argument articulates the form and shape of muse- ums and heritage institutions as dispersed, as fragmented, as interconnected, able to link and contribute to a range of different governmental strategies rationalities and techniques (Cameron 2011). In mapping the notion of plural power theory onto heritage sites, museums and science centres, audiences move from objects for reformatory intervention to subjects for action. This process can be achieved by contributing to and by assembling the ideological positions, views, authoritative opinion, beliefs and values, techniques and technologies of others posing multifarious combinations from which the object as a mobile assemblage of different types of content might emerge. To this end, transdisciplinarity and the practical example of online gaming offers a pathway to explore further the notion of the 'unauthorised' heritage object, the pathways for the tourist and the heritage institution as a liquid institution.

Transdisciplinarity, gaming and the heritage tourist

The aim of this argument is to produce a relational system based on an assemblage dynamic. This allows for a emergent and machinic form of knowledge to be performed rather than knowledge unity, and for elements such as fluidity, uncertainty, complexity and their incumbent dynamical relations to be have their place and to be played out. Each of these interpretations as performed by the various actants and actors in the object assemblage expand and complexify objects' knowledges to which discipline-based knowledge alone cannot inform.

Taking all this into account, it might be more productive to conceive of the liquid institution not just as a symbolic technology but as an influential force – as an assemblage and attractor within these dynamical confederations, bringing together serendipitous elements, and conversely as a border zone where heterogeneous content might meet. Latour's (2005) idea of the 'capable actor' can be brought together with the liquid institution in which the latter takes on the role of translating and integrating these heterogeneous elements seeing each as part of a chain that makes up the complex object.

Clearly a complex approach gestures towards a need to expand the meaning of objects beyond disciplinary boundaries that seek closure, to a role as actors in the constitution of social relations by examining broader categories such as art, landscape, memory, technology, exchange and consumption and the non-human. The collections interpretative space therefore must be thought of as a series of emergent and non-linear dynamical relations in the context of mutual relationships between a number of different actors and actants, both human and non-human as well as technologies and practices. There is also a need to deal with expertise in the museum as participatory, local, experiential knowledge and as jointly generated knowledge) –as different forms of interactions that occur in interdisciplinary and transdisciplinary practice. The role and agentic capacity of the non-human must be acknowledged as an integral part of the object's vitality.

The challenge for this process is how to think of the metaphorical associations between the heritage object as matter (both organic and non-organic), the emotional, social and symbolic and experiential, in a non-reductionist way and yet capture the liminality, fluidity and interactivity of categorisation. In order to manage complexity and to sort out the desirable and undesirable effects of its increase, the heritage system is challenged to realign its cognitive and practical ordering of the world. Disciplinary-based documentation remains, however, a powerful framework for organising and producing knowledge in heritage institutions and as one that is deeply embedded and sustained by networks and communities of practice. The idea is not to do away with these specialisations and the accumulated collections knowledge that heritage institutions hold but to add a level of complexity. That is, for collections interpretative platforms to act as open and dynamic spaces for the interaction and the ongoing translation of the complex object within the institution and the public sphere. Contradictions (and indeed contention) must be regarded as acceptable and integral to an object's becoming. The aim here is to hybridise the heritage order, making the boundaries of classification and description, contextualisation and significance permeable. The aim is also to acknowledge and embrace the contention that there will necessarily be a degree of structural instability in the system of collections information and significance previously denied. The idea of the object interaction and translation makes the distinction between curatorial disciplines, internal (the heritage institution) and external (public sphere) and that of the social and non-human less sustainable.

One approach is to rethink object interfaces as assemblages on the basis of a range of multiple, mobile metaphors – material, solid and linguistic – to which various actants and actors can contribute as a kind of transdisciplinary practice. Here, boundaries between disciplines are able to be transcended and knowledges assembled and commune with each other. Solid metaphors refer to the actional and biographical contexts – how an object is produced, sourced, what its raw materials, exchange and consumption contexts, uses, sequence of events or factual qualities are (Tilley 1999: 263–6). Conceptual metaphors are those taken-for-granted meanings that frame an object's activities. Linguistic metaphors on the other hand are statements for describing significance and are typically opinion based. The aim is to produce a relational system that allows for knowledge emergence and the acknowledgment of the value of communication rather than the performance of knowledge unity. The institution of such practices will allow for uncertainty and complexity which discipline-based knowledge alone cannot take account.

Gaming initiatives utilise transdisciplinary ideas and non-linear dynamical interactions to mobilise collective intelligence and imagination. One of the first and most successful of these was *World Without Oil* (2007), with the tagline 'play it before you live it'. This alternative reality game invited people from all walks of life to contribute 'collective imagination' to confront a real-world concern – namely, the risk that running out of oil has for our economy, climate and quality of life – in a way that had value for policymakers and other authority figures. The game's central site linked to all the player material and the game's characters documented their own lives and commented on player stories on a community blog and individual blogs, plus via instant messaging (IM), webchat, Twitter and other media. *World Without Oil* not only raised awareness about oil dependence, but it also focused thousands of people from all walks of life upon this common concern – sparking peer learning and inquiry-based exploration of the roots, outcomes and prevention of an oil crisis. It also provoked participants to change their everyday approaches to energy use. Similarly, *Superstruct* (2008) is another online game that involved 8,000 citizen future-forecasters from September to November 2008. Players were asked to think about who they will be in 2019, and then fill out a survival profile to create their future identity. Players first learned about 'superthreats' by watching breaking news reports from the future to find out what the year 2019 might be like on planet Earth. The United Nations has also recently developed an online game, *Freerice.com*, run by the United Nations World Food Program. In this game, players earn grains of rice by correctly answering questions on geography, art, mathematics and chemistry, as well as German, Spanish, Italian, French and English. *Freerice* is part of a movement in computer games designed to promote serious messages be they political, philanthropic or social justice orientated. In these instances, different content provided by participants are utilised. While the audience–tourist moves freely, expertise is combined but not enmeshed. This is a space in which the compossibility of the heritage object emerges.

Conclusion

In modernist museological and heritage frameworks, both the object and audience are rendered passive. By contrast, the Reconceptualising Heritage Collections project considered the way objects have agency, act as mediated drivers and as modes of encounters. Here the heritage institution has the opportunity to reconstruct the historical and artistic context of particular experiences, thinking about them as analytical instruments through which to see internal views and external experiences as nuanced exchanges. Through the notion of liquid institutions, heritage sites can be seen as special attractor assemblages, as fluid, porous and as distributed, involving many actors. While internal heritage institutional frameworks remain powerful structures for producing, organising and controlling collections, knowledge production operates through largely uncontested authorised narratives, but the development of social media and new modes of object interaction suggest an alternative reality.

References

Bauman, Z. (1987) *Legislators and Interpreters*, Ithaca NY: Cornell University Press.
Bauman, Z. (1991) *Modernity and Ambivalence*, Ithaca, NY: Cornell University Press.
Bauman, Z. (2000) *Liquid Modernity*, Cambridge: Polity.
Bauman, Z. (2006) *Liquid Times: Living in an Age of Uncertainty*, Cambridge: Polity.
Bennett, J. (2010a) *Agency, Nature and Emergent Properties*. Available online: http://neodoxa.wordpress.com/2010/11/03/agency-nature-and-emergent-properties (accessed 28 September 2011).
Bennett, J. (2010b) *Vibrant Matter: A Political Ecology of Things*, Durham NC: Duke University Press.
Bennett, T. (1995) *The Birth of the Museum: History, Science, Politics*, London: Routledge.
Byrne S., Clarke A., Harrison R. and Torrence R. (eds) (2011), *Unpacking the Collection. Networks of Material and Social Agency in the Museum*, One World Archaeology Series, New York: Springer.
Cameron, F.R. (2007) 'Moral lessons and reforming agendas: history museums, science museums, contentious topics and contemporary societies', in S. Knell, S. Macleod and S. Watson (eds) *Museum Revolutions: how museums change and are changed*, London: Routledge.
Cameron, F.R. (2008) 'Object-orientated democracies: conceptualising museum collections in networks', *Museum Management and Curatorship* 23(3): 229–43.
Cameron, F.R. (2010) 'Liquid governmentalities, liquid museums and the climate crisis', in F.R. Cameron and L. Kelly (eds) *Hot Topics, Public Culture, Museums*, Newcastle upon Tyne, UK: Cambridge Scholars Publishing.
Cameron, F.R. (2011) 'From mitigation to complex reflexivity and creative imaginaries – Museums and science centres in climate governance', *Museum and Society Special Issue: Hot Science, Global Citizens: The Agency of the Museum Sector in Climate Change Interventions* 9(2). Available online: www.le.ac.uk/ms/museumsociety.html (accessed 18 September 2011).
Cameron, F.R. (2012) From "dead" things to immutable combinable mobiles: H.D. Skinner, the Otago Museum and university as centres for the collection and calculation of Maori material culture/taonga during the early phases of the development of anthropology in New Zealand.' Paper presented at Crossroads Conference, Paris, 3–6 July 2012 (in press).
Cameron, F.R. and Mengler, S. (2009) 'Complexity, trans-disciplinarity and museum collections documentation: emergent metaphors for a complex world', *Journal of Material Culture* 14: 189–218.
Cameron, F.R. and Mengler S. (2011) 'Cosmopolitics, border crossings and the complex museum', *International Journal of Heritage Studies*. Online. 1–17. DOI:10.1080/13527258.2011.614629.
Castells, M. (ed.) (2004) *The Network Society: A Cross-Cultural Perspective*, Northampton MA: Edward Elgar.
Dant, T. (2006) 'Materiality and civilization: things and society', *British Journal of Sociology*, 57(2): 289–308
DeLanda, M. (2006) *A New Philosophy of Society: Assemblage Theory and Social Complexity*, London and New York: Continuum.
Deleuze, G. and Guattari, F. (1987) *A Thousand Plateaus*, Minneapolis MN: University of Minnesota Press.

Foucault, M. (1991) 'Governmentality', trans. Rosi Braidotti, in G. Burchell, C. Gordon and P. Miller (eds) *The Foucault Effect: Studies in Governmentality*, Chicago: University of Chicago Press.

Fraser, N. 1997 *Justice Interruptus: Critical Reflections on the Postsocialist Condition*, New York: Routledge.

Gell, A. (1998) *Art and Agency*, Oxford: Clarendon Press.

Gleick, J. (1988) *Chaos*, New York: Cardinal.

Greenhalgh, P. (ed.) (2002) *The Persistence of Craft: The Applied Arts Today*, London: A&C Black.

Harrison, R., Byrne, S., and Clarke, A. (forthcoming) *Reassembling the collection*, Sante Fe: SAR Press.

Hetherington, K. (2006) 'Museum', *Theory, Culture & Society* 23(2/3): 597–602.

Jones, S. (2007) 'Building cultural literacy', Paper presented at *New Collaborations: New Benefits – Transnational Museum Collaboration, International Council of Museums*, Shanghai, 26–27 July.

Latour, B. (1987) *Science in action: How to follow scientists and engineers through society*, Cambridge, MA: Harvard University Press.

Latour, B. 2004 *Politics of Nature: How to Bring the Sciences Into Democracy*, Cambridge, MA: Harvard University Press.

Latour, B. (2005) *Reassembling the Social: An Introduction to Actor-Network Theory*, Oxford and New York: Oxford University Press.

Latour, B. and Weibel P. (2005 eds) *Making Things Public: Atmospheres of Democracy*, Cambridge MA: The MIT Press.

League of Nations (1923) *Mandate for Palestine and Trans-Jordan Memorandum*. Reprinted in the *American Journal of International Law*.

Malraux, A. (1965[1947]) *Le Musée Imaginaire*, Paris: Gallimard.

Merritt, E.E. (2010) 'Where do we go from here: a call to action', in American Association of Museums (ed.) *Demographic Transformation and the Future of Museums*, Washington DC: AAM Press.

Mezzadra, S. and Neilson, B. (2010) *Border as Method or the Multiplication of Labour*, European Institute for Progressive Cultural Policies. Available online: http://eipcp.net/transversal/0608/mezzadraneilson/en (accessed 2 September 2010).

Pinney, C. (2005) 'Things happen: or, from which moment does that object come?', in D. Miller (ed.) *Materiality*, Durham NC: Duke University Press.

Rodríguez, C. (2004) *The Renaissance of Citizens' Media*, Media Development, 2/2004. Available online: www.waccglobal.org/en/20042-citizenship-identity-media/506-The-renaissance-of-citizens-media.html (accessed 28 August 2012).

Smith, J. and Jenks, C. (2005) 'Complexity, ecology and the materiality of information', *Theory, Culture & Society* 22(5): 141–63.

Taylor, R. (2007) 'Pollock, Mondrian and nature: recent scientific investigations' *Chaos and Complexity Letters (Art and Complexity Special Edition)*, 1(3): 112–34.

Tilley, C. (1999) *Metaphor and material culture*, Wiley-Blackwell.

Urry, J. (2003) *Global Complexities*, Oxford: Blackwell.

Young, I. (2002) *Inclusion and democracy*, New York: Oxford University Press.

Part II

Heritage, tourists and the work of representation

Chapter 4

Heritage tourism and its representations

Emma Waterton

Introduction

At most destinations, the haphazard collection of brochures and related paraphernalia can generally be used to piece together an official sanctioning of what a heritage tourism site ought to 'look like'. Images, in this context, operate as perhaps the most critical element. No doubt incorporated so as to simply portray or mirror 'the real thing' – the physical realities of a site or place – they are simultaneously unsettled from this role by their capacity to also 'speak' of embedded, underlying meanings and tensions. Thus, while the images used are likely to be quite blatant in terms of promotion and marketing, their composition will also have far more subtle things to say about matters of power and exclusion. To put it briefly, this occurs by virtue of the role images play in the construction or creation of meaning; a process that is also inevitably filled with hidden silences and obfuscation. This tells us something significant about the act of signification: any negotiation between what is hidden and what is made manifest is meditated by *discourse*.

In the past I have explored the role of discourse with reference to heritage policy in the British context of New Labour government, concluding that a particular 'way of seeing' heritage plays a dominant and complex role in reproducing social relations of inequality (see Waterton 2010a). Significantly, this discourse has continued to dominate *despite* the new Conservative government's political strivings for community cohesion. And so it remains to this discourse that I turn in this chapter, pinpointing the role it plays within British cultural industries and, specifically, within heritage tourism. Why? Because ideas of heritage in Britain seem to operate in much the same way as Nietzsche's 'culture', only in this scenario it is the lie of heritage 'that poses as if it were the only reality' (cited in Webb 2009: 117). To make this case, the chapter closes in on a specific outcome of these mediated processes: the point at which a handful of iconic images, awash with intimations of power, wealth, magnificence, spirituality and longevity, are equated with the complex material and social realities of 'being British'.

Here, the rehearsed and repeated cultural symbols of a particular social group – the elite, middle-classes and the predominantly *white* – are peddled to international and domestic tourists alike, where their reiteration allows them to become 'obvious', 'true' or, at the very least, 'common sense'. While all manner of interesting things can be said about the messages such images convey to international tourists, my focus in this chapter lies with the domestic, because this same set of limited touristic symbols is also presented as 'the true test' of belonging (Hall 1999: 24). Thus, through a process as adept at obscuring the past as it is at marketing it, Britain's multicultural citizenry are asked to positively respond to an exclusive set of representations somehow deemed capable of identifying the nation.

Structurally, the chapter is organised into two sections: (1) an initial qualitative semiology and brief content analysis of a selection of brochures and websites produced by key agencies VisitBritain and English Heritage, and; (2) a more speculative consideration of how these emerging concepts of 'English heritage' are deployed and contested within the associated and ongoing communicative practices of negotiating citizenship and national belonging. In this way, the chapter has itself been structured to move from a consideration of the dependency heritage tourism has upon a small selection of representative practices towards an exploration of how these may be interpreted and negotiated by a specific group of visitors. To achieve this movement in my argument, I borrow from a number of important scholars in the areas of textual analysis and non-representational theory. The first section rests primarily on the work of Norman Fairclough and his rendering of critical discourse analysis (CDA), and Laurajane Smith's convincing attempts to problematise the way heritage is commonly understood within the cultural sector. In combination, the work of Fairclough and Smith allows for an account of more than just language in the processes of heritage meaning-making by drawing in an understanding of the circulation of power. Neither Fairclough nor Smith deal explicitly with the visual, however, and so with this in mind I also turn to scholars such as Jennifer Webb, Annette Pritchard and Nigel Morgan, all of whom have framed the visual as a major discursive category. This initial analysis is used to underscore the second part of this chapter, which explores the *consequences* using a limited heritage imagery has – not only for signifying specific tourist destinations but for constituting and symbolising the nation as well. This, it seems me, is the surest way of bending discussions towards the circulation of feelings and affect, which here will be achieved by considering ethnicity and class. Mike Crang, Divya Tolia-Kelly and Roshi Naidoo provide the theoretical impetus behind this section, which argues that a nationalist-inspired identity (and concomitant sense of belonging) can no longer be presumed to be the universal affective response of visitors when the heritage site in question is already marked out as exclusive or a signifier of difference.

continuity sits well with Benedict Anderson's (1983) 'imagined community' and draws with it a paternalism that presupposes experts in a position of power. Heritage thus becomes something old, beautiful and tangible, certainly of relevance to the nation, selected by experts and *made to matter*, not simply because of the position of power held by experts, but also because of a paternalistic belief in educating and informing the public. As Smith (2006) has gone on to empirically document, these core features emerged from, and continue to privilege, the cultural symbols, experiences and understandings of the white, middle- and upper-classes.

Implicit though many of Smith's points may be, it is still possible to discern the means by which their essentialised and homogenous nature – *along with* their associated message – is used to appeal to potential tourists, and here the work of Annette Pritchard and Nigel Morgan (2000; Morgan and Pritchard 1998) can be used to link the broad brush-strokes of Fairclough's 'discourse' to the field of tourism. In their earlier work, *Tourism, Promotion and Power* (1998; see also Jenkins 2003), Morgan and Pritchard finesse touristic imagery into Stuart Hall's 'circuit of culture', simultaneously pulling our attention away from a sole focus on production to that of consumption, too. Tourism, they insist, is an integral facet of the cultural industries, and is one that is replete with power and dominated by a 'promotional language and imagery [that] privileges the white, male, heterosexual gaze' (1998: 117; see also Kokosalakis *et al.* 2006; Scarles 2004: 49). The obvious corollary to this, of course, is that the stereotypical 'tourist' will subsequently be imagined and positioned as white, male, Western and heterosexual, with the associated 'heritage tourist' emerging out of the literature as wealthy, masculine, predominantly white and almost entirely an economic-being (after Graburn and Barthel-Bouchier 2001). Similar to discourse, visual imagery is at once both constituted *by* and constitutive *of*, recursively embroiled in the production and consumption of a dominant perspective on heritage that is already mediated by gender, age, class and ethnicity. As Watson (2010: 255) points out, drawing on the work of cultural theorist Barbara Kirshenblatt-Gimblett, visual interest thus becomes 'vested interest'. As such,

> 'display not only shows and speaks, it also *does*', and in doing so it orders and organises its material referents in a way that not only sells attractions, but also reflects and affects the underlying meanings, identities, social structures and affinities that determine the society concerned.
>
> (Watson 2010: 255, original emphasis)

With all this in mind, tourism imagery is better understood as a significant site of struggle, within which 'particular ideologies triumph at the expense of others' (Morgan and Pritchard 1998: 242; see also Scarles 2004).

Heritage tourism in England

As Amoamo and Thompson (2010; see also Pritchard and Morgan 2000) point out, those involved in the promotion of tourist destinations are increasingly turning to iconic imagery in order to both create and reinforce a lasting impression of what they have to offer (see Watson in this volume). Indeed, as Amoamo and Thompson go on to argue:

> [p]romoted images come to be perceived as 'real' images of the destination, potential tourists are directed towards particular interpretations at the expense of others, and thus 'reality' is contested via unequal relations of power. The official image marks the 'site' as a 'sight', becoming a marker for both the place and the experience.
> (2010: 41; see also MacCannell 1999)

Britain, recently ranked fourth out of 50 in the Anholt-GfK Roper *Nation Brands Index 2010*, is no exception to this process, and has at its disposal a highly visual tourism product that revolves around a particular notion of heritage and its attendant politicised 'identity' narrative: Smith's AHD. This has clearly proved to be an effective marketing device, evidenced by the fact that heritage tourism is responsible for 84 per cent of the total UK visitor economy. Indeed as an industry heritage tourism is worth in the vicinity of £12.4 million, according to English Heritage (n.d.; see also Abramsky 2010: 1), with heritage highlighted as the main reason 30 per cent of all international visitors come to the UK (Dawe 2010: 4). This measure of success is also supported by research recently undertaken by VisitBritain, the official website of the British Tourist Authority, which concluded that:

> research in 35 countries around the world reveals that our core strengths as a visitor destination are *our heritage*, history, pageantry and culture ... People tell us that they especially value our accessible *heritage* – our museums and galleries, castles and stately homes, our ruins and industrial sites, our palaces and cathedrals.
> (Sandie Dawe, Chief Executive of VisitBritain 2010: 4,
> emphasis added)

> VisitBritain told us that *culture and heritage* 'remain the main appeal of any consumer interest in Britain'.
> (Culture, Media and Sport Select Committee 2006, emphasis added)

As for a domestic comparison, in 2008 an estimated 967.5 million touristic trips were undertaken by the domestic market, 53 per cent of which were undertaken for holiday and/or leisure purposes (VisitBritain 2010: 4). This figure can be whittled down further to reveal the 9 per cent of domestic day-trippers who specifically noted 'heritage' as their main motivation for travel (Heritage Lottery Fund 2010: 11). Intimately tangled up with the notion of heritage captured by the above quotes are assumptions of 'ancient traditions' and 'rich culture', both of which stand alongside a distinct tempering of heritage as metaphor for the nation (McManus 2005: 237, cited in Edensor and Holloway 2008: 489; see also Waterton 2009: 40). This prominence afforded to heritage is not confined to the tourism industry alone, as a similar narrative can also be found replicated in both policy and political discourse, as the following extract from Jeremy Hunt, Secretary of State for Culture, Olympics, Media and Sport, made clear:

> I believe our tourism industry is one of our most undervalued national assets. Which other country can offer our rich heritage and history – our cathedrals, and castles, our stately homes and royal houses? Where else can you see so much culture – our world-class galleries and museums, and the incredible concentration of artistic talent of the West End or Edinburgh Festival? And where else can you find the stunning countryside of the Lake District and Snowdonia, the ecological wonders of the Eden Project and the geological marvels of this heritage coast? Not for nothing are we the 6th most visited country on the planet.
>
> (Hunt 2010: para. 13)

Most striking about the textual constructions of heritage evidenced in two of the extracts above (from Sandie Dawe and Jeremy Hunt) is the logic of meaning nestled within the semantic relations of the sentences (after Fairclough 2003). In both cases, pronouncements of 'heritage' are followed immediately by additive elaborations that mark out equivalence, such that heritage is equated with the sum total of museums, galleries, cathedrals, castles, stately homes, ruins, industrial sites, palaces and cathedrals. Indeed in both the clauses following the utterance 'heritage' can be read as an elaboration of, or addition to, the term. These clauses do not offer an explanation of causal links; rather, they establish, more or less in list form, the parameters of what *ought* to be captured by the word 'heritage'. What emerges is a tangible, monumental and predominantly 'wealthy' image of heritage. As I have argued elsewhere (Waterton 2010a; see also 2009), what this listing signifies is the inevitability of the relationship between the word 'heritage' and its grand and tangible manifestations: no cause and effect need be mentioned as the deeper relationship between them can simply be assumed from their recurrence (after Fairclough 2000: 28).

At the heart of these utterances lies Smith's AHD. What is crucial here, however, is that Smith's empirical observations and conceptualisation of a distinct rendering of heritage move out of their original domain where they can be seen to be taken on and re-encoded by a wider range of agencies and institutions, including destination managers, hoteliers and local councils

(Watson and Waterton 2010: 89; see also Waterton 2010b). In much the same way as speeches and textual documents, the visual modalities of heritage thus become infused with a potent and particular way of seeing. For the majority of tourists entering the UK, brochures remain the more visible – and instant – promotional tool, and are supplemented by both websites and guidebooks (Scarles 2004; see also Morgan and Pritchard 1998). All three elements are highly visual in nature. For this part of the analysis, I have considered the way heritage is indexed within the promotional material produced to market Britain as a destination. The material included was gathered between 2004 and 2010, and is sourced from two of the most influential bodies involved with the promotion of the tourism industry in Britain. The section therefore focuses specifically upon material authored by English Heritage (brochures, guidebooks and website material), the government's statutory advisor on the historic environment, and VisitBritain (brochures, promotional books and website material), the government-sponsored tourism body. It is also supplemented by the inclusion of website material gathered from EnjoyEngland, the official website for tourism in England. This material was then juxtaposed against VisitBritain's Great British Heritage Pass[1], a tourism initiative heavily marketed to both international and domestic travellers, valid for periods of three, seven, 14 or 30 days at over 850 'top heritage locations' (VisitBritain n.d.). What emerged from this loosely framed content analysis was a preponderance towards an explicitly tangible, monumental, grand and aesthetically pleasing sense of heritage, revolving largely around castles, forts and defended houses (32.12 per cent), abbeys and priories (15.96 per cent) and country houses and their estates (10.58 per cent), all of which are saturated with notions of power, wealth and a certain timelessness (see Table 4.1).

These are images that are devoid of people, with 'history', 'wealth', 'tranquillity', 'power' and 'spirituality' providing the assumed orthodoxy, with any subtleties alluding to alternative notions of heritage stamped over by a strident form of national branding. Collectively, what these figures reflect is an extraordinarily high commitment to one version of heritage, earmarked here as both categorical and non-modalised, which is itself reliant upon the continual overuse of distinctive images of icons – Stonehenge, Kenilworth Castle, Bolsover Castle, Whitby Abbey, Rievaulx Abbey (see Figures 4.1 and 4.2) – which subsequently minimises the possibilities for articulating a different, alternative narrative of heritage (after Scarles 2009: 468). Nowhere can one glimpse much in the way of twentieth century history, nor do issues of poverty, grime or migration rate a mention. Instead, this emerging visual index maps itself convincingly into the unreflexive parameters of the AHD, recording an existential assumption about a primordial people – fixed, unchanging and characterised by cultural symbols indicative of power, wealth and *whiteness*. These are the values and cultural preferences that are inculcated by the AHD and collectively hail from the 'golden ages' of 1066, the civil war, Tudor England and so forth. Their narrative tells a

Table 4.1 Type of heritage pictured in a sample of heritage tourism marketing material

	Number	%
Bridges	5	0.96
Buildings		
Ecclesiastical buildings	20	3.85
Traditional buildings	20	3.85
Country houses and estates	55	10.58
Manorial complexes	5	0.96
Railway heritage	1	0.19
Industrial heritage	8	1.54
Heritage falling outside of the authorised heritage discourse	2	0.38
Heritage re-enactments	16	3.08
Landscapes	10	1.92
Miscellaneous (sculptures, statues, Blue Plaques, etc.)	22	4.23
Monuments		
Abbeys and priories	83	15.96
Castles, forts and defended houses	167	32.12
Scheduled monuments	34	6.15
Museums, libraries and archives		
Exhibitions	5	0.96
Visitor centres	5	0.96
Local/regional museums	6	1.15
Libraries	1	0.19
Parks, gardens and battlefields		
Urban parks	2	0.38
Country house estates	20	3.85
Sites		
Archaeological sites	32	6.15
Underwater sites	1	0.19
Total	520	99.6

linear story constituted by tradition, conquest, piety, providence and progress, reflecting, as Edensor (2006: 527) points out, 'a wider obsession with official, historical, elite constructions of national identity'. Indeed, as Edensor goes on to argue, it is upon this terrain – the symbolic and famous landscapes and sites – that implicit performances of identity and belonging are carried out (see also Palmer 1999). A more detailed analysis of the imagery is possible, one that points to particular fields of vision and distancing techniques, or takes account of the viewer's 'gaze' and the hyper-realness of the images (see, for example, Waterton 2009). But, for my purposes here, it is suffice to say that this selection of supply-side imagery, anchored by a single logic to the AHD, effectively communicate to a wider population a seemingly 'complete' picture of what heritage ought to be.

In many ways, it is unsurprising that the tourism sector would turn to these icons as fodder for visitors, but what are the consequences of this visualisation, particularly when it becomes hitched to notions of belonging and identity, at a more personal level? What affects does this presentation of an

Figure 4.1 Dominant images of heritage: Audley End, York Minster, Rievaulx Abbey and Bolsover Castle
Images reproduced with permission from Lila Rakoczy

Figure 4.2 Dominant images of heritage: Warkworth Castle, Bodiam Castle, Bamburgh Castle and Kenilworth Castle
Images reproduced with permission from Lila Rakoczy

entirely built, ruinous and 'magnificent' heritage have, not only for the idea of 'heritage' itself, but for the idea of national belonging conjured within the tourist's imagination? Such touristic sites are enlivened with this particular heritage discourse, but this simultaneously provides its visitors with a truncated range of potential tourist performances and roles. All too often, these roles are provided for a particular social and cultural group only, which, in turn, cannot help but *do things* in terms of how individuals and communities are aligned (or not) with these spaces of national belonging. For Aitchison (2007), who sees the social world as being increasingly dominated by patterns of consumption, tourism has become central to the formation and augmentation of a range of cultural identities. Allcock (1995: 101) takes this one step further, arguing that in gaining control over the past, tourism, in 'validating some appeals to identity and invalidating others establishes and legitimises social relationships over a far wider area than the field of tourism itself'. How, then, can these tourist places communicate a narrative of 'this is me, this is my history, my roots, my place' to a supposedly full spectrum of British society? This is not an idle query on my part. Indeed, both the tourism and heritage sector are now explicitly shackled to processes of inclusion and cohesion in political discourse, a relationship initiated by New Labour government in the late 1990s and nurtured today by David Cameron's Conservative counterpart:

> As well as being a hugely important economic driver, *we believe tourism has much to offer* wider social and environmental objectives. This includes providing opportunities for education and lifelong learning (through visits to properties but also through active engagement and volunteering to help look after these properties), underpinning the viability of a huge range of rural (often small) businesses, *promoting a sense of positive local identity and social cohesion from a shared local history/culture and the resources that it offers.*
>
> (Memorandum submitted by The National Trust cited in Culture, Media and Sport Select Committee 2008, emphasis added)

> And yet our heritage remains defiantly, recognisably British – conserved, maintained and interpreted for *a new generation to understand who we are and in so doing contribute to our economic and cultural wellbeing today.*
>
> (Dawe 2010: 5)

More significant still is the role both heritage and tourism have been afforded in the supposed 'fight' against separatism in the UK, fuelled by the concomitant 'fear of difference' (Naidoo 2008). It is from here that the strangest paradox emerges, as it is to a truncated and exclusionary sense of heritage that marginalised groups – the working classes and ethnic minority groups primarily – are being asked to turn and *tour* in order to heighten their sense of 'felt' ownership and belonging (Palmer 2005; Prentice and Andersen 2007). Now, for the most part, theoretical excursions into the relationship between tourism and identity have tended to revolve around positive feelings and familiarity. Moreover, these positive feelings of belonging, comfort and identity have, in this scenario at least, been applied as if they are somehow universal – touring this heritage will naturally, it is assumed, affect feelings of inspiration, belonging, citizenship and wellbeing. Importantly, though, in this context visitors are directed to the same exclusionary heritage that prompted Stuart Hall (1999: 24; see also Palmer 1999) to lament that 'those who cannot see themselves reflected in its mirror cannot properly belong'. The 'felt' responses, those emotional feelings that are stirred when one engages with identity, may *not* in this case be so universal and positive (after Prentice and Andersen 2007: 662). This is because the touring 'ethnic minority' or 'working class' visitor is being asked to orientate their senses and structure their felt responses against a visual impression of Britain that stands as a clear marker – both historically and contemporarily – of exclusion. Indeed, they are symbols that are inflected with gender, class and ethnicity, places of alienation in which sightings of a multicultural narrative are rather rare (after Tolia-Kelly 2007).

For Crang and Tolia-Kelly (2010: 1) it is precisely in these moments – during the circulation of feelings of alienation – that people come to identify themselves as 'included'/'excluded' or 'insider'/'outsider'. For example, in the *Taking Part* survey conducted by the Department for Culture, Media and Sport in 2007, the affective responses of 'discomfort' and 'rejection' were revealed as the most commonly cited reasons for *not* visiting a heritage site by participants self-identifying as ethnic minorities:

> when we walk into these properties we get a sense of rejection and omission.
>
> (National Audit Office 2009: 9)

> [It's] like you don't belong there. The staff attitude and even the attitude of certain general public on certain sites they look at you like you don't belong there . . . It's almost like 'how did they let you in?'
>
> (National Audit Office 2009: 9)

In these quotes, the heritage sites in question draw from the typical stock of assets discussed in earlier sections of this paper, and at these particular sites the ability of individual tourists to move, respond and be affected *in the same ways* is unsurprisingly compromised by their broader affectual capacities. In other words, as Fortier (2010: 23) points out, 'affect operates differently on different bodies – that is, that affect is differently distributed between different kinds of group formations, and some affects are favoured over others as desirable bases or outcomes of meaningful interaction'. Integral to this example are inflections of power, which mark out some visitors as belonging (and not others) by virtue of the core values nestled at the heart of the AHD. Here, the physical surrounds of the examples of heritage prioritised for both tourist and citizen consumption are *complicit* in a dialogue of belonging that runs between individuals and a much larger, imagined collectivity. Indeed, the backdrop of the stately home, castle, fort or ruinous abbey creates a space within which specific identities are formulated and enacted, with the physical surroundings, to borrow from Askins (2009: 372, original emphasis), working to '*express* identity, *claim* status and convey cultural and personal values'. The point, as Sara Ahmed (2004) makes clear, is that affect, emotions, *do things*.

Examples of this type of emotion and affect were evidenced in a recent qualitative project I undertook at three social history museums (The Potteries Museum, the Gladstone Pottery Museum and the Etruria Industrial Museum) in an area of the West Midlands affectionately known as 'The Potteries' (see Waterton 2011). Work by Laurajane Smith undertaken at Beamish, the National Coal Mining Museum for England and the Tolpuddle Martyrs Museum also revealed similar bodily affects. Both projects revolved around notions of heritage traditionally associated with the working classes (the coal and pottery industries) and recorded a typical visitor profile that was reflective of this. Like the qualitative material gathered by the *Taking Part* survey, a significant theme emerging from the more critical commentary uttered by people visiting these sites also revolved around a discomfort or sense of exclusion from dominant expressions of heritage:

> I mean, anyone under the age of 40, I don't think they always get the opportunity to display much interest in their past – it's not encouraged by the present government, anyway [laughs] . . . it's true! It's true! As far as Tony Blair is concerned, we haven't got a history!
>
> (EIMA123, female, over 60)

> When you hear a lot about heritage it's not usually the heritage of the whole country, it's exclusive, it excludes people. Such as stately homes, they represent the upper echelons of society and not the majority; here [Tolpuddle] it is more inclusive of people's heritage.
>
> (cited in Smith 2006: 211)

Instead, a rich seam of the visitors interviewed at these sites was emphatically *not* searching for cultural cues of citizenship and nationhood at the sort of sites earmarked in this chapter as emblematic of the AHD. Certainly, they were seeking out an alternative heritage narrative, but one that at the same time allowed them the space to think through and express a deeply *felt* reaction to that sense of exclusion:

I'm sick of hearing about Lord Lar-di-da or Lady this or that. The country focuses too much on country houses and all that and forgets that it was built on the blood of the working class. I think it's time we raised the profile of this history – it's horrible and dark and grimy but it happened.

(GMA059, female, over 60, cited in Waterton 2011: 360)

[heritage is] working class history as opposed to seeing a stately home where the landed gentry live [said sneeringly], country houses are interesting in themselves but there is only so much you can learn from them, and why would I pay someone to look around their house – they can pay me 10 quid to look around mine.

(cited in Smith 2006: 212)

These quotes are punctuated with feelings of anger and resentment, thereby prising apart the affective registers presumed to emerge from heritage visitation. Indeed, they stand in contradistinction to the 'affective universals' and 'automatic responses' imagined by English Heritage, for example, an organisation predicated on the assumption that a touristic space offers the sum total of affective pleasures that move through tranquillity, spirituality and indulgence to delight (Crang and Tolia-Kelly 2010: 13; see also Waterton 2009, 2010b; Watson and Waterton 2010). Underpinning this assumption is the related expectation that the domestic heritage tourist will spontaneously feel a sense of belonging to a particular social and cultural group and will align themselves with such spaces of national belonging accordingly. Ignored here is the reality that every visitor is their own peculiar conjuncture of history, gender, ethnicity, age and education, and will thus not experience the touristic spaces that surround them in quite the same ways (Tolia-Kelly 2006). We can see this in the above through responses of opposition and dissonance, aimed specifically at country houses, which are being expressed at social history museums by those who seek out a heritage experience that for them holds more complex meaning.

Conclusion

Although admittedly speculative, this chapter has attempted to document the power of 'the visual' in representations of heritage tourism. Using examples drawing from Britain, I have suggested that heritage representations sustain an understanding of nationhood, or 'Britishness', which privileges the cultural symbols of a particular social group – that defined as elite, middle-class and predominantly *white*. These representations, I have argued, are contingent upon a particular understanding of heritage (as elite, tangible and inherently *white*) and have since moved out of the tourism realm and entered wider political discourse, where they have

become both potent and self-fulfilling, signalling an idea of heritage that is presumed to speak to, and on behalf of, the full spectrum of British subjects. Here, the affective capacity 'to feel' as though one *belongs* is simultaneously assumed to be universal, and thus it is towards a limited set of cultural symbols that excluded groups are shepherded in the hopes that they will come to belong to the wider British citizenry. Neglected in this process are the more negative felt responses engendered by the heritage tourism sites on offer, which, in a complex circulation of feelings of discomfort, alienation and rejection, provide performative roles for the 'excluded' as well as the 'included'. Thus, while the chapter has relied upon Britain as a case study, a broader argument has also been attended to, one that can perhaps sit alongside the more recent outpouring of publications that challenge us to produce new ways of thinking about heritage and the role it plays in our wider experiences as moments of cultural meaning (see Crouch 2010; Selby 2010; Watson 2010). To this end, the chapter has attempted to use a focus upon discourse to pinpoint the futility of hitching a limited notion of heritage with policies of cohesion. This, I have argued, renders such policy essentially *non-performative* (if we use Judith Butler's [1997] notion of performativity), as it can never produce that which it names: cohesion. Indeed, without first understanding *how* and *why* a particular way of thinking about heritage all too often elides the multiplicity of alternatives, the progressive overtones of many current governments that trumpet inclusion, wellbeing, citizenship and a shared identity will effectively mask the problems they were meant to reveal.

Note

1   The Great British Heritage Pass 'gives you the freedom to explore some of Britain's finest castles and forts, palaces and royal residences, stately homes and historic houses, gardens and ancient monuments' (VisitBritain n.d.). See Table 4.2 for details.

Table 4.2 Heritage included with *The Great British Heritage Pass*

Heart of England	Brockhampton Estate	Haughmond Abbey	Shakespeare's Birthplace and the Shakespeare Town Houses
Anne Hathaway's Cottage	Buildwas Abbey	Ironbridge Gorge Museums	
Attingham Park	Charlecote Park	Kenilworth Castle and Elizabethan Garden	Shugborough Estate
Baddesley Clinton	Croft Castle and Parkland		Stokesay Castle
Benthall Hall	Croome	Mary Arden's Farm	The Greyfriars
Berrington Hall	Dudmaston Estate	Moseley Old Hall	The Weir
Biddulph Grange Garden	Farnborough Hall	Much Wenlock Priory	Upton House and Gardens
Boscobel House and the Royal Oak	Goodrich Castle	Packwood House	Warwick Castle
	Hanbury Hall		

Table 4.2 continued

Wightwick Manor and Gardens

Wilderhope Manor

Witley Court and Gardens

Wroxeter Roman City

North West

Acorn Bank Garden and Watermill

Beatrix Potter Gallery

Beeston Castle and Woodland Park

Birdoswald Roman Fort

Brougham Castle

Carlisle Castle

Dunham Massey

Furness Abbey

Gawthorpe Hall

Hare Hill

Hill Top

Holker Hall and Gardens

Lanercost Priory

Levens Hall and Gardens

Little Moreton Hall

Lyme Park

Muncaster Castle and Gardens

Nether Alderley Mill

Quarry Bank Mill and Styal Estate

Rufford Old Hall

Rydal Mount and Gardens

Sizergh Castle and Garden

Speke Hall, Garden and Estate

Stott Park Bobbin Mill

Tatton Park

Townend

Wordsworth House and Garden

South East

1066 Battle of Hastings

Alfriston Clergy House

Arundel Castle and Gardens and The Collector Earl's Garden

Basildon Park

Bateman's

Bayham Old Abbey

Beaulieu

Bembridge Windmill

Blenheim Palace

Bodiam Castle

Borde Hill Garden

Breamore House

Carisbrooke Castle

Chartwell

Clandon Park

Berrington Hall

Cliveden

Deal Castle

Dover Castle

Down House – Home of Charles Darwin

Emmetts Garden

Exbury Gardens and Steam Railway

Greys Court

Groombridge Place and The Enchanted Forest

Hatchlands Park

Hever Castle and Gardens

Highclere Castle and Gardens Hinton Ampner

Hughenden Manor

Ightham Mote

Knole

Lamb House

Leeds Castle

Leith Hill

Lullingstone Roman Villa

Medieval Merchant's House

Mottisfont

Mottistone Manor Garden

Newtown Old Town Hall

Nymans

Osborne House

Petworth House and Park

Pevensey Castle

Polesden Lacey

Portchester Castle

Portsmouth Historic Dockyard

Quebec House

RHS Garden Wisley

Richborough Roman Fort

River Wey and Godalming Navigations and Dapdune Wharf

Royal Pavilion

Sandham Memorial Chapel

Scotney Castle

Shalford Mill

Sheffield Park and Garden

Sissinghurst Castle

Smallhythe Place

South Foreland Lighthouse

St Augustine's Abbey

Standen

Stoneacre

Stowe Landscape Gardens

The Needles Old Battery and New Battery

The Vyne

Uppark House and Garden

Waddesdon Manor

Wakehurst Place

Walmer Castle and Gardens

West Wycombe Park

Winchester City Mill

Winkworth Arboretum

Yarmouth Castle

North East

Alnwick Castle

Aydon Castle

Bamburgh Castle

Barnard Castle

Belsay Hall, Castle and Gardens

Berwick-upon-Tweed Barracks & Main Guard

Table 4.2 continued

Brinkburn Priory
Cherryburn
Chesters Roman Fort
Corbridge Roman Town
Cragside
Dunstanburgh Castle
Etal Castle
George Stephenson's Birthplace
Gibside
Housesteads Roman Fort
Lindisfarne Castle
Lindisfarne Priory
Ormesby Hall
Prudhoe Castle
Seaton Delaval Hall
Souter Lighthouse and The Leas
The Bowes Museum
Tynemouth Priory and Castle
Wallington
Warkworth Castle
Washington Old Hall

East Midlands
Ashby de la Zouch Castle
Belton House
Belvoir Castle
Bolsover Castle
Calke Abbey
Canons Ashby
Chatsworth
Haddon Hall

Hardwick Estate: Stainsby Mill
Hardwick Hall
Hardwick Old Hall
Kedleston Hall
Kirby Hall
Kirby Muxloe Castle
Lincoln Castle
Lincoln Medieval Bishops' Palace
Lyddington Bede House
Lyveden New Bield
Mr Straw's House
Peveril Castle
Rockingham Castle
Rushton Triangular Lodge
St Peter's Church
Sudbury Hall and the National Trust Museum of Childhood
Tattershall Castle
The Old Manor
The Workhouse, Southwell
Thornton Abbey and Gatehouse
Woolsthorpe Manor

London
2 Willow Road
Apsley House
Carlyle's House
Chelsea Physic Garden
Chiswick House
Eltham Palace and Gardens
Fenton House

Ham House and Garden
Jewel Tower
Marble Hill House
Osterley Park and House
Rainham Hall
Red House
Royal Albert Hall
Shakespeare's Globe Exhibition and Theatre Tour
St Paul's Cathedral
Sutton House
Syon House
The Wernher Collection at Ranger's House
Wellington Arch

Yorkshire
Aldborough Roman Site
Beningbrough Hall and Gardens
Brodsworth Hall
Byland Abbey
Castle Howard
Clifford's Tower
Conisbrough Castle
East Riddlesden Hall
Fairfax House
Fountains Abbey and Studley Royal Water Garden
Harewood House
Helmsley Castle
Kirkham Priory
Middleham Castle
Mount Grace Priory
Nunnington Hall
Pickering Castle

RHS Garden Harlow Carr
Richmond Castle
Rievaulx Abbey
Rievaulx Terrace
Roche Abbey
Scarborough Castle
Skipton Castle
Treasurer's House
Whitby Abbey
York Cold War Bunker

North East
Alnwick Castle
Aydon Castle
Bamburgh Castle
Barnard Castle
Belsay Hall
Berwick-upon-Tweed Barracks and Main Guard
Brinkburn Priory
Cherryburn
Chesters Roman Fort
Corbridge
Cragside
Dunstanburgh Castle
Etal Castle
George Stephenson's Birthplace
Gibside
Housesteads
Lindisfarne Castle
Lindisfarne Priory
Ormesby Hall
Prudhoe Castle
Seaton Delaval Hall

Table 4.2 continued

Souter Lighthouse and The Leas

The Bowes Museum

Tynemouth Priory and Castle

Wallington

Warkworth Castle

Washington Hall

East of England

Anglesey Abbey, Gardens and Lode Mill

Audley End House and Gardens

Blickling Estate

Bourne Mill

Castle Acre Priory

Coggeshall Grange Barn

Felbrigg Hall, Gardens and Estate

Framlingham Castle

Great Yarmouth Row Houses

Grime's Graves

Horsey Windpump

Houghton Mill

Ickworth

Lavenham Guildhall

Melford Hall

Orford Castle

Oxburgh Hall

Paycocke's

Peckover House and Garden

RHS Garden Hyde Hall

Saxtead Green Postmill

Shaw's Corner

Sutton Hoo

Tilbury Fort

Verulamium Museum

Wicken Fen

Wimpole Estate

Woburn Abbey

Wrest Park

South West

A la Ronde

Antony

Arlington Court

Avebury

Barrington Court

Bath Assembly Rooms

Berkeley Castle

Berry Pomeroy Castle

Bradley

Brownsea Island

Buckland Abbey

Castle Drogo

Chedworth Roman Villa

Chysauster Ancient Village

Cleeve Abbey

Clevedon Court

Clouds Hill

Clovelly Village

Coleridge Cottage

Coleton Fishacre

Compton Castle

Corfe Castle

Cotehele

Cotehele Mill

Dartmouth Castle

Dunster Castle

Dyrham Park

East Pool Mine

Eden Project

Farleigh Hungerford Castle

Finch Foundry

Glendurgan Garden

Godolphin

Great Chalfield Manor and Garden

Greenway

Hailes Abbey

Hardy's Birthplace

Hartland Abbey and Gardens

Hidcote

Killerton

Killerton: Budlake Old Post Office

Killerton: Clyston Mill

Killerton: Marker's Cottage

Kingston Lacy

Knightshayes Court

Lacock Abbey

Lanhydrock

Launceston Castle

Levant Mine and Beam Engine

Lodge Park and Sherborne Estate

Lundy

Lydford Gorge

Lytes Cary Manor

Mompesson House

Montacute House

Muchelney Abbey

Newark Park

Okehampton Castle

Old Sarum

Old Wardour Castle

Overbeck's

Pendennis Castle

Portland Castle

Powderham Castle

Prior Park Landscape Garden

Restormel Castle

RHS Garden Rosemoor

Saltram

Sherborne Castle

Sherborne Old Castle

Snowshill Manor and Garden

St Mawes Castle

St Michael's Mount

Stonehenge

Stourhead

Sudeley Castle Gardens and Exhibition

The Courts Garden

The Fashion Museum

The Lost Gardens of Heligan

The Roman Baths

Tintagel Castle

Tintagel Old Post Office

Tintinhull Garden

Totnes Castle

Trelissick Garden

Trengwainton Garden

Trerice

Tyntesfield

Westbury Court Garden

White Mill

Wilton House

References

Abramsky, J. (2010) 'Foreword: investing in success', in *Investing in Success: Heritage and the UK Tourism Economy*, London: Heritage Lottery Fund.

Aitchison, C.C. (2007) 'Marking difference or making a difference: constructing places, policies and knowledge of inclusion, exclusion and social justice in leisure, sport and tourism', in I. Ateljevic, A. Pritchard and N. Morgan (eds) *The Critical Turn in Tourism Studies: Innovative Research Methodologies*, Oxford: Elsevier.

Allcock, J.B. (1995) 'International tourism and the appropriation of history in the Balkans', in M-F. Lanfant, J.B. Allcock and E.M. Bruner (eds) *International Tourism: Identity and Change*, London: Sage.

Ahmed, S. (2004) 'Affective economies', *Social Text* 22(2/79): 117–39.

Amoamo, M. and Thompson, A. (2010) '(Re)imaging Māori tourism: representation and cultural hybridity in postcolonial New Zealand', *Tourist Studies* 10(1): 35–5.

Anderson, B. (1983) *Imagined Communities: Reflections on the Origin and Spread of Nationalism*, London: Verso.

Askins, K. (2009) 'Crossing divides: ethnicity and rurality, *Journal of Rural Studies* 25(4): 365–75.

Butler, J. (1997) *Excitable Speech: The Politics of the Performative*, New York: Routledge.

Crang, M. and Tolia-Kelly, D.P. (2010) 'Nation, race, and affect: senses and sensibilities at national heritage sites', *Environment and Planning A* 42(10): 2315–31.

Crouch, D. (2010) 'The perpetual performance and emergence of heritage', in E. Waterton and S. Watson (eds) *Culture, Heritage and Representation: Perspectives on Visuality and the Past*, Aldershot: Ashgate.

Culture, Media and Sport Select Committee (2006) *Third Report of the Session 2005–06.* (Memorandum submitted by VisitBritain). Available online: www.publications.parliament.uk/pa/cm200506/cmselect/cmcumeds/912/912we115.htm (accessed 18 February 2011).

Culture, Media and Sport Select Committee (2008) *Tourism: Eighth Report of Session 2007–08, Volume II*, London: HSO.

Dawe, S. (2010) 'Commentary: valuing heritage tourism', in *Investing in Success: Heritage and the UK Tourism Economy*, London: Heritage Lottery Fund.

Graburn, N.H.H. and Barthel-Bouchier, D. (2001) 'Relocating the tourist', *International Sociology* 16(2): 147–58.

Edensor, T. (2006) 'Reconsidering national temporalities', *European Journal of Social Theory* 9(4): 525–45.

Edensor, T. and Holloway, J. (2008) 'Rhythmanalysing the coach tour: the Ring of Kerry, Ireland', *Transactions of the Institute of British Geographers* 33(4): 483–501.

English Heritage (n.d.) *Heritage Fact Sheet 2: Tourism.* Available online: www.english-heritage.org.uk/content/imported-docs/f-j/heritage-fact-sheet-2.pdf (accessed 10 February 2011).

Fairclough, N. (1995) *Critical Discourse Analysis: The Critical Study of Language*, Harlow, Essex: Pearson Education Limited.

Fairclough, N. (2000) *New Labour, New Language?* London: Routledge.

Fairclough, N. (2003) *Analysing Discourse: Textual Analysis for Social Research*, London: Routledge.

Fairclough, N. (2010) *Critical Discourse Analysis*, Harlow, Essex: Pearson Education Limited.

Fortier, A-M. (2010) 'Proximity by design? Affective citizenship and the management of unease', *Citizenship Studies* 14(1): 17–30.

Hall, S. (1999) 'Whose heritage? Un-settling "the heritage", re-imagining the post-nation', *Third Text* 49: 3–13.

Heritage Lottery Fund (2010) *Investing in Success: Heritage and the UK Tourism Economy*. London: Heritage Lottery Fund.

Hunt, J. (2010) *Tourism Keynote Speech*. Available online: www.culture.gov.uk/news/ministers_speeches/7162.aspx (accessed 1 February 2011).

Jenkins, O. (2003) 'Photography and brochures: the circle of representation', *Tourism Geographies: An International Journal of Tourism Space, Place and Environment* 5(3): 305–28.

Kokosalakis, C., Bagnall, G., Selby, M. and Burns, S. (2006) 'Place image and urban regeneration in Liverpool', *International Journal of Consumer Studies* 30(4): 389–97.

McManus, R. (2005) 'Identity crisis? Heritage construction, tourism and place marketing in Ireland', in M. McCarthy (ed.) *Ireland's Heritages: Critical Perspectives on Memory and Identity*, Aldershot: Ashgate.

MacCannell, D. (1999) *The Tourist: A New Theory of the Leisure Class*, Berkley: University of California Press.

Morgan, N. and Pritchard, A. (1998) *Tourism, Promotion and Power, Creating images: Creating Identities*, Chichester: John Wiley and Sons.

Naidoo, R. (2008) 'Fear of difference/fear of sameness: the road to conviviality', in S. Davidson and J. Rutherford (eds) *Race, Identity and Belonging: A Soundings Collection*, London: Lawrence and Wishart.

National Audit Office (2009) *Promoting Participation within the Historic Environment*. Available online: www.nao.org.uk/publications/0809/historic_environment.aspx (accessed 15 February 2011).

Palmer, C. (1999) 'Tourism and symbols of identity', *Tourism Management* 20: 313–21.

Palmer, C. (2005) 'An ethnography of Englishness: experiencing identity through tourism', *Annals of Tourism Research* 32(1): 7–27.

Prentice, R.C. and Andersen, V. (2007) 'Interpreting heritage essentialisms: familiarity and felt history', *Tourism Management* 28: 661–76.

Pritchard, A. and Morgan, N.J. (2000) 'Constructing tourism landscapes: gender, sexuality and space', *Tourism Geographies* 2(2): 115–39.

Scarles, C. (2004) 'Mediating landscapes', *Tourist Studies* 4(1): 43–67.

Scarles, C. (2009) 'Becoming tourist: renegotiating the visual in the tourist experience', *Environment and Planning D: Society and Space* 27(3): 465–88.

Selby, M. (2010) 'People-place-past: the visitor experience of culture heritage', in E. Waterton and S. Watson (eds) *Culture, Heritage and Representation: Perspectives on Visuality and the Past*, Farnham: Ashgate

Smith, L. (2006) *Uses of Heritage*, London: Routledge.

Smith, L. and Waterton, E. (2009) *Heritage, Communities and Archaeology*, London: Duckworth.

Smith, L. and Waterton, E. (2012) 'Constrained by commonsense: the authorised heritage discourse in contemporary debates', in J. Carman, R. Skeates and C. McDavid (eds) *The Oxford Handbook of Public Archaeology*, Oxford: Oxford University Press.

Tolia-Kelly, D.P. (2006) 'Affect – an ethnocentric encounter? Exploring the 'universalist' imperative of emotional/affectual geographies', *Area* 38(2): 213–17.

Tolia-Kelly, D.P. (2007) 'Fear in paradise: the affective registers of the English Lake District landscape re-visited', *The Senses and Society* 2: 329–51.

van Dijk, T. (1986) *Racism in the Press*, London: Arnold.

van Dijk, T. (2008) *Discourse and Power*, Basingstoke: Palgrave Macmillan.

VisitBritain (2010) *England: A Strategic Framework for Tourism 2010–2020*, UK: British Tourist Authority. Available online: www.visitengland.org/Images/7049_Strategic_Framework_LR_singles2_tcm143-197943.pdf (assessed 19 January 2011).

Waterton, E. (2009) 'Sights of sites: picturing heritage, power and exclusion', *Journal of Heritage Tourism* 4(1): 37–56.

Waterton, E. (2010a) *Politics, Policy and the Discourses of Heritage in Britain*, Basingstoke: Palgrave Macmillan.

Waterton, E. (2010b) 'Branding the past: the visual imagery of England's heritage', in E. Waterton and S. Watson (eds) *Culture, Heritage and Representation: Perspectives on Visuality and the Past*, Aldershot: Ashgate.

Waterton, E. (2011) 'In the spirit of self-mockery? Labour heritage and identity in the Potteries', *International Journal of Heritage Studies* 17(4): 344–63.

Watson, S. (2010) 'Constructing Rhodes: heritage tourism and visuality', in E. Waterton and S. Watson (eds) *Culture, Heritage and Representation: Perspectives on Visuality and the Past*, Aldershot: Ashgate.

Watson, S. and Waterton, E. (2010) 'Reading the visual: representation and narrative in the construction of heritage', *Material Culture Review* 71: 84–97.

Webb, J. (2009) *Understanding Representation*, London: Sage.

Data sources

English Heritage (2008) *2007/8 Members' and Visitors' Handbook*, London: English Heritage.

English Heritage (n.d.) *Power and Value, Piety and Peace* (Historic Yorkshire Brochure), London: English Heritage.

English Heritage (n.d.) *Medieval Wealth and Spiritual Vision* (Rievaulx Abbey Brochure), London: English Heritage.

English Heritage (n.d.) *16 Great Places to Visit* (Exploring Historic Northumbria Brochure), London: English Heritage.

English Heritage (n.d.) *Treasures and Tranquility* (Audley End House and Gardens Brochure), London: English Heritage.

English Heritage (n.d.) *History and Landscape* (Cumbria and the Lake District Brochure), London: English Heritage.

English Heritage (n.d.) *Indulge in Floral Delights* (Belsay Hall, Castle and Gardens Brochure), London: English Heritage.

enjoyEngland (n.d.) *EnjoyEngland Web*. Available online: www.enjoyengland.com/ (accessed 20 February 2011).

VisitBritain (2007) *Heritage Britain*, London: VisitBritain Publishing.

VisitBritain (n.d.) *The Great British Heritage Pass Website – Featured Properties*. Available online: www.britishheritagepass.com/ (accessed 20 February 2011).

VisitBritain (n.d.) *VisitBritain Web*. Available online: www.visitbritain.com/en/AU/ (accessed 20 February 2011).

Chapter 5

Swords, sandals and togas

The cinematic imaginary and the tourist experiences of Roman heritage sites

Russell Staiff

> Movies are the lingua franca of the 20th century.
>
> (Gore Vidal 1992)

Introduction

> Priscus was a gladiator of the Thracian type, wearing a broad-brimmed helmet with a grille that covered his face and a griffin ornament; greaves covered his legs up to his thighs, and he carried a small round shield and a curved sword. Verus was a Murmillo, the traditional opponent of the Thracian . . . he was armed like a Roman legionary with a short sword and a tall, oblong shield.
>
> The two fighters were so evenly matched that neither seemed able to draw blood from the other, but the gracefulness of their movements was so striking and the violence of their sudden clashes so thrilling that theirs was by far the most exciting contest of the day.
>
> (Extract from Steven Saylor's novel *Empire* 2010: 329)

In our mind's eye – 'the virtual world of the mind' according to Robert Dunbar (2008) – it is easy to 'see' the scene. The clues in the text readily create a 'picture' of gladiatorial contests in ancient Rome. If we have seen enough illustrations of gladiators in books, museums, movies, documentaries, video games and so on, we may even have a clear impression of the two types of gladiators, especially the Thracian outfit that, in some ways, has perhaps become the archetypal image of the gladiator.

Consider the possibility of these mental images being brought to bear on a visit to an extant Roman arena. Such a communication between the viewer and the viewed is informal, particular to the subject viewing, unauthorised and, to a certain degree, anarchic and spontaneous. And yet this intercourse between heritage site and visitor, this imagined narrative, must surely be considered a crucial part of the visitor/place engagement. We know that what the visitor brings with them when they enter heritage spaces and museums (material, represented and imagined) is a fundamental dynamic within the heritage experience (Black 2005; Harris 2010; Hein 1998). In the case of ancient Rome, the mental imagery of the visitor is not likely to be directly derived from Roman antiquity, that is, from the images that have survived in mosaics, frescoes, pottery, sculpture and jewellery. Rather, such imaginings are likely to be contemporary (or near contemporary) in origin. In other words, the iconography that informs the mental image of the viewing subject will be recent and, further, it is likely to have cinematic connections (Solomon 2001; Wyke 1997).

Ancient Rome and the cinematic imaginary

It is difficult to find recent commentaries about heritage and heritage interpretation that refer directly to the imagination, imagining and the imaginative (Fairclough *et al.* 2008; Graham and Howard 2008; Logan and Reeves 2009; Smith 2006; and Watson 2010). Imagination is mentioned, of course, but more than not it is about heritage places provoking powerful imaginative responses not how the imagination conjures the heritage place (with the notable exception of Schouten 1995). This is perhaps surprising given recent interest in intangible heritage and embodiment, denoting as it does a shift to subjective relationships with heritage (e.g. Ruggles and Silverman 2009; Smith and Akagawa 2009). Certainly the coupling of heritage and memory has been a dominant theme in recent heritage studies (e.g. Anheier and Isar 2011; Benton 2010; Byrne 2007; Graham and Howard 2008; Logan and Reeves 2009; Moore and Whelan 2007; Ruggles and Silverman 2009; Waterton and Watson 2010; Winter 2007). Where the terms 'imagination' and 'imagining' and the 'imaginative' do have an enduring significance, however, is in travel literature (e.g. de Botton 2002; Dessaix 2008; Durrell 1962; Morris 1983; Theroux 2008). Here the terms arise in a number of registers and in a number of circumstances, not the least its use in the context of tourist encounters with heritage places.

Like so many words associated with the experiential, 'imagination' is a difficult, quite concise and yet slippery notion. It is concise because there is general acceptance about what the phenomenon is. After all, it is something that is a central part of consciousness and perception and it operates almost continuously whether awake or asleep. But beyond this, imagination becomes complex because the term is linked to a constellation of other phenomenon: dreams, make-believe, fantasy, memory and remembering, perception, the 'mind's eye', understanding, world-views, learning, storytelling (in all its many forms) and so forth. Slippery, because the imagination is an embodied and intensely personal experience that seems to operate in a way not simply tied to the somatic; it is internal but can be projected onto the external; it is immaterial but 'real'; and it appears to be unbounded by time and space in its inner manifestation of psychological states but is rooted in the time–space moment of the person imagining.

Further, it is slippery because it inhabits a world of fantasy, desire, dreams and reality where the imaginings can easily and fluidly combine these entities in mental creations that are often borderless and boundless. It's a shape-changing phenomenon and it's utterly central to the human experience (for a multifaceted analysis of the imagination, see McGinn 2004).

This chapter is an exploration and meditation about some aspects of the imagination as it applies to the ways in which certain iconic heritage sites are visualised. It takes seriously the power of the imagination in visitor engagement and in the 'dialogue' that is established when the visitor encounters material culture that has already been marked out as both 'heritage' and 'historical'. In particular, the spotlight is on material culture that is overdetermined by the sheer density of representations under the descriptor of 'Ancient Rome'. The proposition is thus. There operates a type of heritage iconography when it comes to certain sites and certain periods of history: for example, ancient Rome and ancient Greece, Medieval Europe, Feudal China, eighteenth century aristocratic and revolutionary Europe, especially France, nineteenth century rural and urban European landscapes and various twentieth century war sites. The tourist brings to the encounter/production of place a strong set of mental images and associations that, in a sense, 'give life' to the materiality and distinctly lifeless forms of ruined buildings, crumbling walls, traces of road or remnants of the past now dwarfed by subsequent urban developments. In the case of ancient Rome, the tourist (seemingly marked neither by geography nor culture in a globalised economy) carries in their imagination a strong image of life in the time of the Romans. Imagination and memory, of course, are intimately connected (McGinn 2004), but the focus here is not on memory *per se*, but on the visual repertoire that memory conjures.

The cinema is a particularly rich archive for the evolution of a heritage iconography although it is, of course, not the only one. Museum objects, illustrated histories, television documentaries, paintings, computer games, photography, Google images, descriptions in historical novels and in histories (etc.) all contribute to what has become a standardised and profoundly ahistorical and ageographical set of images about life in ancient Rome. My particular interest is cinematic representations (including television series) because cinematic virtual worlds are complete in a way that archaeological sites never can be. And these virtual worlds feed the tourist imagination.

Let me begin with an anecdote about a visit to the Colosseum. I was spending a couple of days in Rome while I was awaiting the arrival of a colleague and before travelling to northern Italy for a conference. Because I hadn't been to the Forum, the Palatine and the Colosseum for some time, I was interested to see the progress of the restoration work and in particular the re-opened Colosseum. I was leaning on a parapet looking down into the arena of the famous Flavian amphitheatre. To my left was a small group of tourists from the UK and on my right three visitors in their early 20s from

New Zealand. The UK tourists had a guide and they were having the structure of the amphitheatre explained to them – the galleries, the tiers of
seating (and which strata of Roman society sat where) and the hypogeum,
the subterranean network of tunnels clearly visible because the wooden
floor of the arena has long gone. The New Zealand trio, sans guidebook,
audio tour and guide was far more excited by their being there than the
staid group on my left. They were recalling the 2000 film *Gladiator* (directed
by Ridley Scott with Russell Crowe the leading actor, himself born in New
Zealand). They were conjuring the gladiatorial contests, the use of chariots
and wild animals in the arena, the life of the gladiators in the tunnels below
the arena, the elaborate mechanisms used to hoist men and machines to the
arena level and above all the atmosphere of the gladiatorial spectacles. They
shared the memories of the 'fickle crowds', the imperial family, the use of
African drummers, the sheer excitement generated by the contests and
their deep ambivalence about blood sports and the cruelty and violence of
the displays, the opulence of the occasions and the inhumanity of slavery
and gladiatorial games. It was very clear from their animated interaction
that the film provided not only a lavishly detailed representation of the
Colosseum to augment their experience (in ways not dissimilar to a guide or
audio guide of the site) – it framed the visual experience of a heritage place
(Rojek 1997; Urry 2002; Waterton and Watson 2010) – but enabled a powerful imaginative interaction. The lifeless and the partial were in their minds
and in their discussion transformed into a complete 'world' where the
computer generated imagery of the film had given them not only a fully
'restored' image of the Colosseum, some 100 years after its construction,
but 'brought it to life' in ways that the verbal descriptions of guides could
not. The young travellers could imaginatively 'see' what may have been and
hear it as well (Hillis 1999; Marcus *et al.* 2010).

The intersection of the cinematic imaginative with the tourist experience of ancient Rome produces many possible analytical trajectories. My
interest is threefold: the dimensions of visual culture, particularly film,
which create an active dynamic in the heritage experience; a preliminary
investigation into the way 'Ancient Rome' has crystallised into a profoundly
ahistorical iconographic tradition via the moving image, and; third, the
notion of the cinematic imaginative in history, heritage and the heritage
experience.

Understanding the image/world relationship has a long history in western epistemology stretching back to debates that have come down the
centuries from ancient Greece about the nature of images, their mimetic
capacity and their power to kindle emotional responses. More recently, as
Ron Burnett (2005) has shown us, the digital-imaging techniques now so
commonplace in medical science, archaeology, geology, geography, conservation, weather and climatology (and so on) have illustrated anew that
visualisation can change and shape both perceptions themselves and the

knowledge attached to them. Within visual theory such capacities have already been explored. For example, the idea of 'pictured vision', which we see the landscape in terms of pictorial conventions that have become culturally inscribed and naturalised has been widely accepted (Alpers 1983; Bryson 1983; Crary 1992; Wartofsky 1984), as has the way cartography and map-making powerfully intervened into the way we 'see' and 'know' the world around us (Alpers 1983; Carter 1987; Cosgrove 1999; Turnbull 1989). While these studies have, on the whole, been circumscribed by cultural theory, cognitive psychology has played its part and the work of James Gibson (1979) on the ecology of vision was groundbreaking in its time and continues to inform debates about the relationship between seeing, images, experience and knowledge. For Gibson, seeing is direct and a complex neurological process that is not in any way dependent on visual representation but, paradoxically, pictorial representations become the template for our understanding of vision. So, for example, Gibson has shown that we do not see, in the biophysical sense, in western three-dimensional perspective but we use geometric perspective, a cultural construction, to explain how we see so that, over time, the two have become enmeshed (Gibson 1979).

The study of iconography in art history (e.g. Adams 1996) has taught us that the meanings of images constitute much more than what is being seen and what is being depicted in a picture, whether drawn, painted, engraved, photographed or filmed. Meaning is not confined to the image itself. Instead, the visual representation connects the image to the world beyond its frame, to the subjectivities of the viewer, including their emotions, and to the meaning-making machinery of the socio-cultural environment within which the image is embedded. In other words, the referent of pictures is complex: a picture's subject matter may be connected to a pictorial tradition, or genre; it may be completely idiosyncratic and linked to the imaginative 'world' of the painter, photographer or filmmaker; it may be connected to performance and ritual; it may form part of an ensemble where the picture annunciates in a context of sound, music, other images, smells, touch and architectural spaces; or, as is often the case, all of these simultaneously. This partly explains why the cinematic iconography of ancient Rome has a degree of uniformity built into it.

Gladiator, the Ridley Scott epic and the second biggest income-making movie of 2000 (Russell 2007), quite consciously re-worked scenes from earlier films especially Stanley Kubrick's *Spartacus* (1960) and Anthony Mann's *The Fall of the Roman Empire* (1964). It also drew on iconography associated with images of the Third Reich quite specifically *Triumph of the Will* (1935) the Nazi propaganda film by Leni Riefenstahl that documented the Nuremberg Rally of 1934 with its 700,000 participants (for an analysis of the visual sources in *Gladiator*, see Burgoyne 2008). What such borrowings do is create something that is visually familiar. The television series

Rome (series I, 2005; series II, 2007) also used Nazi iconography in the re-creation of Julius Caesar's military encampments (especially series I, episode 1) but coming after *Gladiator*, the exact inspiration, always the case with iconographic traditions, is somewhat diffuse.

All the films set in ancient Rome draw on the extant architecture of both the Republic and the Empire with scant interest in archaeological veracity (Rosenstone 2001). The entry of Cleopatra into Rome in the 1963 version of the film *Cleopatra* conforms not only to the notion of Roman spectacle, that has an iconographic history going back to D.W. Griffith's *Intolerance* (1916) and re-invigorated in the 1959 version of *Ben Hur* (Burgoyne 2008), but employs monumental Roman architecture to underscore the grandeur and opulence being depicted. It is the Arch of Constantine (312–315 CE) that is used as the portal for the entry of Cleopatra's cavalcade, but in this scene, re-decorated and re-located to the Roman Forum. This is not to mention that Cleopatra's visit to Rome was in the first century BCE, some three centuries before the Arch of Constantine was built (Solomon 2001). The architecture of Roman villas as markers of the lifestyle of patrician families – the wealthy and the powerful – extensively employs Pompeii as its model. The frescoed walls, the atrium, the gardens of the peristyle, Hellenised columns, mosaics, water features and a colour scheme that in the television series *Rome* – particularly the house of Atia, the mother of Octavian Caesar and seen throughout the series – heavily employs the red and black walls of Pompeian villas (for a comparison, see Clarke 1991).

The link to frescoes and mosaics is less easily defined. Frederico Fellini, in his *Fellini Satyricon* (1969) – the self-absorbed elegiac meditation on excess, debauchery and eroticism within the ever-oppressive shadow of life's transience – regarded frescoes as a major scenic inspiration (Solomon 2001). More importantly, the aesthetics of *Satyricon* re-established an 'ancient Roman mood' of decay, deprivation, poverty and hardship of the 'lower classes' amid the decadence and excess of the rich. The two worlds in *Satyricon* are intimately mired in claustrophobic intensity. And so it is in both *Gladiator* and *Rome*.

Other sources, distinctly cinematic, along with contemporary tastes in popular culture have also had a powerful influence on the *mise-en-scène* of the recent depictions of ancient Rome. The epic Hollywood films of the 1950s – especially *Spartacus* – seem, from the viewpoint of the twenty-first century, to be highly stylised and theatrical. The Roman Forum looks like a stage set for an opera and the crowd scenes are highly choreographed, again much like a theatrical production. The Forum has an air of expansive space (the camera is always elevated) and is remarkably sterile with not a piece of rubbish to be seen. However, the arrival of 'bad new futures' in film (for example, Ridley Scott's *Blade Runner* in 1982 and James Cameron's *Aliens* in 1986), the gritty realism and the sheer manic nature of television series like *ER*, the use of hand-held cameras, the impact of Asian cinema (particularly martial arts films and anime), the influences of a whole range of aesthetic styles from popular culture (punk rock, grunge, hip-hop, graffiti art and Japanese comics to mention just a few) and, most importantly of all, the advent of computer generated images (CGI) have radically changed the look and the feel of the Roman Forum in the early twenty-first century. In *Rome* the camera is always low, often hand-held. The Forum is cramped and dirty; crowds of every social class cheek-by-jowl compete with animals of many descriptions. The atmosphere is menacing, claustrophobic, sweaty, chaotic and smoky. The streets are littered with rubbish, are straw-strewn and an aesthetic profusion of activities. The 'signature' buildings, like the Temple of Jupiter and the Senate, are not grand architectural wonders but simply big structures rising up from the mayhem of their social environment. The inspiration seems to be the contemporary *medina* of North African cities rather than the phlegmatic pictorial reconstructions and museum models of the Roman Forum (see the digital reconstruction of UCLA CVRLab and the Gismondi model in the Museo della Civilta Romana). The achievement, however, relies on CGI.

Over 400 feature films – excluding television series like *I, Claudius* (1976) and *Rome* (series one 2005, series two 2007) and docu-dramas like the BBC's *Ancient Rome: the Rise and Fall of an Empire* (2006) – have been set in ancient Greece and Rome (Solomon 2001). This repetition of subject matter has contributed to what Gilles Deleuze (1986) has called 'universal history', a nineteenth century German historiography that had three aspects: monumental history (the architectural environments), antiquarian history (the details of customs, dress, rituals, everyday objects, weaponry and the like) and critical/ethical history (like the dilemmas, challenges, obstacles and judgements the 'hero' of the story enacts in the historical scenario). Roland Barthes (1972) has discussed this stereotyping of the past as a necessary function of the way the semiosis works in films set in 'ancient Rome'. Umberto Eco (1986) refers to it as a loss of difference. The emergence of a uniform iconography is, therefore, a necessary way for audiences to immediately establish an understanding of the diegetic world they enter into. The visual codes are familiar and well established. Maria Wyke, a classicist, in her study of ancient Rome in cinema makes the point that 'cinema has been crucial to the formation and wide dissemination of an historical consciousness of ancient Rome ... knowledges of "Rome" have become effects of its reconstruction in moving images' (1997: 3).

Consequently, the cinematic imaginary cannot be divorced from the 'dialogue' between visitors and ancient Roman heritage sites. Chris Rojek (1997) has examined this 'transference' in a rather different analytical register within the context of tourism.

Heritage, the cinema, the tourist and visual culture

Rojek's starting point is that heritage/tourist places are socially constructed as spaces that signify something extra-ordinary, their 'aura' pertaining to a fusion of visual power (including the iconographic and, therefore, the symbolic), discursive power (including descriptions – whether empirical or mythological or fictional – and disciplinary expositions like history, art history archaeology, for example) and imaginative power. Places like ancient Roman ruins are already semiotically dense because they are rich in associations through the intersection of numerous representations: those of history, myth, archaeology, literature, image, art, music, associated cuisine (and so on). Heritage places are often already imbued with wonder, reverie and speculation, writes Rojek. And antique Roman sites are an excellent example. The imaginative power of heritage places relies on a wellspring of intoxicating and various (and often simultaneous) desires: spiritual, aesthetic, sensual, intellectual, fantasy, power, identity, knowledge, overcoming alienation, nostalgia and even the desire to journey/travel itself (see also de Botton 2002; Leed 1991).

Because of the reach and the pervasive nature of visual culture, the 'aura' of heritage is not confined to a particular place or site but is a constant eruption within the everyday. Rojek (1997: 53) writes of 'files of representation' which he defines as 'the medium and conventions associated with signifying a sight'. In other words, the visual and discursive representations of heritage places, like those marked out as 'ancient Roman', produce semiotic density and engender imaginative power. For Rojek, what erupts into the everyday is an 'index of representation', a phenomenon made up of those representations from the file that produce familiarity in the everyday. To the notions of 'file' and 'index' Rojek adds 'dragging', a process whereby a number of players in heritage site visitation (managers, guides, interpretation designers, education officers, curators and the visitors themselves) combine elements from the 'file of representation' and, in so doing, 'create new value'. Dragging, therefore, refers to an ongoing process of first, using existing grids of representation and, second, creating new representations some of which are by design and some of which are improvised and are performative in nature (see also Staiff 2010). In Rojek's view, following the ideas of Walter Benjamin, the physical site – its originality, its uniqueness – is mired in endless reproductions (particularly images but also texts) so that, in a sense, the original is always 'corrupted' or, to use less rhetoric, the 'original' is *always* mediated. No heritage site can be seen in some pure pre-epistemic way; the viewing and the viewed will always be implicated with representations/discursive practices that mark heritage as 'heritage' (see also Smith 2006; Waterton and Watson 2010). In other words, the viewing and the viewed will be 'pictured' and infused with the technologies of vision whether the still image or the moving image (Crary 1992).

Rojek's insights can be extended beyond the geographic precision of specific locations, specific topographies (necessary in his regard for particular tourist destinations or particular heritage sites) to a more general relationship between heritage and 'files of representation'. In particular, this refers to something that may be termed a 'visual repertoire': that constitutive part of heritage place construction, whether 'real' or imagined, and which is powerfully 'present' in certain types of heritage visitation precisely because the visual repertoire becomes entangled with the place/site/landscape/object in a way that is personal and spontaneous. Places like the Colosseum or the Roman Forum or Pompeii are perfect examples. While the reference to a visual repertoire relates to all the dimensions of contemporary visual culture and the files of representation it spawns, the particular concern here is the moving image.

According to the BBC documentary series *How Art Made the World* (2005), in the year 2004 seven billion people, worldwide, went to a cinema to watch a movie, a figure that obviously includes multiple visits by one person. This figure, however, excludes DVD movie rentals and purchases. Cinema has an impressive and unprecedented reach. And the moving image has a unique position in contemporary visual culture for another reason: its considerable and unique ability to captivate the viewer and take hold of our imaginations. The promotional byline for James Cameron's immensely popular *Avatar* (2009) was 'Enter the World. Avatar'. This experience of suspending disbelief (about the fact that we, the viewers, sit in a room watching a series of moving images produced by a computer and projected by a light source onto a screen) and the sense of being transported, as it were, into another world is the contemporary surrogate experience once related to other fusions of images, sound, music, movement, text – performance, religious rituals and so forth. However, the cinema seems to surpass these other fusion experiences. Movies enchant, captivate and enthral. They are intense sensorial experiences involving images, sounds, music, narrative, action, emotions and our imaginations (our internal world of images and imaging). Like all technologies of vision, film involves us knowing how they work and we learn how they work not from filmmaking courses but through the years of sustained exposure to the cinema experience (see also Crary 1992). We understand the fast edit and multiple views and perspectives, simultaneous plot lines, character development, complex manipulations of time, panning, zooming, the use of sound effects and music, the conventions of titles and credits and so forth. Today, the moving image has become ubiquitous and (almost) universally understood, especially if we also include video and television.

Because of the sheer power of the moving image to not only connect to our imaginations but to create indelible memory images, in other words, a memory iconography or a memory 'file of representations', it has over time produced and contributed to a repertoire of visual images that has standardised a visual interpretation of history and this is precisely where it potentially produces a visual heritage interpretation that is independent of site-based interpretation. Such a visual interpretation, this visual repertoire we carry around in our heads, is at our constant disposal. When the words 'ancient Rome' are uttered what *images* come to mind? And more importantly, what is the *source* of these memory images? These 'worlds' of the imagination exist in a mode that has never been so vivid or as detailed. Earlier generations – for example, those of the late-nineteenth century – relied on the pictures or illustrations in books, supplemented by material culture in museums (and for the few, travels to the ancient sites) along with their reading of history and classical literature or Shakespeare and so forth. This is not to say that their imaginative understanding of ancient Rome was any less than in the twenty-first century but arguably the repertoire is, today, (1) more vivid (2) more detailed (3) has greater conformity and (4) is more widely known. This iconography of places/times like ancient Rome is fed and fuelled by the representations of ancient Rome in movies, books, video games, travel books and magazines, documentaries, novels, the internet (Google images, Wikipedia, virtual tours and/or reconstructions) and so on. And similar (but different) to the late-nineteenth century, these visualisations are supplemented with museum visits and, increasingly significant, tourism to the heritage sites the representations refer to.

A cursory survey of the available visual material on ancient Rome reveals a rich ecology of interconnected visualisations. What is extraordinary about this ecology of imagery is the complete dissolution of the borders between fiction and the archaeological, and the dissolution of time itself. (Compare this with Foucault's [1986] discussion of heterotopias.) The cinematic iconography of ancient Rome may make important distinctions about the Rome of Sulla (c. 138–78 BCE) compared to the Rome of Julius Caesar (100–44 BCE) or the Rome of Constantine (272–337 CE), but in the mind's eye these distinctions dissolve and in the end through constant visual reinforcement of certain standard images about the dress and armaments of Roman soldiers and generals, the details of villa interiors (invariably of the rich and powerful Roman elites), the dress and jewellery of Roman patrician women, of senators and slaves, of Roman architecture (especially the Forum, the Colosseum, temples, theatres and aqueducts), chariots, Roman triremes, gladiators, roads and so on, a generalised and somewhat uniform memory iconography of ancient Rome becomes established. Thus the question about the ways this visual repertoire is activated and the ways it is connected to heritage places. Can those who vividly remember the chariot race in *Ben Hur* (1959, directed by William Wyler) not recall, in a general sense, this cinematic representation of both the place and the event when standing looking at the present-day sad remnants of the Circus Maximus in

Rome? Can we look at the Colosseum without being informed by the way it was represented in *Gladiator*? The use of this visual repertoire is not reliant on language-based interpretation, rather it is the fusion of memory images with our direct perception of a heritage site and our imaginative capacities. Of course, language-based knowledge is implicated but it is not the primary mechanism being described here.

Often what the visitor to archaeological sites sees is disconnected remnants. Pompeii, for example, is relatively easy for the visitor because the site has what heritage conservationists might term 'topographical and historical integrity' and the buildings of Pompeii do not compete with other 'remnants' of historical developments over the centuries nor modern developments like in Rome. Nevertheless, while the streets can be walked down and villas can be entered and the forum can be sensed as a civic space and a baker's shop and a wine tavern can be identified and the chariot grooves in the road and the remaining frescos can be marvelled at, the town today requires imaginative engagement. Trying to imagine a living, vibrant and complete urban landscape is quite difficult. And so into this space of the imaginative steps visual culture: films, docu-dramas, pictures and visual reconstructions (by artists and now by CGI). What cinema does so well is create total urban environments to give the viewer the illusion of 'being there', as it ostensibly was at some moment before the city's destruction. The BBC production *Pompeii: The Last Day* (2003) directed by Peter Nicholson, and noted for its use of CGI, is the most recent English-language film but also recently released on DVD was the television miniseries from 1984, *The Last Days of Pompeii* starring Lawrence Olivier, a series that had French, German and Spanish versions. These films do what no visit can, and that's (re)construct places into lived-in environments peopled with characters enmeshed with these virtual worlds, where the streetscape of archaeology is transformed into complete urban places as though we can somehow see and hear in the twenty-first century how it 'really' was just before the cataclysm of the eruption. The filmic versions of Pompeii fill the town with action and an iconography of daily life (whether historically accurate or assumed is beside the point). We see markets full of produce, social class and status played out semiotically with different costumes and activities (slaves carry, the patricians are carried), transport of various kinds, we experience the internal calm of a courtyard garden in a villa, we observe a Roman feast with guests lying on couches, we sense the politics of the *imperium* through the different roles played by the various social classes, by the relationships between men and women (and the position of the *pater familias*), by harsh punishments, we are exposed visually to a world that seems obsessed with order, with superstitious beliefs and the randomness of divine favour and we are introduced to a world of licentiousness and exotic past times, of whores and gladiators. And equally powerfully, the images are heard. Sound effects and music are integral to movies.

Film powerfully transcends the reality of (historical and heritage) fragments and disparate remnants with its illusion of complete worlds. The viewer of a film set in ancient Rome is instantly 'transported' into this 'virtual world' and the dramatic sequences simultaneously occur as the viewer is connected to the semiotics of the historical moment – the costumes, the types of weapons and armoury, the style of the architecture, the modes of transport, the symbols of power and powerlessness, gender differences and poverty are all visually created. It is a textbook lesson in the construction of a history (and heritage) iconography that then deeply resonates because of the connections between the particular film 'text' and all the others that reinforce this iconography (paintings, descriptions, other movies, museum objects, Roman architecture, computer games and so forth). The veracity of a film set in ancient Rome lies not in its historical accuracy or otherwise, but in the way it communicates a visual rendition that is increasingly standardised. We recognise the visual signs of ancient Rome (Barthes 1972).

And it is not only a question of visual seduction. In a way all visual images *enhance* reality and have always done so. It is almost as though unmediated reality were not enough. As Blanche DuBois so memorably says in Tennessee Williams' *A Streetcar Named Desire* (1947): 'I don't want realism. I want magic!' (Scene 9). In visual culture there is a propensity to exaggerate and enhance (Spivey 2005). This exaggeration, paradoxically, increases abstraction. This is one of the reasons why the experience of a movie – highly abstract with its multiple camera shots, its editing and its multiple narratives and manipulation of clock-time – can seem more 'real' than viewing physical reality. So the propensity to exaggerate and to increase abstraction (potentially producing hyper-real states) is a culturally inscribed quality (Spivey 2005). But more than this, it gives visual images (static or moving) a comparative edge over the 'real' world of the everyday. The urge to exaggerate in image construction is part of what causes images to demand our attention, to activate our engagement and to enchant us (Spivey 2005). The way heritage places are marked out semiotically (as not the everyday, as significant, as special, as vital and so on) shares something with images and when the two are fused – image and heritage site – a complex interplay is established. The visual imagery of heritage places gives rise to the magic Blanche DuBois craved.

The cinema and the imagination in history, heritage and the heritage experience

In his important book *History on Film/Film on History* (2006) Robert Rosenstone asks a series of questions about the narrative of the past in visual media and points out that such questions are still not, in his opinion, seriously asked, let alone answered. These questions can be equally applied to heritage. Do the depictions of places and monuments in the cinema really count as 'heritage'? Do films add or detract from our knowledge of the past and the protection of the past for the future? Can the depiction of heritage places and monuments in film be taken seriously? Can historical films set in places like ancient Rome count as 'heritage thinking' and contribute to 'heritage understanding' (adapted from Rosenstone 2006: 12)? Setting aside the not insignificant matter of films being part of heritage and having a significance that is equal to other forms of cultural expression within heritage-signifying practices, the questions derived from Rosenstone point to a virtual absence of cinema in heritage discourse and practices, particularly in the interpretation of heritage places by tourists/visitors.

Heritage and history share a common cultural environment: in the twenty-first century visual media has become the main means by which public history is consumed and historical knowledge engendered. Terence Wright, in his book *Visual Impact*, begins the preface with this far-reaching claim:

> In today's media age the visual image has become the predominant mode of communication. Indeed, for most people, pictures have become the primary channel through which we gain knowledge of the world.
>
> (2008: ix)

Even if this seems far-fetched, what cannot be ignored is the profusion of documentaries made for the likes of the National Geographic Channel, the History Channel and the Discovery Channel, for the public broadcasting corporations such as BBC, the CBC and the ABC and then the subsequent release of all these programmes on DVD. Add into this mix, period – or so-called 'costume' – dramas produced for the BBC and historical series in the USA beginning with the groundbreaking and profoundly affecting *Roots*, all the films set in 'historical times' in the last two decades. Consider also the range of computer/video games, for example, *Rise and Fall: Civilizations at War* (set in the first millennium, BCE), *Assassin's Creed* (set in Renaissance Italy), *Victoria: Empire Under the Sun* (economic simulation between 1836 and 1920), and the sheer density of visual representations of the past involving the moving image becomes apparent. And this list only refers to the Anglo-phonic world.

A fiercely debated scholarship has arisen around the heritage, cinema, history and tourism nexus (e.g. Higson 2003; Hughes-Warrington 2009; Landy 2001; Lowenthal 1998; Monk and Sargeant 2002; Rosenstone 2006). Much of it hinges on the veracity of each form of representation (does cinema 'Disnify' heritage and history?), on film as history (what are the distinctions between historical and costume films and documentaries?), on the eternal debates about the 'nature' of history and heritage (does heritage cannibalise history and what role for narrative and reconstructions in both enterprises?) and on the ideological inscriptions at work (Tory history, Whig history, gender, class and identity, branding 'nation' and so forth). Only Andrew Higson (2003) gives a prominent place to the imaginary in this ongoing critique. Heritage, he notes, is mobilised by the cinema and by tourism because all three are both temporal and spatial in character and, consequently, the three have become entwined in the process of imagining. Filmic narratives always and literally take place somewhere and these landscapes and settings, in turn, invite the viewer into the diegetic reality created by the film. The success of tourism to places depicted in movies underscores the way the imagination links films, heritage places and tourists (Higson 2003) and, simultaneously, links to the scopic nature – the spectatorship – of the entwined experience of all three.

The debates about film as history (and in comparison there is very little that is directly about film as heritage) do make one thing clear. Film more than any other form of representation allows the audience to 'see' and 'hear' the past. It allows the fantasy of time-travel to be realised on one experiential level that is a different order of embodied experience to reading a history book or visiting a heritage site or visiting a heritage/history theme park (Sobchack 2004). While the debates rage about the distrust of historical films, their inaccuracies, their distortions of the past, their tendency to fictionalise, trivialise, romanticise and falsify (for a summary, see Rosenstone 2001) – and such debates could easily be applied to heritage places and the cinema – the concern in this chapter has been the imaginative engagement with the past through the cinema. The creation of a 'heritage iconography' that is consciously or unconsciously transferred to particular types of heritage places in the tourist engagement as a crucial, but rarely acknowledged, part of the communication process between a site, such as the Colosseum, and the tourist in an age of visual media.

In the 2008 International Council on Monuments and Sites (ICOMOS) Charter on the Interpretation and Presentation of Cultural Heritage Sites, what was implicit in earlier heritage charters is made more explicit: the heritage site itself generates the communicative act. So everything from the conservation and protection process itself, including statements of significance, through to the engagement of tourists/visitors via media technologies, the locus of the communication act is the heritage place and its various custodians (ICOMOS 2008). However, it seems to me that the imagination of the tourist potentially subverts this neat formulation of the communicative power of heritage places and bypasses the powerful role that representations more generally have in the construction of heritage places and the engagement of visitors (Waterton and Watson 2010). These systems of representations are, by nature, constantly dynamic, always open-ended, have a life beyond that which they ostensibly represent and cannot be controlled (Hall 1997). Imagination is similar and, in any case, is inter-twined with representation.

However, the relationship between cinema and the viewer's imagination is not clear-cut because of the certainties and the uncertainties associated with our understanding of imagination (for a philosophical analysis of the imagination, see McGinn 2004). It is suffice to say that 'mindsight', as Colin McGinn calls it, is a process that is linked to and is similar in character to external visualisation by the eye but is not the same. McGinn concludes his study in this way:

> The imagination is a ubiquitous and central feature of mental life. It pervades nearly every mental operation. It never rests, day and night... It plays a constitutive role in memory, perception (seeing-as), dreaming, believing, meaning – as well as high level creativity.
>
> (2004: 163)

When the cinema is involved in the creation of an imaginary, as Umberto Eco (1986) explains, it strips away distinction and dissolves the boundaries between past–present–future. Geography and time are compressed into a procession of events. It produces what he calls the 'continuous return' that results in the formation of historical archetypes. The imagined ancient Rome inspired by the movies (together with all the other visual represen-tations) becomes a template for experiencing ancient Rome in the present. It makes the unfamiliar familiar and herein lies one of the paradoxes asso-ciated with a stereotyped set of images, what I've called a 'heritage iconography', being employed imaginatively in the communication between tourists and sites. The 'ancient Rome' of archaeological and historical research is only ever a hypothesis and the historical city – like most of the past – is ultimately unknowable, hard to fathom, fragmented, distant, obscure and abstract. Our archaeological knowledge and our historical knowledge are incomplete and we know that the epistemological regimes of the ancient Romans is incompatible with that of contemporary western thought (Foucault 1973). So any meaningful interaction between tourists and Roman heritage sites requires a translation of the unfamiliar into the familiar and cinema is one of the dominant representational processes for doing this. When we think 'Roman soldier' or 'Roman chari-oteer' or 'Roman banquet' our mental image is most likely to be, in some degree, cinematically informed, more indebted to the circulation of contemporary visual imagery rather than ancient Roman iconography based on frescoes, pottery, mosaics and sculpture. And with today's digital technologies, the propinquity of the heritage visit and the cinema is no longer a matter of imagination and memory, but imagination and visual culture. In the anecdote I told about the tourists at the Colosseum, the group from New Zealand were recalling from memory their viewing of

Gladiator. It is now possible, thanks to iPhones and G3 and G4 digital technology, to watch a clip of the second century (re)constructed gladiatorial
contest on YouTube as the tourist stands in the Colosseum.

When Foucault proposed the eclipse of (historical) time by space, the
shift away from the nineteenth century obsession with time and history,
could he, in the 1980s have envisaged the swiftness with which history as a
project would be so utterly abandoned? Can we any longer say with any
certainty that history is a foundational epistemology? I think not. This is
not the same thing as saying the past has lost its imaginative power. But it
is a past of spaces and sites not a past of chronologies and a belief in the
power of the past to explain the present and point to the future, in a
progressive and utopian ideology (Foucault 1986). Intersections between
the cinema, heritage and tourism further emphasise the dominance of
space over time. Simultaneously, visual culture has become a major source
of historical knowledge. The cinema, along with the panoply of other visual
representations is a potent way for tourists to imagine and engage with
particular types of heritage places.

References

Adams, L. (1996) *The Methodologies of Art*, New York: IconEditions.
Alpers, S. (1983) *The Art of Describing*, Chicago: University of Chicago Press.
Anheier, H. and Isar, Y. (eds) (2011) *Heritage, Memory and Identity*, London: Sage.
Barthes, R. (1972) 'The Romans in films', in M. Hughes-Warrington (ed.) (2009)
    The History on Film Reader, London and New York: Routledge.
Benton, T. (ed.) (2010) *Understanding Heritage and Memory*, Manchester:
    Manchester University Press.
Black, G. (2005) *The Engaging Museum: Developing Museums for Visitor Involvement*,
    London and New York: Routledge.
Bryson, N. (1983) *Vision and Painting: The Logic of the Gaze*, London: MacMillan.
Burnett, R. (2005) *How Images Think*, Cambridge, MA and London: MIT Press.
Burgoyne, R. (2008) *The Hollywood Historical Film*, Malden MA and Oxford: Blackwell.
Byrne, D. (2007) *Surface Collection: Archaeological Travels in Southeast Asia*, Lantham
    and New York: Altamira Press.
Carter, P. (1987) *The Road to Botany Bay: An Essay in Spatial History*, London: Faber
    and Faber.
Clarke, J. (1991) *The Houses of Roman Italy 100BC-AD250: Ritual, Space and
    Decorations*, Berkeley: University of California Press.
Cosgrove, D. (ed.) (1999) *Mappings*, London, Reaktion Books.
Crary, J. (1992) *Techniques of the Observer*, Cambridge, MA: MIT Press.
de Botton, A. (2002) *The Art of Travel*, London: Penguin Books.
Deleuze, G. (1986) *Cinema I: The Movement-Image*, Minneapolis: Minnesota
    University Press.
Dessaix, R. (2008) *Arabesques*, Sydney: Pan Macmillan.
Dunbar, R. (2008) 'Why humans aren't just great apes', *Issues in Ethnology and
    Anthropology* 3(3): 15–33.

Durrell, L. (1962) *Prospero's Cell*, London and Boston: Faber and Faber.

Eco, U. (1986) *Travels in Hyperreality*, London: Picador.

Fairclough, G., Harrison, R., Jameson, J. and Schofield, J. (eds) (2008) *The Heritage Reader*, London and New York: Routledge.

Foucault, M. (1973) *The Order of Things: An Archaeology of the Human Sciences*, New York: Vintage Books.

Foucault, M. (1986) 'Of other spaces', *Diacritics* 16(1): 22–7.

Gibson, J. (1979) *The Ecological Approach to Visual Perception*, Boston: Houghton Mifflin.

Graham, B. and Howard, P. (eds) (2008) *The Ashgate Research Companion to Heritage and Identity*, Farnham and Burlington: Ashgate.

Hall, S. (ed.) (1997) *Representation: Cultural Representations and Signifying Practices*, London: Sage.

Harris, A. (2010) 'Everyone has a story to tell', unpublished Ph.D thesis, University of Western Sydney, Australia.

Hein, G. (1998) *Learning in the Museum*, London and New York: Routledge.

Higson, A. (2003) *English Heritage, English Cinema: Costume Drama since 1980*, Oxford: Oxford University Press.

Hillis, K. (1999) *Digital Sensations: Space, Identity and Embodiment in Virtual Reality*, Minneapolis and London: University of Minnesota Press.

Hughes-Warrington, M. (ed.) (2009) *The History on Film Reader*, London and New York: Routledge.

ICOMOS (2008) *Charter on the Interpretation and Presentation of Cultural Heritage Sites*, Québec. Available online: www.international.icomos.org/charters/interpretation_e.pdf (accessed 13 June 2012).

Landy, M. (ed.) (2001) *The Historical Film: History and Memory in Media*, London: Athlone Press.

Leed, E. (1991) *The Mind of the Traveler*, New York: Basic Books.

Logan, W. and Reeves, K. (eds) (2009) *Places of Pain and Shame: Dealing with 'Difficult Heritage'*, London and New York: Routledge.

Lowenthal, D. (1998) *The Heritage Crusade and the Spoils of History*, Cambridge: Cambridge University Press.

Marcus, A., Metzger, S., Paxton, R. and Stoddard, J. (2010) *Teaching History with Film*, New York and London: Routledge.

McGinn, C. (2004) *Mindsight: Image, Dream, Meaning*, Cambridge MA and London: Harvard University Press.

Monk, C. and Sargeant, A. (eds) (2002) *British Historical Cinema: The History, Heritage and Costume Film*, London and New York: Routledge.

Moore, N. and Whelan, Y. (eds) (2007) *Heritage, Memory and the Politics of Identity*, Farnham and Burlington: Ashgate.

Morris, J. (1983) *Venice*, revised edn, London and Boston: Faber and Faber.

Rojek, C. (1997) 'Indexing, dragging and the social construction of tourist sights', in C. Rojek and J. Urry (eds) *Touring Cultures: Transformations of Travel and Theory*, London and New York: Routledge.

Rosenstone, R. (2001) 'The historical film: looking at the past in a Postliterate Age', in M. Landy (ed.) *The Historical Film: History and Memory in Media*, London: Athlone Press.

Rosenstone, R. (2006) *History On Film/Film On History*, Harlow, Essex: Pearson Education.

Ruggles, D. and Silverman, H. (eds) (2009) *Intangible Heritage Embodied*, London and New York: Springer.

Russell, J. (2007) *Historical Epic and Contemporary Hollywood*, New York and London: Continuum.

Saylor, S. (2010) *Empire: The epic novel of Imperial Rome*. London: Constable and Robinson.

Schouten, F. (1995) 'Heritage as historical reality', in D. Herbert (ed.) *Heritage, Tourism and Society*, Pinter: London.

Sobchack, V. (2004) *Carnal Thoughts: Embodiment and Moving Image Culture*, Berkeley and Los Angeles: University of California Press.

Solomon, J. (2001) *The Ancient World in the Cinema*, New Haven and London: Yale University Press.

Smith, L. (2006) *Uses of Heritage*, London and New York: Routledge.

Smith, L. and Akagawa, N. (eds) (2009) *Intangible Heritage*, London and New York: Routledge.

Spivey, N. (2005) *How Art Made the World*, London: BBC Books.

Staiff, R. (2010) 'History and tourism: intertextual representations of Florence', *Tourism Analysis* 15(5): 601–12.

Theroux, P. (2008) *Ghost Train to the Eastern Star*, London: Penguin Books.

Turnbull, D. (1989) *Maps Are Territories*, Geelong: Deakin University Press.

Urry, J. (2002) *The Tourist Gaze*, 2nd edn, London: Sage.

Vidal, G. (1992) *Screening History*, Cambridge MA: Harvard University Press.

Wartofsky, M. (1984) 'The paradox of painting: pictorial representation and the dimensionality of visual space', *Social Research* 51(4): 863–83.

Waterton, E. and Watson, S. (eds) (2010) *Culture, Heritage and Representation*, Farnham: Ashgate.

Winter, T. (2007) *Postconflict Heritage, Postcolonial Tourism*, London and New York: Routledge.

Wright, T. (2008) *Visual Impact: Culture and the Meaning of Images*, Oxford and New York: Berg.

Wyke, M. (1997) *Projecting the Past: Ancient Rome, Cinema and History*, Routledge: New York and London.

Chapter 6

Country matters

The rural–historic as an authorised heritage discourse in England

Steve Watson

Introduction

My purpose in this chapter is to explore ways in which a distinctive cultural construct, which I have termed the 'rural–historic', has permeated the production and experience of heritage tourism in England. The chapter suggests that in doing so the rural–historic has sustained a pervasive and enduring version of the national past that contrasts strongly with England's urban–industrial history. The latter, with its cultural motifs of modernity and production, social class division and multiculturalism, represents something of an unwelcome intrusion on these representations of the country's heritage. The rural–historic on the other hand presents a narrative that, on the surface at least, presents a more socially cohesive and collective vision of cherished national mythologies and imaginary values. Laurajane Smith's (2006) concept of an 'authorised heritage discourse' (AHD) provides a theoretical framework through which to examine the rural–historic both in theory and in practice and, using the touristic representation of English parish churches as an example, I demonstrate the abiding strength of a cultural construct that works to express a binding sense of nationhood and identity.

Contexts

As the first urban society associated with industrial modernity, Britain consumed raw materials from around its global empire and transformed them into manufactured goods that were in turn exported to emerging markets in its colonies and other industrialising nations. To service this first expression of industrial global capitalism, the country itself was transformed from a rural agricultural economy into an urban powerhouse characterised by the movement of people to expanded towns, cities and conurbations in the midlands and the north. As a result, the population of countryside diminished and a newly and largely urban population grew from 8.3 million in 1801 to over 30 million a century later (Jefferies 2005: 3) and this trend continued through the twentieth century. The England of the imagination, however, neither absorbed nor reflected these changes. There is a paradox, therefore, in the construction of English identity; a radical disconnect between what is known and what is represented, reproduced and believed about the country. The 'Dickensian' conditions in the new towns and cities, with their factories and mills, were masked by a cultural dislocation in which a remembered past came to be replaced, appropriately, by a manufactured one. As the cities grew they also acquired the trappings of a cultural resurgence seen most clearly in architecture (Dellheim 2004). Town halls resembled renaissance palaces while museums, galleries and theatres became essays in revived gothic. Even the factories were adorned with period detail as if to deny their real purpose.

The English, however, persisted in representing to themselves and to others an identity drawn from an idealised, bucolic past and an image of nationhood that represented anything but the 'urban–industrial' that was at the heart of its economic progress. Instead there emerged a pervasive and durable cultural construct that I refer to here as the rural–historic, centred on the English countryside, landscape and buildings. This image has endured to the present day at the core of discourses about national identity, especially the more elegiac of them (Scruton 2001), but also those which appear in popular media representations. With this in mind it is hardly surprising that it has also suffused the national tourism 'product' with its imagery, to the extent that destinations not only reflect the rural–historic itself but also its representations in literature, cinema and television programmes, especially costume dramas and those which offer entertaining, comforting and ultimately nostalgic visions of the past. Such representations are the stock-in-trade of destination marketers ever eager to develop products that already resonate in the minds of potential visitors or which confirm their stereotypes of what England is or should be, both visually and experientially.

The countryside itself is a place where change is rejected and repudiated, and where landscapes full of castles, country houses, villages, customs and 'folk' combine in official heritage and touristic discourses to create comforting illusions of continuity and stability. These illusions are substantiated and maintained by the monumental materiality of the past as well as less-tangible expressions of tradition and 'way of life' that are essentially conservative, white, middle-class and exclusionary. People lower down the rural social order are inevitably represented either as well-meaning and earnest, the sons and daughters of honest toil or as 'salt of the earth' picaresques with hearts of gold, such as Pop Larkin in H.E. Bates' *Darling Buds of May* or Claude Greengrass in *Heartbeat* – both of which were television adaptations of a novel series.

This vision of rural life is also presented as 'authentic' and in polar opposition to urban–industrial culture which is inscribed with modernity and multiculturalism and therefore not quite English (Askins 2009). As

Christopher Tilley (2006: 14) has put it: 'It is through making material reference to the past that identification with place occurs through the medium of 'traditional' material culture and representations of life-styles, urban and rural, that no longer exist'. The rural–historic, therefore, is an expression of this disconnect between a past as lived, found or discovered and another that is still represented by signifiers of an imagined Englishness, an artefact of the industrial revolution, a powerful cultural construct and now a valuable resource for heritage tourism.

Official guidebooks and marketing communications draw much attention to the rural–historic with country houses and medieval castles forming the archetypes, and an imagined countryside equipped with hedgerows and villages with medieval churches, manor houses, rose-draped cottages and an all-pervasive quaintness is populated with friendly police constables, district nurses on bicycles, country doctors and any number of engaging and colourful 'characters'. In a curious historical inversion, the rural–historic, a MacCannellian 'staged-authenticity', opposes an 'aberrant' modern–urban–industrial. As Tim Edensor (2002: 40) has expressed it, to be in the English countryside is 'to achieve a kind of national self-realisation, to return to 'our' roots where the self, freed from its inauthentic – usually urban – existence, is re-authenticated'.

As a tourist resource, the rural–historic can be neatly contrived in marketing narratives and sold to audiences from overseas and natives alike, its performance as such reproducing an authorised discourse that makes further representation recognisable, knowable, and experientially possible through heritage tourism. The English rural–historic is thus animated by performative and representational practices that timelessly evoke a past-in-the-present, the empirical reality of which is displayed in the selected materiality of the nation's past and a 'particular idea of heritage in England' (Waterton 2009: 52). But how is it that the cradle of industrial capitalism and urbanism, where most of the population have lived in towns and cities since the nineteenth century, came to be defined by the historical imagery of its much diminished countryside?

Discourse, performance and representation

Much of the heritage debate as it has developed over the last 20 years has been encapsulated by Smith's (2006) notion of an AHD, which provides both the context and a powerful theoretical framework within which the eclectic mix of places, buildings and objects, the monumental and the material that constitute heritage can be understood in their cultural context. The AHD thus recognises heritage as a form of cultural production that comes to represent something about the world in which it is active in representing objects to which value has been ascribed. Taste, connoisseurship and expertise sustain this value that in turn supports a narrative

of naturalness. Even the wild and natural-looking moorlands and heaths are the result of clearance activities that began in the Bronze Age. Nonetheless, it has developed an aesthetic value, validated and supported in cultural production that appears to be more dependent on art than nature. Paradoxically, therefore, the English landscape is as much the product of human activity as the towns and cities with which it is conventionally contrasted. The distinction between country and city is exceptional in England, however, in being established relatively early and decisively, with the industrial revolution as its motive force, and the polarity it has engendered remaining pervasively ingrained in expressions of national culture (Askins 2009; Harrison 1991; Williams 1973). As such, and despite its obvious artifice, it acts in a similar way to the more natural landscapes of the Alps and Canada in authenticating notions of nationhood and national identity.

If nature can be so easily dismissed in the English landscape it is also difficult to make any real claim for its historicity. The conventional view adopted by Fred Inglis (1987) is that the imagery of the English countryside is a feature of the Romantic movement from the late-eighteenth century and a reaction to industrialisation and urbanisation. For Edensor it is the rural, or the 'rhetoric of the rural' that expresses the national *genius loci* where the 'essential national spirit resides' (2002: 40). He considers rural England to be a 'supreme marker of national identity' (2002: 40–2) not least because, as David Lowenthal (1994) has discussed, it signifies an imagined stability and sense of order, the constituents of an ideological current that while essentially conservative is couched in terms of aesthetics, nostalgia and patriotism. Crucially, this is presented in a way that is apolitical, naturalised and woven into the nation's sense of itself and it is specifically the south of England that provides the appropriate signifiers:

> Parish churches, lych gates, haystacks, thatched or half-timbered cottages, rose-laden gardens, village greens, games of cricket, country pubs, rural customs, hedgerows, golden fields of grain, plough and horses, hunting scenes, and a host of characters including vicars, squires, farmers, gamekeepers, are part of a series of interlinked cues which are widely shared at home and abroad.
>
> (Edensor 2002: 41)

At the same time, as Edensor goes on to suggest, the ideal of the countryside masks a multitude of less-desirable qualities, such as rural poverty and gendered and racial exclusiveness, a point developed more recently by Kye Askins (2009), Emma Waterton (2009) and Mike Crang and Divya P. Tolia-Kelly (2010). The point, however, is not just what the rural–historic is and what it excludes, but also what it *does* in the identity politics of nationhood, property ownership and the power politics of social change. Evidence of the brutal politics of the countryside lies in the patterns of land ownership from the beginning of the industrial revolution when the English country-side can be seen as the product of little more than an eighteenth century land grab. As John Rennie Short has stated:

> The so called 'typical English Scene', of a patchwork of Green fields, is in origin the spatial imprint of an eighteenth century commercial enterprise. [This] supercharged image of English Environmental ideology, which can still conjure up notions of community, unchanging values and national sentiments, is in reality the imprint of a profit-based exercise which destroyed the English peasantry and replaced a moral economy of traditional rights and obligations with the cash nexus of commercial capitalism.
>
> (1991: 77)

The power nexus is also expressed in what Olwig (2008) has described as 'Elysian Britain', the construction in the eighteenth century of a United Kingdom that shared in some sense the same mythical origins as ancient Rome. The landscape was thus remodelled by a variety of landscape artists to reflect this elective antiquity with the parkland around country houses (built or remodelled on Vitruvian principles) variously enhanced, embellished and decorated with Palladian summerhouses, temples and other classical follies:

> Whereas the old nobility legitimized their right to the land through ancient inheritance, the new landed class naturalized their rights in property by surrounding their land with a pastoral/Elysian style of park and garden that was seen to be 'natural'.
>
> (2008: 85)

Lowenthal (1991) affirms that the visual cliché that is the English land-scape is 'quite recent' in its recognised form and is difficult to trace back beyond the pre-Raphaelites. For David Matless (1998) it is a contested terrain of tradition and modernity and fluctuating definitional narratives that settled into its present form after the Second World War. In short, the English countryside is neither particularly natural, nor particularly old, and yet despite this it is a place of contested verities: in the face of urban development, road-building and industrialised agriculture all of which are seen as social and economic necessities, it is protected, protested about, celebrated, evoked, memorialised, enjoyed and adored. The object of legislation, planning regulations and development control, it animates a variety of official and quasi-official agencies – pressure groups, local authorities, the National Trust and a multitude of local amenity groups.

The 'historic' in terms of the built environment is equally problematic, with buildings and archaeological remains selected as heritage objects on the basis of their accessibility and visuality as much as any inherent historical or architectural qualities. I use the word visuality here as a metaphor for the social and cultural significance that links them to AHD (Smith 2006). Thus, many of the most ancient and archaeologically significant sites are rarely recognised as heritage tourism attractions because they lack this significance. The ubiquitous country house on the other hand or the ready supply of medieval castles, conveniently 'slighted' by Oliver Cromwell in the English Civil War, provide a ready resource for heritage tourism, because they are easily assimilated into narratives about the national past that make them easy to represent through the AHD. Add these to a stock of abbeys and monasteries made picturesquely and conveniently ruinous by Henry VIII's commissioners after the dissolution in 1538, and it is hardly surprising that touring the medieval has long been a national pastime (Watson 2001). The country houses, particularly, when added to this mix, support a rich discourse that speaks of a particular essentialised view of the national past, and this same past as a cohesive factor in the formation of a national identity (Deckha 2004; Mandler 1997; Smith 2006).

For Waterton this heritage is both selective and definitional, and

> [...] shares too much in common with a dominant and exclusive understanding of heritage and its associated identity categories. The categories include the 'nation', as immaculate Englishness, 'expertise' and 'us', as white, middle- and upper-classes.
>
> (2009: 53)

The involvement of the rural–historic in linking national identity with the physical fabric of the land and its history, according to Patrick Wright, produces a version of the past that is very clearly an artefact of the present, especially when expressed as a *national heritage* replete with uniquely expressive objects:

> Far from being 'behind' the present, the past exists as an accomplished presence in public understanding. In this sense it is written into present social reality, not just implicitly as a residue, precedent or custom and practice, but explicitly as itself – as History, National Heritage and Tradition.
>
> (1985: 25, 142)

These places and these historic objects, whether vernacular, stately or academically sanctioned by architectural connoisseurs, have come to epitomise what Krishnan Kumar (2003: 209) calls 'a certain kind of "Englishness" ' that became the stuff of postcards and tourist posters. This cultural axis reflects something of what Chris Rojek and John Urry (1997: 15) note in some places as a 'timelessness' expressed in their survival over such long periods that they seem to be appreciated as places apart from the instantaneous *placelessness* of modernity.

What exists in England, therefore, is a confluence of the rural and the historic which is signified by the instantly recognisable 'soft landscape' of the lowlands and, of course, the ubiquitous country house (Smith 2006). Here are a clear set of signifiers that associate the countryside with the nation and what Stephen Daniels and Denis Cosgrove (1988: 8) describe as the 'conservative picture of a "deep" England with its stable layers of historical accretion'. It is also an abiding cultural construction that symbolises and actively represents the social structures that created it and in ways that help to reproduce them.

However, this ensemble has little to do with any objective evaluation of archaeological, historical or artistic contexts and is, rather, conditional on the processes by which the AHD is configured in a particular setting. This results in a process of selection, the outcomes of which are coterminous with the socio-cultural priorities that the AHD supports. In other words there has to be a reason to select and a reason to display, and the AHD either provides this and links it with a proven narrative, or it does not. In the case of the Northumberland hillforts in the UK, for example, the lack of an appropriate and pre-existing narrative prevents these archaeologically important Iron Age monuments from entering that portion of the heritage on display through tourism (Watson 2009: 36–7). Their lack of cultural *visuality* works against their selection despite their archaeological significance and tangible appearance in the landscape.

The rural–historic in populating the AHD with images and objects replaces both nature and history with a powerful cultural construct that is, in itself, a product of history, the social and economic history of England. There is more than an echo here of Eric Hobsbawm and Terence Ranger's (1983) 'invented tradition', an invention that enables England to be imagined in the way that it is, especially when it is reproduced and reinforced by the representational practices of tourism and other cultural productions. This semiotic code is both expressed and reinforced by art and literature and latterly, by movies and TV, all of which construct a countryside that is rich in the opposites of the urban–industrial.

Here is not a natural, but rather a *naturalised* countryside wrapped up in the benign spirit of an imagined England, posed in joyful and heroic counterpoint to the paraphernalia of modern, urban life. The media representations of the rural–historic reinforce the role of selected places as tourist attractions and destinations to the extent that, as has often been noted, the places themselves become known, at least for tourism, by their media representations (Mordue 2001). As places become extensions of literary and media brands they also serve to create a representational nexus around accepted and reproducible meanings. For Jodi Wallwork and John A. Dixon (2004: 36), such representations can become embedded in everyday discourse and form a link between the representation of place and the construction of identity, such that even ordinary talk and text becomes suffused with this kind of meaning. The discourse, as it has developed, has positioned an imagined England in a way that is radically differentiated from its urban alter ego, separated by processes of selection and representation which are associated with the cultural work of the heritage industry expressed through the AHD.

Deepest darkest England

In England there is an intensity and longevity about the fascination with the rural that has become definitional in cultural terms. England is 'Olde England' or 'Merrie England' and crystallised in later Victorian literature such as Tennyson's *English Idylls* and a host others (Wiener 1982: 42–64). A variety of cultural movements and artefacts sought inspiration from the mythical past, including the garden city movement in urban planning and the wistful, elegiac orchestral music of the early twentieth century. Edward Elgar, Ralph Vaughan Williams, Gustav Holst and others provided a musical English *neverland*, an introspective counterpoint not only to modernity, but also to the assertive imperial pride of the period before the First World War (Crump 1987: 186; Wright 1985: 105). It was at this time that the suburbs were forming on the edges of towns and cities, growing around the roadsides in so-called 'ribbon developments' and extending into and subsuming the countryside. The actual built-up area of London quadrupled in size between 1900 and 1939 (Harrison 1991: 22). It is perhaps not surprising that this gave rise to another bout of rural eulogising and painful nostalgia, what Marilyn Strathern (1982) refers to as 'Englishness as architecture', and the importation into the suburbs of explicitly rural forms and imagery. Avenues of mock Tudor houses thus perfectly complemented Vaughan Williams' mock Tudor music. The expansion of motor tourism also led to the building of large hotels and pubs on major arterial roads, the so-called 'road houses', in a style that came to be known as 'Brewer's Tudor', with names like *Ye Olde Royal Oak* and similar reflections of national myth and folklore. Even the pubs of the inner cities began to recall rustic Elizabethan Inns haunted by the ghost of Falstaff.

The suburbs began to look like a series of sprawling extruded villages evoking the English imaginary in timber, brick and plaster rendering, as if the urban–industrial was like the grit in an oyster that has to be coated with smooth layers of rural–historicity in order for it to be accepted and assimilated. The image of the countryside was projected onto the new urban spaces so that these too became constitutive of the nation itself, with the rural–historic acting as a cypher for national identity so that a walk in the suburbs became as much the experience of an authorised national past as any visit to a country house. Tourism, however, became one of the most significant routes to this narrative, supporting and reinforcing its core messages of identity and social cohesion.

Throughout the twentieth century the rural–historic also came to symbolise concerns about the erosion and disappearance of the conventional appearance and extent of the countryside, something that can be detected in the work of those two stalwarts of the *Englishness* genre in the 1930s: J.B. Priestly and H.V. Morton (Giles and Middleton 1995: 73). H.V. Morton's (1927) book, *In Search of England*, ran to 25 editions between 1927 and the Second World War. This reflects another recurrent theme, an elegiac sense of loss combined with an acute political sensibility based on the need for social and political change (Wright 1985: 104), something that by the late twentieth century had been profoundly stirred by the experience of two world wars (Giles and Middleton 1995; Kumar 2003; Matless 1998).

It is clear, therefore, that in the interwar and post-war periods there was an increasing desire to aestheticise the rural–historic as an object of wider cultural interest, something to be valued (even treasured) and invested with this value, as an object of tourism. Here it retains its abiding role as a place of both identity formation and leisure consumption, with a discourse that ranges from the beauty of the rural and what are seen as the intrinsic attractions of old buildings to some rather extreme formulations, at least by today's standards:

> If I had no duties I would spend my life not in driving briskly but in walking slowly, not in the distracting society of a pretty woman, but just gazing into the fair face of my country. That her face is her fortune is allowed by every visitor, but few faces grow lovelier as they grow older. The face of Britain is most lovely where it is most ancient.
>
> (Mais and Stephenson 1951: 7)

S.P.B. Mais had something of a track record in this kind of purple prose, producing two or three books a year through the 1930s, with titles such as *England's Character*, *England's Pleasance*, and *Weekends in England*. His books are well populated with a variety of colourful characters each perfectly suited to their role as representatives of their region. He even misses them when they are absent: 'what I wanted was the genial and time-encrusted atmosphere of a true North Riding (Yorkshire, UK) inn filled with men speaking in the rich native idiom'. (1951: 148). Mais became famous, as an author, raconteur, journalist and a radio broadcaster, someone whose job it was to speak to us, in an accent that my family would have described as 'posh', and yet reminding us, at the same time, that we are all the same, sharing a rich heritage that binds us together. The reality of this social cohesion could then be materialised and demonstrated on a 'day out' in the country where the nation would speak of its past and the tourist would listen, and return every summer weekend for more of the same.

After the Second World War the National Parks were established, and joined the already existing National Trust and Ministry of Public Building and Works in providing the organisational framework for protecting and representing the material basis of the rural–historic. English Heritage later absorbed the government property portfolio, in presenting to the public its stock of medieval rubble and ruins. The aristocratic owners of country houses were also impelled by a combination of taxes and the profit motive to open their doors (or at least their gates) to the newly motorised tourist. The background to these developments is well rehearsed, which in many ways culminated in the 1980s heritage boom, so effectively deconstructed in Robert Hewison's (1987) well-known book. A lively 'heritage debate' ensued. Critics and defenders, baiters and beraters and an *antiheritage animus*, as Lowenthal (1998) described it, with philistine tourism the chief villain, and at whose door accusations of commodification, inauthenticity and elitism would be laid. Academic debates, of course, mattered little in the clamour for novel and interesting forms of tourism that could draw in new kinds of objects and 'assets', for new kinds of tourists (Munt 1994). The rural–historic was very much a part of this movement, especially where it was linked, in a market-led way, with all the other paraphernalia of a national obsession with the past (Samuel 1994). But again it is the strength of the affinity that is notable here, so that the countryside is:

> commodified not only as a physical place, but as a place with spiritual resonances, with connotations of romantic simplicity and golden tradi-
> tionality. In many cases, the countryside is portrayed as a container of traditional cultures, national identities, and authentic lifestyles.
>
> (Kneafsey 2001: 763)

The expansion of touristic significance in specific places with distinct place imagery is a recent cultural development that contrasts strongly with the mass recreational tourism of the past. Typically these are places that were once used for other purposes, such as industry, agriculture or buildings such as fortifications, stately homes and churches. As Fraser MacDonald (2002: 62) has observed, 'the reorganisation of space around heritage and tourism is now the dominant strategy of economic revival'.

For Rojek (1997) the process involves the social construction of touristic significance from available resources in a process he describes as 'indexing and dragging'. Tourism is defined by movement through spaces that are constructed from 'files' of indexed representations linked to an original object, 'that is a range of signs, images and symbols which make the sight familiar to us in ordinary culture' (1997: 53). The system operates at both conscious and unconscious levels and may involve 'privileged readings', authoritative or authorised meanings derived from other cultural productions. These might include hegemonic images and even the cinema – a source to which people are particularly receptive and which has been manifest in the many ways that literary, cinema and television 'locations' have been attached to touristic space (1997: 54–5). For the purposes of tourism development, these official designations are easily generated by the activities of locally and regionally based public sector destination managers who identify all manner of cultural and heritage assets that can be duly packaged and re-represented for the purposes of destination marketing.

Interest in English identity was renewed towards the end of the millennium although the reasons for this are obscure. It may have been related to the heritage 'boom' of the 1980s, or possibly it was a response to multiculturalism, or even the implementation of Scottish and Welsh self-government. Either way, a number of writers from the 1980s onwards have sought to revivify the search for, and expression of, English identity, and from a variety of viewpoints: sociological (e.g. Edensor 2002; Kumar 2003; Wright 1985) historical (e.g. Mandler 2002; Paxman 1998) and aesthetic (e.g. Ackroyd 2004; Scruton 2001). This interest fed and was in turn fed by an affective response that Catherine Palmer (2005) explains in terms of an imagined intimacy based on something 'deeply felt', rather than on chronological history. In examining a number of important sites of national heritage she observes distinctive processes of identity creation:

> The sites thus communicate different yet interlinked components of nationness and in doing so create a gaze of Englishness. However...the discourse of nationness reflects the intentions and agenda of those organisations that own and manage the sites. It is a hegemonic discourse devoid of the nuances, complexities and contradictions inherent in both defining the characteristics of a particular identity and in the reading of history.
>
> (2005: 24)

This intimacy is based around three themes: unbroken tradition, kinship ties and love of freedom. Each of these, according to Palmer, ties the individual to the imagined community of nationness, a clear link is thus made between the materiality of the heritage and the discursive realm of nationhood:

> It is a discourse where nationness is presented as unifying and where tourists are invited to celebrate and commune with the core characteristics of Englishness.
>
> (2005: 8)

Palmer's approach reflects Michael Pretes' (2003) attempt to draw parallels between the role of heritage tourism sites and that of museums in validating a common identity or 'imagined community' to use Benedict Anderson's (2006) well-known formulation. The producers of heritage tourism thus:

> Project their values of national identity and national inclusivity. Such sights may function in the same way as museums, guarding national heritage and history and preserving it for public display.
>
> (Pretes 2003: 139)

For both Palmer and Pretes heritage tourism provides a medium through which a hegemonic discourse around identity and nationhood can be transmitted, a discourse that Smith has labelled as the AHD and which is represented here in the rural–historic, a cultural construct with a long-standing and sustained expressive power. Having explored the antecedents of the rural–historic it is time to examine a specific example in context to gain an understanding of its pervasive influence in touristic discourse.

The country church and the rural–historic

Supported by nearly 200 years of representational practice in which the countryside and its contents have come to symbolise a nation lost to industry and urbanisation, the rural–historic has become a powerful cultural axis by which specific objects of heritage are signified as part of an AHD. Among these objects country churches, not least because of their often medieval origins, are both significant and abundant. They may lack the well-managed attraction value of the country house or castle ruin, but their emblematic quality and presence in virtually every country village almost guarantees their place in the pantheon of the rural–historic. As such the rural church is a significant cultural object and one that is reproduced and reinforced through the medium of the tourist guide book and gazetteer, especially those with a strong visual emphasis, and where the link is made with vague notions of spirituality expressed through pastness and tranquillity.

As part of a wider study of church tourism, a survey of English local government tourism websites was undertaken over a three-year period. Of the 324 websites investigated, just over a third (116) made explicit references to churches either as attractions or as aspects of local heritage. The majority of local authorities representing churches on their websites were in predominantly rural locations: a total of 79 (68 per cent) of the 116 authorities that referred to churches were representing them in rural contexts. Even local authorities in large urban centres would often confine their representation of churches to those whose setting looked less urban. At Bradford, for example, an industrial city in northern England, no urban churches other than the Cathedral were represented. According to the diocesan tourism officer, who was interviewed as part of the research, this was because the urban space was thought too challenging for touristic representation, with its generally run-down appearance and the risk (or rather the fear) of crime. In other urban areas, local tourism officials even sought to *ruralise* their urban settings often with surprising results:

> The picture on the cover of the guidebook to Luton Parish is almost comical. The photographer contrives an angle that gives it a site in rural woodland. In reality, this fine perpendicular church is set in some of the worst urban development that even the Home Counties have to offer, a horror of car parks, one-way systems and hostile shopping centres.
>
> (Jenkins 1999: 9)

So, despite many examples of culture and heritage being used in urban regeneration, it is to the countryside that representational practice constantly returns. Local authorities are representing churches as a part of their rural attraction value, even where there is a major urban area within their boundaries. An authorised version of spatial representation thus develops, one that will only admit selections based on culturally conditioned notions of attractiveness that are of long standing, and related to mythologised concepts of English rurality: the historic building, the picturesque scene and the landscape setting. Bella Dicks contextualises the process in terms of its organisational setting and objectives: the management and marketing of local qualities for the purposes of inwards investment:

> Increasingly, the particular resources and attractions that local areas can offer capital are configured as *representational* challenges. Each locality is catapulted into a competition to market those qualities that will allow it to gain a competitive edge over its rivals.
>
> (2000: 55, original emphasis)

While this motive factor was found in the representation of churches in both urban and rural locations, it was the latter that found the greatest celebration of the church in its physical setting, in this case as an essential component of English rurality and the growing interest in rural tourism as a new and predominant form of capital accumulation (Butler 1998).

The role of churches in the rural attraction 'portfolio' was demonstrated clearly in Lincolnshire, in the East Midlands. At North Lincolnshire, church tourism is represented as a tranquil resort from the stresses of everyday life:

> We will develop and celebrate the cultural diversity of North Lincolnshire
> through initiatives such as vibrant local events and church tourism. We
> will work with attractors to develop quality leisure breaks, positioning
> North Lincolnshire as a destination to escape the stresses of everyday life.
> (North Lincolnshire Council 2003: 11)

Perhaps the most developed form of this representation was where
churches were represented not only as components of rurality, but also as
essentially characteristic of it, free-standing symbols of the rural–historic.
Evidence of this 'symbolic' representation was found in 13 per cent of the
local authorities that referred to churches in their tourism 'offer', and it
was typical of areas that possessed a particular type of building. For example, the limestone or flint that characterises buildings in some areas, or the
style of building, such as the Cotswold 'wool churches', the spires of
Northamptonshire or the round towers of Norfolk and Suffolk. The information provided by Wycombe District Council is typical of such practices:

> The District's churches are one of the key features of the landscape.
> Most of the Chiltern villages are centred around a centuries old
> church, built of stone and flint. The towns have large parish churches
> and other smaller ones to cater for different denominations.
> (Wycombe District Council 2005)

These are old formulations, and the abiding influence of the rural–historic
as a cultural construct is apparent in the text. What can be seen here, then,
is the use of a construction of the English countryside with churches as an
essential component, and as a cultural artefact with a symbolic quality.

Such mythologies are central to the touristic representation of rural
tourism and with at least 200 years of cultural practice to build on, it is
hardly surprising to see churches represented as part of an English rural
iconography, the continuity of which is amply demonstrated in a comparison of Constable's well-known painting *Dedham Vale* (1802) with a
contemporary image from the Shropshire tourism website (see Figures 6.1
and 6.2). In both, the countryside is represented as an aestheticised space.
In the picture of Clun, in Shropshire, the countryside is cultural capital
worthy of inclusion in the attraction portfolio, and of the attentions of the
intending tourist. Apart from the wide vista, the photograph includes the
same visual elements as Constable's painting of 200 years earlier: trees,
fields, farm animals and church, neatly arranged to refer to a well-established semiotic of timeless tradition and tranquillity. The two images
occupy and represent the same cultural space, that of the rural idyll that is
mythologised by the purveyors of rural tourism, the cult of the country
house and the deracinated view of rural life that symbolises an established
concept of heritage as a kind of cultural constant: the rural–historic.

Figure 6.1 Denham Church and Vale
John Constable, 1800. Pen, ink and watercolour on paper, Whitworth Art Gallery,
University of Manchester

Figure 6.2 Clun village
Image from promotional website for South Shropshire District Council 2006,
reproduced with permission from Shropshire Tourism [UK] Ltd

This set of cultural referents continues to support the imagery of 'towns and villages' as a basis for attraction value and as an important context for representational practice. Thus, 24 per cent of the authorities surveyed were employing this representative context in relation to churches. Some of the constructions seem rather laboured. Visitors to East Northamptonshire, for example, are offered the 'Home of Spires and Squires' (East Northamptonshire District Council 2004). Similar examples are plentiful: 'The villages of Hart are perfect examples of all that is typically English' (Hart District Council 2004). Alfriston in East Sussex is made irresistible with the addition of afternoon tea, just to make sure that every possible aspect of the English rural image is conveyed:

> With its narrow streets and quaint cottages...it is everything an English Village should be. St Peter's Church and the Clergy House are popular attractions, as are the numerous cafes serving traditional cream teas.
>
> (East Sussex District Council 2004)

After reading a few similar paragraphs we can begin to feel immersed in the narrative and as tourists the rural–historic can not only be seen, it can be felt. You can even eat it and drink it in cafes and pubs, a just reward for all that leafy exploration, as here in the North Norfolk Broadland:

> Most of Broadland's towns and villages have a beautiful church and many interesting streets of quaint houses and cottages that give each its own character and charm. There are leafy lanes that are delightful to explore, where you will find secluded country pubs and ancient churches.
>
> (Broadland District Council 2004)

At Horsham in West Sussex things take a more aesthetic turn. The churches constitute a 'fine collection', as if assembled by some connoisseur of medieval buildings for the benefit of discerning visitors, 'their towers and spires forming a distinctive feature of the landscape' (Horsham District Council 2004). The following examples point to similar forms of representational practice:

> At Adur, the parish churches are amongst the District's most striking features.
>
> (Adur District Council 2004)

> The District's landscape is breathtaking and rich in heritage, including numerous examples of outstanding historic buildings, castles and ancient churches.
>
> (South Shropshire District Council 2004)

The District of Ashfield has a fine selection of churches well worth a visit. Dating from 11th Century Norman architecture to the modern day, each church has its own unique attraction to offer.

(Ashfield District Council 2004)

Once a church is fully achieved as touristic space, representational practices are initiated in which every scrap of attraction value is wrung from whatever resource is available, however, obscure or eclectic:

The twelfth century Church of St Thomas, Stanhope is described by many as the little Cathedral of the Dale and even has a 250 million year old fossilised tree stump in the church yard.

(Wear Valley District Council 2005)

Elsewhere words referring to particular styles such as *perpendicular*, or periods such as *Saxon* or *Norman* are employed without comment, explanation or expansion as though something in the symbolic value of the word itself is sufficient to confer attraction value.

For representational practice to be fully achieved, however, it has to engage the processes of marketing, such as 'product development' and marketing communications. In tourism, this involves linking the various components of attraction value together in the kinds of systematic ways previously described. The rural–historic figures largely in this process and this in turn leads to the production and representation of a broad portfolio of attractions. Evidence of the kind of systemic representation described above was found in 39 per cent of the local authorities, and of these 15 per cent either represented their church tourism within the context of 'church trails' or 'Christian heritage'. In south Staffordshire, for example, a *Historic Churches Trail* is supported by a downloadable leaflet and the invitation to 'enjoy the buildings', because 'they represent the richness of our heritage and something for current and future generations to protect'. (South Staffordshire District Council 2006).

This is very much the language of heritage tourism, a discourse that meets the needs of a definable market, and which can carry out cultural work in affirming identity and presenting a single narrative about a past conveniently abstracted from the messy politics of history. Represented as heritage and meeting the needs of tourists, it appears as a given thing when in fact it is heavily mediated, selected and represented in a way that separates it from less appealing accounts of the past. It is inconceivable, as Kirshenblatt-Gimblett (1998: 172) reminds us, that such 'display techniques' can ever be neutral, when the purpose they serve is so focused on both capital accumulation and a suitably authorised narrative.

Dellheim, C. (2004) *The Face of the Past: The Preservation of the Medieval Inheritance in Victorian England*, Cambridge: Cambridge University Press.

Dicks, B. (2000) *Heritage Place and Community*, Cardiff: University of Wales Press.

East Northamptonshire District Council (2004) 'Spiritual dimensions of peace and beauty' *East Northamptonshire Council Web*. Available online: www.east-northamptonshire.gov.uk/site/scripts/documents_info.aspx?documentID=792 (accessed 1 February 2006).

East Sussex District Council (2004) 'Historic Towns and Buildings', *A Day Out Visiting Historic Towns and Buildings*. Available online: www.eastsussex.gov.uk/leisureandtourism/countryside/daysout/historic.htm (accessed 8 August 2005).

Edensor (2002) *National Identity, Popular Culture and Everyday Life*, Oxford: Berg.

Giles, J. and Middleton, T. (1995) *Writing Englishness: An Introductory Sourcebook on National Identity*, London: Routledge.

Harrison, C. (1991) *Countryside Recreation in a Changing Society*, London: TMS Partnership Ltd.

Hart District Council (2004) 'Places to Discover', *Hart District Council Web*. Available online: www.hart.gov.uk/index/community_living/guide-to-hart/discover.htm (accessed 3 May 2006).

Hewison, R. (1987) *The Heritage Industry: Britain in a Climate of Decline*, London: Methuen.

Hobsbawm, E. and Ranger, T. (eds) (1983) *The Invention of Tradition*, Cambridge: Cambridge University Press.

Horsham District Council (2004) 'Churches and Chapels, Leisure and Tourism', *Horsham District Council Web*. Available online: www.horsham.gov.uk/leisure_and_tourism/leisure_2690.asp (accessed 9 April 2006).

Inglis, F. (1987) 'Landscape as popular culture', *Landscape Research* 12(3): 20–4.

Jefferies, J. (2005) 'The UK population: past, present and future', in *Focus on people and Migration*, London: United Kingdom Office for National Statistics.

Jenkins, S. (1999) *England's Thousand Best Churches*, Harmondsworth: Penguin.

Kaufmann, E. and Zimmer, O. (1998) 'In search of the authentic nation: landscape and national identity in Canada and Switzerland', *Nations and Nationalism* 4(4): 483–510.

Kirshenblatt-Gimblett, B. (1998) *Destination Culture: Tourism, Museums, and Heritage*. Berkeley: University of California Press, 1998.

Kneafsey, M. (2001) 'Rural cultural economy, tourism and social relations', *Annals of Tourism Research* 28(3): 763–83.

Kumar, K. (2003) *The Making of the English National Identity*, Cambridge: Cambridge University Press.

Lewis, P.F. (1979) 'Axioms for reading the landscape, some guides to the American scene', in D.W. Meinig (ed.) *The Interpretation of Ordinary Landscapes*, New York: Oxford University Press.

Lowenthal, D. (1991) 'British national identity and the English landscape', *Rural Studies* 2(2): 205–30.

Lowenthal, D. (1994) 'European and English landscapes as national symbols', in D. Hooson (ed.) *Geography and National Identity*, London: Wiley-Blackwell.

Lowenthal, D. (1998) *The Heritage Crusade and the Spoils of History*, Cambridge: Cambridge University Press.

MacDonald, F. (2002) 'The Scottish Highlands as spectacle', in S. Coleman and M.

Crang (eds) *Tourism, Between Place and Performance*, Oxford: Berghahn Books.

Mais, S.P.B. and Stephenson, T. (eds) (1951) *Lovely Britain*, London: Odhams.

Mandler, P. (1997) *The Rise and Fall of the Stately Home*, Newhaven: Yale University Press.

Mandler, P. (2002) *History and National Life*, London: Profile Books

Masson M.A. (ed.) (1955) '*De l'esprit des lois; Essai sur les causes qui peuvent affecter les esprits et les caractères*', in M. André Masson (ed.) *Oeuvres complètes de Montesquieu*, III, Paris: Editions Nagel.

Matless, D. (1998) *Landscape and Englishness*, London: Reaktion Books.

Meinig, D.W. (ed.) (1979) *The Interpretation of Ordinary Landscapes*, New York: Oxford University Press.

Mordue, T. (2001) 'Performing and directing resident/tourist cultures in heartbeat country', *Tourist Studies* 1(3): 233–52.

Morton, H.V. (1927) *In Search of England*, London: Methuen and Co. Ltd.

Muir, R. (1999) *Approaches to Landscape*, Basingstoke: MacMillan Press.

Munt I. (1994) 'The "other" postmodern tourism: culture, travel and the new middle classes', *Theory, Culture and Society* 11: 101–23.

North Lincolnshire Council (2003) *A Tourism Strategy for North Lincolnshire, 2004–2007*. Available online: www.northlincs.gov.uk/leisure/tourism/north-lincolnshire-tourism-strategy/ (accessed 13 April 2006).

Olwig, K.R. (2008) ' "Natural landscapes" in the representation of national identity', in B.J. Graham and P. Howard (eds) *The Ashgate Research Companion to Heritage and Identity*, Farnham: Ashgate.

Palmer, C. (2005) 'An ethnology of Englishness: experiencing identity through tourism', *Annals of Tourism Research* 32(1): 7–27.

Paxman, J. (1998) *The English, A Portrait of a People*, London: Penguin Books.

Pretes, M. (2003) 'Tourism and Nationalism', *Annals of Tourism Research* 30(1): 125–41.

Rojek, C. (1997) 'Indexing, dragging and the social construction of tourist sights', in C. Rojek and J. Urry (eds) *Touring Cultures: Transformations of Travel Theory*, London: Routledge.

Rojek, C. and Urry, J. (eds) (1997) *Touring Cultures, Transformations of Travel and Theory*, London: Routledge.

Romani, R. (2001) *National Character and Public Spirit in Britain and France, 1750–1924*, Cambridge: Cambridge University Press.

Samuel, R. (1994) *Theatres of Memory*, London: Verso.

Schama, S. (1995) *Landscape and Memory*, London: Harper Collins.

Scruton, R. (2001) *England an Elegy*, London: Pimlico.

Selby, M. (2010) 'People-place-past: the visitor experience of cultural heritage', in E. Waterton and S. Watson (eds) *Culture Heritage and Representation, Perspectives on Visuality and the Past*, Farnham: Ashgate.

Short, J.R. (1991) *Imagined Country*, London: Routledge.

Smith, L. (2006) *The Uses of Heritage*, London: Routledge.

South Shropshire District Council (2004) 'Spires and Cycles', *South Shropshire District Council Web*. Available online: www.cycle-n-sleep.co.uk/local%20routes/shropshire/spires%20and%20cycles%20-%20cleobury%20mortimer.htm (accessed 12 March 2006).

South Staffordshire District Council (2004) 'Tourism', *South Staffordshire District*

Council Web. Available online: www.sstaffs.gov.uk/Default.aspx?page=13321 (accessed 23 April 2006).

Strathern, M. (1982) 'The village as an idea: constructs of village-ness in Elmdon', in A. Cohen (ed.) *Belonging. Identity and Social Organisation in British Rural Cultures,* Manchester: Manchester University Press.

Tilley, C. (2006) 'Introduction, identity, place, landscape and heritage', *Journal of Material Culture* 11(7): 7–32.

Wallwork, J. and Dixon, J.A. (2004) 'Foxes, green fields and Britishness: on the rhetorical construction of place and national identity', *British Journal of Social Psychology* 43: 21–39.

Waterton, E. (2009) 'Sights of sites: picturing heritage, power and exclusion', *Journal of Heritage Tourism* 4(1): 37–56.

Waterton, E. (2010) 'Branding the past: the visual imagery of England's heritage', in E. Waterton and S. Watson (eds) *Culture Heritage and Representation, Perspectives on Visuality and the Past,* Farnham: Ashgate.

Waterton E. and Watson, S. (2010) *Culture, Heritage and Representation, Perspectives on Visuality and the Past,* Farnham: Ashgate.

Watson, S. (2001) 'Touring the medieval: tourism, heritage and medievalism in Northumbria', *Studies in Medievalism* 11: 239–61.

Watson, S. (2009) 'Archaeology, visuality and the negotiation of heritage', in E. Waterton and L. Smith (eds) *Taking Archaeology Out Of Heritage,* Newcastle upon Tyne: Cambridge Scholars Publishing.

Watson, S. (2010) 'Constructing Rhodes: heritage tourism and visuality', in E. Waterton and S. Watson (eds) *Culture Heritage and Representation, Perspectives on Visuality and the Past,* Farnham: Ashgate.

Watson, S. and Waterton, E. (2010) Reading the visual: representation and narrative in the construction of heritage, *Material Culture Review* 7: 84–97.

Wear Valley District Council (2005) 'Tourism', *Wear Valley District* Web. Available online: www.wearvalley.gov.uk/index.cfm?articleid=5551 (accessed 30 May 2006).

Wiener, M.J. (1982) *English Culture and the Decline of the Industrial Spirit, 1850–1980,* Cambridge: Cambridge University Press.

Williams, R. (1973) *The Country and the City,* London: Chatto and Windus.

Winter, T. (2007) 'Landscapes in the living memory', in N. Moore and Y. Whelan (eds) *Heritage, Memory and the Politics of Identity: New Perspectives on the Cultural Landscape,* Farnham: Ashgate.

Wright, P. (1985) *On Living in an Old Country,* London: Verso.

Wycombe District Council (2005) 'Tourism Services', *Wycombe District Web.* Available online: www.wycombe.gov.uk/sitePages.asp?step=2&categoryID=3597 (accessed 23 April 2006).

Part III

Tourism and performance at heritage places

Chapter 7

Cuzcotopia

Imagining and performing the Incas

Helaine Silverman

In their introduction to this volume, the editors write that heritage is framed by its own discourses and practices and that heritage activates an imaginative capacity fuelled by Hollywood and other cinematic representations, by historical fiction and by traditions of visual renderings – all interacting to produce a historical/heritage iconography of immense power. The city of Cuzco, Peru – inscribed on UNESCO's World Heritage List in 1983 – is exemplary of this process, particularly in terms of a theatrically staged revival of an ancient Inca rite called Inti Raymi.

Whereas much previous heritage scholarship approached its object of study as fixed, something that can be apprehended because it is 'there' (whether tangible or, more recently, intangible), recent critical approaches emphasise the dynamic process of heritage production and its vernacular performativity. As David Crouch observes, 'heritage is continually emergent in living' (2010: 57), what he calls 'perpetual performance', which is intrinsically related to cultural practice in a Bourdieuian sense. In addition, there is the deliberate, temporally finite performative act – as analysed by Barbara Kirshenblatt-Gimblett (1998) in her treatment of 'performing culture', notably festivals: 'All the senses – olfactory, gustatory, auditory, tactile, kinaesthetic, visual – are engaged. The experience tends to be environmental, as episodes of the drama are enacted in various locations' (1998: 58). Inti Raymi is such a festival and more. It is a performance and process of heritage, identity building, historical commemoration and narration and contemporary political negotiation. As in less official festival practices, Inti Raymi's participants draw on elements of the past to operationalise their lives in the present.

As a formally staged event Inti Raymi is, and has been since its inception in 1944, organised by dominant cultural institutions. The great cultural theorist Theodor Adorno (1991: 118) criticises such formal festivals saying, 'Festivals are to be celebrated as they come; they are not to be organized ... Administrative reason which takes control of them and rationalizes them banishes festivity from them. This results in an intensification into the grotesque'. But I argue, *contra* Adorno, that it is the very sponsored nature of formal festivals and, for my purpose here, of Inti Raymi, that makes these cultural performances and performances of culture so intellectually engaging for critical heritage scholars. We should be interested when the nation–state or other official entity expresses interest in them or exerts control (e.g. Bruner 2001; Charassri 2004) because 'choices in repertoire and style are ideologically charged' (Kirshenblatt-Gimblett 1998: 65; see also Guss 2000) and 'contingent: they are not generally made to stand alone, set off for exclusively aesthetic attention' (Kirshenblatt-Gimblett 1998: 64). Moreover, proprietary rights may be implicated (Kirshenblatt-Gimblett 1998: 65), thus engaging cultural heritage with intellectual property and cultural rights (e.g. Coombe 1998, 2010).

Inti Raymi is a highly manufactured and contrived cultural performance – an extravaganza involving several stage sets (already in existence as part of the Cuzco landscape as well as newly constructed), physical actions (behaviour) of human actors in their role-supporting costumes, ritualised verbal discourse that both channels the ancient Incas and espouses contemporary political viewpoints (speech acts) and a public constituted by the Cuzqueños and their hordes of tourist guests who are engaged in a two-way communicative interaction with varying mutual intelligibility (see West 2010: 279). This paper examines the performativity of Inti Raymi, tracing and contextualising the festival's origin and evolution into its present-day configuration.

The early twentieth century production of Inca Cuzco

Inti Raymi's origins are found in *indigenismo*, an elite Peruvian intellectual, moral and political movement over the 1910s to 1930s that 'sought to root the image of Peru in its pre-Hispanic Incan tradition' (de la Cadena 2000: 63). *Indigenismo* was especially resonant in Cuzco where physical remains of the great Inca Empire and Indigenous cultural traditions were everywhere evident. Surrounded by ancient grandeur, the *indigenistas* lamented that the Indian descendants of the Incas lived in the most abject poverty under conditions of extreme exploitation by the mestizo class. Indeed, the *indigenistas* regarded mestizos 'as former Indians who had decayed morally after leaving the haven of their agricultural community' (de la Cadena 2000: 65). Importantly, *indigenismo* did not 'revive Indigenous history and culture as archaeology' for this, as Mary-Louise Pratt has argued in a critique of the European colonialist imagination, would be 'to revive them *as dead*' (1992: 134, original emphasis; see also Smith and Waterton 2009; Waterton and Smith 2009). Rather, history and archaeology were used by the *indigenistas* to attend to Peru's Indian population as *living* peoples abused by structural obstacles, ongoing since the Spanish Colonial era.

Cuzqueñismo was a local cultural and political movement that built on *indigenismo*. It propounded 'a decided faith in the eternal superior quality of immortal Cuzco' (Aparicio Vega 1994: 14; here and henceforth, all Spanish translations are mine). In a country whose government and power were centralised in Lima, the flourishing, modern mestizo capital on the coast, *Cuzqueñismo* re-presented Cuzco – a small provincial city of faded glory in the early twentieth century – as the 'cradle of Peruvianness' and also, therefore, a 'nationally relevant political center' (de la Cadena 2000: 67).

Incaismo is an important component of *Cuzqueñismo*. As described by the distinguished Cuzco anthropologist, Jorge Flores Ochoa (1990: 11–12), it is a nativistic ideology expressing the sentiment of identification with the Incas and with the real or supposed glories of their empire. It is a feeling learned from childhood in the home and at school that is shared among Cuzqueños that refers to and nostalgically evokes a past that is distant or near according to the circumstances at hand. It is pride in one's ancestry and even a longing to return to ancient times. It is the actions of resistance, persistence and continuity that make the idea of 'Inca' active today in everyday life in Cuzco.

Cuzqueñismo and *incaismo* were supported by the great archaeological finds that galvanised local, national and international attention in the early twentieth century. Machu Picchu was scientifically discovered in 1911–12 by Hiram Bingham (1913a, 1913b, among others). Large-scale excavations around Cuzco in 1933–34 revealed yet more monumental Inca architecture (Valcárcel 1946). Indeed, in 1933 Cuzco was named the 'Archaeological Capital of South America' by the International Congress of Americanists. At the same time, Inca plays were being performed in full costume by the *indigenista* intellectual elite and enthusiasts (Chambi 1993: 102), sometimes staged at Inca ruins themselves – such as Sacsayhuaman, the megalithic Inca site above the city, which would soon become the setting for Inti Raymi.

Cuzco Day (*El Día del Cuzco*) was created in 1944, the brainchild of a local intellectual and school teacher Humberto Vidal Unda, in association with the private Instituto Americano de Arte del Cuzco. Its explicit goal was to 'stimulate a true spiritual revolution in the sons of Cuzco in particular and the country in general with respect to the meaning of our land' (*Revista de la Semana del Cusco* I [1]: 7–8), to 'remember the worth of Cuzco, what it was in the past and the preponderant role it played in American history' (Vidal Unda cited in Nieto Degregori 1994a: 16). Cuzco Day was to be 'the idealization of the Inca past and the projection of this ideal to the future in a kind of Andean messianism that considers Cuzco to be sacred land, centre of the universe, navel city that is called to govern the future of the country and continent' (Nieto Degregori 1994a: 17). The date of Cuzco Day, 24 June, was chosen to coincide with the ancient Inca celebration of Inti Raymi (the Inca ritual initiating a new agricultural year, always occurring around the time of the winter solstice) and was close to the religious calendar celebration of Corpus Christi, already a popular festival in this Catholic city.

The re-creation of the Inca festival of Inti Raymi – embedded in the creation of Cuzco Day and its centrepiece – was the maximal expression of *Cuzqueñismo*. In reviving Inti Raymi, Vidal and his collaborators plumbed Spanish sources for information about the original Inca ceremony. Garcilaso de la Vega's 1609 description was the major source through which the Cuzco intellectuals imbued the modern version of *Cuzqueñismo* with as much accuracy as possible (de la Cadena 2000: 159). Various committees created the scenery and costumes for the pageant (Barreda Murillo 2000). The resulting Inti Raymi is both an invented tradition (Hobsbawn 1983) and a somewhat historical re-enactment with an abundance of dramaturgical license.

From the beginning, Inti Raymi has been a celebration intended for the entire population of Cuzco, a paean to Cuzco's former Inca glory, but with cognisance of Cuzco's regional position *vis-a-vis* the rest of Peru and with an eye towards economic development and tourism. Indeed, although it is Vidal's *Cuzqueñismo* discourse about Cuzco Day that has been emphasised since the time he proposed it, Vidal's own statements also revealed practical goals in his creation of the event: 'Cuzco has unlimited possibilities for economic development', which would be enhanced by the fairs and expositions occurring within the festivities of Cuzco Day (Nieto Degregori 1994a: 16). Cuzco Day also would give the city the opportunity to become 'the leading tourist centre of the continent and the great celebration of Inti Raymi could become one of the greatest celebrations in the world' (*Revista de la Semana del Cusco* III [2]: 3–5). Thus, Vidal drew a direct connection between Inti Raymi, tourism and economic benefits.

Consciously exploiting Cuzco's stunning monumentality, the first Inti Raymi was staged above the city at Sacsayhuaman – as it has been in all the decades since – notwithstanding occasional protestations of concern for the preservation of the archaeological site (see Figures 7.1A and B). More than 5,000 spectators witnessed the first modern performance of Inti Raymi at Sacsayhuaman (Barreda Murillo 2000: 8; for a reconstructed description, see also de la Cadena 2000: 158–62). It was a public ritual and cultural and political expression of *Cuzqueñismo*, enhanced by the presence of the Peruvian president at the inaugural event. Indeed, here we begin to appreciate the scalar significance of Inti Raymi as a local performance, in what Tim Edensor would evaluate as a 'parochial setting' (2002: 35) but one which connects with the nation and, ultimately, the production of national identity.

Tourism

Even before the creation of Cuzco Day and Inti Raymi in 1944, Peru's early tourism industry was enthusiastic about Cuzco. The National Tourism Corporation (NTC) already had organised a branch office in Cuzco in the

Figure 7.1 Inti Raymi celebration at the site of Sacsayhuaman, overlooking Cuzco. The
Inca Emperor is carried on a litter (above) towards the platform (below)
where ceremonies will be conducted
Photo: Helaine Silverman 1999

1920s (de la Cadena 2000: 139). A monthly magazine called *Turismo* was published by the NTC (which changed its name to Touring Automóvil Club del Perú in 1940, again with a branch office in Cuzco). Articles in the early 1940s (the issues available to me) were laudatory about the sights/sites of Cuzco, highlighting Inca and Colonial monuments, souvenir purchases that could be made, as well as side trips to the great Inca centres in the Urubamba Valley, including Machu Picchu (accessible by rail by 1927 and already important in motivating tourism to Cuzco). Indeed, in 1942 alone there were five articles on Cuzco in *Turismo*.

Writing well before the first Cuzco Day and Inti Raymi, Phyllis Snyder (1936) observed of the pre-staged Cuzco: 'The scenes that you will encounter on the streets will make you believe you are in Hollywood'. This was the Cuzco vividly described by Luis Valcárcel (1981), the great Peruvian *indigenista*, in his memoir, and incomparably recorded by the renowned Cuzqueño photographer, Martín Chambi (1993). It was an 'authentic' Cuzco unscripted by tourism, a city where horrifyingly unequal social statuses and roles were played out in an exceptional built environment.

Cuzco's 'Hollywood-esque' character did not escape Paramount Studios, which filmed *Secret of the Incas* (1954, starring Charlton Heston) on location in Cuzco and Machu Picchu. As vividly depicted in the movie, foreign tourism to Cuzco was for the rich, adventurous and well-travelled. There were not many of these tourists at this time for although there were daily flights to Cuzco from Arequipa at least by 1942, commercial flights from Lima did not become regular until 1948.

The Peruvian state was involved in promoting tourism to Cuzco, creating 'a sumptuous Hotel de Turistas' (Holguin de Lavalle 1943),[1] which was inaugurated soon after that description was written. The hotel had a capacity of 180 guests lodged in 93 rooms with ten collective bathrooms, serving 'international food' and having 'ample garages', the latter feature indicating the mode of arrival of most guests (*Revista del Instituto Americano del Arte*, Cuzco, Año IV, vol. 1, 1ero y 2do semestre, 1945). Several scenes in *Secret of the Incas* were shot in the hotel. The hotel briefly antedated the invention of Cuzco Day and recreation of Inti Raymi. Those spectacles soon filled it to capacity.

In 1947 Cuzco was named 'Tourist Capital of Peru' with Inti Raymi 'its most important marketable image' (de la Cadena 2000: 173). But, in 1947, this largely referred to domestic tourism – Cuzco was not yet a significant presence in the recurring international tourism circuit, as I indicated above.

Cuzco suffered a devastating earthquake in 1950 and tourism (both domestic and foreign) was set back for several years as the entire city's infrastructure had to be rebuilt. Nevertheless, by 1959 tourism was on the rise with more than 23,000 visitors (*El Sol*, 6 January 1960). In the early 1960s, thanks to the airline (introduction of jet planes, accessible airfares – note the 1963 song 'Come Fly With Me', which, coincidentally, features Peru) and hospitality industries, tourism to Peru significantly increased, including that to Cuzco. Just as *National Geographic* had earlier played a defining role in producing Machu Picchu as 'the lost city of the Incas' (Bingham 1913b), so its later article 'The Five Worlds of Peru' (Weaver 1964) informed readers of the ancient, exotic and tourable cultural heritage of this nation. And although Peru is not identified as the setting for the action in Disney's *The Emperor's New Groove*, this 2000 film also contributes to the cinematic construction of 'Inca Peru' (see Silverman 2002a). Thus Cuzco exemplifies this volume editors' interest in 'looking, seeing, mediated vision, images, vision and visuality, the technologies of vision [and] the fundamental and powerful role of seeing/representation in the heritage/tourist dialogue'.

Inti Raymi redux

Perhaps responding to tourism, but overwhelmingly deeply embedded in Cuzco's own social dynamic, grander celebrations of Inti Raymi were created. By 1952 and notwithstanding the devastating 1950 earthquake, the fame and significance of Inti Raymi had risen to such a level that cultural authorities representing the Peruvian state intervened to ensure the so-called historical accuracy of the performance for its national and international audience and simultaneously elevated Inti Raymi to the level of a 'national symbol of Inca history' (de la Cadena 2000: 167, 169–70). This official sanctification of one version of Inti Raymi would constrain improvisations and inhibit varying interpretations into the future (de la Cadena 2000: 171) – at least for a while.

Tim Edensor (2002: 6) has observed that 'large-scale performances frequently aim for fixity', although this is difficult to accomplish. While the freezing of the performance of Inti Raymi ritualised local culture practice, 'inscribing a particular world view that is circulated in mediated popular culture' (Crouch 2010: 57), nevertheless interpretation was not so easily controlled – for Inti Raymi is polysemic and has continued to mean different things to various sectors of local, national and international society. Its script and performance, while canonised, are flexible and accommodating. Inti Raymi has that quality that Crouch (2010: 58) has posed as 'the potential relationality of "new" heritage [to] other, pre-existent and also emergent contemporary pasts and their heritages'. Herein, surely, lies the explanation of Inti Raymi's continued success, including the interest that later power wielders have manifested in it, most especially Daniel Estrada, who became Mayor of Cuzco in 1984.

Mayor Estrada's political priorities were to combat hunger and poverty, provide better healthcare, create more adequate housing, institute educational reforms, improve public sanitation and transportation, diversify the economy so as to correct Cuzco's over-reliance on tourism, generate more employment, and overall to conduct city business transparently in the interest of the citizenry. His progressive political platform sought to achieve social justice, political redress and economic opportunity for the large number of impoverished and historically downtrodden residents of the city. His politics were informed and formed by Cuzco's political culture and objectionable social realities, the latter originating in the Colonial period.

In addition to the many necessary practical policy actions taken by Estrada during his three terms in office (1984–86, 1990–92, 1993–95), he also operated in a dynamic discursive field, selectively appropriating Cuzco's Inca – *not* Spanish Colonial – cultural heritage as a tool to advance his philosophy of responsive governance. Estrada preached the 'recuperation' or 'recovery' of Inca identity, believing that the glorious Indigenous past should and could be the font of self- and local pride upon which to undertake new achievements and propel Cuzco toward prosperity and modernisation. In addition to his flamboyant verbal political discourse, Estrada deployed a dramatic visual discourse, creating a new iconographic urban landscape of ancient and modern monuments referring to the Incas (Silverman 2002b; see also Waterton and Watson 2010 on heritage and visuality). Recognising that cultural heritage is also embodied action, that heritage and its meanings are constituted through performance, and that heritage is experienced dynamically, Estrada also organised grand public inaugurations of the municipality's monument projects at which his eloquent and impassioned speeches reiterated his political philosophy and mobilised popular support for his other pragmatic political actions.[2]

Nowhere were Estrada's theatrical politics greater than in his controversial intervention in the institutionalised 1952 script of Inti Raymi. Already a well-established and beloved local celebration and enthusiastically embraced by the domestic and foreign tourism industry by the time Estrada came to office, the Mayor nevertheless commissioned a new script, thereby adding performance to his creative mayoral tool kit and adding a new register of meaning to Inti Raymi. Estrada was as able as Inti Raymi's early proponents to understand and manipulate Cuzco's multiple relations and produce them for consumption by multiple parties.

Working with the Cuzco actor and theatre director Guido Guevara, Estrada created two new morning acts (Acts One and Two) before the traditional (1944) afternoon performance at Sacsayhuaman (thus, Act Three).[3] Act One is an opening prayer ceremony at Coricancha, the still-standing Inca Temple of the Sun (see Figure 7.2).[4] The performers then move slowly in procession to the Plaza de Armas, where Act Two unfolds in two scenes. Act Two, Scene One is a historically and ethnographically based rite in which coca leaf is offered to the sacred mountains of Cuzco. Act Two, Scene Two is the ideologically radical innovation introduced by Estrada. It is discursively quite different from the rest of Inti Raymi, because

Figure 7.2 The Inca Emperor recites a prayer, standing on the original outer curving wall
of Coricancha (the Spanish Colonial church of Santo Domingo was
constructed over the sacred Inca sun temple)
Photo: Helaine Silverman 2004

the modern era is deliberately brought into the action through the
'encounter of the times' (*el encuentro de tiempos*, henceforth, the *encuentro*).
This scene was imbued with great political meaning by Estrada, for it
reaches across the centuries to link the ancestral Inca leader with his
modern counterpart, the Mayor of Cuzco. The *encuentro* thus generated an
important new site of political engagement and cultural production.

The choice of the Plaza de Armas for the *encuentro* was apt because it has
long been the locus of transcendental events and historical process in
Cuzco. It is not an exaggeration to say that every Cuzqueño knows the 600-
year history of the Plaza: it was Haukaypata – the Great Plaza of the Incas;
it was the conquered space of the Conquistadores and then the centre of
Colonial Era power; it was the setting of the 1781 martyrdom of the inde-
pendence-seeking José Gabriel Condorcanqui; it was the premier social
space of the slowly evolving city (see Valcárcel 1981) through the 1950
earthquake; and it has undergone dramatic functional transformation
since the 1960s as it became reconfigured for tourism. The Plaza de Armas
is a dramatic palimpsest encapsulating all of Cuzco's history.

In choosing to situate the *encuentro* in the Plaza de Armas, in front of the great Cathedral (built by the Spanish in the mid-sixteenth through mid-seventeenth centuries with blocks of stone from dismantled Inca buildings), Estrada consciously evoked not just the history of this specific location but also the entire complex panoply of social, economic and political relationships of the city. Indeed, the coherence of Inti Raymi, as revised by Estrada and Guevara, specifically depends on its being performed in this particular 'theatre'. Thus, we are obliged to recognise the construction of the space of heritage – a symbolic space whose intended and diverse meanings are co-produced by the performers and audience.

Estrada's populist ideology was expressed through the scripted dialogue between the Inca Emperor and the Mayor (including all mayors who would follow Estrada):

INCA EMPEROR: Everything makes us think that my father, the Sun, today will be magnanimous with us. [...] High Priest, wise older brother! Look for he who now guides my beloved people, Cuzco, and return with him. I know that he is present in this grandiose plaza of Haukaypata. (*Note how the words call the image of the pre-Conquest Plaza into existence.*)

HIGH PRIEST: Warrior! Fulfil the orders of our Inka Pachacutec. Bring our Mayor to him! (*Note that the Mayor is thus hierarchically lower than the Inca Emperor.*)

WARRIOR: Older brother, Mayor of Cuzco, our father, the Inka, calls you. Please come with me. (*Note that the Mayor is treated with respect and inexorably linked to history through the inescapable ties and duties of this fictive kinship.*)

INCA EMPEROR: Leader (*referring to the Mayor*) who now leads my people of Cuzco! Time and life get confused in the infinite mystery of the universe and here I appear before you as if a dream, leaping over the unbreachable in spite of the centuries. You have before you the revived Inka, son the Sun, father of all these people! I have come to fortify with my words the energy that must exist in your honest arms, in your good heart and in your keen mind. I tell you that you yourself will rediscover in the deepest part of our wise ancestry the fundamental principles of good government.[5] (*As performed under Estrada's first mandate, the Mayor now walks out from the line of city officials standing on the steps of the Cathedral, arrives at the centre of the Plaza and ascends the huaca/stepped platform on which the Inca Emperor stands, so as to receive the verbal admonition and the khipu from the hand of the emperor.*)

Govern with generosity, with honour, with truth, and with justice! At the same time, be aware that communal work and the unity of all my people will resolve the difficulties, no matter how difficult they are. And so that you don't forget I leave in your hands this sacred *khipu* (*mnemonic knotted string device of the Incas used for accounting and for narrating history*), a legacy from our forefathers. In it are contained the three powers that are the life of our people and whose history is embedded in the beginning of time: To Want! To Know! To Work! You be the light that illuminates your good government and the destiny of our race. Don't forget this!

MAYOR: I promise you, father Inka Pachacutec, to take the greatest care of this marvellous legacy! I promise you, great sir, to work for your people, Cuzco, and to work tirelessly for its happiness. (*The Mayor returns to the steps of the Cathedral where the other members of his government are standing. Like him, all are wearing suits with a rainbow sash, representing the Inca flag, across the chest.*)

INCA EMPEROR: People of Cuzco! Now, yes, we go quickly to Sacsayhuaman. We go united, like the single force that we are. Let's go.

Estrada deployed the *encuentro* as a cultural performance whose discursive form ultimately was a field of action, not just a codified text. My use of the word 'field' here is deliberate. I am recalling Victor Turner's (1974: 17) proposal of 'field' as 'the abstract cultural domain where paradigms are formulated, established, and come into conflict'. The *encuentro* explicitly facilitated political debate and social examination. Competing claims could be heard and evaluated. And, as David Guss (2000: 23) has argued, 'festive forms ... are the sites of continual struggle, public stages on which competing interests converge to both challenge and negotiate identity'. For identity is always foregrounded as dynamic in performance and is always in the process of production and reconstitution through performance (see Edensor 2002: 69).

In 1984 Estrada went beyond his newly introduced spoken interaction between Inca Emperor and Mayor that obligated the municipal officer to practice good government as, implicitly, the emperor had in the Inca era.[6] Estrada also commissioned the construction of a temporary *huaca* in the centre of the Plaza de Armas (see script, above), to cover the imported Belle Epoque fountain that has existed there since before the turn of the twentieth century (see Figure 7.3). Estrada thereby created a more visually compelling stage set for the important dialogue of the *encuentro*. It is important to indicate that few Inca wall remnants exist in the Plaza de Armas, and so here Estrada was trying to remediate the overwhelmingly colonial milieu by reasserting and reinserting the Incas into the Plaza, again reflecting his awareness of the power of iconography in the political domain.

Rather than the addition of Act One at Coricancha, or Act Two, Scene One's coca rite, or Act Two, Scene Two's spoken words of the *encuentro*, it was the temporary physical alteration of the Plaza de Armas that caused controversy in Cuzco. Critics expressed concerns that the superstructure would damage the fountain or be a pretext to remove the fountain altogether so as to replace it with an Inca monument (Silverman 2008). Estrada retorted:

> we can never deform and much less ignore our Inca essence that has an extraordinary presence in all actions in the Andean world, rural as well as urban...We are reliving our past with a dialectical vision that projects us toward the future...We march steadily toward the conquest of a new social and economic order that vindicates us historically.
>
> (*Diario El Sol*, 23 June 1984)

But the use of a *huaca* for the *encuentro* was short-lived because of the controversy.

Figure 7.3 The Inca Emperor (immediately left of the vertical banner) speaks, just prior to the *encuentro* with the mayor. Note the fountain, which engendered the *huaca* controversy in Estrada's first term of office. Note the surrounding built environment of the Plaza de Armas
Photo: Helaine Silverman 2004

The rest of Estrada's innovations to Inti Raymi, however, have remained untouched, insofar as I can determine. It is that complete version of Inti Raymi (morning: Coricancha and Plaza de Armas; afternoon: Sacsayhuaman) that six years after Estrada left office (on 4 March 2001) was declared 'cultural patrimony of the nation and principal ritual ceremony of national identity' by Article 1 of Law 27431. Article 2 of the law charged the Municipality of Cuzco with maintaining the authenticity of the script in its contemporary iteration. Article 3 exhorted the Ministry of Education and the Ministry of Industry, Tourism, Integration and Commercial Affairs to 'promote and disseminate Inti Raymi as a cultural act evoking the Incas and as touristic interest'. The tourism alluded to in Law 27431 is both domestic and foreign.

Today Inti Raymi is a professionally choreographed 'cast of thousands' performance that is managed by a discrete city office, Empresa Municipal de Festejos del Cuzco/Municipal Office of Cuzco Festivities (EMUFEC). According to some local critics, EMUFEC has so commercialised the event that the historical aspects of the script are being lost to ever-increasing theatrics for the purpose of income generation (see Barreda Murillo 2000; EMUFEC 2012). EMUFEC was created by the Municipality of Cuzco in 1987, during the interregnum between Estrada's first and second periods of office. Although Mayor at the time, Carlos Chacón Galindo belonged to a rival political party and was accused by Estrada of having won the race through fraud. When Estrada regained the mayoralty he expanded the purview of EMUFEC. In particular, EMUFEC assumed the promotion of Inti Raymi as the main tourism product of Cuzco, undertaking to 'unfold integral promotion strategies and a policy of access to information, working with the private sector and various civil society institutions'.

I quoted EMUFEC above because it is important to consider its role within the social history of Inti Raymi. Inti Raymi was the creation of elite Cuzqueño intellectuals who made calibrated choices about how to represent Cuzco's historic past and sociological present, as de la Cadena (2000) correctly argues. She also deconstructs Inti Raymi as a venue of philosophical debate between these intellectuals, some being more 'purist' towards the Indian heritage (*indigenismo, incaismo*) and some reworking that view toward a favouring of mestizo heritage (*neoindianistas*). While I understand this argument, I would isostatically minimise its significance in tandem with the diachronic growth of tourism around Inti Raymi and ongoing social and political change in Cuzco due to local, regional and national forces. Thus, although Cuzco intellectuals were engaging in their own debates about cultural identity and social hierarchy in Cuzco, I contend that especially since the 1960s and exponentially increasing to the present day, Inti Raymi is being understood and enjoyed by the local population in different terms – as an exuberant validation of Cuzco's centrality in the national historical narrative, and as a spectacular (*sensu stricto*) expression of

Cuzqueñismo in its most basic essence: pride of place; pride of heritage. Whatever control Cuzco's elite still may have – or think they have – over Inti Raymi (see de la Cadena 2000: 234; see also van den Berghe and Flores Ochoa 1999: 12) – their stratospheric ideas are superseded on the ground by EMUFEC's business-oriented management of Inti Raymi, by public opinion and local concerns and by the pressures exerted by the international tourism industry.

Political ritual and the built environment

Tim Edensor has observed, correctly, that 'tradition can be dynamic, contested and claimed by different groups at different moments in time' (2002: 6). I am interested in expanding that view to concurrent time in which the same observation remains true. The different local claims on and expectations of Inti Raymi (those of the population in general, the intellectual elite, the municipality, EMUFEC specifically) simultaneously create and enable different registers of meaning among the diverse stakeholders. Supporting my argument is Raymond Williams' (1977) concept of culture as a constant production involving the negotiation of dominant, residual and emergent cultural practices, which are mediated by processes of selective tradition and incorporation. His thesis conveys the dynamic, even competitive, aperiodicity of culture whereby not only can people (individuals) hold multiple consilient and discordant views at the same time, but – in a more factionally embodied manner – dominant, residual and emergent cultural arrangements (ideologies, practices, etc.) can simultaneously exist among the sectors of a society. Williams' argument recalls George Kubler's (1970) denunciation of relative chronology charts in archaeology/art history, since no stylistic phase (read: dominant) ever occludes that which preceded it (read: residual) and new elements (read: emergent) are always appearing.

The script of Inti Raymi that was sanctified as cultural heritage in 2001 was a significant evolution from the official 1952 presentation, which was staged only at Sacsayhuaman. Although some tourists watch the ceremonies at Coricancha and in the Plaza de Armas along with locals, it is the pageantry at Sacsayhuaman that attracts a larger attendance (and has greater capacity for such), captures the imagination and transports the willing viewer (local and tourist) back in time – for there are no visually conflicting later buildings or contemporary political officials to jar with the performance. By contrast, in the absence of language translation and situational translation, the local meaning of the *encuentro* in the Plaza is lost to tourists and is not performed for them. Thus, we have a shared but differently motivated interest in a revived past history (see van den Berghe and Flores Ochoa 1999: 8). But tourists are certainly not complaining. Indeed, being in Cuzco during Inti Raymi is a target for most tourists if they can swing it. A statement by Barbara Kirshenblatt-Gimblett is apt here. She writes: 'Public and spectacular, festivals have the practical advantage of offering in a concentrated form, at a designated time and place, what the tourist would otherwise search out in the diffuseness of everyday life, without guarantee of ever finding it' (1998: 59). Inti Raymi and its associated Cuzco Week celebrations provide the concentrated Andean experience that motivates foreign tourism to Cuzco, 'backstage-frontstage', 'tourist gaze' and 'post-tourist gaze' factors aside (Bruner 2005; MacCannell 1976; Urry 1990, 1992).

This is not to say that the local Cuzco population does not enjoy Inti Raymi as a spectacle too, for they do (except for the most recalcitrant conservative Catholic residents of the city). Moreover, Inti Raymi is repeatedly emphasised as Cuzco's cultural heritage both by the microphone of the official master of ceremonies (MC) of the event and by the 'talking heads' cultural experts of the national news media. This is the mediation of heritage in popular culture that Crouch (2010) speaks about. But unlike the tourists, for Cuzqueños all three venues of Inti Raymi are significant. (This does not, of course, necessarily mean that the same political opinions are held by all Cuzqueños.) The *encuentro*, especially, which occurs in the Plaza de Armas and that theatrically enjoins the Mayor to pay obeisance to the Inca Emperor as the latter exhorts (in Quechua) Cuzco's civic authorities to practice good governance, is readily understood by the public as political ritual, just as Daniel Estrada intended. The *encuentro* fulfils a number of Kertzer's observations about the relationships between ritual, politics and power:

> ... ritual can provide an important safety valve for political tensions.
> (1988: 131)

> ... ritual fulfills important organizational needs, it helps provide legitimacy at the same time as it mystifies actual power relations, it facilitates popular solidarity even where consensus is conspicuously absent, and it leads people to conceive of their political universe in certain ways.
> (1988: 153)

> ... There can be no politics without symbols, nor without accompanying rites.
> (1988: 181)

As van den Berghe and Flores Ochoa (1999: 16) astutely observe, Inti Raymi is a ritual of mass participation among the Cuzqueños. Although it has attracted significant international tourism, the event is not held for the benefit of tourists; rather, tourism has adopted but not co-opted Inti Raymi. Most especially, the script created by Estrada and Guevara was intended for, and still serves, the vast Cuzco public. Thus, although Inti Raymi is staged, it does not conform to Dean MacCannell's (1976: 91–107) famous concept of 'staged authenticity', which is produced specifically for the tourist (see van den Berghe and Flores Ochoa 1999: 16). Inti Raymi is first and foremost produced for Cuzqueños.

Nestor García Canclini's insights in *Hybrid Cultures* are also relevant to Cuzco. He says:

> To understand the essential relations of modernity with the past requires an examination of the operation of cultural ritualisation. In order for traditions today to serve to legitimise those who constructed or appropriated them, they must be staged. The patrimony exists as a political force insofar as it is dramatised.
>
> (1995: 109)

Estrada was genius at this dramatisation. Not only did he inscribe the city with new monuments referring to the Incas (as above; see also Silverman 2002b, 2008), the institutionalisation of the *encuentro* has served to perpetuate the political challenge Estrada bequeathed to all subsequent municipal governments in Cuzco: to live up to the social contract embodied in the impersonated Inca Emperor's exhortation of civil authority to perform for the populace. Although the fountain in the centre of the Plaza de Armas is no longer covered with a temporary *huaca* and although few Inca walls are visible from the point in the Plaza where the *encuentro* takes place, the costumed performers themselves are the visual scenery. Furthermore, it also could be argued that the surrounding Colonial Period architecture is a reminder of the fall of that idealised pre-Columbian realm of better governance, rather than being an unavoidable visual distraction.

The controversy surrounding the construction of a temporary *huaca* in the Plaza de Armas powerfully illustrates the importance of the built environment in the construction of social life, for the 'landscape is never inert, people engage with it, rework it, appropriate and contest it' (Bender 1993: 3). Urban landscapes are not semiotically or spatially arbitrary endeavours: they are the materialisation of aesthetic, social, political and economic values, networks and processes. The physical script of the Plaza de Armas can either support or refute the memory history, and heritage that different segments of Cuzco society hold dear and actively deploy by their embodied practices. Estrada regarded the Incas as the fundamental element of Cuzco's identity. It is an identification that many Cuzqueños still feel (Nieto Degregori 1994b; Silverman 2002b), but which they situationally and strategically rather than ubiquitously deploy. As if speaking of our case study, García Canclini sees 'the historical patrimony [a]s a key stage for the production of the value, identity, and distinction of the modern hegemonic sectors' (1995: 135). Similarly, Pierre Nora's (1996–98) 'lieux de mémoire' – the places where memory is crystallised as a part of real, everyday experience – is an appropriate concept for understanding the controversy over Estrada's *huaca*, temporary though it was intended to be.

Estrada sought to create a more inclusive space in the Plaza by re-historicising it to more fully reflect the events that had occurred there, and thereby to empower the descendants of the Incas whom he wished to transform into true stakeholders, modern subjects and agents in their own present and future. The *huaca* was part of his plan. But, as Kertzer (1988: 175) has recognised, 'There can also, however, be conflict over which symbolic understandings are appropriate: what roles should exist…and which are worth fighting over'. For Estrada, the *temporary* Inca-like *huaca* in the Plaza de Armas for the single day of the Inti Raymi celebration was not worth the fight (what people in the USA would phrase as the spending of 'political capital'). Rather, as I have shown elsewhere, Estrada was willing to fight to inscribe the Plaza de Armas with *permanent* markers of Inca heritage and identity – a fight, however, which he also lost (Silverman 2008).

As Mayor, Estrada's dominant frame of reference was Cuzco and in that context the Plaza de Armas, specifically, was the greatest, most compelling site of enduring and unresolved struggles for space and memory in the city. Its ambiguities, tensions, omissions and overwritings are characteristic of living heritage cities worldwide. UNESCO, International Council on Monuments and Sites (ICOMOS), Organization of World Heritage Cities (OWHC) and other assorted agencies issue declaration after declaration to facilitate historic preservation, sustainable tourism and equitable life-ways in these places, but the concerns in Cuzco that motivated Daniel Estrada went far deeper than these. He reached to the very core of heritage stimulation and management and sought to manipulate these to produce a socially just, holistic modernity within the context of high capitalistic commodification and globalisation. In his efforts he deployed political rituals and symbolic means of communication (both tangible and intangible) quite effectively.

But Estrada did not work in a vacuum. The *encuentro* is a historically contingent cultural performance. Estrada's intervention in Inti Raymi was possible only because of that festival's existence and Estrada's profound engagement with the intellectual movements, social realities, and political history that contextualised the creation of this spectacle. Estrada ultimately lost the battle over the *huaca*, but he won in the long term with the *encuentro*. Kertzer writes, 'The power of rite is based in good part on the potency of its symbols and its social context. Political rites can be spectacular failures or, more routinely, simply fail to be spectacular'. (1988: 179). The *encuentro* is a spectacular (in all senses of the word) success. Cuzco has a vibrant political culture and mayors are still voted in and out of office on the basis of how they perform for the public. The *encuentro* is a reckoning in the eyes of the Cuzqueños as they make their own political calculations about how well a mayor is living up to the exhortation of the Inca Emperor.

Estrada's choice of the Plaza de Armas as the locus of the *encuentro* had a predominantly local context, but we also must be aware of Cuzco's insertion in the global tourism market and of Inti Raymi as a major attraction. During the *encuentro*, the Plaza de Armas is a contact zone, defined by Mary-Louise Pratt (1992: 6) as 'the space of colonial encounters, the space in which peoples geographically and historically separated come into contact with each other and establish ongoing relations, usually involving conditions of coercion, radical inequality, and intractable conflict'. While 'intractable conflict' is too strong a representation of the situation of tourism in Cuzco, I think Pratt's concept is otherwise applicable as heritage and tourism encounter (pun intended) each other in the historic district, generating all manner of interactions and constantly shifting interfaces and conditions of contact (Silverman 2002b, 2005, 2006, 2007).

It is also worthwhile to recontextualise Manuel Castells' (1992: 217) discussion of the 'informational city' to call attention to 'the spatial coexistence of very different social groups in an increasingly valuable space' that occurs with tourism in historic districts. In effect, tourism creates a dual city in which physical space is shared but a divergent production of meaning occurs daily, and most particularly when symbolic performances are beyond the ken of the outsider – as happens with the yearly *encuentro* of Inti Raymi.

Let us recognise, however, that there are limitations to the sharing of physical space. The Plaza de Armas has a central, open park-like space ringed by a historic architectural frame: the *portales*. Cuzqueños and tourists move freely around the gardens, each group constructing its own social space but occupying the same physical space in the centre of the Plaza. However, over the past 40 or so years the former shops (of all kinds) of the *portales*, which attended the needs of the local population, have been converted to an exclusively tourist-orientated function. The final blow came in 2009 when the beloved Café El Ayllu was forced to close by the Archdiocese of Cuzco so as to rent its privileged location to Kentucky Fried Chicken, although not without a mass protest and petition drive by Cuzqueños. Tourism is a contested space in which local and global forces compete for dominance or, more realistically from the local perspective, for a fair share at least.

During Cuzco's celebration of its major cultural patrimony – Catholic Corpus Christi and revivalist Inca Inti Raymi – local interests massively occupy the premier physical, social and political space of the city, temporarily overcoming the neoliberal economic restructuring of the centre of the historic district. The visually stunning performance of Cuzco's Inca heritage is, at the same time, a proud manifestation of ethnic and regional identity. Like Kertzer (1988), Takeshi Inomata and Lawrence S. Coben (2006: 11) have argued compellingly for the role of public events 'in which agents of political power presented themselves in front of a large number of spectators and the participants shared experiences through their bodily copresence'. Inti Raymi creates what Inomata and Coben (2006: 16) call 'clear spatial and temporal frames, in which participants witness and sense the presence of others and share a certain experience'. But I have cautioned in this paper that shared experience through bodily copresence is not necessarily predicated upon nor does it necessarily generate shared interpretations. Nevertheless, although multiple perspectives are held by the local viewing and local performing populations during Inti Raymi (especially as concerns the *encuentro*) the vast number of participants in the Plaza de Armas does speak to the meaningful *essence* of the event among all Cuzqueños.

As for tourists, here too we see the analytical and theoretical importance of recognising that the expectations of participants in a heritage performance depend on 'the cultural values of the themes presented in these events as shaped in specific social and historical contexts' (adapting Inomata and Coben 2006: 16). Whereas the experience of Cuzqueños and production of meaning by Cuzqueños has been shaped by clusters of locally contingent events and processes, tourist interpretation of Inti Raymi has been especially scripted by travel ads, brochures, magazines and agents as well as by literature and movies, most of which visually and textually emphasise the essentialist trope of a timeless Andean land (Lutz and Collins 1993). In this way, Inti Raymi's 'cultural values' are received and interpreted by tourists according to their 'specific social and historical contexts' as has occurred among the Cuzqueños.

Conclusion

Cuzco's 170-hectare historic district is composed of the remains of magnificent Inca stone walls, towering Spanish baroque churches and impressive colonial mansions. Although this zone has undergone dramatic depopulation in recent decades and now has fewer than 25,000 inhabitants, the rest of the city has a burgeoning population of over 358,000 inhabitants (Estrada Iberico and Nieto Degregori 1998). Like other provincial cities in Peru and throughout the developing world, Cuzco contends with a range of problems. Some of these are exacerbated by international tourism, others are ameliorated by it, and still others are structural, having little or no relationship to the global tourism industry that markets this remarkable place.

Inti Raymi is an ephemeral tourist and local site within the permanent built environment of Cuzco. It is an 'especially rich performative arena...where the organisation and interpretation of space provides a framework within which locals and visitors ascribe and contest meaning'. (Mordue 2010: 174). It is remarkable that the three officially scripted, iconographically powerful acts of Inti Raymi – each presented on its own stage set – satisfy the diverse actors and varied audience. The explanation lies in the multiple registers of meanings produced by each group and enabled by the fundamental invented character of all three acts in their current iterations and context.

The versatility of Inti Raymi is demonstrated by its long-term survival, even as its context has changed. I would argue that the greatest change in Inti Raymi occurred under Mayor Estrada when he introduced the *encuentro* as what Judith Butler (1997: 161) might well regard as 'the political promise of the performative', whereby the speech act is insurrectionary. The *encuentro*, which was redolent with political reality and emotionally shared meaning between Estrada and the Cuzqueño public during his periods in office, nevertheless has been able to survive his premature death under less charismatic, less progressive mayors.[7] The *encuentro*, post-Estrada, has indeed become a performance.

In this chapter I have analysed and theorised Inti Raymi, and the *encuentro* within it, through approaches that this volume's editors call 'contingent' and 'negotiated'. 'Contingent' refers to the way that heritage and tourism are structured by representational narratives; 'negotiated' refers to the meanings of heritage and tourism in more open, performative situations. No one theoretical perspective is adequate for this analysis and I have referred to theorists of space, vision, identity, ritual and performance.

Inti Raymi is both a construction of a social imaginary and, especially under Daniel Estrada, an act of political recuperation. Inti Raymi is simultaneously the recreated performance of an ancient ritual and a new narration of personal and local identity in the context of national-scale inequities and intrusive global tourism. Inti Raymi intensifies the contact zone that exists between 'hosts' and 'guests', and – while not facilitating a process of cultural translation – Inti Raymi nevertheless satisfies the goals of its diverse public, thanks to its producers who have been responsive to all courted audiences. Inti Raymi exemplifies the potential of any recurring large celebration to become a site of subversion and, over time, a new authorised discourse. Inti Raymi is fascinating because of its imbricated relations: generic, structural, referential, interpersonal, medial (pertaining to media) and silential (what is unsaid or unsayable) (see Becker 1984: 136).

Now approaching its seventieth anniversary in a city that has evolved during this time from provincial backwater to UNESCO World Heritage site and prime node in the global tourism circuit, one can only wonder if Inti Raymi will need to undergo another script revision so as to maintain its relevance for its own local population. With the ongoing residential depopulation of the historic centre, with the surrender of the Plaza de Armas – Cuzco's main social, economic and symbolic space – to the inexorable property acquisitiveness of tourism, with Cuzco's tourism-generated cyber connectivity to the entire world, and with an abundance of young

Cuzqueños living in a Cuzco far different from that of their parents and, especially, grandparents, we must ask if Inti Raymi will become just 'playing Inca', without the historically deep sentiments of attachment to that cultural heritage and the political dynamics that anthropologists have observed there. Put simply – will Cuzco become Cuzcotopia? The historic centre is almost at that point in its development, providing a fertile field for continued study.

Notes

1   The Hotel de Turistas has been long closed but the building is still standing. I have vivid memories of this hotel from my first visit to Peru in 1973 by which time it was no longer sumptuous. It was most famous for its large bar with magnificent woodwork and, when I saw it, long red curtains stamped with images of Colonial Cuzco from Felipe Guaman Poma de Ayala's early seventeenth century *Crónica del Perú y Buen Gobierno*. On 15 December 2010 an article in Cuzco's newspaper, *El Sol*, announced that after decades of legal wrangling over title to the property (after the hotel had ceased to function), the building would be refurbished and 'in two years it will be the best hotel in Cuzco'. We'll see.

2   These include the monument to Manco Capac and his wife, an enormous monument to Pachacutec, the Pumaqchupan mosaic wall and fountain, the 'puma city' *maquette*, an immense mural depicting the grand sweep of Inca history and a huge sculpted condor atop a towering obelisk (see Silverman 2002b).

3   In Act Three the impersonated Inca Emperor is carried by vassals on a litter to a platform in the centre of Sacsayhuaman. Hundreds of performers in the roles of the 'virgins of the sun' and soldiers of the imperial army delight the crowd. A llama is sacrificed and the future is prognosticated from its entrails; libations are made to the gods; the *Sapa Inca* delivers a prayer in Quechua; and the unifying power of the Inca Emperor over the geographically vast and ethnically diverse empire is manifested. The emperor's subjects offer presents to him in 'reverent obedience and subservience'. (de la Cadena 2000: 160). The Inca Emperor makes his final speech, imploring the ancient gods to provide fertility to the people, their crops and animals: 'let there be food and let hunger disappear forever... ¡Que viva el pueblo del Qosqo!'

4   This is what happens at Coricancha: The imperial cast of characters appears on the terraces of the Sun Temple in formation. The song 'To the Sun God' is sung as everyone turns to face the sun. The Inca Emperor then speaks ceremonially, praising the deity. Then, in hierarchical order, the cast rearranges itself by group – almost 20 – for the procession to the Plaza.

5   Good government: *buen gobierno*. Estrada and Guevara surely appropriated the phrase from Felipe Guaman Poma de Ayala's *Nueva Corónica y Buen Gobierno* a massive illustrated letter to the King of Spain that sought to explain to him the efficacy of authochthonous Inca rule and the deficiencies of the Spanish Colonial government. The phrase is immediately recognisable to Peruvians.

6   Marisol de la Cadena (2000: 165) interviewed the first and most famous impersonator of the Inca Emperor in Inti Raymi, Faustino Espinoza Navarro. He said that in the role of the Inca he advised President Manuel Prado, who attended the inaugural ceremony in 1944, to be as wise as Pachacutec, the great emperor who created the statecraft of the Inca Empire and began its dramatic imperial expansion. I have no evidence that Daniel Estrada was aware of this when he

initiated the *encuentro* in 1984. During Inti Raymi 1991 de la Cadena (2000: 175) observed a new Inca Emperor address then Peruvian president, Alberto Fujimori, by radio, exhorting him to follow the three precepts that traditionally are said to have guided Inca governance: 'Do not steal; Do not lie; Do not be lazy'.

7   The current mayor, Luis Florez García, breaks that characterization of his post-Estrada predecessors, being an exceptionally dynamic and effective public official.

References

Adorno, T. (1991) *The Culture Industry: Selected Essays on Mass Culture*, London: Routledge.

Aparicio Vega, M.J. (1994) 'El creador de la Semana del Cusco, Humberto Vidal Unda', *Parlante* 49: 14–15.

Barreda Murillo, L. (2000) 'Inti Raymi o Fiesta del Sol', *Parlante* 70: 8–9.

Becker, A.L. (1984) 'Biography of a sentence: a Burmese proverb', in E.M. Bruner (ed.) *Text, Play, and Story: The Construction and Reconstruction of Self and Society*, Washington DC: American Ethnological Society.

Bender, B. (1993) 'Landscape: meaning and action', in B. Bender (ed.) *Landscape, Politics and Perspectives*, Oxford: Berg.

Bingham, H. (1913a) 'The discovery of Machu Picchu', *Harper's Magazine* 127: 709–19.

Bingham, H. (1913b) 'In the wonderland of Peru', *National Geographic* 24: 387–573.

Bruner, E.M. (2001) 'The Masaai and the Lion King: authenticity, nationalism, and globalization in African tourism', *American Ethnologist* 28(4): 881–908.

Bruner, E.M. (2005) *Culture on Tour*, Chicago: University of Chicago Press.

Butler, J. (1997) *Excitable Speech. A Politics of the Performative*, New York: Routledge.

Castells, M. (1992) *The Informational City. Information, Technology, Economic Restructuring and the Urban-Regional Process*, Cambridge: Wiley-Blackwell.

Chambi, M. (1993) *Martín Chambi. Photographs, 1920–1950*, Washington DC: Smithsonian Institution Press.

Charassri, N. (2004) 'The role of performing arts in the interpretation of heritage sites', *SPAFA Journal* 14(3): 37–44.

Coombe, R. (1998) *The Cultural Life of Intellectual Properties: Authorship, Appropriation and the Law*, Durham: Duke University Press.

Coombe, R. (2010) 'Property forms and heritage politics', Paper presented at *Critical Heritage Studies: Knowledge Identity and Power*, 109th Annual Meeting of the American Anthropological Association, New Orleans.

Crouch, D. (2010) 'The perpetual performance and emergence of heritage', in E. Waterton and S. Watson (eds) *Culture, Heritage and Representation. Perspectives on Visuality and the Past*, Farnham: Ashgate.

de la Cadena, M. (2000) *Indigenous Mestizos: The Politics of Race and Culture in Cuzco, Peru, 1919–1991*, Durham: Duke University Press.

Edensor, T. (2002) *National Identity, Popular Culture and Everyday Life*, Oxford: Berg.

EMUFEC (n.d.) *Empresa Municipal de Festejos del Cusco*. Available online: www.emufec.gob.pe/es/inti-raymi-.html (accessed 30 August 2012).

Estrada Iberico, E. and Nieto Degregori, L. (1998) 'Cuzco en la encrucijada. Análisis del registro catastral del centro histórico', *Crónicas Urbanas VI* (6–7): 3–37.

Flores Ochoa, J. (1990) 'Incanismo, resistencia y continuidad cuzqueños', in *El Cuzco: Resistencia y Continuidad*, Qosqo: Centro de Estudios Andinos.

García Canclini, N. (1995) *Hybrid Cultures. Strategies for Entering and Leaving Modernity*, Minneapolis: University of Minnesota Press.

Guss, D. (2000) *The Festive State. Race, Ethnicity and Nationalism as Cultural Performance*, Berkeley: University of California Press.

Hobsbawm, E. (1983) 'Introduction: inventing traditions', in E. Hobsbawn and T. Ranger (eds) *The Invention of Tradition*, New York: Cambridge University Press.

Holguin de Lavalle, J. (1943) 'De regreso del Cuzco. La voz del deber', *Turismo* 84(June).

Inomata, T. and Coben, L.S. (2006) 'Overture: an invitation to the archaeological theater', in T. Inomata and L.S. Coben (eds) *Archaeology of Performance. Theaters of Power, Community and Politics*, Lanham: AltaMira.

Kertzer, D. (1988) *Ritual, Politics and Power*, New Haven: Yale University Press.

Kirshenblatt-Gimblett, B. (1998) *Destination Culture. Tourism, Museums and Heritage*, Berkeley: University of California Press.

Kubler, G. (1970) 'Period, style and meaning in ancient American art', *New Literary History: A Journal of Theory and Interpretation* 1(2): 127–44.

Lutz, C.A. and Collins, J.L. (1993) *Reading National Geographic*, Chicago: University of Chicago Press.

MacCannell, D. (1976) *The Tourist: A New Theory of the Leisure Class*, Berkeley: University of California Press.

Mordue, T. (2010) 'Time machines and space craft: navigating the spaces of heritage tourism performance', in E. Waterton and S. Watson (eds) *Culture, Heritage, and Representation. Perspectives on Visuality and the Past*, Farnham: Ashgate.

Nieto Degregori, L. (1994a) 'Cincuenta años de la creación del Día del Cusco', *Parlante* 49: 16–17.

Nieto Degregori, L. (1994b) 'Una aproximación al Cusqueñismo', *Allpanchis XXVI* (43–44): 441–76.

Nora, P. (1996–98) *Realms of Memory: Rethinking the French Past*, New York: Columbia University Press.

Pratt, M-L. (1992) *Imperial Eyes. Travel Writing and Transculturation*, New York: Routledge.

Silverman, H. (2002a) ' "Groovin" to Ancient Peru: a critical analysis of Disney's *The Emperor's New Groove*', *Journal of Social Archaeology* 2(3): 298–322.

Silverman, H. (2002b) 'Touring ancient times: the present and presented past in contemporary Peru', *American Anthropologist* 104(3): 881–902.

Silverman, H. (2005) 'Two museums, two visions: representing cultural heritage in Cusco, Peru', *The SAA Archaeological Record* 5(3): 29–32.

Silverman, H. (2006) 'The historic district of Cusco as an open-air site museum', in H. Silverman (ed.) *Archaeological Site Museums in Latin America*, Gainesville: University Press of Florida.

Silverman, H. (2007) 'Contemporary museum practice in Cusco, Peru', in P. Duke and Y. Hamilakis (eds) *Archaeology and Capitalism: From Ethics To Politics*, Walnut Creek: Left Coast Press.

Silverman, H. (2008) 'Mayor Daniel Estrada and the Plaza de Armas of Cuzco, Peru', *Heritage Management* 1(2): 181–217.

Smith, L. and Waterton, E. (2009) 'Introduction: heritage and archaeology', in E. Waterton and L. Smith (eds) *Taking Archaeology Out Of Heritage*, Newcastle upon Tyne: Cambridge Scholars Publishing.

Snyder, P. (1936) 'Cusco', *Turismo* 105 (July).

Turner, V. (1974) *Dramas, Fields and Metaphors: Symbolic Action in Human Society*, Ithaca: Cornell University Press.

Urry, J. (1990) *The Tourist Gaze*, London: Sage.

Urry, J. (1992) 'The tourist gaze revisited', *American Behavioral Scientist* 36(2): 172–86.

Valcárcel, L.E. (1946) 'Cuzco archaeology', in J.H. Steward (ed.) *Handbook of South American Archaeology*, vol. 2, Washington DC: Bureau of American Ethnology, Smithsonian Institution.

Valcárcel, L.E. (1981) *Memorias*, Lima: Instituto de Estudios Peruanos.

van den Berghe, P.L. and Flores Ochoa, J. (1999) 'Tourism and nativistic ideology in Cuzco, Peru', *Annals of Tourism Research* 27(1): 7–26.

Waterton, E. and Smith, L. (2009) 'There is no such *thing* as heritage', in E. Waterton and L. Smith (eds) *Taking Archaeology Out Of Heritage*, Newcastle upon Tyne: Cambridge Scholars Publishing.

Waterton, E. and Watson, S. (eds) (2010) *Culture, Heritage and Representation: Perspectives on Visuality and the Past*, Farnham: Ashgate.

Weaver, K. (1964) 'The five worlds of Peru', *National Geographic*, 125(2): 212–65.

West, S. (2010) 'Heritage as performance', in S. West (ed.) *Understanding Heritage in Practice*, Manchester: Manchester University Press.

Williams, R. (1977) *Marxism and Literature*, London: Oxford University Press.

Chapter 8

Using immersive and interactive approaches to interpreting traumatic experiences for tourists

Potentials and limitations

Andrea Witcomb

Dark encounters

> Entering
> You will find yourself in a climate of nut castanets
> A musical whip
> From Torres Straits, from Mirzapur a sistrum
> Called Jumka, 'used by aboriginal
> Tribes to attract small game
> On dark nights', coolie cigarettes
> And mask of Saagga, the Devil Doctor,
> The eyelids worked by strings.
>
> (Fenton 1984: 81–4)

In this stanza from a poem about the Pitt Rivers Museum at Oxford University, the English poet James Fenton conjures up an image of this Museum not only as a place of wonder and curiosity but also as a metaphor for travel, for encounters with 'the other'. Museums are, for him, places of the imagination in which one can perform a multitude of identities, largely because one can lose a sense of self in them. Travel, imagination and immersion are, in this image of museums, a productive constellation of ideas that capture some of the experiential aspect of visits to museums and heritage sites.

Traditionally, these encounters have been understood in terms of either the beautiful or the exotic (Dolff-Bonekamper 2008). However, as the growing literature on dark tourism (e.g. Stone 2006) indicates, visits to museums and heritage places increasingly include encounters with the abject – with horror, depravity or terror. This trend is evident, for example, in recent developments in re-unified Berlin which offer tourists, as well as locals, the opportunity to explore that city's and Germany's role in a geography of terror – that of the Holocaust as well as the Cold War. According to Elke Grenzer (2002: 94) 'about 600 new placards, monuments and memorials now commemorate a past that Berlin had left unacknowledged'.

Much of it comes from a desire for redemption, the need to memorialise in order to grieve and the need to demarcate the present from the past while also recognising the ongoing effects of the past on the present. But it also comes from the recognition that Germany's unique position in the history of twentieth century terror is a commodity that can be traded – it brings visitors.

Under these circumstances, and others like it, what are the parameters for ethical and socially responsible forms of interpretation? The question is particularly acute for those forms of interpretation that encourage tourists to encounter the abject by explicitly taking on the identity of those who were either social outcasts or victims of atrocities and disasters through immersive interpretation strategies. These forms of interpretation provide a particularly challenging context for asking this question as they frequently use strategies of role-playing, re-enactments and reconstructions as part of their attempts to cast visitors in the role of victim. This particular form of privileging immersive experiences poses a series of important questions that need our critical attention. Among them is the question of whether interpretative strategies that attempt to place visitors in the subject position of the other – victim, perpetrator or social outcast – can live up to the aim of achieving empathy in ways that go beyond didactic forms of moralism or which avoid the problems of further objectification. In exploring my own experiential encounters with three very different immersive sites dealing with themes of incarceration, death through disaster and genocide, this chapter explores the conditions under which these strategies either aid or complicate our ability to sensitively and ethically engage with the abject. My aim is to contribute to the exploration of the potentials and limitations of immersive experiences in the hope that the increasing interest in dark tourism does not eclipse critical and reflexive approaches to museological and heritage practices.

The Melbourne Watch House Experience

My first case study, The Melbourne Watch House Experience, comes from a gaol complex owned and managed by the National Trust of Australia (Victoria). Built in 1906–7 and closed in 1994, The Melbourne Watch House was the site where every potential criminal who had been arrested by police was placed in a cell, under crowded conditions awaiting their court appearance – a process that could take months. Caught in its net were hardcore criminals as well as petty offenders. In amongst the dangerous criminals were housewives, naïve youths, innocent people and the mentally ill. The site also includes the Court House, where those held in the Watch House were either convicted or freed. Next door is the Old Melbourne Gaol, an older structure famous as the site of Ned Kelly's hanging – a bushranger who, through his death, achieved a mythological status

in Australian bushranging stories and who many liken to a Robin Hood-
type figure.

From the point of view of marketing and finances, the immersive
approach developed at The Melbourne Watch House is extremely successful. Before its opening in October 2007, the National Trust had been
experiencing financial difficulties culminating in a loss of AUD 1.59 million
in the Trust's 2006/07 budget (National Trust of Australia Victoria 2008: 3).
By 2008 the new interpretation at The Melbourne Watch House, marketed
as the 'Crime and Justice Experience', contributed to a profit of AUD 2.1
million in (2008: 3). The complex received 153,000 (2008: 22) of the
250,000 visitors to the Trust's properties in the 2007–8 financial year (2008:
5), a figure that is quite remarkable given the Watch House Experience was
only opened in October 2007. By the end of the 2008–9 financial year, the
complex had received 163,780 visitors – an increase of 7 per cent on the
previous year (National Trust of Australia Victoria 2009a: 27). The Old
Melbourne Gaol Crime and Justice Experience also won the State tourism
award in November 2008 for the best Heritage and Cultural tourism attraction in Victoria, and the National award in the same event in 2009, as well as
the 2009 Interpretation Australia (IA) Gold Award for Excellence in
Heritage Interpretation (National Trust of Australia Victoria 2009b).

The Watch House complex presents an opportunity to understand the
nature of the justice and penal system over the twentieth century: the experience of awaiting trial while locked up, police culture, social attitudes
towards criminals, the cultural practices of those in gaol, the dreams, fears
and aspirations of those caught in its net and the social situations that led
to people being incarcerated there. Moreover, the longevity of the working
life of this watch house means the potential to undertake an interpretation
strategy that analyses these factors in the recent past. Apart from the physical presence of jailors and jailed (and the smells and sounds), all the
infrastructure still exists – the police office where people were arrested, the
cells in their original condition, including all the graffiti (which has not
been whitewashed) (see Figure 8.1).

The ambiguous position of those in power (the police) and those under
their power (the prisoners), however, make this potential a difficult thing
to achieve. Unlike victims of the Holocaust or of autocratic despots, the
inmates of this prison are not subjects that can easily attract our sympathy.
Unless they were a colonial convict who is often understood as a victim of
the system within Australian popular culture, gaol prisoners are not 'us' but
'the other'. The figure of the police also presents any attempt to interpret
their role with difficulties. They are not the standard perpetrator who is
clearly in the wrong. Though they might abuse power, they also represent
a socially given permission to arrest and incarcerate individuals who are
accused of not staying within the confines of the law. Who audiences are
going to identify with and why is not, therefore, straightforward, and nor is

Figure 8.1 Graffiti on the bench in one of the cells in the Watch House
Photo: Andrea Witcomb

the question of who they should identify with. The question of ethical integrity in the case of this site is therefore a complex one and is perhaps best served by exploring the complexity of the subject positions of gaoler and gaoled. How then is this potential realised through the immersive, interactive interpretation strategies for the site?

Playing on the double meanings of 'arrest', the Trust advertises the site as an 'arresting experience with performers playing the part of Charge Sergeants, allowing the visitors the experience of being apprehended and incarcerated in the Watch House'. (National Trust of Australia Victoria 2008: 20). The main substance to the tour is thus the experience of being arrested *en masse*. An individual actor, playing the role of a Police Sergeant, does their best to intimidate, harass and generally disempower their audience by replicating the process of conducting an arrest on the audience who are put in the subject position of being criminals. Members of the audience are indiscriminately shouted at, made fun of, ridiculed through the use of abusive language, stripped of any social standing. Phrases used all the time include 'move your carcass', 'saw-dust brain', 'you – here. Move!', 'Quiet!' Everyone is given a charge sheet and told to memorise it and is then subjected to questioning concerning their sex and sexuality, age, physical marks, charge and name of arresting officer. Other than short answers to this question based on the charge sheet, no audience member is allowed to interrupt or ask questions of any sort and they must answer 'Yes Sir!' or 'No Sir!' to any question thrown at them. Neither are they allowed to talk to one another.

It quickly becomes clear that it is better to do as one is told or suffer the embarrassment of being pulled out and made fun of. As men and women are separated and told to march in separate lines, they are taken into the gaol where a physical search is conducted to indicate the kinds of things police are looking for – mainly drugs. You are given to understand this is only the soft version and what a serious physical search would involve. Each group is given a few minutes in a locked cell with no natural light and told to stand against the back wall. It is the first moment where we can catch our breath, have a laugh, check everyone is alright and not stressed and comment on how good or not the actor is. Interestingly, in my two visits there, I have not come across any discussion about the meaning of what is being experienced. The focus is on the performance, not the content, a response that indicates that the thrill of the experience is more important than any moral message the show might be intending to deliver. After that we are given a small lecture on the prison regime and given about ten minutes to explore the site. We are told about the existence of sound and video installations but constantly shouted at to move and keep going – the performance never lets up and the consequence is that the other side of the story (that of the prisoners) is hardly allowed through despite the intensely powerful ambience of the site itself, an ambience which is made even more palpable by the presence of multimedia installations, particularly soundscapes, within the site.

My impression of these, from my intense but necessarily short experience of listening, is that these multimedia-based installations add to the powerful ambience of the site itself by filling in some of the absences – the sounds of voices and dialogues in the exercise yards, the sound of toilets being flushed, showers running. Among these sonic installations are snatches of dialogue meant to give some insight into the thoughts of the prisoners, representing a variety of people and experiences. But the 'forced march' nature of the tour makes it impossible to take in this multiple layering of the stories and people associated with the place. The curatorial intent to provide a layered interpretation aimed at providing a level of complexity to the interpretation of the site by personalising individual circumstances and thus render what has become silent palpable (Gibson 2008) is lost in the overwhelming experience of the theatrical nature of the tour and the pressure of the clock (which times each tour) to maximise the economic return to the institution rather than the range of meanings its audiences might construct from their experience while at the site. At the end of the tour, audiences have slightly more time to read a number of panels dealing with various inhabitants of the Watch House but, by this time, the majority of the tourists have only inhabited the experience of being arrested rather than the opportunity to explore the various circumstances in which a wide variety of people might have gone through that experience. Therefore, it is not surprising that they are more interested in being photographed playing the role of prisoner and taking that away as their memento of the experience than in exploring the nature and purpose of the justice system.

On reflection, what comes across is not a sensitive exploration of power relations and how they are produced. Rather, what comes across, as Jacqueline Wilson (2008) has put it, in relation to prison sites that use former prison guards to conduct tours, are the perspectives of the prison establishment. While the actors work hard at communicating the brutality of the system, they also work hard at communicating the brutality of the inmates, often with recourse to sexual innuendo and references to the insane. No reference is made to the more complex explorations of fear and dashed hopes found in some of the multimedia installations. Nor is an interpretation offered of the graffiti found in the cells or the exercise yards. And yet, as the work of Jacqueline Wilson (2008) has shown, the graffiti in this prison is a unique record of the culture and experiences of the prisoners, offering an insight into their friendships, the ways in which it was essential to have friends within the prison population who were feared by others as protection, their attitudes towards the police force and to the place itself.

In working so hard to provide an experience of what dehumanisation is like, the actors end up continuing the practice of 'othering' the prison population. The result is that it is impossible to explore the social matters that often lead to criminal activity, ask questions about the nature of today's prison population, the nature of the justice system or about police practices in these places and how they might have changed over time or to explore attitudes towards criminals. The fact that the tour guides are actors rather than education officers only emphasises these difficulties. I tried to engage one of them in conversation by asking them how they felt people responded to the tour after the tour was finished. Her concern was with whether they were realistic enough, hard enough. She then proceeded to share with me some of the comments other visitors had made to her, which included the line that prison nowadays was 'too soft' and that criminals 'deserved everything they got'. She went on to support these views herself, by saying with quite a straight face 'what happens when all these people are out on the street? We are all going to get blown up'. Clearly her education at the site had not extended to any discussion of the social, political and economic matters embedded in the police and justice system. She had no critical distance from the discourse she herself was mouthing as an actor.

The problem is made worse by the fact that it is very hard to maintain site itself. This outcome is achieved through the juxtaposition of two narratives. The first is the explicit narrative that provides the dramatic impetus of the show, namely the tension between the naïve faith at the time of the sinking in technological progress and the knowledge that a simple iceberg destroyed that naïvety and with it well over a thousand lives. The second narrative is far more subtly produced but supports a significant commercial machine by proposing that only the modern technological knowhow of this enterprise makes it possible to honour the memories of those who suffered and died that cold night in 1912 through the retrieval, conservation and display of objects that once belonged to them. Supported by an interpretative strategy that encourages identification with the victims of this disaster, it becomes relatively easy to encase the exhibition within a narrative of memorialisation. The result is not only to support an exclusive commercial enterprise but also to re-enchant our faith in technological progress and its desirability.

Using a simple passenger card as the entry to the exhibition, the organisers invite their audience to experience the story of the *Titanic* from the point of view of those who travelled on it. We experience the excitement of the story of its production, the sumptuous and not so sumptuous interiors, meet some of our fellow travellers and experience the tragedy of its sinking. This is followed by the story of the discovery of its location, the process of recovering and conserving the artefacts and the memorialising aims of that effort, a memorial gallery where it is possible to find out whether the passenger we were given at the beginning survived or not and finally, in the Melbourne case, a little display on passengers with an Australian connection and their fate. The exit is through the inevitable exhibition shop where it is possible to get replicas of various personal items carried on board – mainly jewellery – as well as replicas of the third-class blankets and first- and third-class dinner sets.

It is the emotional trajectory of the exhibition, however, and how that is achieved that is of interest, as it is this trajectory that underpins the exhibition maker's ability to defend their existence and institutional aims. Essentially, the exhibition works through a series of sensory contrasts, using music, different levels of light, changing temperatures and the contrast between sumptuous recreations and the fragility of recovered objects to achieve an emotional narrative to support the attempt to get visitors to identify with the victim through the strategy of the passenger card. The experience, for the visitor, is somewhat akin to a Hollywood epic *à lá* Cecil B. de Mille, much like the film *Titanic*, in which the sumptuous stage set is contrasted with the minutiae of the protagonists' lives who carry the emotional focus of the viewer.

The visitor experience begins with our placement in Ireland at the beginning of the exhibition by a soundscape of traditional Irish music. Upbeat in feel, it captures the working-class nature of the men who built the ship and offers a pleasant background against which we can sense the optimism of the period, the faith in technology that lay behind the design and construction process and the ambition of the White Star Line who built the ship to control the lucrative trans-Atlantic trade. The large-scale black and white photographs of the shipyard, the ship itself in different stages of construction, the men who financed, drew up plans and finally of those who built her, and a few small pieces from the ship itself helped to tell the story. These are supported by the industrial nature of the exhibition space itself – hard wooden floors and black industrial-looking walls. This section of the exhibition provided great opportunities for inter-generational conversations as grandfathers happily explained to their grandsons the intricacies of building a ship while others excitedly looked at their boarding cards to find out who they were, willing to participate in the game to be a passenger on board this most famous of ships.

This sense of playing a game continued into the next space as we were led through a gangplank into the upper first-class deck of the ship itself. This was the space for 'oohs' and 'aahs' as we were led from one reproduction of the ship's luxurious interior to another. The sets were brightly lit by crystal chandeliers setting off the dark oak panels of the grand staircase, the rich surfaces and decorations of marble, brass and wrought iron in the first-class areas. We gazed in wonder at the splendour of the ship and those rich enough to pay for this luxury while listening to the strains of Strauss's *The Blue Danube*, which gently took us back into another time. Amid the sumptuous reproduction of the ship's interior spaces, such as the grand staircase where one could be photographed, the Verandah Café and a first-class suite, small vitrines held a range of artefacts recovered from the sea bed leading to a different kind of 'ooh aah' experience – that of wonder that such objects survived in the first place, followed by the realisation that they once belonged to someone. As one child put it to their mother, 'is that really real mum? Did it really come from the ship?', while another visitor I overheard, this time a young adult, said: 'Someone's boot. Just imagine, someone wore that!' This sense of wonder was clearly effective in leading people to identify with the passengers. The contrast between the sumptuous reproductions and the fragility of the objects on display, as well as their ephemeral and everyday nature, made for an experience of wonder which only heightened the emotional encounter with the moment in which such grandness and the dreams and aspirations of those aboard the ship, whose stories we had just come into contact with as we leaned over the vitrines and studied their possessions, came to a sudden halt.

As we continued our tour deep into the ship, along a narrower passage and past a third-class cabin recreation, the ambience changed. The lighting got darker, the strains of Strauss disappeared to be replaced by the sounds of the ship's engine and the air temperature became noticeably cooler. The mood of the audience changed to one of apprehension. At the end of the passage we arrived in the ship's boiler room which, instead of hot and smelly, was dark and cold. Here we heard how the men reacted to the *Titanic*'s encounter with an iceberg. We then emerged into a cold dark room, in which a large sheet of ice (masquerading as the iceberg) was dramatically lit against a black, starry night. The soundscape was appropriately sombre and quiet. There, largely in silence, in stark contrast to the first-class recreations before where lively chatter was the order of the day, we encountered the drama of that terrible night – the life and death decisions people made to separate from each other or not, the realisation that there were not enough lifeboats for everyone and a few eye-witness descriptions of the moment in which the *Titanic* sank with over a thousand people still on board. A silent digital recreation of the moment of the sinking in which the ship broke into two completes the picture. Visitors watched it in horrified silence.

Suitably chastened into a recognition of the power of nature against human naivety, greed and faith in technology, the exhibition moved on towards the redemptive aspect of its narrative strategy – that modern-day technology enables us to appropriately memorialise the tragedy by salvaging, conserving and display items from the wreck site. Without a hint that such a narrative stands in contradiction with the critique in the faith in technology we have just experienced or, as Marcus Westbury (2010) has argued, any admission of the debates that have occurred over such an enterprise, RMS Titanic Inc. goes on to glorify its own role in the tragedy. This is a role that, as they describe it, requires courage, a sense of moral duty and technical expertise at the use of modern technology. As one looks around at these fragments from the ship, in wonder not only at their survival but at their very presence in front of our eyes, the 'company's goal' to 'preserve and display these objects in memory of those who perished aboard *Titanic*' seems not only worthwhile but necessary, given that the ship is slowly disintegrating due to the action of metal-eating bacteria.

The exhibition ends with a memorial gallery where one can find out what happened to each and every passenger on the ship as well as some of the personal stories of those on board. These include that of the last survivor, Elizabeth Gladys Dean, a child travelling in third class who survived along with her mother and brother but whose father died. Millvina, as she was known, died in 2008 and the exhibition is dedicated to her memory. As we walk out through a small corridor, there are some panels accompanying the display of a few ephemeral objects from the ship-wreck site which link its story to the stories of a small number of Australians on board as both staff and passengers. We come out into the bright glare of the shop where we can purchase photos of ourselves taken as we entered the exhibition and later on the grand staircase, as well as any number of replica objects from the ship. If we did not catch on to the exhibition as a marketing exercise for the company to fund and rationalise its salvaging activities, if not to make a profit, it becomes clear here. Not that that reali-sation has had any impact on the desire of people to purchase – a quick scan on the web reveals that many have come to this exhibition in locations around the world just to purchase and collect that first-class dinnerware or third-class blanket. *Titanic* mania, much of it driven by the box office success of the film starring Leonardo di Caprio and Kate Winslet, now includes the collecting of exhibition merchandise.

The exhibition has had a number of critics, some of whom point to the commercial interests of the salvage company and the lack of any acknowl-edgement within the exhibition of the debates surrounding their activities and the limited nature of its formulaic account of the disaster which, as Edward Rothstein pointed out (in relation to the Times Square version), offered

> no exploration of the cause of the Titanic's failure, barely a hint of the difficulties of that night's rescue and only a cursory nod at the event's impact. There is little here that will challenge preconceptions or offer reinterpretations. It is, in other words, a package: effective, intriguing, but stopping short of what the best museums might demand.
>
> (2009: para. 12)

What I hope to have shown is how these problems are a direct outcome of this exhibition's immersive strategies which play to people's emotional engagement but not necessarily to any deepening of their historical under-standing. A separate but linked matter, then, is how public institutions should position themselves. This I grant is not an easy question. Engaging the public with history in the enormous numbers that this exhibition does all over the world is an achievement. There is intense public interest in the story of the *Titanic* and an argument could certainly be made as to their right to see this material and engage with it at an emotional level. But the fact also remains that there is contest over this particular company's activi-ties and that this contest is not recognised within the structure of the exhibition. The battle for exclusive rights only makes the use of emotional narratives to control how people view their activities more distasteful. How should public institutions engage with commercial entities when it comes to heritage and what controls or ability to add value through debate should they be able to exact for the price of granting them the status that inevitably comes with display in a public institution?

The memorial for the murdered jews of Europe

Producing strategies of interpretation which position visitors in the role of victim in order to give them a heightened emotional experience is not, however, the only way to use our attraction to other human beings. Instead, taking my cue from critics such as Young and La Capra, I am interested in exploring how a more complex focus on the impact of personifying the victim might lead to a questioning of one's own relationship to other human beings and thus to the production of 'empathic unsettlement'. My final case study is one where the identification of visitors with victims is not achieved through attempts to step into their shoes either through role-playing or the ubiquitous identity card supported by a highly emotive journey. Instead, I wish to explore how the interaction between a focus on personal narratives and the aesthetic qualities of an exhibition can encourage both an empathetic response with the victims and a critical position which requires a process of self-examination that asks about our relationship to both victim and perpetrator. My example comes from the exhibitions at the information centre that supports the Memorial for the Murdered Jews of Europe in central Berlin.

The need for this centre was established as part of the deliberations in the Bundestag which led to the German government's decision to support and pay for the building of the Peter Eisenman-designed Memorial in 2000 (Schlusche 2007). Its tone is set by the aesthetics of the Memorial above which, as Schlusche (2007: 28) argues, resists identification with any one individual and uses the sombre nature of cemetery forms (stelae, sarcophaguses and gravestone slabs) to reference the millions who perished during the Holocaust in a sensorial experience that resists any final understanding or absolute knowledge of what occurred. The intention is to create a field of disquiet as well as the quietness appropriate to a Memorial space – that is we are meant to think as well as feel.

One of the difficulties posed by the building of this Memorial and its dedication as a Memorial for the Murdered Jews of Europe was the perception that its existence precluded the necessity for the German State to build a national memorial that served as a warning to itself and its citizens. The identification with the victims was understood as leaving out any confrontation with the perpetrators (Benz 2007: 31). That perception changed as Germany itself went through a process of debate which, as Jürgen Habermas (1999, cited in Benz 2007: 31) argued, resulted in a widespread understanding that memorialising the victims involved accepting the question of responsibility – an acceptance that is reflected not only in the decision of the Bundestag to add an interpretation centre to the Memorial but also in the eventual form of the exhibition itself. It is that form, I want to argue, which prevents any simplistic identification with the victim while eschewing the question of one's relationship to the perpetrators.

At first glance, the narrative provided within the Centre is not that different from other memorial sites. A summarised version of what occurred between 1933 and 1945 is provided in the introductory space. Four thematic rooms deal respectively with the range of experiences from Western to Eastern Europe; they offer representative family histories from across Europe before, during and after the Holocaust, provide a space for the naming of victims and a cartographic representation of the sites of persecution and extermination of European Jewry. Mention of other victims also takes place within these rooms. Finally, the foyer area is used to point visitors towards other memorials and museums that explore similar themes.

The genre and content of the material is familiar from other exhibitions dealing with the Holocaust. The museological contribution of the space however is different and lies in the productive use of the tension between the role of memorialisation above ground and the role of information below ground. Not simply a documentary centre, its displays, I want to argue, use aesthetics as well as documentary evidence, much of it in the voice of the victim, to produce disquiet as well as remembrance on the part of the visitor. It is within that space of disquiet that our own position in relation to both victim and perpetrator and our future role as a defender of democratic values emerges. How then was this achieved?

The first strategy is not to attempt any vicarious identification with the victim by attempting to put visitors into their position. There are no re-enactments, no role-play and no identity cards of any sort. The visitor, then, is not explicitly positioned in relation to either the victims or the perpetrators. The fact that they are within a memorial space is allowed to signify whom that space stands for.

Instead, the focus is simply on individual stories that give meaning and immediacy to the scale of the disaster. Indeed, the aim of the Foundation's Board of Trustees was to provide a cognitive space that would counter the emotional experience of the Memorial sculpture itself by bringing the reality of the six million people who were being commemorated down to the level of what the Holocaust meant for individual people and their families. Their aim was that the information centre should 'personalize and individualise the horrors of the Holocaust' (Quack 2007: 41) and show its impact throughout Europe. At the same time, the Centre also sought to educate their visitors, including German citizens, as to the basic contours of the Nationalist Socialist policies and their applications. Hence a visit to the Centre ends with information on other memorial sites where the atrocity itself occurred. Responsibility for what occurred is clearly owned.

It is in the space of the encounter between information and aesthetic experience, however, that the educational potential of this narrative is realised. Those involved in the development of the exhibition had two main aims, both of which were driven by the location of the Memorial in Europe, as well as in German capital itself. First, they wanted to ensure that visitors would be able to sympathise not only with the fate of individuals and their families but begin to understand the impact on entire communities and European Jewry at large (Quack 2007; Rürup 2007). Given that the history of remembrance of the Second World War in both Western Europe and the former USSR tended to embed the Jewish experience as just another victim of the Nazis among many others, this was regarded as an important aim (Rürup 2007). Knowledge about the fate of Eastern European Jews who had tended not to be commemorated during the socialist period was seen as particularly important. The second aim was that people would make the connection between the collapse of democracy in Germany and the fate of the Jewish People, taking on the role of guardians of modern day democratic societies (Rürup 2007). In a country that was newly reunited and facing its own process of educating its expanded citizenry into democratic values, this aim also took on an added importance. It is also this aim that requires visitors to make the connection between empathising with the victims, essentially an emotional journey, with undertaking a degree of self-examination that requires them to confront the role of perpetrator and their relationship to it. It is this aim that is catered for, I want to argue, at the level of the aesthetic experience rather than the straightforward narrative informational content provided within the exhibition space.

As Dagmar von Wilcken (2007), the designer of the space points out in his contribution to the commemorative book about the Centre, it is the tension between the function of information provider and reflective memorial space that drives the aesthetic experience. For von Wilcken it made sense to continue the visual language of the memorial above into the information centre below. This language, of stelae and grave, is embedded within the walls, floors and ceilings of the space, as well as the colour scheme with its tones of black, grey and white. For her, it is this language that provides the space necessary for reflection appropriate to a memorial space. For me, as a visitor, it is this language, in conjunction with the documentary material on display that allows me to empathise with the victims and, at the same time, explore my own relation to them in the present rather than simply relegate them to history.

The experience is particularly strong in the first thematic room dealing with the European dimensions of the Holocaust. At first sight this room appears largely empty. An electronic frieze around the upper perimeter of the room records the names of all the countries affected and the number of their victims. The large scale of the event equals the incomprehensibility captured in the Memorial above where the stelae appear to disappear into the horizon. A sense of absence and emptiness is the first experience. However, on entering the room proper it becomes evident that it is the floor that carries the main message. For the pattern of the stelae above is repeated on the floor where rectangular light boxes carry quotations from the diaries and writings of the victims. On the floor, these rectangular light boxes become gravesites. Looking downwards, to read them is not only a chance for inner reflection, a point made by von Wilcken (see Quack and von Wilcken 2007: 46). It is also a point of ethical choice – I did not see a single person walking across each gravesite and thus desecrate them. How one walks in the space involves a conscious choice to treat the information as sacred and precious, and thus showing respect for the testimony of those who went to such efforts to speak to others beyond their shortened life-time. In showing that respect, visitors are engaging in exactly what those victims did not have at the time of their murder – a recognition of their humanity (see Figure 8.2).

Figure 8.2 Looking, feeling and apprehending the significance of what happened and our own relationship to it
Photo: Henry Benjamin

The point is not only that the authors of these extracts from fragments of diaries, letters and postcards sent or thrown out of train windows at the moment of deportation wished to testify to posterity what was occurring to them in the hope their names would not be forgotten. While, as many authors have argued, these writings are part of an extraordinary effort on the part of individual Jewish victims to make it impossible to erase their existence from European history, to ask of survivors to speak their names as is customary in Jewish commemorative tradition, they are also attempts to recover their status as human beings. As Annette Auerhahn and Dorothy Laub (1990) argued in relation to the giving of testimony on the part of survivors, testifying was not only based on a desire to document what happened. It was also based on a desire to have an audience, to be heard.

According to them, the experience of the Holocaust was the experience of being left alone, of not being able to establish a relationship between themselves and others. In our listening of these testimonies, then, we are to some extent, giving them their humanity back. We have become their listeners, receiving, as Roger Simon (2006) would argue, 'their terrible gift' – a gift that comes laden with political responsibility.

That this is happening inside the German capital, so close to the former site of the Reichstag, is of course of enormous metaphorical significance. It is this decision, embodied in our sensorial or affective response to the aesthetics of the display and the recognition of the import of the informational content (the personal testimony) that takes this exhibition away from a representation of the past to a request to engage in the present. The space produced out of the tension between the form or aesthetic quality of the display and the informational content, particularly its documentary, testimonary nature in the first person is what makes this exhibition an immersive space that encourages rather than shuts off a process of self-reflection. The process is somewhat like that put forwards by Bertold Brecht in his epic theatre productions, which produced a critical space by allowing each element – words, music and dramaturgy to stand on their own, creating meaning through their relationship to one another. The point was not to produce a closed narrative but one where representation was open to critique as was the relationship of audience members to that representation.

Conclusion

Techniques of immersion can be structurally very different from one another and have very different outcomes for the visitor. The three case studies explored here suggest that there is a real need to understand these differences. Closed immersive experiences that do not allow sufficient time for different voices to emerge from within the experience close off any form of exploratory learning based on a notion of critical engagement. If they do so using a form of delivery that borders on farce for its dramatic effect, they function only at the level of entertainment posing serious ethical concerns. Immersive experiences aimed at producing closely structured emotional encounters on a grand, almost filmic scale, as in the *Titanic* exhibition, make it difficult to have any external perspective on the narrative being produced. The problem with these is not that they function only as entertainment, which could, in some scenarios, be a sufficiently worthy aim. The problem is that it is too easy to use them to hide either ideological or commercial motivations. Finally, immersive strategies that create a space for reflection and critical engagement, while also being successful in terms of box office appeal, are those that create a spatial and aesthetic environment where the dialogue between the nature of the material on display and the form of the display work together to create a space for affective as well as cognitive forms of interaction. It is only then, I would suggest, that such interpretation strategies, particularly in the context of dark tourism, can achieve full ethical integrity.

Note

1   An earlier version of this argument was published as a review of *Titanic: The Artefact Exhibition* in *ReCollections* 5(2). Available online: http://recollections.nma.gov.au/issues/vol_5_no_2/exhibition_reviews/titanic (accessed 20 May 2012).

References

Auerhahn, N.C. and Laub, D. (1990) 'Holocaust testimony', *Holocaust and Genocide Studies* 5(4): 447–62.

Benz, W. (2007) 'A memorial for whom?', in Foundation for the Memorial to the Murdered Jews of Europe (ed.) *Materials on the Memorial to the Murdered Jews of Europe*, Berlin: Nicolai.

Dolff-Bonekamper, G. (2008) 'Sites of memory and sites of discord: historic monuments as a medium for discussing conflict in Europe', in G. Fairclough, R. Harrison, J.H. Jameson Jnr and J. Schofield (eds) *The Heritage Reader*, London and New York: Routledge.

Fenton, J. (1984) 'Pitt-Rivers Museum', in *Children in Exile: Poems 1968–1984*, New York: Random House.

Gibson, R. (2008) 'Palpable history', *Cultural Studies Review* 14(1): 179–86.

Grenzer, E. (2002) 'The topographies of memory in Berlin: The Neue Wache and the Memorial for the Murdered Jews of Europe', *Canadian Journal of Urban Research* 11(1): 93–110.

Habermas, J. (1999) 'Der Zeigefinger, Die Deutschen und ihr Denkmal', in *Die Zeit*, 31 March, in Benz, W. (2007) 'A memorial for whom?', in Foundation for the Memorial to the Murdered Jews of Europe (ed.) *Materials on the Memorial to the Murdered Jews of Europe*, Berlin: Nicolai.

La Capra, D. (1998) *History and Memory After Auschwitz*, Ithaca and New York: Cornell University Press.

National Trust of Australia (Victoria) (2008) *Annual Report for the Financial Year 2007–2008*, Melbourne: National Trust of Australia Victoria.

National Trust of Australia (Victoria) (2009a) *Annual Report for the Financial Year 2008–2009*, Melbourne: National Trust of Australia Victoria.

National Trust of Australia (Victoria) (2009b) *Media Release: Old Melbourne Gaol Crime & Justice Experience wins National IAA Award*. Available online: www.nattrust.com.au/about_the_trust (accessed 29 August 2012).

Quack, S. and von Wilcken, D. (2007) 'Creating an exhibition about the murder of European Jewry', in Foundation for the Memorial to the Murdered Jews of Europe (ed.) *Materials on the Memorial to the Murdered Jews of Europe*, Berlin: Nicolai.

Rothstein, E. (2009) 'Relics from the Deep and the Dawn of Man', *New York Times*, 25 June. Available online: www.nytimes.com/2009/06/26/arts/design/26discovery.html?_r=1&pagewanted=all (accessed 29 August 2012).

Rürup, R. (2007) 'National socialism, war and genocide of the Jews' in Foundation for the Memorial to the Murdered Jews of Europe (ed.) *Materials on the Memorial to the Murdered Jews of Europe*, Berlin: Nicolai.

Schlusche, G. (2007) 'A memorial is built', in Foundation for the Memorial to the Murdered Jews of Europe (ed.) *Materials on the Memorial to the Murdered Jews of Europe*, Berlin: Nicolai.

Simon, R.I. (2006) 'The terrible gift: museums and the possibility of hope without consolation', *Museum Management and Curatorship* 21: 187–204.

Stone, P.R. (2006) 'A dark tourism spectrum: towards a typology of death and macabre related tourist sites, attractions and exhibitions', *TOURISM: An Interdisciplinary International Journal* 54(2): 145–60.

Westbury, M. (2010) 'Do blockbuster exhibitions dumb down history for entertainment?' *The Age*, 24 May: 19.

Wilson, J.Z. (2008) *Prison: Cultural Memory and Dark Tourism*, New York: Peter Lang.

Young, J.E. (2001) 'Foreword: Looking into the mirrors of evil', in N.L. Kleeblatt (ed.) *Mirroring Evil: Nazi Imagery/Recent Art*, New Brunswick, New Jersey and London: The Jewish Museum, New York & Rutgers University Press.

Part IV

Heritage, 'tradition', tourism and the politics of change

Chapter 9

Cultures of interpretation

Tim Winter

Introduction

As tourists we frequently find ourselves acting as amateur anthropologists. If a trip to a heritage visitor centre involves encountering visitors or tour groups from other countries it is hard to resist leaping to conclusions about the behaviour – sometimes perceived as rude – of those Germans, Italians, Americans or Koreans across the room. All too often those conclusions rest on clichés. But to dismiss such observations out of hand would be to close down a fascinating and potentially fruitful line of enquiry. Clearly, it would be foolish to suggest that our spectrum of cultural differences are somehow erased or transcended as we take on the role of 'the tourist'. But to identify national traits risks the criticism of sweeping generalisations, or worse, of even being racist. So how are we to safely read and differentiate between the behaviours of tourists originating from different parts of the world? The boundary that separates rigorous, analytically sound accounts from unfounded generalisations is not always readily apparent. Perhaps most treacherous is identifying appropriate geographical scales or ethno-cultural axes for making assertions about motivations, desires or discernible characteristics. At what point is it valid to speak of Asian, European, Western, French, Hindu Indian, or North American traits? By analysing the changing nature of tourism in Asia today and the impact this will have on the presentation or 'interpretation' of heritage sites, this chapter ventures down such treacherous and murky roads. Moving between a number of geographical and historical scales, the account is schematic rather than being narrowly prescriptive, and as such, it incurs the risks that accompany generalisations. Nevertheless, various avenues of enquiry are pursued here in the hope that they offer some fresh perspectives on heritage interpretation and cast light on matters that have yet to receive the attention they deserve.

Understood in its broadest sense, heritage is about conserving or restoring the past, and preserving tradition or traditions. But as Eric Hobsbawm (1983) succinctly reminded us, the notion of tradition is an invented one. More specifically, it is vital to remember that a language of 'tradition' and 'the traditional' have evolved within the rapid and seemingly irrevocable changes inflicted by industrialisation and modernity. Accordingly, over the last 20 years or so it has become increasingly apparent that a language of World Heritage has emerged within, and been forged by, the broader contexts of a European cum Western modernity. As we know, momentum for the creation of UNESCO, along with the subsequent protection instruments of the 1964 Venice Charter and 1972 World Heritage Convention largely came from Europe and North America. For a number of reasons – not least the massive destruction caused by two world wars and the twentieth century's unstoppable march towards industrialisation and urbanisation – World Heritage emerged as an overwhelmingly 'fabric'-based discourse. Understandably, the primary concern was the protection of cultural and natural landscapes, which together constituted an endangered 'heritage of mankind'. Implicit to a language of 'mankind' was the idea that certain frameworks for protecting heritage could be universally implemented and ratified. One of the main precepts of the Venice Charter was the protection of the authenticity of the physical fabric. While the term authenticity vividly captured the philosophical orientations towards conservation at that time, its use also pointed towards a series of underlying fears. Quite naturally calls for preservation would stem from a fear of losing the irretrievable. The discourse of heritage that emerged strongly reflected fears about the rapid social and environmental changes of modernity, postwar reconstruction, urbanisation and globalisation. There was also a fear of how the degenerative forces of capitalism would incur a loss of that authenticity. Industries such as tourism, for example, have been consistently perceived as threatening the authenticity of sites and landscapes, and thus resisted or kept at a safe distance.

While the broad concept of World Heritage has proved extremely successful, concerns about the validity of universalist approaches, and the semantics of 'universal value', have continued to grow. In the face of such critiques, there has been a widespread shift away from earlier 'top down' models of heritage management in favour of more democratic approaches that valorise concepts like 'stakeholders' or 'values'. These terms reflect a concern for incorporating multiple perspectives, and a plurality of voices. Heritage planners are now required to incorporate – and balance – the views of local residents, academics, local businesses, government offices and non-governmental organisations, with the needs of those consuming the heritage: tourists. As a result, the opinions and interests of central government or outside experts are now countered by more localised, everyday perspectives.

To complement the recognition given to these global, local tensions, more regionalised, culturally sensitive paradigms have also evolved via the Burra Charter, Nara Declaration, and the more recent Hoi An Protocols and China Principles. One of the main challenges for those involved in the China Principles – an initiative of the State Administration of Cultural

Heritage in China, The Getty Conservation Institute and the Australian Department of the Environment and Heritage – has been the incorporation of 'international best practice while maintaining traditional attitudes to China's rich inheritance and its values' (Sullivan 2005: 281). To help resolve such socio-cultural differences, these regional charters and guidelines have shifted attention away from the authenticity of the fabric towards ideas of continuity and renewal, the preservation of craftsmanship and more values-based approaches (for further details see Agnew and Demas 2002). While initiatives like the China Principles have admirably helped overcome many of the Eurocentric biases inherent to today's globally roaming discourse of heritage, it will be suggested over the coming pages that many of the field's core ideas and assumptions – forged within European and North American experiences of modernity – continue to be deployed in universalist, global ways. It is a situation that leaves the heritage conservation sector poorly equipped to understand the various ways in which different societies produce their own cultural norms and shared ideas of how to negotiate, mediate and delineate the traditional from the modern, the authentic from the inauthentic.

Much the same can be said about our understandings of tourism and tourists. Even within those approaches that have sought to differentiate between a variety of stakeholders, the need to balance inside versus outside, or local versus non-local, values invariably results in the homogenisation of 'the tourist' as the outsider. Although numerous attempts have been made to differentiate cultural-tourists from eco-tourists from mass-tourists, the seeming inability of these categories to map onto the complex empirical realities of tourism has meant 'the tourist' remains a generic, universally proclaimed term. As such, the tourist conjures up certain identifiable characteristics, desires, aspirations and habits. But I would argue to recognise these characteristics is to identify with a long cultural history of medieval travel, the European enlightenment and the rise of industrialised modernity in the West. The dominance of European languages in today's global heritage movement means understandings of the social, cultural and moral values associated with the 'tourist' are empirically grounded within histories of pilgrimage, the European grand tour, colonial exploration, the rise of leisure and the growth of mass travel during the twentieth century.[1] As a consequence, in the arena of heritage policy, the analytical frameworks for interpreting tourism have been overwhelmingly directed towards west-to-east and north-to-south encounters. In countless studies exploring the impact of a *global* tourism industry on a *local* environment or destination the tourist has been conceptualised as the wealthy westerner travelling in search of pre-modern authenticity. In essence then, the argument presented in broad strokes here, is that today's globally roaming discourse of heritage policy implicitly draws upon Western-centric ideas of tourism and tourists and deploys them in universalist ways.

It is a situation that is rapidly being rendered unsustainable in regions like Asia because of the rise of domestic and intra-regional tourism. The significant increases in the number of Asians travelling for leisure mean that heritage tourism across the region can no longer be read through the conceptual lens of Eastern, Southern hemisphere hosts and Western, Northern hemisphere guests. More specifically, it demands a reappraisal of how terms such as 'tourist' and 'cultural tourism' are used and deployed within the heritage industry. This chapter focuses on Asia as a region that sharply brings in to focus the multitude of unfamiliar challenges for managing and presenting heritage sites, arising from large-scale non-Western forms of travel, tourism and leisure. More specifically, it considers the industry familiar discourse of 'site interpretation' against a backdrop of Asian modernities in order to ask questions about aesthetics and the politics of heritage narration. As we head into what many are referring to as 'the Asian century', the scale of the expansion of the region's educated, middle-class will be staggering. In less than a decade, India and China alone will be home to more than half a billion urban middle-class citizens, many of whom will have the disposable income and inclination to travel.

In observing this trend in their 2004 book, *The New Consumers: The Influence of Affluence on the Environment*, Norman Myers and Jennifer Kent gave particular focus to the rising levels of consumption associated within rapid economic development in the developing world. Accordingly, they defined these new consumers as 'people within an average of four-member households who possess purchasing power parity (PPP) of at least PPP$USD10,000 per year, or at least PPP$USD2500 per person'. (2004: 8). Myers and Kent suggest they are typically:

> the long-standing members of the middle and upper class classes that can include senior managers, small business owners, investment bankers, physicians, lawyers, marketing executives, real estate agents, Internet engineers, architects, journalists, private school teachers, home designers, and insurance salespeople, [as well as] more recent members that can include computer programmers, junior managers, accountants, bank tellers, secretaries, and many others of similar status.
>
> (2004: 16)

Myers and Kent offer a list of 'new consumer societies', which they populate with 20 countries. Among a range of analytic considerations, inclusion in this category requires a population exceeding 20 million, and an economic growth rate that exceeds 5 per cent per year.[2] In examining the consumption practices of these new consumers they point to a number of distinct, upwards trends, such as private car ownership, the daily consumption of meat and the demand for electricity at the household level driven by a rapid growth in the number of energy-intensive domestic appliances being purchased. Crucially, they argue that the number of 'the new consumers' will continue to 'soar' both in the medium and longer term. Asia, home to ten of the 20 new consumer economies, is rapidly becoming 'the center of gravity for the new consumer phenomenon' (Myers and Kent 2004: 18). Writing in 2004, they estimated the region would be home to around 900 million 'new consumers' by 2010; a figure that, despite the economic downturn of 2008–2009, seems plausible given the double-digit growth in GDP that both China and India experienced over this period. Interestingly, their account pays less attention to the propensity of these new consumers to become increasingly mobile. The liberalisation of cross-border travel in Asia, together with the massive upgrading of physical infrastructures and the ongoing acquisition of the cultural capital required for travel and tourism all mean the region's new consumers will be visiting sites of heritage in ever greater numbers.

Narrating the past and non-universal histories

The editors of this volume rightfully question the all-pervasive notion of providing a particular heritage message or narrative. Given such approaches are likely to dominate professional conservation practice for some years to come, however, it is worth considering in some detail how the trends noted above bear upon this area. As noted elsewhere in this book, the field of interpretation has grown out of a desire to remain rigorous about how the past is presented. In the quest for historical accuracy, speculation is to be avoided. The idea of 'authenticity' has provided the semantic vehicle for ensuring this paradigm is upheld. Early approaches to heritage management privileged authenticity in order to ensure the meanings and values were extracted from a heritage landscape in a genuine, faithful and systematic manner. The focus was on authoritative, credible truths. The move towards notions of plurality and contestation clarified the limitations of these earlier prescriptions. However, the ongoing use of the term reflects the idea that meanings and voices, however disparate, can still be extracted from a heritage site as stable, intrinsic values.

The term also implies that narratives and places are consumed and interpreted by the audience in stable, universally shared ways. All too often, this homogenisation of the audience rests on the assumption that the tourist is, by default, prototypically Western. Crucially, however, in regions like Asia this has continually reproduced Eurocentric understandings of how the past or heritage sites are narrated. To illustrate this I want to focus on the World Heritage site of Angkor in Cambodia.

Visitors to Angkor today invariably suffer from an overload of information. Tour guides and guidebooks bombard the visitor with a seemingly endless amount of information about the kings of Angkor, their dates of rule, chronological shifts in architectural style, transitions between styles of sculpture and a bewildering list of gods, demons and their various avatars. The information tourists receive is derived from a field of scholarship that has studied the temples of Angkor as the legacy of a once glorious, classical civilisation. At the heart of Angkorean scholarship lies the Ecole Française d'Extrême Orient (EFEO). Over the course of nearly 100 years of research EFEO has built up an immense wealth of information on Angkor. They are rightfully seen as the authorities of knowledge about the temples and their history. This situation does, however, mean that Angkor has been inter- preted through an intellectual prism of European origin.

Like many other historic sites around the world, one of the defining myths in the story of Angkor relates to its supposed loss and 're-discovery' by the French botanist Henri Mouhot in 1860. It is commonly recounted that Mouhot battled his way through the north Cambodian jungle to rescue the decaying architectural remnants of a civilisation which had supposedly abandoned its capital in the mid-fifteenth century. Arriving just over 400 years later, Mouhot entered history as the man that awakened the Khmers from an era of decay and cultural degeneration. As I have detailed at length elsewhere this account of historical rupture and resurrection has played a pivotal role in shaping recent discourses of heritage and conservation in Cambodia (Winter 2007). Not surprisingly, the tourism industry which has evolved around Angkor has also thrived off the romantic, mysterious and adventurous tales of rediscovering lost antiquities. But as heritage and tourism have converged and come to shape each other, a period of history spanning around 400 years has been eclipsed.

The problems with this account have been highlighted by a number of recent studies focusing on temple graffiti, monasteries, ceramics or vernac- ular traditions. By turning to such areas, scholars like Ashley Thompson (2004) and Ang Choulean (Apsara 2000) provide evidence of ongoing occupation in order to refute the overly simplistic narrative of Angkor being 'abandoned'. In an article entitled 'Pilgrims to Angkor: A Buddhist "Cosmopolis" in Southeast Asia?', Thompson also draws our attention to a detailed and rich history of Asian travel to Angkor spanning several centuries. Her account reveals Angkor's role as a major destination for Buddhist pilgrims travelling from around Asia. Together these studies represent important departures from the currently dominant narrative of the post-Angkorean era as a 'middle period' of cultural dormancy (for further details see Apsara 2000).

In many instances, the framing of Angkor's history today also repro- duces the broad classifications offered by colonial historians regarding Asia's 'greater' and 'lesser' civilisations. Over the course of the twentieth century Angkorean historiography has focused its gaze on the former, plac- ing far greater emphasis on the influence of a classical Indian culture and religious iconography. In her piece 'Taj Angkor; enshrining l'Inde in le Cambodge', Penny Edwards describes a process of 're-Indianization' whereby early-twentieth century 'Buddhist worship at Angkor presented unwelcome challenges to colonial desires to compartmentalize Cambodia both vertically, through time, and horizontally, through the categorization of religion' (2005: 17). Given that most Cambodians practised a form of Theravada Buddhism that integrated animist beliefs and the veneration of figures like Vishnu and Shiva, the presence of monks and Buddhist icons detracted from the colonial imagining of a once-glorious 'Hindu' past represented by a pristine Angkor. Considered to be an eyesore, the community of monks living in front of Angkor Wat were removed by EFEO in 1909 (Anderson 1991: 182). This was followed by the consolidation of all of the temple's Buddhist statues within a single space on the ground floor; an area that was subsequently coined 'the gallery of a thousand Buddhas'. According to Edwards such ' "Buddhist" identities spoiled the "Hindu" template presented to tourists [and] disturbed the colonial presentation of Angkor as both monument *and* frozen moment, a material archive to the "golden" era of Khmer greatness and glory'. (2005: 17–18, original emphasis).[3] The reification of an Indian influence also defined EFEO's epigraphic research. The meticulous translation of Sanskrit inscriptions found on numerous stelae or doorways revealed elaborate stories of kingship and devoted populations, of battles and conquests and of deities and religious cults (see, for example, Coedès 1968; Dumarcay and Groslier 1973).

In piecing together Angkor's history, much less attention has been given to the Khmer inscriptions found among the temples or the evidence pertaining to the ongoing presence of animism. Indeed, within an account of architectural splendour and pristine glory, anthropological accounts which might reveal oral histories or the transmissions of cultural traditions across generations have been largely overlooked. In other words a fascination with the rise and fall of classical civilisations – a theme central to late-nineteenth century European historiography – has created a real obstacle for the presentation of narratives addressing localised belief systems, vernacular traditions or Angkor's enduring role within a pan-Asian Buddhist tradition.

In essence then we can see that the heritage industry surrounding Angkor today reproduces and prioritises certain readings of Angkor. These narratives have also emerged in tandem with a Eurocentric discourse of Angkorean tourism. Angkor has become the quintessential lost ruin, the untouched pristine landscape. Encapsulated in a French imagining of *Indochine*, Angkor, as tourist site, has stood as an embodiment of the exotic, the romantic and the mysterious. As Edward Said pointed out, for France in particular 'theirs was the orient of memories, suggestive ruins, forgotten ruins' (1995: 169). With their appeal extending far beyond France, these themes have strongly resonated with a long tradition of Western tourism orientated towards ideas of exploration, adventure, discovery and individuality.

But if we look at Angkor as a site of Asian tourism a very different set of themes begin to appear. For Thai, Chinese, Korean and Taiwanese tourists, the story of 'discovery' by a French botanist carries significantly less weight. Within Asian history, Angkor represents the capital of an imperial power, and one of the most significant pre-modern polities in the region. Within a pan-Asian Buddhist history, Angkor is revered as a site of pilgrimage. And within an Asian social history, Angkor was an important hub of commerce, attracting people and their objects of trade from across Southeast Asia, Southern China and beyond. Stories of Japanese Buddhist pilgrims or Chinese traders need to become part of the interpretation narrative presented at Angkor today. Equally, for Cambodians, Angkor is a living space; a landscape studded with monasteries, villages and an array of animist traditions. Community-based programmes for restoring and modernising its pagodas and *vihears* vividly illustrate how the boundaries between past and present, modern and traditional are far less marked for Cambodians. But within an interpretative framework of world heritage that prioritises monumental glories, stories of a Hindu pantheon or the aesthetic beauties of ancient relics, these narratives and values receive little attention.

The rise of Asian tourism makes such situations increasingly unsustainable. It brings into view the endurance of Eurocentric interpretations. In the case of Angkor, this has involved the museumification of the landscape via representations of the past as linear narrative. Asian tourism therefore suggests the need for more Asian-centric accounts of place and history. This, in turn, means being aware of the origins of expert knowledge. In a parallel to Angkor, Michael Aung-Thwin shows how the accepted history for Pagan in Myanmar rests upon a series of mythical events invented by late-nineteenth and twentieth century colonial historians. Accordingly, he traces the 'intellectual, political and social trends in nineteenth and twentieth century Burma that likely shaped the historiography' of the country (1998: 3). It is therefore important that interpretation experts remain alert to such historical processes, in order to avoid today's heritage industry serving as an unwitting residue of colonial power.

Of course the incorporation of more Asian-centric histories poses fresh challenges. A number of recent academic studies on Asian tourism have highlighted how attempts to capture the Renminbi, Indian Rupee or Korean Won have involved a shift in the narratives presented. To preserve harmonious relations with their northern neighbours in China, government officials in Vietnam have instructed local tour guides to skim over histories of invasion and inter-state conflict. In turning to a regional tourist audience, rather than just a Western one, Vietnam is having to reconfigure the way it represents war and conflict. Similar challenges face China itself, with the memorialisation of the Nanjing Massacre of 1937. As the site becomes increasingly popular with domestic tourists, it seems to engender

simultaneous feelings of hatred and peaceful reconciliation towards Japan
(Ross 2006). Equally, in Singapore whether to recognise Little Japan as a
heritage space endures as a political dilemma. Once again, the geographical proximity of intra-regional tourism is raising uncomfortable questions
about the narration of stories of invasion and violence (Blackburn 2006).
Clearly, such examples also point towards unfolding possibilities for
governments to manipulate heritage towards their ideological biases. In
this respect, it is worth remembering how intra-regional and domestic
tourism in Asia raises the temperature on historically sensitive sites and the
politics of their interpretation.

The aesthetics of modernity

Growth in Asian travel and tourism is taking place against a backdrop of
extremely rapid social change. Urbanisation, mechanisation, industrialisation and information technologies – processes which spanned several
decades in Europe and North America – are now being completed in just
a few short years. It also goes without saying that this accelerated modernisation of Asia is also occurring within very different, non-Western, cultural
and societal contexts. In the case of China, for example, tourism has
emerged as a post-Maoist phenomenon. As Pal Nyíri (2006) shows, the
eventual arrival of mass tourism in China was dependent upon the Chinese
Communist Party's efforts to recast its citizens as modern consumers. While
tourism would form part of the party's desire to privatise the country's
economy, it would also be a mechanism for promoting a state-centred
nationalism.

To interpret such changes requires a subtle reading of multiple modernities. Few observers suggest that the experience of modernity across Asia
is uniform and that the region is merely following the same trajectories as
the West (Hosagrahar 2005). In fact, pursuing this line of enquiry sheds
light on a very different set of social, economic and cultural dynamics
surrounding heritage and heritage tourism. Asia's various pathways of
modernity require us to revisit our core assumptions about these two public
spheres, including how we understand heritage as the interface between
past and present, how the past is presented and narrated and how traditions come to be venerated, ignored or deliberately discarded (Winter and
Daly 2012). The current destruction and removal of architectural structures regarded as less than 'modern', coupled with the insertion of
re-created 'pre-modern' cultural landscapes, across countless Asian cities
suggests familiar questions about heritage are being met with unfamiliar
answers (see, for example, Becker 2004). How do we make sense of the
management and presentation of architectural heritage in cities like
Singapore, for example? Or of the modernisation of the templed landscape of Pagan in Burma? Should the approaches adopted in these places

merely be pejoratively described as post-modern? It was noted earlier that these questions are now being addressed within debates about the philosophies of conservation and regionalised approaches to restoration. However, the impact they hold for the field of interpretation has yet to be fully explored.

To help frame such a discussion it is important to note that the distinction between the 'authentic' and 'inauthentic' is not as clearly articulated in Asia as it is in Western discourses of heritage and tourism. Indeed, as Nobuo Ito points out, the Japanese language has 'no proper word for authenticity' (1994: 35). As a consequence, conservation and modernisation are not seen as inherently in tension or as antithetical processes as they invariably are in the West. This raises interesting questions about the presentation of sites and the aesthetics of interpretation. In the case of China, for example, ideas of sustainable management often involve the modernisation of a site and the improvement of its facilities. As Nyíri illustrates, the management authorities of historic *mingsheng*, or scenic spots, are not afraid of adding concrete and glass ticket booths, large gates and conspicuously located retail outlets. It is perceived that adding these facilities enhances the tourist experience. Instead of blending buildings in with their local environment through the use of low-pitched roofs, muted colours or native timbers, they are designed to look distinctly modern, and conspicuously new. Crucially, given that such interventions are not perceived as intrusions threatening the authenticity of the site, there is little concern for a language of 'harmonising the old with the new', or using 'materials sympathetic to the environment'.

For Nyíri 'the Chinese tradition suggests a different way of approaching and responding to nature, lacking the modern western taboo on human intervention'. (2006: 67). By examining the aesthetics of current heritage site-management practices in China we can see that the fear of modernisation and commercialisation which pervades a Western discourse of heritage is often absent. Such differences can also be seen within the context of tourist souvenir aesthetics. As I have shown elsewhere, the purchasing patterns of tourists visiting Cambodia from Northeast Asia speak of radically different relationships between tradition and the modern (see Winter 2008). Rather than buying miniature stone carvings or 'traditional Khmer' silks, tourists from Korea, Taiwan and China are returning home with glass sculptures illuminated by LEDs, metal ornaments or plastic figurines. A trip to the temples of Angkor is not remembered by the locally crafted, traditional but by the modern, mass-manufactured. But do such examples mean the aesthetics of heritage and tourism in Asia are fundamentally and intrinsically different from those in the West? Or is Asia essentially evolving along the same aesthetic and cultural trajectories as other parts of the world? These are two simple but challenging questions that have yet to be fully addressed.

The spectrum of practices being employed for heritage site presentation across Asia today suggests these questions will deliver complex answers. If we look at sites that have been primarily designed for domestic visitors and/or have been managed by local authorities or entrepreneurs, it is apparent that the position and style of signboards, retail units and information kiosks, as well as the positioning of viewpoints and walkways differ significantly from many of the conventions recognised as 'best practice' within Western heritage discourse.

A number of recent studies on the practices of tourists from across the region have also revealed various cultural practices that would seem unfamiliar to a student of Western tourism. In her account of mainland Chinese tourists in Macau, Hilary du Cros (2007) observes particular behavioural norms that pose new challenges for the city's heritage-management authorities. She also identifies how some sites, such as churches, linked to Macau's historical connections with Europe receive scant attention, a matter I shall return to shortly. According to Yuk Wah Chan (2008) Chinese tourists travel to Southeast Asia in search of signifiers of modernity and futurity. She offers a framework of 'disorganized tourism space' to interpret how sites of consumption are encountered and made meaningful through particular embodied practices. In the case of Bali, Thirumaran (2008) develops a framework of cultural affinity to make sense of Indian tourism to the island. Rather than rehearsing the account of Balinese culture as the quintessential exotic 'other', Thirumaran explains how the cultural referents of a 'shared heritage' between the Indian tourists and Balinese dancers are pivotal to the consumption and interpretation of traditional dance.

The risk of offering sweeping generalisations ensures conclusions remain tentative. Nonetheless, when seen together, these studies suggest that tourism in contemporary Asia remains bound up in collective identities and communal affinities, rather than the search for individualised expression, independence and self-actualisation familiar to Europe and North America. By implication, rather than absorbing information individually via guidebooks, there is a greater tendency for many Asian tourists to learn about a destination via DVDs or videos played on airplanes or tour buses. The widespread popularity of airline magazines, television documentaries or the glossy brochures produced by local authorities means that information can be disseminated across a wide variety of media. It is also equally important to consider how sources of information are perceived. For American, Australian and European tourists, brands such *Lonely Planet*, *Baedeker or National Geographic* are consumed as reliable, authoritative sources of knowledge. In many Asian countries, however, the concept of the branded guidebook has yet to solidify. Consequently, Chinese, Vietnamese, Indian or Indonesian tourists tend to rely more on publications by ministries of tourism, airlines or recognisable bodies like

UNESCO. Once again, it is common to find that content offered via CDs or DVDs from these sources is as popular as text-based publications. More research also needs to be conducted concerning how heritage visitor centres are read and perceived by domestic and intra-regional tourists in Asia. It appears that rather than being orientated around conservative, fact-based narratives of the past, visitor centres for Asian tourists place greater emphasis on performance and re-enactment. The dozens of 'cultural villages' now dotted across the region provide a parallel illustrating how the cultural, whether it be historic sites or ethnic communities, is performed, modernised and aesthetically stylised for consumption as a tourist product.

Visitor centres have become a commonly used tool for managing tourist flows as well as raising awareness about a heritage resource. In countries like China, the addition of such modern facilities can actually transform sites previously considered as unattractive into 'tourable' destinations (Nyíri 2006). Not surprisingly, throughout Asia today, local developers and entrepreneurs are preparing and modernising heritage sites for the domestic and intra-regional tourist dollar. For many Western observers, the addition of neon signage or glass and concrete shopping malls or visitor centres might be regarded as 'tacky' or 'kitsch'. Of course however, such critiques, along with suggestions for more 'tasteful' or 'sympathetic' alternatives, are value judgements that stem from particular cultural and historical contexts. The question of cultural differences in aesthetics and what constitutes good or bad taste is a very familiar one, and the thoughts outlined here offer nothing new to these debates and arguments. However, the matter is raised as a highly pertinent one in light of a burgeoning Asian consumer market. The rise of the Asian tourist now means that it is more important than ever to revisit and re-work these concerns and questions into the field of heritage interpretation. Should heritage experts, for example, revert to what might be seen as elitist readings by eschewing loudspeakers or brightly painted kiosks and labelling them as kitsch?

Of course it would be extremely misleading to suggest that heritage and tourism in Asia have a single, all-encompassing set of aesthetics. There will always be a spectrum of opinions and tastes. The management of heritage sites within the region involves the typical discordant views and disputes between government bureaucrats, local entrepreneurs, land owners and academics. Indeed, it is not difficult to find scholars or bureaucrats lamenting the ways in which their local environment has been transformed in recent years. The extensive destruction in the name of beautification in readiness for the 2008 Olympics in Beijing and the Shanghai Expo in 2010 provides cases in point. And in Asia, as elsewhere, deciding on the appropriate type and style of site interpretation does not necessarily mean following the popular, or indeed populist, view. In offering this brief overview I do not want to argue that there is an 'Asian way', a perspective that would lead us back to the Asian values debates. Rather, the aim here is to suggest that the rise of the Asian tourist opens up important questions about what constitutes 'best practice' in heritage interpretation. It should not be assumed that the conventions adopted in Europe or North America can continue to be deployed uncritically. Equally, it should also not be assumed that the rise of Asian tourism renders all Western approaches as 'bad' or Eurocentric. Instead, the field of interpretation needs to pursue a path that straddles the polarised positions of universalism and cultural relativism. Adopting such an approach will help us find solutions to the difficult questions about what is 'tasteful', appropriate and successful.

In summary then, the various examples offered over the course of this chapter begin to illustrate why the field of heritage interpretation needs to revisit the concept of 'the tourist'. In focusing on Asia, it has been argued that the rapid changes now occurring in the region raise unfamiliar and challenging questions regarding the heritage tourism interface. The changing situation in Asia suggests if heritage sites are to be successfully and appropriately protected, presented and interpreted, more nuanced, differentiated and culturally sensitive readings of tourism and tourists are now required.

Acknowledgement

The editors would like to thank Taylor and Francis for granting permission for material previously published by Tim Winter in the article 'The modernities of heritage and tourism: interpretations of an Asian future' *Journal of Heritage Tourism*, Vol. 4, No. 2, May 2009, 105–115, within this chapter.

Notes

1   The ascription of oneself as 'traveller' and others as merely 'tourists', for example, speaks much about everyday social hierarchies, the need for expressing individualism, and/or the moral benefits of self-education. Equally, to interpret the aesthetics of tourism is to trace histories of landscape, beauty or nature. The legacy of *The Picturesque*, for example, can still be seen in the photographic practices of many Western tourists who commonly define some scenes and viewpoints as iconic, while disregarding all around them.
2   The 20 countries listed are as follows – in Asia: China, India, South Korea, Philippines, Indonesia, Malaysia, Thailand, Pakistan, Iran and Saudi Arabia; in Africa: South Africa; in Latin America: Brazil, Argentina, Venezuela, Colombia and Mexico; in Eastern Europe: Turkey, Poland, Ukraine and Russia (Myers and Kent 2004: 16).
3   An example of this hierarchical division can be found in the account presented in the opening chapter of Henri Parmentier's (1959) 'Guide to Angkor'. Dominated by explanations of the Indian pantheon of Hindu deities, little attention is given to other religious forms or aspects of Angkorean history.

References

Agnew, N. and Demas, M. (2002) *Principles for the Conservation of Heritage Sites in China* (English translation of the document issued by China ICOMOS), Los Angeles: Getty Conservation Institute.

Anderson, B. (1991) *Imagined Communities: Reflections on the Origin and Spread of Nationalism*, London: Cornell University Press.

Apsara (2000) *Udaya No.1 April 2000,* Phnom Penh: Dept. of Culture and Monuments, APSARA.

Aung-Thwin, M. (1998) *Myth and History in the Historiography of Early Burma*, Ohio: Ohio University Center for International Studies.

Becker, J. (2004) 'Faking it: Chinese burn their bridges with the past', *The Independent* 2 April, 20–21.

Blackburn, K. (2006) 'Representing Singapore's "Little Japan" in heritage and tourism', Paper presented at *'Of Asian Origin': Rethinking Tourism in Contemporary Asia*, 7–9 September, National University of Singapore, Singapore.

Chan, Y-W. (2008) 'The emergence of non-Western tourism: Chinese tourists in Hong Kong, Singapore and Vietnam', in T. Winter, P. Teo and T.C. Chang (eds) *Asia on Tour: Exploring the Rise of Asian Tourism*, London: Routledge.

Coedès, G. (1968) *Inscriptions du Cambodge, Collection de Textes et Documents sur l'Indochine, 1937–1966, vols. I–VIII,* Paris: EFEO.

du Cros, H. (2007) 'Too much of a good thing? Visitor congestion management issues for popular World Heritage tourist attractions', *Journal of Heritage Tourism* 2(3): 225–38.

Dumarçay, J. and Groslier, B.P. (1973) *Le Bayon*, EFEO *Mémoires Archéologiques, III-2,* Paris: EFEO.

Edwards, P. (2005) 'Taj Angkor: Enshrining L'Inde in le Cambodge', in K. Robson, and J. Yee (eds) *France and "Indochina"; Cultural Representations*, Lanham: Lexington Books.

Edwards, P. (2007) *Cambodge: the Cultivation of a Nation 1860–1945*, Honolulu: University of Hawaii Press.

Hobsbawm, E. (1983) 'Introduction: inventing traditions', in E. Hobsbawn and T. Ranger (eds) *The Invention of Tradition*, New York: Cambridge University Press.

Hosagrahar, J. (2005) *Indigenous Modernities: Negotiating Architecture and Urbanism*, London: Routledge.

Ito, N. (1995) ' "Authenticity" inherent in cultural heritage in Asia and Japan', in L.E. Larson (ed.) *Nara Conference on Authenticity,* Japan: UNESCO World Heritage Affairs/Agency for Cultural Affairs Japan.

Myers, N. and Kent, J. 2004, *The New Consumers: The Influence of Affluence on the Environment*, Washington: Island Press.

Nyíri, P. (2006) *Scenic Spots: Chinese Tourism, the State, and Cultural Authority*, Washington: University of Washington Press.

Parmentier, H. (1959) *Henri Parmentier's Guide to Angkor*, Phnom Penh: E.K.L.I.P.

Ross, K. (2006) 'Re/visiting the Nanjing massacre', Paper presented at *"Of Asian Origin": Rethinking Tourism in Contemporary Asia*, 7–9 September, National University of Singapore, Singapore.

Said, E. (1995) *Orientalism*, Harmondsworth: Penguin.

Sullivan, S. (2005) 'Loving the ancient in Australia and China', in J. Lydon and T.

Ireland (eds) *Object Lessons: Archaeology and Heritage in Australia*, Melbourne: Australian Scholarly Publishing.

Thirumaran, K. (2008) 'Renewing bonds in an age of Asian travel: Indian tourists in Bali', in T. Winter, P. Teo and T.C. Chang (eds) *Asia on Tour: Exploring the Rise of Asian Tourism*, London: Routledge.

Thompson, A. (2004) 'Pilgrims to Angkor: a Buddhist "Cosmopolis" in South East Asia?', *Bulletin of the Students of the Department of Archaeology*, (3 July): 88–119.

Winter, T. (2007) *Post-Conflict Heritage, Postcolonial Tourism: Culture, Politics and Development at Angkor*, London: Routledge.

Winter, T. (2008) '"Of Asian destination": rethinking material culture', in T. Winter, P. Teo and T.C. Chang (eds) *Asia on Tour: Exploring the Rise of Asian Tourism*, London: Routledge.

Winter, T. and Daly, P. (2012) 'Heritage in Asia: converging forces, conflicting values', in T. Winter and P. Daly (eds) *The Routledge Handbook on Heritage in Asia*, London: Routledge.

Chapter 10

Heritage for sale

Indigenous tourism and misrepresentations of voice in northern Chile

Juan Francisco Salazar and Robyn Bushell

Introduction

Tiny San Pedro de Atacama is a precordillera oasis village turned into a tourist boomtown, and is also the gringo gathering point of northern Chile. Its popularity stems from its position in the heart of some of northern Chile's most spectacular scenery. A short drive away lies the country's largest salt flat, spotted pink with flamingos and its edges crinkled by volcanoes. Here too are fields of steaming geysers, a host of otherworldly rock formations and weird layer-cake landscapes. San Pedro itself seems hardly big enough to absorb the hordes of travellers that arrive; it's little more than a handful of picturesque adobe streets clustering around a pretty tree-lined plaza and postcard-perfect church. However the last decade has seen a proliferation of guest-houses, restaurants, internet cafés and tour agencies wedging their way into its dusty streets, and turning the town into a kind of highland adobe-land. And sure enough, San Pedro suffers from the classic draw-backs of any tourist honey pot: high costs, irritating restaurant touts and lackadaisical tour agencies. However, the town has an addictively relaxed atmosphere and an enormous array of tours that can hook travellers for weeks. And at the end of every trip, there's the comfort of a creamy cappuccino, a posh meal and a soft bed waiting in San Pedro.
(*Lonely Planet Chile and Easter Island*, McCarthy *et al.* 2009)

One of the major sources of information for international travellers to San Pedro de Atacama is the *Lonely Planet* guide which, as this quote suggests, describes something more akin to a theme park than a place of a vibrant living Indigenous culture. The heritage of the area is often overlooked, and the voices of the Atacameño or Lickanantay Indigenous peoples frequently rendered silent (Bushell and Salazar 2009) in the presentation to visitors.[1] Rather, San Pedro de Atacama, a small town in the Atacama Desert of northern Chile, 1,670 kilometres north of Santiago, is commonly portrayed as a geological marvel and magnificent pre-Columbian archaeological site.

Settlements such as the village of Tulor that date back 2,500 years are often used to promote San Pedro as the 'archaeological capital' of Chile. Besides the rich archaeological heritage of San Pedro some of the main activities promoted to tourists include trekking, climbing, tours to natural landscapes, adventure and extreme sports. Little attention is given to the opportunity to have a meaningful exchange with Atacameñian communities who welcome visitors and offer homestays.

A reciprocity between heritage tourism and the loss of Indigenous identity and cultural control continues due in part to a policy vacuum. In this chapter we explore lost opportunities at several levels: for the Indigenous community; for heritage tourism to the region and country and for the visitor. We also consider ways in which cultural signifiers such as the 'Atacameño brand' are appropriated and at the same time Indigenous place names replaced.

(Mis)representation through tourism in San Pedro de Atacama

Extracted from Wikipedia (2012) under the heading of 'Tourism', the following is typical of the content of many websites about San Pedro de Atacama, including those of the local government and the national tourism authority:

There are various activities for tourists and adventurers...

- R.P. Gustavo Le Paige Archaelogical Museum, displaying ceramics and pottery crafts from the first inhabitants of the area.
- Church of San Pedro, a national monument, built with adobe, a building material used in colonial times.
- El Tatio, a geyser field with over 80 active geysers.
- Salar de Atacama, a giant salt area in the middle of the Atacama Desert.
- Chaxas Lagoon, part of Los Flamencos National Reserve in the Salar de Atacama, inhabited by pink flamingo.
- Pukara de Quitor, a fortification built by the Atacameño people in the 12th century
- Puritama hot springs
- Laguna Miscanti and Laguna Miniques, two neighbouring altiplanic lagoons at the altitude of 4,200 m.
- Licancabur, a notable volcano near San Pedro de Atacama.
- Valle de la Muerte (Death Valley) where gigantic dunes and rocks abound.
- Valle de la Luna (Valley of the Moon) a moon-like landscape with ruins of old Chilean salt mines and workers huts.
- Llano de Chajnantor Observatory, a radio telescope site home of ALMA the Atacama Large Millimeter Array.

Notably, this representation of place and its 'attractions' is bereft of reference to the Atacameño people, or any allusion to Atacameños as a thriving, living community. The only reference is to a fort 'built in the 12th century'.

The past 15 years or so has witnessed a significant growth in tourism in San Pedro de Atacama. The name refers to both the local government area (*comuna*) made up of 14 communities (*ayllus*) as well as the town of San Pedro de Atacama (see Figure 10.1). It has a population (2002 Census) of 4,969 permanent residents (around 55 per cent Indigenous) that has grown rapidly from 2,829 (1992 Census) due mostly to immigration for employment, initially in mining, but these days mostly in tourism (Meyer and Gonzalez 2008). This growth in the local population is dwarfed by the more than 120,000 international visitors who travel each year to San Pedro and other sites of the Salar de Atacama area, and Antofagasta region

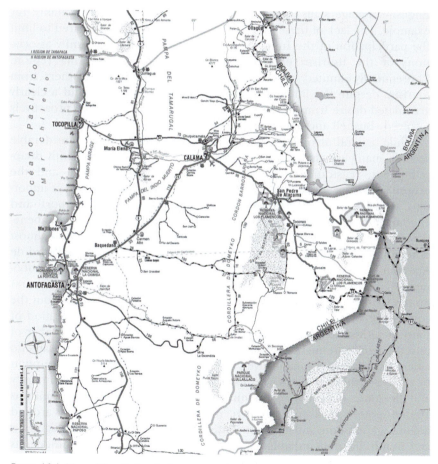

Figure 10.1 Map of San Pedro de Atacama region
Source: www.turistel.cl

(SERNATUR 2010).[2] The growth has accelerated predominantly in the last 5 years, with San Pedro de Atacama now ranked as the second most important tourism destination within Chile in terms of international visitor numbers, after Patagonia (Torres del Paine National Park) and now ahead of Easter Island (ARDP 2008a, 2008b; SERNATUR 2010). Until very recently, tourism development has been largely unregulated and, in particular, lacking any specific policies in relation to the socio-cultural or economic rights and needs of local Atacameño peoples. This includes their appropriate and ethical role in the planning and policy development for tourism, given its reliance on and integration with their control over cultural heritage.

This absence of a clear heritage and/or tourism policy framework during a phase of rapid economic development has been compounded by a lack of investment or financial acumen, business or management experience among the Indigenous community. Few Atacameño people have English-language skills or formal training in tourism and hospitality, for example. The lack of these important competencies has conspired to limit the participation of the Indigenous people and their community associations in the tourism enterprises of the Salar de Atacama region. Consequently, limited revenue returns to the traditional owners from tourism, despite the impressive growth in visitor numbers, and a clearly articulated desire from the local Indigenous associations to be proactively involved (Bushell and Salazar 2009).

While a handful of Indigenous enterprises are enjoying considerable success, many are struggling, leaving numerous communities with disappointment, frustrations, loss of confidence and enthusiasm and the eruption of internal tensions. And, while the growth in tourism is important to the regional economy, receiving government support and encouragement, it is non-Indigenous tourism operators who are the beneficiaries. As noted earlier, this period has seen the local population almost double in order to capitalise on the potential of tourism in San Pedro de Atacama. As the *Lonely Planet* and Wikipedia extracts imply, and corroborated by fieldwork, the influx of visitors (most especially domestic visitors) do not visit San Pedro with an intention or expectation to learn about the contemporary Indigenous community. Subsequently, the proliferation of tourism without particular regard for these peoples has had a number of unintended consequences. Social matters of concern to the Atacameño elders include unacceptable levels of noise, drug and alcohol consumption by visitors within the main centres in townships, affecting the community and its sense of wellbeing in numerous ways. Unequal opportunity is another potent social concern. Perceived inequities create tensions around income generation and the distribution of benefits between Indigenous and non-Indigenous inhabitants as well as within and among Indigenous groups. These challenges featured prominently among concerns raised by community members during a series of workshops conducted to investigate the potential of heritage tourism to support the Atacameño/Lickanantay people.

Each social issue is important and worthy of detailed attention. For the purposes of this chapter, we focus on the appropriation of identity and the silencing of the Indigenous voice that is perpetuated, ironically, through 'heritage tourism'. To the visitor, all tours and the guides, all souvenirs and products, are 'authentic' if they carry the Atacameño nomenclature. Silverman (2005) describes 'nomenclatural borrowing' in Peru, a wide-spread phenomenon in tourism. The appropriation of cultural signifiers in San Pedro de Atacama and the sanctioned appropriation of the Atacameño 'brand' by various levels of government is alarmingly commonplace, deserving interrogation.

To introduce the social milieu, this chapter engages with contemporary Latin American post-colonial and Indigenous writings to contextualise heritage tourism in relation to the radical emergence of Indigenous politics across the continent since the early 1990s. The advent of new ethnic formations is occurring in Chile in response to the loss of cultural control, agency and rights over heritage. This is a reaction not only to unregulated tourism, but also to a number of industrial/commercial enterprises including mining, which has long been the economic and political powerhouse of the region and nation.

Tourism is a relatively new layer of contestation within Indigenous struggles for self-determination, cultural autonomy and political rights, and one that frequently polarises debate. On the one hand, it is regarded as yet another tool of colonisation, dispossession or subjugation of Indigenous peoples. On the other hand, tourism is often idealised and promoted as a vehicle for new opportunities for Indigenous community and socio-economic development. Development is, however, an inherently unstable and fluid entity, necessarily grounded in local contexts and knowledges. While development may be regarded as a step towards self-determination (Salazar 2009), in most cases it continues to operate as a construction grounded in Western idealism and analytical thought. As Mosse (2005) poignantly demonstrates through his analysis of international aid, development works to maintain itself as a system of representations as much as an operational system, and mostly serves to produce particular policy models and authoritative views. Here, we argue that the tourism practices of Lickanantay Indigenous associations emerging in the last five years can be regarded as performative acts of ethnic citizenship, that is, as sites of resistance and cultural expression that serve to legitimise Indigenous views about the cultural and environmental heritage of the area.

Incipient examples exist of relatively successful Indigenous tourism enterprises in many Latin American countries. Relevant examples include the Achuar in Ecuador or the Kuna in Panama. Yet, despite an increased demand for Indigenous tourism globally within the broad growth of heritage-based tourism, in most cases Indigenous peoples continue to be marginalised and confront countless barriers to becoming active participants in tourism development. Underlying this disadvantage is the vicious cycle of poverty, which excludes many people, including Indigenous peoples, from available opportunities in education, health and productive development (Bushell and Powis 2009), consequently jeopardising their cultural wealth (Ashley, Boyd and Goodwin 2000; Ashley, Goodwin and Roe 2001) as well as natural justice and access to vital environmental resources. Pro-poor tourism (Ashley, Boyd and Goodwin 2000) – centred on local cultures – is intended to allow people in circumstances of poverty to improve their quality of life through tourism, opening up opportunities, encouraging their participation and proactively tilting tourism developments towards their benefit. It can also enable the generation of wealth, not only in terms of monetary gain but also the achievement and fulfilment of social, cultural and spiritual aspirations and, via this opportunity, it can enable generations to derive a decent income from tourism and the many affiliated activities arising within communities. In turn, tourism can stimulate contemporary cultural expression (Trau and Bushell 2008). The Paris Declaration of the International Council on Monuments and Sites (ICOMOS) (2011) acknowledges the legitimate and important role of heritage as a driver of development.

Despite the potential, in places where inequitable development models operate and/or where development strategies are not well designed and managed, tourism as an economic activity has been a catalyst for cultural disintegration and, through the degradation and contamination of ecosystems, has contributed to the loss of biodiversity and damage to natural systems and resources. Likewise tourism has been shown to actually generate greater levels of entrenched poverty by displacing agricultural lands, reducing access to potable water and energy resources and diverting community resources from basics to tourism infrastructure (Bushell 2008; Figgis and Bushell 2007; Fisher *et al.* 2008). In such cases, often associated with a lack of adequate administration and planning, tourism also generates poorly paid or unappealing employment opportunities for Indigenous peoples, especially for those lacking formal education and /or commercial or managerial experience. Such scenarios do little to stimulate confidence or interest in younger generations for whom tourism may represent one of the main employment options in increasingly service-led economies. Our workshops and interviews in San Pedro de Atacama confirmed that among high school-aged Atacameñian students, despite witnessing the growth of tourism around their everyday lives, it is not regarded a desirable employment prospect. Most cited personal experience of parents working long hours in unskilled positions for very low salaries, with few prospects for workplace advancement – despite the prosperity of others who own the tourism businesses.

Lead international agencies concerned with the preservation of cultural and natural heritages (including United Nations Educational, Scientific and Cultural Organization [UNESCO], United Nations Environment Programme [UNEP], the UN World Tourism Organization [UNWTO]), together with various non-governmental organisations (NGOs) committed to conservation (for example the Global Heritage Fund, The Nature Conservancy, The Rainforest Alliance), and other international organisations such as the World Bank, have developed a range of financing systems to support local Indigenous groups develop tourism projects in heritage sites. As more people travel to remote places in search of unique high-quality experiences, seeking unspoilt environments and places, heritage tourism generates good returns to those capable of providing a quality destination and exceptional visitor experience: a diversity of offerings, good attractions, a variety of styles and levels of accommodation, very good standards of service, engaging interpretations and stories around the heritages and histories of the place. There is, it seems, adequate demand and potential but the barriers persist. Readiness of the local people, local policies and the attitudes and intentions of others involved in tourism in an area are all tangibly important to the success or otherwise of heritage tourism.

Indigenous heritage tourism in northern Chile has received very little attention in international tourism studies, with no empirical studies published explicitly examining the role of heritage tourism in promoting economic development or cultural empowerment. Unlike other Latin American countries, Indigenous tourism in Chile is relatively underdeveloped, despite a significant increase in interest from Chilean government agencies, NGOs and tourism business associations identifying opportunities. Since 2000 a more cohesive national tourism policy has been developed. This is supported by a series of strategic reports with the overall aim to reposition Chile as a world-class destination and to put in place regulatory frameworks to ensure enhanced tourism service delivery and products (Bushell and Salazar 2009). However, the emphasis is firmly on improving the perceived visitor experience and the competitiveness of Chile as a destination, rather than on social outcomes of tourism development. In spite of this concentration of effort, there remains a weak public policy environment in relation to Indigenous tourism.

We are interested in the processes of misrepresentation that proliferate as opportunities in tourism grow due to this policy gap, and that enables heritage tourism to continue irrespective of the lack of engagement with Indigenous communities or appropriate capacity building to encourage Indigenous-led tourism enterprises. The analysis is grounded in research conducted in 2008 and 2009 that included participant-observation based fieldwork, interviews and focus groups with local Atacameñian communities, Indigenous Associations, local, regional and national government bodies and non-Indigenous tourism businesses in San Pedro de Atacama. Through this we explore the processes of appropriation of Indigenous heritage by non-local entrepreneurs and critically examine how the promotion of the San Pedro de Atacama natural and archaeological 'attractions' render the living Lickanantay culture almost invisible and voiceless to the visitor.

Heritage tourism in the context of the emergence of Indigenous social movements

Among the most impressive and radical transformations in Latin America since the 1990s is the emergence and political positioning of diverse Indigenous social movements. These movements are not precisely 'new' as Indigenous resistance movements in Latin America can be traced back to the eighteenth century and earlier (Bengoa 2000). Rather, these movements convey a resurgence of a latent ethnic political consciousness, which today takes place under a very different context: an advanced stage of capitalist globalisation, co-occurring with emerging neo-socialist movements and the formation of new neo-liberal democracies and deregulatory policy reforms that, in the case of Chile, also takes place concurrently with contested post-dictatorship democratisation processes.

In this context of expanded globalisation, Indigenous social movements began resurging strongly in Latin America after the 'commemoration' in 1992 of the quincentenary of the European 'discovery' of the Americas. The most important and paradigmatic uprising is the Zapatista insurrection in Chiapas, Mexico, in early 1994 (Bengoa 2000). Since the early 1990s several countries including Mexico, Peru, Guatemala, Colombia and Bolivia have formally acknowledged the multicultural base of their societies in their national constitutions in line with a number of other nations around the world (i.e. Norway, Denmark, New Zealand) that have begun 'to support the unconditional right of self-determination of Indigenous peoples and have called it a precondition for the full realization of their human rights' (Muehlebach 2003: 249). Two decades of sustained social mobilisation by Indigenous organisations demonstrate the strength of the insurrection of subjugated Indigenous knowledges and the eruption of Indigenous discourses that challenge not only centuries of imposed silence and racist denial, but also the core underlying principles of citizenship in Latin America (Bengoa 2000; Salazar 2011) which takes place 'both within the realm of Afro and Indigenous community-based struggles, and within the frame of State constitutions, rights, and politics' (Walsh 2011: 51). In Chile, Indigenous movements have been very active since the 1990s (particularly Indigenous Mapuche mobilisations in the south of the country and to a lesser extent Rapa Nui people in Easter Island). In most cases these movements have been severely and violently disavowed by successive governments since at least 1994. In fact, Chile was one of the last countries in Latin America to sign Convention 169 of the International Labour Organization (1989) in 2009, 20 years after the Convention was drafted.

The first point we want to make is that this emergence of Indigenous social movements in Latin America after 1992 is an important factor to consider in any critical examination of Indigenous heritage tourism in the region, and particularly in northern Chile, as it connects directly with current struggles for cultural self-determination. Self-determination involves a substantive transfer of decision-making power from government to Indigenous peoples in the management of cultural assets. This by definition should include tourism, most particularly any destination marketed primarily for its heritage values. Indigenous tourism should ethically involve a complex process of decolonising tourism practices and knowledges, with care taken to understand how critical historical relations of power and knowledge production have and do shape tourism practices and how, importantly, these could be reshaped based on principles of Indigenous self-determination. These principles are outlined in the United Nations Declaration on the Rights of Indigenous Peoples (2007), which require that Indigenous peoples have 'Free, Prior and Informed Consent' of any actions that may affect their wellbeing, and makes clear that this principle applies to enterprises of Indigenous self-managed tourism enterprises. As Linda Tuhiwai Smith (1999) articulates, self-determination is not just a political goal, it is a goal of social justice. Do these principles inform heritage tourism that is not Indigenous self-managed? In the case of San Pedro de Atacama, sadly there is little evidence of awareness or concern for these matters. Indigenous tourism is intricately linked to questions of human rights and Indigenous rights, which include intellectual, cultural and environmental rights. Johnston (2003) argues that self-determination is vital in the exercise of Indigenous rights in tourism, particularly in contexts where Indigenous communities are vulnerable to 'market-driven tourism, losing access to their customary lands and resources, their right to religious freedom at sacred sites, and as a result, their capacity for self-sufficiency' and/or facing a process of 'accelerated voyeurism' (Johnston 2003: 116–17). However, tourism also presents itself as an opportunity to strengthen self-management and leadership within Indigenous communities (Castro and Llancaleo 2003). Despite the inherent complexities of Indigenous tourism, it is possible to observe in recent years an increasing process of insertion in tourism practices and business by Indigenous peoples and nations in Latin America. These must be taken into consideration in relation to the possibilities opened up by tourism to exercise control over natural and cultural assets (both tangible and intangible) assets, acting against the often predatory and exploitative activities of national and transnational corporations.

As mentioned previously, the San Pedro de Atacama Basin region attracts the second largest number of international visitors in Chile, after Patagonia. While there have been no published studies to indicate visitors' experiences in these places or the values and motivating interests of international visitors,[3] our preliminary research suggests most of the visitors (especially domestic Chilean tourists) are not a new kind of 'politicized tourist' (Coronado 2008) who visits, for example, the southern region of Chiapas in Mexico, 'attracted by the [Zapatista] Indigenous movement and its relevance as a global social movement' and where as a response, Indigenous and non-Indigenous tourist agents generate 'new strategies for economic recovery, including changes in the organizational networks and marketing symbols and ideologies as commodities' (Coronado 2008: 53). Rather, like Ed Bruner's (2005) experiences in Indonesia, we found visitors occupied in touristic presentation, rather than engaging reflexively with contemporary cultural expressions. This meaning making opportunity has perhaps been inadvertently denied, and it is to the detriment of all.

The second point we make is that the resurgence of Indigenous and Afro-descendant activist politics in the early 1990s points to a reinvigorated interest in 'decolonial thinking' (Castro-Gomez and Grosfoguel 2007; Mignolo 2000; Quijano 2003) across Latin American social research circles and among Latin American scholars in the United States. Broadly defined, with roots in the work of Amílcar Cabral, Aimé Césaire and Frantz Fanon in the 1960s, the new embodiment of a decolonial sensibility is an attempt to rethink critical theory at a moment in time when what takes place is 'a number of global and pluriversal revolutions anchored in local stories that during the past 500 years could not avoid contact, conflict and complicity with the West' (Mignolo 2000: 25). Besides this decolonial thinking within Latin American academics and scholars, there has been an important emergence of Indigenous intellectuals that Zapata regards as:

> Indigenous subjects whose intellectual production revolves around the commitment to their original cultural groups that recognize the weight of the historical circumstances in their work and are constituted as intellectuals around them. A complex subject in social and cultural terms, that nevertheless opted at a moment in time for an ethnic identity and a historical project of liberation to which expects to contribute from writing.
>
> (2008: 116)

This positioning resonates with Maori critical decolonial thinking, also strongly emerging around the same time (Smith 1999). As an epistemic turn, decolonial thinking in Latin America – as in Africa or Aotearoa/New Zealand – has been a reflexive and practical critique of the matrix of colonial power that calls for a detachment from the political project of modernity. In this regard, Indigenous social movements (and other ethnic movements such as the Afro-Colombian) are an important analytical key to understanding the current crisis in the idea of the modern nation–state in Latin America. This is particularly relevant for in Indigenous tourism as it is the ancestral cosmologies and future life-visions (Walsh 2011) of Indigenous peoples that are increasingly made visible/invisible through tourism infrastructures.

As discussed in the following sections, visitors to San Pedro de Atacama and surrounding satellite towns and villages are attracted and encouraged to visit the region because of the spectacle of a unique natural landscape and a number of important archaeological sites. The ways in which both government and the private sector promote the region and its attractions results in rendering the Lickanantay culture invisible through complex processes of appropriation and misrepresentation. Despite some innovative projects being undertaken by small community-based organisations in San Pedro de Atacama, tourism has yet to bring about a sense of collective well-being (Bushell and Salazar 2009), and Indigenous Atacameño peoples, with a few exceptions, continue to be presented through the discourse of touristic accounts and tourism information, as subjugated subjects within a colonial biopolitical matrix.

In most cases, and particularly for international tourists, the visitors remain quite ignorant to the fact that they are in Indigenous territories with few opportunities to discern what is 'local', what is imported and what is fabricated. This extends to tours to villages and archaeological remains without permission or the involvement of local people as guides and with no payment of any sort to the local community. 'Local' tour companies on the whole are at best Chilean, but not from San Pedro. Most business owners moving from Santiago as tourism opportunities have flourished, but very few are Indigenous owned or employ Atacameñian people as guides or other frontline staff. Despite this, most businesses deliberately and liberally utilise the 'brand' 'Atacameño' in the naming of their enterprises, leading the undiscerning and ill-informed visitor to 'understand' the guides and products are 'local'. Souvenirs sold in local government-managed craft markets as well as private shops have an indiscernible heritage: most are not local, but imported from Bolivia because of availability and price. The craft markets are not in the service of local people or cultural expression. Foods served in the many cafes are not specifically local. The names of important heritage and sacred sites, such as 'Moon Valley' and 'Death Valley', are recent inventions without permission from the Indigenous peoples whose place names have been replaced on local and national government signs, maps, websites and tourist brochures. The descriptions of place and the sanctioned activities undertaken at these sites are frequently adventure-orientated (such as sandboarding, for example), something quite inappropriate given the fragile ecological values of the place, and quite disrespectful given the important cultural values attached

to these sacred sites. Such practices are in stark contrast to the UN principles of Indigenous self-determination. This style of 'heritage tourism' is not
in the service of local people or intangible heritage. These effects are not
confined to tourism in Chile. ICOMOS (2011: 1) notes the effects of globalisation, manifest in 'the attrition of values, identities and cultural
diversity'. In San Pedro de Atacama this is despite the fact that the local
mayor is herself an Atacameño woman. Again, the current Wikipedia
(2012) entry exemplifies the way the discourse (mis)represents place and
renders the Indigenous people invisible:

> San Pedro de Atacama is a Chilean town and commune in El Loa
> Province, Antofagasta Region. It is located east of Antofagasta, some
> 106 km (60 mi) southeast of Calama and the Chuquicamata copper
> mine, overlooking the Licancabur volcano. It features a significant
> archeological museum, the R. P. Gustavo Le Paige Archaeological
> Museum, with a large collection *of relics and artifacts* from the region.
> *Native ruins* nearby now attract increasing numbers of tourists inter-
> ested in learning about *pre-Columbian cultures*. Tourists also visit for
> other popular activities including sandboarding and stargazing, with
> the views of the stars from the Atacama unrivalled across the continent.
> (emphasis added)

This erasure of the Indigenous people as a living culture makes a respectful or reflexive understandings very difficult for visitors. The official
government website 'This is Chile' (Government of Chile 2012) is equally
dismissive and insensitive to Atacameñian heritage and culture, entirely
missing the opportunity proffered by their own national policies to
encourage Indigenous tourism. The website describes San Pedro de
Atacama as 'a picturesque town with a special charm, at the foot of the
Licancabur Volcano, in the middle of the driest desert in the world'. With
a photo of a geyser, it goes on to say:

> 314 kilometers from Antofagasta lies San Pedro, the land of the
> Indigenous Atacameños or kunzas, an ancient culture that developed
> around a fertile oasis. Hundreds of years later, the town is a bustling
> international tourist centre. This desert, the driest in the world,
> contains numerous attractions that have turned San Pedro town into a
> hot spot for travelers from all over the world. On its dirt streets one can
> see hundreds of tourists with a mix of languages and experiences from
> the various journeys that can be taken through the desert geography.
> San Pedro de Atacama offers a large variety of places to stay, from
> budget rooms to sophisticated boutique hotels. The variety of restau-
> rants allows for choosing between various options, from small inns with
> typical Chilean cuisine to fusion restaurants on Caracoles Street. At

night it is also the place to relax with a drink or eat a meal of Patasca, which is prepared with peeled corn, beef or lamb and a stew. San Pedro de Atacama is also well known for its nightlife.

This national government website perpetuates a 'party town' image, which is the antithesis of that desired by Indigenous peoples. Yet, similarly to the other websites already mentioned, 'This is Chile' portrays the Atacameño as an 'ancient culture' with only the faintest hint of a living culture:

> This road, the main street of San Pedro, is the starting point for those looking for tours of the diverse sectors of the area. There are several tourist offices, bicycle and sandboard rental stations, and the international milieu blends with the Atacameño community. The community itself takes on the task of safeguarding their own natural and architectural wealth. A visit to the Church of San Pedro is a must. Although it has required various repairs, its walls date back to 1744, and ever since, it has been the center for the main festivities. The Museum of Father Le Paige is another important spot, where you can learn more about the rich heritage of the 'Acameños', the pre-Columbian culture.

Erasures such as the use of non-Atacameñian naming of significant places and attractions, and the many levels of misrepresentation, pose serious challenges for future developments of heritage and Indigenous tourism in the area, particularly in a region with a fragility of complex social and political relationships. This fragility is partly explained by the fact that this is one of the driest places on earth (and hence significant factors around water scarcity), and some of the world's richest deposits of minerals (copper, lithium, iodine) have led to a century of extensive mining activities in the region. The mining sector contributes 15.2 per cent of the total gross domestic product (GDP) of the country (Central Bank of Chile 2011: 34) and brings considerable wealth to the government (through royalty laws) and private corporations, but imposes on local peoples in many ways, not least through the excessive consumption of water resources, a major concern that has been disregarded.

These erasures and enduring fragilities pose a threat to the viability of the tourism enterprise as a whole. While sadly, the Indigenous people themselves can be, and are, frequently ignored by government agencies and the tourism industry, the international visitor may be able to demand greater respect. Heritage tourism is regarded a higher yielding proposition compared to the 'mass' alternatives, due to a willingness by these visitors to stay longer in places offering significant attractions and a propensity to pay more for high-quality experiences. The heritage market is, perhaps, better informed and becoming more discerning, expecting not only that the experiences and products sold will be 'local' and have strong local content, but that the tourism in such places would support heritage conservation and local-community development. In an era of visitor-authored critiques via social networking tourism websites, any dissatisfaction with a place is readily broadcast far and wide. Ethical travel companies and tourism investors may in the future be reluctant to be involved in bringing their visitors to places where the heritages of a place are exploited and/or visitors are expressing dissatisfaction. To successfully market a heritage destination in the long term requires conscientious effort to ensure the custodians of the heritages presented are themselves appropriately involved, as well as the protection of the fabric of place.

Performing heritage as acts of ethnic citizenship

According to the national tourism body, SERNATUR (2010), 2.7 million tourists visited Chile in 2010, with some 700,000 from outside South America. The Chilean tourism industry to date has focused on its natural attractions, with a total of 95 Wildlife Protected Areas (comprising 32 national parks, 48 national reserves and 15 natural heritage sites) covering almost 14 million hectares or 19 per cent of the country's area. The contribution of tourism to the national GDP in Chile was around 3.5 per cent, an average figure by world standards.

In recent years, sustainable community tourism projects have began to emerge, particularly in Indigenous Development Areas such as La Araucanía, Tarapacá, Antofagasta, Rapa Nui and San Pedro de Atacama. Considering that almost 40 per cent of all international visitors to San Pedro de Atacama are younger than 35 years of age and 55 per cent are from Europe, it might be expected that information and communication technologies would play a pivotal role in visitor information and the planning of their travel. Despite a relatively ample range of online sites promoting San Pedro de Atacama to inform visitors of the wide range of attractions, most are in Spanish, few offering any information in English. These online sites range from official websites promoting the main tourist attractions (government sites such as those already cited), private businesses and increasing numbers of websites by small Indigenous tour operators offering a Lickanantay perspective. This is an unexplored area of study, which may shed light on the relative importance of the use of web-based information, such as social media, web mapping service applications like Google Maps or Google Places, or mashups and smartphone applications for international tourists. Given the fact that there is relatively poor information available, Web 2.0 has an important role to play in informing international visitors to San Pedro de Atacama, providing Indigenous community and operators with considerable agency to address the shortcomings of tourism policies and practices.

According to a study by SERNATUR (2010) on international visitors profiles, 55 per cent of international visitors inform themselves about San Pedro de Atacama through the internet, significantly above the 22 per cent who reportedly do so through specialised travel literature, and 20 per cent who are informed through travel agencies. Interestingly, 34 per cent of international visitors surveyed indicated their source of information prior to the visit was direct information from friends or relatives who had previously visited the area. During a fieldwork trip in 2009 we also noted that international tourists rely on online information about the area. We observed, for example, a German couple in our hotel reviewing user-uploaded images and videos of nearby attractions and places to visit in Google Maps. Of particular interest was a 10-minute video on Google Maps produced by other German tourists where an Atacameño man explained the traditional way of building a house. The question that arises is to what degree do sites like Google Maps and Google Places provide the potential to provide a different perspective about San Pedro de Atacama and surrounding satellite communities? Moreover, considering that presently there is a relatively low penetration of Web 2.0 technologies and applications on tourism enterprise websites in San Pedro de Atacama, there exists a potential for developing a culturally appropriate perspective of the Atacama area, given the ease with which visual information can be uploaded and shared. Many of the local tourism enterprises, especially Indigenous ones, are in the early stages of applying Web 2.0 concepts to the way they engage with visitors. With enhanced skills and experience this technology offers a very potent mode of communication.

The development of information communication technologies (ICTs) and the various associated forms of social networking media add an additional layer to the already complex forms in which heritage is performed. This is particularly so with the attractions and villages in the region where Indigenous knowledges are yet to be appropriately and significantly incorporated into the repertoire of visitor's information available for San Pedro de Atacama. This is important, as knowledge can be a participative and transformational social process performed actively through bodies, discourses, images and things. Problematically though, whether in brochures, videos or online, Indigenous epistemologies continue to be misrepresented, silenced and invisible in northern Chile. This is deserving of attention, as the performance of heritage is crucial not only to foster Indigenous representation but to understand Indigenous social participation and embodied forms of ethnic citizenship. As Denzin (2003) implies, the performative can be seen as a way of being, as a way of knowing and as a way of being political. The performative is where the soul of the culture resides. The performative haunts the liminal spaces of culture (Denzin 2003; Salazar 2009) and while culture may always be intertwined with (and not just derived from) the processes of political economy, heritage tourism can not be understood outside the world system of global capitalism or without consideration of the way racial discourses organise the world's population in an international division of labour that has direct economic implications. In San Pedro de Atacama, new initiatives to develop community Indigenous tourism or so-called *special interest tourism* (as opposed to a 'mass' tourism) implicitly incriminates the fact that Lickanantay people perform the most coerced and worse remunerated labour: from handicrafts, to hotel cleaners, occasionally tourist guides, but seldom hotel manager or policymakers. In order to achieve appropriate benefits, significant capacity building and reimagining the role of Atacameño people in this enterprise is essential.

It is also necessary to note that until the 1992 National Population Census, Lickanantay or Atacameño people were not distinguished as a distinct Indigenous nation. Since then, Indigenous peoples in Atacama have engaged in processes of 'ethnogenesis' or 'self-ethnification', concepts that have received wide, critical and contrasting views from Latin American scholars (Bengoa 2000). As processes for articulating a reinvented rather than imagined community, Indigenous people have made use of official population statistics in their self-representation as peoples, and this is an important matter in San Pedro de Atacama. Reinvented communities are not based on fictional accounts. They require a credible narrative with at least a partial grounding in traditions, documents and collective memories, implying that a community can begin to recognise itself from a reconstruction and reinvention of the past, the present and the future. Tourism in San Pedro de Atacama has the potential to be a foundational element in the processes of re-ethnification of Lickanantay people (see Figures 10.2a and 10.2b).

The processes of ethnic reinvention flow in varied forms, from Indigenous communities and leaders as well as from governments and local bureaucrats. A major initiative for Indigenous tourism development in the Atacama Development Area of El Loa was undertaken in the late 1990s and early 2000s by the regional government (CONADI 2006). Titled *Programa Orígenes* (Origins Program), one of its primary objectives was to revitalise local traditions through processes of folklorisation, which in some instances did not coincide with the cultural dynamics within the communities (Morawietz 2008). Carried out as an initiative of the Chilean Government and financed through the Inter-American Development Bank, *Programa Orígenes* is an example of what Bascopé calls the 'multiculturalist machine' to refer to the 'indigenist' policies that mark the 'last escalation of the liberal techniques of government in post-dictatorship Chile' (2009: 27). For Morawietz, *Programa Orígenes* converges with the 'fiction of the folklorised ethnicity, of participation and authenticity that tourism pursues' (2008: 6).

While the large majority of commercial and tourist establishments in San Pedro de Atacama exhibit symbols and products that overtly rely on the

Figure 10.2 a & b The black flag protest in San Pedro de Atacama represents ongoing frustration by Indigenous and non-Indigenous community members at failure of government to take action on matters of significance to the Indigenous community
Photo: Robyn Bushell

Atacameño 'label', very few demonstrate any appreciation of the intrinsic value and importance of genuine or ethical respect for Atacameño people and their culture. The Atacameño ventures are, of course, the exception to the rule but most of these have serious visibility problems because of the poor marketing by local and state tourism bodies and the very remote location of many of these emerging enterprises in small villages. There are a few emerging enterprises worth mentioning, such as the Asociación Indígena Valle de la Luna (Moon Valley Indigenous Association), the EcoRed Lickanantay and Terrantai Lodge.[4] Each constitutes a different approach to an Indigenous tourism model for the viability of a high-quality product based on tangible and intangible natural and cultural resources of the area, and represents Atacameño culture in a respectful and holistic way.

These are businesses that, in one way or another, embody relevant values elicited from the communities themselves. Terrantai Lodge is a very successful private enterprise owned by an experienced and well-known non-Atacameño local tourism businessman who is committed to a healthy and very respectful model of high-end tourism. The Asociación Indígena Valle de la Luna is composed of an association of six Atacameño communities of the Atacama basin (Solor, Sequitor, Larache, San Pedro, Coyo and Quitor). They have an associative contract with the Chilean Government (Corporación Nacional Forestal [CONAF]) to co-manage Sector No. 6 of the Flamingos National Reserve, a UNESCO-designated biosphere reserve because of its outstanding cultural and ecological heritage values, and better known worldwide by its invented label 'Moon Valley'. The management model has been in place since 2000, and in 2009 generated approximately US$1 million dollars from 102,356 visitors (CONAF 2011). This association of Indigenous communities has a clear goal of administering the site to promote the protection and conservation of their territories and, in order to achieve this goal, a percentage of the revenue is reinvested in the site. For the association and Indigenous tourism entrepreneurs, tourism is also utilised as a way to recover, highlight and make known their ancient and living culture and as a way to support the economic growth and social development of local communities. Globally, land rights factors are at the heart of the experience of Indigenous tourism and in this San Pedro is no exception. The Asociación Indígena Valle de la Luna initiative is, at the core, a programme of self-determination because it gives partial co-management rights to ancestral territories claimed by the Atacameño people. The Association also functions as an incipient tourism operator, concentrating on a differentiated offer in areas of special interest such as speleology, Indigenous astronomy, Indigenous history and mining history. In similar fashion, EcoRed Lickanantay is an Indigenous Association (as defined in the Indigenous Act of 1993) formally established in 2009 which today consists of 27 partners and community members that offers an Indigenous community tourism experience centred specifically on the Salar de Atacama basin, mainly in the ayllus of Coyo, Solor and Sequitor that surround the town of San Pedro de Atacama and the town of Socaire.

The network grew out of community leaders' concerns that Indigenous peoples were witnessing the growth of a dynamic tourism industry in their territories without their involvement or any concern for socially or environmentally sustainable practices. The network emerged as an attempt to

participate directly in tourism, marketing their own original cultural products, obtaining a profit that provides distribution of revenues among the
community participants and contributing effectively to achieving adequate
living standards for Indigenous communities. As their website indicates,
'we see it as our opportunity to continue developing our traditional activities and keep our culture alive while we improve our standard of living'
(EcoRed Lickan Antay 2012). These businesses should be the focal point of
government promotion if the rhetoric of heritage tourism where genuine.
At present they, and others like them, are not privileged and have to
compete with all others for visibility and business.

A values-based approach

These three initiatives, Valle de la Luna Indigenous Association, the
EcoRed Lickanantay and Terrantai Lodge, demonstrate that tourism
development is as much about quality of life and projection of an
Indigenous life-vision as it is an economic strategy, as much about performing an ancestral heritage and permanently negotiated cultural identity, as
it is about developing new revenue streams for communities. These
Indigenous initiatives show promising engagement with a values-based
approach, grounded in the needs, hopes and aspirations of individuals and
groups (Bushell 2008). Planning for appropriate outcomes demands
sophisticated strategies that are capable of attending to the complex and
dynamic requirements of cultural and generational differences, both ethically and equitably. Because of the extent and speed with which economies
and human populations grow, it often becomes difficult to improve the
quality of life for some people without adversely affecting the values of
others (Prescott-Allen 2001, cited in Bushell 2008).

   In a region like Antofagasta and the San Pedro de Atacama area, this
effect has been dramatically demonstrated by the impact of mining. The
industry is a most important source of employment and prosperity but at
the same time, as noted earlier, it generates serious threats to environmental quality and water availability (RIDES 2005). Hence it represents a major
threat to the towns that are dependent on this economic activity.
Consequently, like tourism, mining too is a double-edged sword; both a
support and a threat to survival. Water availability, air quality and the natural habitat are fundamental to survival in this harsh desert environment. As
the RIDES report states, the problematics of environmental degradation
from mining dramatically bind tourism with economic development and
productive growth. As Blanco (2007) identifies, environmental degradation (such as deforestation, air pollution, water scarcity) continues to be a
cost outsourced by the export sector rather than redressed by these highly
profitable mining companies. And, just as mining is a highly contentious
activity, so too is tourism. For some, particularly Indigenous-community

members, the changes brought about by tourism are the very antithesis of 'progress'. Growth and development are not necessarily productive in the long term, nor are the changes necessarily for the common good. For this reason, tourism planning should ideally be based around shared values elicited through discussions and consensus regarding appropriate strategies that ensure management and monitoring systems that espouse, reflect and support those values. The principles of sustainable development articulated in the RIDES (2005) report *Human Welfare and Sustainable Development in San Pedro de Atacama, Chile* are well aligned with such a position, recognising an unequivocal link between human and ecological wellbeing. Any community-development strategy, be it tourism or any other industry, should be centred on the wellbeing of the local population, especially in such a remote and fragile setting. Competing demands on the water supply system in the most arid desert on the planet, a growing mining industry and population of mining workers, and the water consumption of a very extensive floating population of visitors and tourists have become crucial concerns (RIDES 2005). It not only signifies a serious clash in values regarding long-term-sustainability interests but also exemplifies the loss of control by Indigenous people over their heritages.

The following value statements were collated from many sources, including reports and documents, personal observations, meetings and interviews conducted as part of our research. Shared values were elicited and compiled then validated. The validation process involved workshops with representatives of the Atacameño communities and associations, and others involved in tourism, seeking any feedback or amendments, and some ranking of relative importance. The process corroborated these as being representative of the values important to local people as they related to tourism and their community development. The order, a consensus of those consulted, asserted what was important to the people of San Pedro de Atacama:

1   A desire to keep young people connected to their community and culture.
2   The need for education to improve quality of life and opportunities.
3   Indigenous people must be decision-makers about how their heritage is presented.
4   That Indigenous heritages are centrally important to tourism and must be utilised with respect, not exploited.
5   Concern for the protection of natural resources especially water and energy – no water – no agriculture – no life – no culture.
6   Recognition of Atacameño culture as living and dynamic.
7   Support for innovation and entrepreneurship relating to sustainable and responsible practices.
8   A desire for Indigenous and non-Indigenous people to work collaboratively.

9 Work with and for the community is as important as the individual –
   the Lickanantai custom of Ayllu solidarity.
10 The need for the protection of traditional knowledge and culture.
11 That intangible heritage is a key to uniqueness of place – there is a
   need to revitalize Kunza language using tourism as a means to do so.
12 A desire within the Indigenous communities to proactively care for
   country – through traditional relationship with nature as part of their
   cultural landscape.
13 Recognition of the threats from tourism that need to be managed very
   carefully.
14 That tourism in San Pedro de Atacama region should be high quality
   and high yield, not mass tourism.
15 A desire to ensure small and medium businesses are supported to be
   financially viable.
16 That competitiveness and attractiveness of the destination be improved
   to attract visitors who appreciate and respect the natural and cultural
   heritage.

(Bushell and Salazar 2009)

Many of the people interviewed in the Indigenous communities visited,
conveyed a deep discomfort with and a mistrust of the tourism operators in
San Pedro de Atacama, especially those who employed guides with no
cultural connection to the area or its heritage. These guides possess good
English, French or German language skills, and good tourism experience,
but often little or no knowledge of the history, geology or spirituality of the
area. This is unacceptable to local custodians.

During our study we enquired specifically about the use of local
Indigenous guides among the tour companies. Invariably we were assured
that 'all guides are "local"'. By this they invariably meant Chilean or
Bolivian. Only one tour company, EcoRed Lickan Antay, offered
Atacameñian guides. A number of local guest houses and attractions – also
Indigenous owned or supportive – ran their own tours with Indigenous
guides, but these businesses were not operating as tour companies and did
not have a shopfront in town, so only guests at these particular guest houses
had this opportunity. Likewise the handicrafts available were a confusing
mix of local and imported goods. Some were 'imported' from other parts
of Chile; some from across the Bolivian border, which provides a reliable
source of mass-produced, cheap 'Andean' souvenirs. The average, unin-
formed tourist is oblivious to the heritage of these goods (handicrafts,
tours, accommodation and cafes) due to the sanctioned trade names (by
local and national government) that create the illusion of being
Atacemeñian. Most tourism operators were quite knowingly exploiting visitor naivety and the brand. We were told quite candidly in a recorded
interview by a prominent entrepreneur from Santiago and a major figure

Figure 10.3 The sanctioned misuse of the Atacameno 'brand'
      Photo: Robyn Bushell

in the local Chamber of Commerce running numerous tourism operations in San Pedro that 'we appropriate in a friendly way the brand and Atacameño culture' (see Figure 10.3).

Strategic opportunities are necessary to allow quality Atacameño services and products to be privileged and stand out above others on offer locally, to provide meaningful employment in a variety of roles, with appropriate training and career progression for Atacameñian people. Heritage tourism should provide respect and voice to the custodians of the heritage that is being offered to others to share. Government agencies need to provide frameworks to ensure integrity in heritage tourism.

Conclusions

To be effective, tourism policy development in Chile requires the formulation of regulations and guidelines to foster and promote quality Indigenous tourism in order to protect the interests of the Indigenous communities. The perceived increasing demand for heritage-based tourism and enthusiasm among Indigenous leaders for involvement in tourism has yet to translate into tangible outcomes for the Atacameño or other Indigenous peoples experiencing similar problems. Like disadvantaged peoples elsewhere, the Indigenous communities need to be afforded respect, voice and the skills required to manage their way of life and appropriate process tools to control such developments. At this stage, it is outsiders who are better prepared and able to capitalise on the advantages that an expanding tourism industry offers.

Despite heritage tourism being performed around the rich natural and Indigenous heritages of the region, the living heritage and voice of the Atacameño peoples are frequently ignored and cultural signifiers such as the 'Atacameño brand' appropriated. The reciprocity between heritage tourism and loss of identity adds to ongoing Indigenous frustrations over control of their cultural heritage.

Notes

1 In this chapter we use the spelling of Lickanantay as used by the Council of Atacameño Peoples (Consejo de Pueblos Atacameños). The Spanish name of Atacameño derives from the name of the inhabitants of Atacama Desert. Lickanantay is the Kunza language word for 'people from the village'. The Atacameño or Lickanantay territory is made up of 26 communities divided in two Indigenous Development Areas (ADIs): El Loa and Atacama la Grande (Greater Atacama). These represent political–territorial dispositions created by the Chilean Government in 1997 to support Indigenous development. San Pedro de Atacama is the municipal capital and main centre of the Atacama La Grande ADI.
2 According to a 2009 survey by the Chilean National Tourism Service 4.5 per cent of the international tourists that visit Chile travel to San Pedro de Atacama and surrounding areas, representing a total of approximately 123,000 tourists. Of these, about 68 per cent come from long-haul markets such as Europe (55.3 per cent) and North America (12.7 per cent) (SERNATUR 2010).
3 An exception is the SERNATUR (2009) study of profile of international visitors, although it is limited in scope.
4 The power of the dominant touristic discourse is evident through the adoption by these Indigenous communities of the now 'common' name Valle de Luna (Moon Valley), rather than traditional place names, so that they are clearly seen to be associated with this site.

References

Agencia Regional de Desarrollo Productivo de Antofagasta (ARDP) (2008a) *Descripción del Cluster de Turismo de Intereses especiales en San Pedro de Atacama, Región de Antofagasta*, Antofagasta: Documento estrategico ARDP.

Agencia Regional de Desarrollo Productivo de Antofagasta (ARDP) (2008b) 'Lanzamiento de Acciones Programa de Mejoramiento de la Competitividad "Destino Desierto de Atacama"', Presentación Pública San Pedro de Atacama, 15 de Octubre de 2008.

Ashley, C., Boyd, C. and Goodwin, H. (2000) *Pro-Poor Tourism: Putting Poverty at the Heart of the Tourism Agenda*, London: Overseas Development Institute.

Ashley, C., Goodwin, H. and Roe, D. (2001) *Pro-Poor Tourism Strategies: Making Tourism Work for the Poor. A Review of the Experience*, Nottingham: Overseas Development Institute.

Bascopé, J. (2009) *La Invasión de la Tradición: Lo Mapuche en Tiempos Culturales*, Guatemala y Santiago de Chile: CoLibris.

Bengoa, J. (2000) *La Emergencia Indígena en América Latina*, Santiago: Fondo de Cultura Económica.

Blanco, H. (2007) *International Trade and Sustainable Tourism in Chile: Preliminary Assessment of the Sustainability of Tourism in Chile in the Context of Current Trade Liberalization*, Winnipeg: International Institute for Sustainable Development (IISD).

Bruner, E.M. (2005) *Culture on Tour: Ethnographies of Travel*, Chicago: University of Chicago Press.

Bushell, R. and Salazar, J.F. (2009) *Indigenous Tourism in San Pedro de Atacama, Chile*, Report on Scoping Study for Fundación Minera Escondida, Antofagasta, Chile, Parramatta: University of Western Sydney.

Bushell, R. (2008) 'Tourism, quality of life and wellness', in R. Bushell and P. Sheldon (eds) *Wellness and Tourism: Mind, Body, Spirit, Place.* New York: Cognizant.

Bushell, R. and Powis, B. (2009) *Healthy Tourism*, Report to ASEAN plus Three Initiaitive on Healthy Travel & Tourism, ASEAN Secretariat.

Castro-Gómez, S. and Grosfoguel, R. (2007) *El Giro Decolonial: Reflexiones Para Una Diversidad Epistémica Más Allá Del Capitalismo Global*, Bogotá: Siglo del Hombre Editores; Universidad Central, Instituto de Estudios Sociales Contemporáneos y Pontificia Universidad Javeriana, Instituto Pensar.

Castro, K. and Llancaleo, P. (2003) 'Turismo: una apuesta al desarrollo de las comunidades Indígenas de Chile', *Programa Integral de Desarrollo Indígena – Orígenes*, Santiago: Ministerio de Planificación y Cooperación.

Coronado, G. (2008) 'Insurgencia y turismo: reflexiones sobre el impacto del turista politizado en Chiapas Pasos', *Revista de Turismo y Patrimonio Cultural* 6(1): 53–68.

Corporación Nacional de Desarrollo Indígena (CONADI) (2006) *Programa Origenes Memoria I Fase 2002–2005*, Region de Antofagasta.

Corporación Nacional Forestal (CONAF) (2011) 'Cuenta Pública 2009–2010', *Reserva Nacional Los Flamencos*. Available online: www.conaf.cl/cms/editorweb/part_ciudadana/cuentas-publicas/CP-RN_Los-Flamencos.pdf (accessed 6 May 2012).

Denzin, N.K. (2003) *Performance Ethnography: Critical Pedagogy and the Politics of Culture*, Thousand Oaks, CA and London: Sage.

Figgis, P. and Bushell, R. (2007) 'Tourism as a tool for community-based conservation and development', in R. Bushell and P.F.J. Eagles (eds) *Tourism and Protected Areas: Benefits Beyond Boundaries*, Wallingford, Cambridge, MA: CABI Publishing.

EcoRed Lickan Antay (n.d.) *Turismo Indígena*. Available online: www.ecoredturismo.com (accessed 6 May 2012).

Fisher R., Maginnis, S., Jackson, W., Barrow, E. and Jeanrenaud, S. (2008) *Linking Conservation and Poverty Reduction: Landscapes, People And Power*, London: Earthscan.

Government of Chile (2012) *This Is Chile*. Available online: www.thisischile.cl/Article.aspx?ID=1371&sec=344&eje=Turismo (accessed 11 April 2012).

ICOMOS (2011) *The Paris Declaration*. Available online: www.international.icomos.org/Paris2011/GA2011_Declaration_de_Paris_EN_2 0120109.pdf (accessed 6 May 2012).

International Labour Organization (2009) *Indigenous & Tribal Peoples' Rights in Practice: A Guide to ILO Convention 169. Programme to Promote ILO Convention No. 169 (PRO 169)*, International Labour Standards Department, ILO.

Johnston, A. (2003) 'Self-determination: exercising Indigenous rights in tourism', in S. Singh, D.J. Timothy and K.R. Rowling (eds) *Tourism in destination Communities*, Wallingford: CABI Publishing.

McCarthy, C., Benchwick, G., Raub, K., Patience, V. and Carillet, J-B. (2009) *Lonely Planet Chile & Easter Island*, Melbourne, Victoria: Lonely Planet.

Meyer, F.A. and Gonzalez, R.M. (2008) *Inside: San Pedro de Atacama*, Santiago: Editorial Chanar.

Mignolo, W. (2000) *Local Histories/Global Designs: Essays on the Coloniality of Power, Subaltern Knowledges and Border Thinking*, Princeton: Princeton University Press.

Morawietz, L. (2008) 'La comunidad como efecto de la comunidad', *Los gobiernos de la Concertación, el Programa Orígenes y las comunidades indígenas de San Pedro de Atacama*, Informe final del concurso: Las deudas abiertas en América Latina y el Caribe. Programa Regional de Becas CLACSO.

Mosse, D. (2005) *Cultivating Development: An Ethnography of Aid Policy and Practice*, London: Pluto Press.

Muehlebach, A. (2003) 'What self in self-determination? Notes from the frontiers of transnational Indigenous activism', *Identities: Global Studies in Culture and Power* 10: 241–68.

Quijano, A. (2003) 'Colonialidad del poder, eurocentrismo y América Latina', in E. Lander (ed.) *La Colonialidad del Saber: Eurocentrismo y Ciencias Sociales. Perspectivas Latinoamericanas*, Buenos Aires: CLACSO.

RIDES Corporacion (2005) *Bienestar Humano y Manejo Sustentable en San Pedro de Atacama, Chile – Resumen Ejecutivo*, Santiago, Chile: RIDES.

Salazar, J.F. (2009) 'Self-determination in practice: the critical making of Indigenous media', *Development in Practice* 19(4): 504–13.

Salazar, J.F. (2011) 'Indigenous media in Latin America', in J.D.H. Downing (ed.) *Encyclopedia of Social Movement Media*, Thousand Oaks CA: Sage.

SERNATUR (2010) *Perfil del Turista Extranjero que Visita San Pedro de Atacama y Valle de la Luna*, Santiago, Chile: Departamento de Planificación, Unidad de Análisis Económico y Estadísticas.

Silverman, H. (2005) 'Embodied heritage: identity politics and tourism', *Anthropology and Humanism* 30(2): 141–55.

Smith, L.T. (1999) *Decolonizing Methodologies: Research and Indigenous Peoples*, Dunedin and Otago: University of Otago Press.

Trau, A. and Bushell, R. (2008) 'Tourism and Indigenous people', in S. McCool and N. Moissey (eds) *Tourism, Recreation and Sustainability*, Wallingford: CABI.

United Nations (2007) *Declaration on the Rights of Indigenous Peoples*, Document N° A/RES/61/295, 10 December, Paris: UN.

Walsh, C. (2011) 'Afro and Indigenous life – visions in/and politics: (de)colonial perspectives in Bolivia and Ecuador', *Bolivian Studies Journal/Revista de Estudios Bolivianos*, 18(1): 49–69.

Wikipedia (2012) *San Pedro de Atacama.* Available online: http://en.wikipedia.org/wiki/San_Pedro_de_Atacama (accessed 10 April 2012).

Zapata, C. (2008) 'Los intelectuales indígenas y el pensamiento anticolonialista' *Discursos/prácticas* 2(1): 113–40.

Chapter 11

Discourses of development
Narratives of cultural heritage as an economic resource

Neil Asher Silberman

Introduction

The importance of narrative communication in shaping the character and quality of tourist experiences has been demonstrated by a large and varied body of research (for an overview, see Bruner 2005). To be clear from the outset, the story form that I here identify as 'narrative' – a recognisable linear literary sequence that includes a beginning situation, a complication or crisis, struggle, reversal, and concluding transformation (see Bruner 1991; Campbell 1968; Propp 1968) – has been identified as a crucial tool for facilitating and analysing a wide range of specific factors in tourist activities, including the lure of self-discovery (Noy 2004), opportunities to address environmental concerns (Campbell 2002), place marketing and branding (Lichrou, O'Malley and Patterson 2010), visitor motivations (Poria, Reichel and Biran 2006), and the quality of visitor interactions (McCabe and Foster 2006). It has also been seen as an effective communication medium for a wide variety of interpretive forms, ranging from interpretation of Indigenous cultures (Hall 2007), mobile digital applications (Epstein and Vergani 2006), and tourism information systems (Gretzel 2006). Narrative has also been identified as a crucial element of the archaeological and historical discourse (e.g. Landau 1993; Silberman 1995; White 1990) on which most heritage tourism narratives are based. To tell an unfolding story – rather than merely recite a collection of facts or statistics – is to cultivate a potentially powerful subjective emotional engagement, while simultaneously offering a subtle meta-narrative about the inevitability of certain kinds of cause and effect (Bruner 1991).

In the following pages I want to analyse a new class of narrative that has come to exert a significant impact on the public administration and presentation of cultural heritage. I refer to the narrative of 'heritage as an economic resource' or 'heritage as a driver of (sustainable) development' which has now become the leitmotif of international development agencies (see Hawkins and Mann 2007), international organisations (Arezki, Cherif and Piotrowski 2009), and a wide range of public and private stakeholders who have come to identify narrative as an attractive model for action

(Albernaz, Bandarin and Hosagrahar 2011). Put most simply, the story suggests that a city or region's current economic stagnation can be overcome by physically developing and widely promoting heritage sites or historic urban districts as attractive venues for large-scale outside visitation. It is further implied, and sometimes explicitly promised, that the income derived from the expected flow of tourists will stimulate and develop the local economy. I would like to analyse this emerging narrative and highlight its main actors, villains, and storyline to distinguish more clearly its presuppositions, value judgements, and promised goals. No less important is an assessment of its correspondence to real-world outcomes to discover if it represents a sustainable solution to economic underdevelopment or whether it is just, well, a fairy tale.

The anatomy and morphology of the tourist tale

Underlying the heritage-as-development narrative is the basic story of the tourist–adventurer, for the appeal of that familiar trope to paying visitors creates the demand for the kinds of heritage-venue construction that is now currently linked with 'sustainable development'. Its wide dissemination in TV documentaries, travel books, and trek and cruise ship advertising is a modern consumer variant of the universal literary structure that Joseph Campbell (1968) called the 'monomyth'. Though the characters inevitably vary, the basic pattern remains the same:

> The mythological hero, setting forth from his common day hut or castle, is lured, carried away, or else voluntarily proceeds to the threshold of adventure. There he encounters a shadow presence that guards the passage. The hero may defeat or conciliate this power and go alive into the kingdom of the dark…Beyond the threshold, then, the hero journeys through a world of unfamiliar yet strangely intimate forces, some of which severely threaten him (tests), some of which give magical aid (helpers). When he arrives at the nadir of the mythological round, he undergoes a supreme ordeal and gains his reward…or again – if the powers have remained unfriendly to him – his theft of the boon he came to gain…The final work is that of return. If the powers have blessed the hero, he now sets out under their protection (emissary); if not, he flees and is pursued (transformation flight, obstacle flight). At the return threshold, the transcendental powers must remain behind; the hero re-emerges from the kingdom of dread. The boon he brings restores the world…
>
> (1968: 245–6)

Five elements are essential: a central or viewpoint character, the 'Hero'; a disruption to or departure from normal life; the exotic Realm of Darkness or Chaos where the hero's adventure unfolds; the Challenge or Struggle against opposition; and, the capture or theft of the 'Boon' that restores the world. These are the components of the basic European folktale, and even if Campbell was not correct in calling it universal it certainly encapsulates a Western idea of travel, discovery, and imperial quests. In its own more modest way, the tourist narrative places the traveller in the position of the hero who departs from his or her daily routine to visit exotic climes or cultures, struggle with unfamiliar language or customs and return home with a rich collection of stories, snapshots, and souvenirs. Dean MacCannell (1999) characterised the tourist quest as a search for authenticity that he or she could not find in their workaday lives. Whether the destination is an exotic locale or the monuments of an ancient civilisation, the fare-paying, hotel-staying, souvenir-buying tourist becomes something of an adventurer leaving his or her common day hut or castle and returning with memories and keepsakes that can – if not restore the world – at least demonstrate to the folks back home that the tourist had escaped the daily grind for at least a little while.

Within the macro-narrative of the tourist adventure, an embodied sequence of movement reproduces the same adventure motif. In the visitor's carefully programmed and directed progress from the car park, through the ticket booth and attraction entrance, along the designated paths of novel exhibits, sights, and interpretations, finally reaching the cafeteria and gift shop, the visitor emerges back into the 'normality' of the car park again. It is an adventure story read with the feet and experienced with the sensations of the body (Silberman 2007) that offers the same sense of virtual adventure: experiencing the 'authentic' through a personal passage through the physical setting of a carefully planned and managed natural or cultural heritage site. Indeed, the visitor's everyday identity can sometimes be changed or viewed from another perspective in the course of the heritage journey/experience. Whether through immersive virtual reality environments in which the visitor experiences the sights and sounds of distant epochs or battles (Tost and Economou 2009) or accepts the virtual identity of a hero or victim in an historical narrative (Greeff and Lalioti 2001; Liss 1993), a visit to a recently designed and electronically equipped heritage site is increasingly focused on some form of personal enrichment or transformation, however temporary or fleeting it may be (Breathnach 2006).

Thus by the turn of the 21st century, the social meaning of the cultural heritage tourist experience is composed of several distinct and overlapping narratives that all convey the same message: 1) authenticity is to be found elsewhere than home and the present; 2) the value of the past is as a coherent and well-constructed story, and, 3) it requires personal participation in an experience/adventure that does not come for free. Yet far from offering a permanent connection with useful, sources of serious, continuing historical reflection, it is often the product of artifice and illusion (Silberman

2004). Ironically, the same could be said of the new hyper-narrative of 'heritage as an economic resource'.

Heritage and development: from opponents to allies

It might once have seemed strange that professionally curated cultural heritage would ever be widely seen by both academics and regional planners as an exploitable economic resource, for the idea of 'conservation' and the goal of 'development' make an unlikely – not to say oxymoronic – pair. Indeed, heritage preservation and conservation groups and development organisations have been long-time rivals, often seeing past and future in starkly contrasting terms. Conservationists zealously protected the idea of exemplary monuments of historic cultures and did everything it could to prevent their destruction or alteration by the relentless forces of modernity. As stated most recently by former International Council on Monuments and Sites (ICOMOS) President Michael Petzet (2009: 10), 'instead of an a priori "tolerance for change" based on whatever standards…we should stick to our fundamental principles and fight for cultural heritage in a dramatically changing world'. Developers, on the other hand, often saw the material remains of ancient and traditional cultures of the past as burdens or mere obstacles, especially if they interfered with urban investment or construction plans (e.g. Fang and Zhang 2003; Gotham 2001). But the devastating effects of social dislocation (Fullilove 2005), the growing appeal of gentrification (Smith 1979), and 'heritage-themed' shopping environments (Eisinger 2000) gave the idea of scrubbed historic facades and cobblestone streets a higher value than ever before.

Indeed the World Bank, in particular, slowly began to change its policy toward cultural heritage. From an initial passive attitude of 'do no harm' (i.e. avoidance or diversion of roads and other infrastructural projects from conspicuous historical and archaeological monuments), the Bank shifted in its 1999 Framework For Action, encouraging investment and infrastructural improvement of built heritage and historic urban centres in some of its poorest borrowing states (Serageldin and Martin-Brown 1999). The spectacularly successful 1997 opening of the new Guggenheim Museum in Bilbao, Spain – though a cultural institution, rather than cultural heritage – had raised expectations about the effect cultural tourism could have on the economy of regions long in post-industrial decline (Baniotopoulou 2001). And what had occurred in Bilbao, it was believed, could surely happen in other places. And thus with the recognition that cultural attractions and historic urban landscapes gentrified into expensive vacation homes and exotic high-end markets, a new narrative was born.

But this time the narrative's hero was not an adventurer or defender of heritage against the forces of modernity, but rather far-sighted political leaders whose adventure was risking their political prestige (not to mention their nations' credit) in the realm of cultural heritage. For as the World Bank and a growing number of development agencies defined it:

> The patrimony represents a vast collection of cultural assets, but these assets also have a huge economic value. Markets only imperfectly recognize this economic value because of insufficient information and inadequate pricing mechanisms. Historically, the economic value of the patrimony's endowments has been given much less attention than its cultural significance. Largely because of this limited recognition, policy makers and planners in developing countries have been little concerned, and little able, to activate and harvest the economic value of their country's patrimony. Bank policy has come to unambiguously recognize this economic value. It holds that the patrimony can become an auxiliary engine for generating economic growth and development.
> (Cernea 2001: 33)

The past, in its material, money-making form, had become the treasure for the political leader bold enough to grasp this apparent opportunity. For de-industrialised, de-agriculturalised cities and regions, the existential crisis was their hopelessness; the solution lay in investing in the past to build a better future, even at the cost of selling their cultural souls. A new transnational industry grew up to support the so-called 'harvesting' of the economic value of heritage resources (Peacock and Rizzo 2008), their (often outsourced) management (Palumbo 2006), and their design and marketing (Leighton 2006). Borrowing concepts from theme parks and interactive museums, site planners now also began to utilise digital applications, 3D reconstructions, and virtual reality experiences with a wide enough range of vivid images and impressions to satisfy almost every visitor's taste. So like bauxite, coal, or rainforest hardwoods, the material remains of the past were seen as an economic resource. What this amounted to – at least in the new narrative – was the creation of lucrative, job-creating leisure time entertainment, marketed with the same modes of tour booking, entrance fees, restaurants, gift shops, and overnight accommodations as other packaged visits of the modern tourist industry.

Though they were at first resistant to the idea of heritage as commerce, many of the academics and working professionals of the heritage conservations sector eventually were persuaded to go along. Although the 1972 United Nations Educational, Scientific and Cultural Organization (UNESCO) World Heritage Convention warned of 'serious and specific dangers' to the world's cultural heritage due to, among other causes, 'large-scale public or private projects or rapid urban or tourist development projects' (UNESCO 1972: article 11.4) and in its preamble, the 1994 Nara Document on Authenticity bemoaned the threat to heritage in 'a world that is increasingly subject to the forces of globalization and homog-enization' (Larsen 1994), hard economic realities played their own role. Significant budget cuts to monuments and antiquities services in an age of neoliberal restructuring left the cultural heritage sector ravaged and in desperate need of alternative sources of support (Yúdice 2003). And so heritage and development – long-time rivals – now wove together a story about how heritage could be useful – about how development and tradition could create a productive synergy.

The Memorandum of Understanding concluded between UNESCO and the World Bank tells the whole story (UNESCO 2011). After decades of on-and-off discussion of conflicts and common interests, the world's most influential cultural heritage body and the world's most powerful economic development agency openly acknowledged how entwined their respective missions had become:

> By joining forces, UNESCO and the World Bank can provide very posi-tive input for the improvement of aid effectiveness, and make the most of culture as a motor for social development and poverty alleviation, through employment and job creation. We believe also we can give impetus and concrete follow up to the recent resolution of the United Nations General Assembly which underlined the links between culture and development.
> (Irina Bokova, Director-General of UNESCO at the signing ceremony, cited in UNESCO 2011).

In agreeing to collaborate on a series of global initiatives, the two organi-sations officially endorsed the new narrative, which was further validated later that year by the theme of the ICOMOS 17th General Assembly (held at UNESCO headquarters in Paris): 'Heritage as a Driver of Development' (International Council on Monuments and Sites 2011).

The shared story now told to governments, investors, and visitors to rehabilitated historic urban areas and heritage sites is a narrative in which the remains of the past are seen as a path to economic rebirth for devel-oping nations and regions whose economies and societies are in crisis, or at the very least in serious, disruptive decline. The World Bank, as usual, expressed the new narrative succinctly on the 'Cultural Heritage and Sustainable Development' section of its vast website:

> Culture is a resource for economic and social development. Poor communities helped in recognizing and preserving their cultural assets are provided with new economic opportunities and enabled to build development on their diverse social, cultural, and physical back-ground. The possibility to generate income from cultural assets creates employment, reduces poverty, stimulates enterprise development by

the poor, fosters private investment, and generates resources for environmental and cultural conservation. From a human and social perspective, the appreciation of their own cultural patrimony brings to poor communities awareness in their identity. Awareness boosts confidence; it's an input for social mobilization and empowerment, promotes inclusion, and complements capacity building and good governance strategies.

(World Bank n.d.)

But this and all the other related scenarios were filled with assertions – hopeful and positive, certainly – but nevertheless rather vague and empirically unverified. The very redefinition of cultural heritage as an economic resource represents a particular vision of development in which the remains of the past and the products and services derived from it can be commodified while the culture of commodification remains unquestioned and unseen. And yet narratives have their own motivating power, even in a purely business environment (Alvarez and Merchán 1992). And so the global investment in cultural heritage tourism continues. But on purely economic, balance sheet terms, does the fable often come true?

The Empire's new clothes?

For those observers who had neither faith nor financial interest in the 'heritage as economic resource' story, things were not exactly what they were promised to be. Hard statistics on the economic performance of many heritage development projects were hard to come by, and the various methods of calculating the economic valuation of cultural heritage were often contradictory and in dispute (Bowitz and Ibenholt 2009; De la Torre 2002). Yet encouraged by the tautologically supportive promotional 'how-to' guides by international organisations and academics who enthusiastically supported the new story (e.g. Arezki, Cherif and Piotrowski 2009; Chhabra 2009; du Cros 2001; McKercher and du Cros 2002), municipal, regional, and national governments borrowed and invested significant sums to make the infrastructural and management improvements to enter the heritage tourism market, often with the additional expense and effort of nominating sites for the World Heritage List or the various 'Cultural Capitals' competitions that were held throughout the world.

Ironically, the development of cultural heritage sites, built to the standards of access, visitor facilities, and interpretation required to attract international tourism, was part of a seemingly unstoppable process of modernisation in every region and country it occurred. Not only did it almost always require the removal and transfer of resident businesses and populations, but in 'developing' the heritage value through redesign and place-branding, it effectively erased the painful memories of economic decline and abandonment that had actually preserved the old buildings of the historic urban core. And indeed despite all the talk of sustainability, it became clear that investments in heritage had a finite life-span: after an initial period of publicity and fanfare, the level of tourism dropped far below the revenue required to recoup investment costs (Russo 2002). Sometimes even the initial revenue failed to justify the initial outlay, as was seen in Sophia Labadi's (2008) enlightening, if bleak study of the socio-economic impacts of 'regenerated' heritage sites in Europe, where the meagre or non-existent economic regeneration diverged sharply from the widely accepted narrative.

Even in the relatively few sites where the income was enormous, the benefit was rarely seen to be shared equally. Whether the revenue was controlled or mismanaged by the central government, leaving little in the way of trickle-down economic stimulation (Zan and Lusiani 2011), or by international travel firms and cruise lines (Slyomovics 1995; Weaver 2005), leaving little leakage of tourist cash into the local economy, the hidden costs of borrowing, investment credits, and increased public services were seldom taken into account. More troubling still was the social effect when a community's heritage was turned into an industry. When revenue generation becomes a primary objective of urban development, and outside visitors the target, alienation of the local population and mistrust of the motives for investment can result (Eisinger 2000). More subtly and insidiously, the marketing of heritage can blur the line between modern commercial interests and the collective past (for an outlandish example from northeastern China, see Wilson 2009).

The effect of these multiplying critiques of the simple equation of heritage with economic development can be seen as coalescing into something of a counter-narrative – though this one has no hero, only villains, victims, and dupes (e.g. Briedenhann and Wickens 2004; Lansing and de Vries 2006; Liu 2003; Mitchell 2002). In this counter-narrative metropolitan consultants and developers who seek to extract profits from commodified heritage victimise an often idealised local community. The result is a monetary gain (even if only temporary for the developers) and a loss of property, dignity, and ultimately cultural integrity for the local community that is forced out and/or forced to play an increasingly caricatured role for the sake of the heritage display (Macleod 2006).

Yet this counter-narrative offers no solution, no hope to possibility of revitalising and energising the role of heritage and local tradition in a rapidly globalising world. Unlike the story it responds to, there is no treasure or magic elixir to be found at the end of the quest.

Conclusion: towards a story without an end

So what are we to do with the conflicting narratives about heritage as economic resource that are so diametrically opposed? They call for opposite actions; each is a zero-sum tale. One encourages profit-driven excess and commodification, while the other sees no practical or feasible economic alternative to stagnation and decay. The truth – if we can use such a word when speaking of narrative constructions – obviously lies somewhere in between. For history's tangible and intangible traces are not objects with unequivocal meaning; they are rather to be seen as 'vessels of value' (Araoz 2011), whose social context determines how they best should be used. In some cases, heritage monuments can indeed serve as lucrative tourist attractions, so long as the displacement or disruption of the lives of the many does not outweigh the economic benefit of the few (Miura 2005). Sometimes heritage sites can better be 'sites of conscience' for serious historical reflection, rather than for snapshots and souvenirs (Sevcenko 2010). Other sites – sacred places and houses of worship – should perhaps not be declared official heritage sites at all (Zimmerman 2007). Each community has its own range of narrative connections to elements of the historic landscape; no single use or development method can possibly be appropriate for all. Questions about the value and usefulness of cultural heritage for insiders and outsiders, for visitors and locals, transcend specific economic and ideological considerations, no matter how persuasive the particular narrative.

Perhaps it is the power of narrative itself as a means of public discourse and discussion that can animate a more inclusive connection to the past. Narrative is 'powerful speech'; it is the fabric of culture (Niles 2010) – the closest thing we can ever have to a specific collective memory. It is also a call to action that conveys visions of disruption, change, and struggle that cultural heritage itself represents. Yet both the narratives and anti-narratives of 'heritage as an economic resource' look down from on high, from an expert's perspective, concerned primarily with the heritage objects, largely ignoring individual interpretive agency. All must share in the power to weave creative, reflective narratives about the impact of the past on the present. For the right of all stakeholders – insiders, outsiders, tourists, entrepreneurs, and local communities, to contribute their own narrative visions at every stage of public heritage planning, conservation, and presentation – not merely accept 'authoritative' versions – may be the greatest value of cultural heritage in the 21st century.

References

Albernaz, M.F.S., Bandarin M.F. and Hosagrahar, J. (2011) 'Why development needs culture', *Journal of Cultural Heritage Management and Sustainable Development* 1(1): 2.

Alvarez, J.L. and Merchán, C. (1992) 'The role of narrative fiction in the development of imagination for action', *International Studies of Management and Organization* 22(3): 27–45.

Araoz, G. (2011) 'Preserving heritage places under a new paradigm', *Journal of Cultural Heritage Management and Sustainable Development* 1(1): 55–60.

Arezki, R. Cherif, R. and Piotrowski, J. (2009) *Tourism Specialization and Economic Development?: Evidence from the UNESCO World Heritage List*, Washington DC: International Monetary Fund.

Baniotopoulou, E. (2001) 'Art for whose sake? Modern art museums and their role in transforming societies: the case of Guggenheim Bilbao', *Journal of Conservation and Museum Studies* 7. Available online: www.jcms-journal.com/index.php/jcms/article/view/19 (accessed 7 May 2012).

Bowitz, E. and Karin I. (2009) 'Economic impacts of cultural heritage – research and perspectives', *Journal of Cultural Heritage* 10(1): 1–8.

Breathnach, T. (2006) 'Looking for the real me: locating the self in heritage tourism', *Journal of Heritage Tourism* 1(2): 100–20.

Briedenhann, J. and Wickens, E. (2004) 'Tourism routes as a tool for the economic development of rural areas – vibrant hope or impossible dream?' *Tourism Management* 25(1): 71–9.

Bruner, E.M. (2005) 'The role of narrative in tourism', Paper presented at On Voyage: New Directions in Tourism Theory, Berkeley CA, October 7–8. Available online: www.nyu.edu/classes/bkg/tourist/narrative.doc (accessed 18 May 2012).

Bruner, J. (1991) 'The narrative construction of reality', *Critical Inquiry* 18(1): 1–21.

Campbell, J. (1968) *The Hero with a Thousand Faces*, 2nd edn, Princeton NJ: Princeton University Press.

Campbell, L.M. (2002) 'Conservation narratives in Costa Rica: conflict and co-existence', *Development and Change* 33(1): 29–56.

Cernea, M.M. (2001) *Cultural Heritage and Development*, Washington DC: World Bank.

Chhabra, D. (2009) 'Proposing a sustainable marketing framework for heritage tourism', *Journal of Sustainable Tourism* 17(3): 303–20.

du Cros, H. (2001) 'A new model to assist in planning for sustainable cultural heritage tourism', *International Journal of Tourism Research* 3(2): 165–70.

Eisinger, P. (2000) 'The politics of bread and circuses building the city for the visitor class', *Urban Affairs Review* 35(3): 316–33.

Epstein, M. and Vergani, S. (2006) 'History unwired: mobile narrative in historic cities', *Proceedings of the Working Conference on Advanced Visual Interfaces*, Venezia, Italy, 23–26 May.

Fang, K. and Zhang Y. (2003) 'Plan and market mismatch: urban redevelopment in Beijing during a period of transition', *Asia Pacific Viewpoint* 44(2): 149–62.

Fullilove, M. (2005) *Root Shock: How Tearing up City Neighborhoods Hurts America, and What We Can Do About It*, New York: One World/Ballantine.

Gotham, K. F. (2001) 'Urban redevelopment, past and present', *Research in Urban Sociology* 6: 1–31.

Greeff, M. and Lalioti V. (2001) 'Interactive cultural experiences using virtual identities', *ICHIM* 1: 455–65.

Gretzel, U. (2006) 'Narrative design for travel recommender systems', in D.R. Fesenmaier, K.W. Wöber and H. Werthner (eds) *Destination Recommendation System: Behavioural Foundation and Applications*, Wallingford: CABI.

Hall, N. (2007) 'Telling the story: performance and narrative as reflective frameworks for Indigenous tourism', in I. MacDonnell (ed.) *CAUTHE 2007: Tourism –*

Past Achievements, Future Challenges, Sydney: University of Technology Sydney.

Hawkins, D.E. and Mann, S. (2007) 'The World Bank's role in tourism development', *Annals of Tourism Research* 34(2): 348–63.

International Council on Monuments and Sites, (2011) 'Final communiqué – results of the 17th ICOMOS General Assembly Paris', 28 November?1 December. Available online: www.international.icomos.org/Paris2011/GA2011_Press_release_EN_20120109.pdf (accessed 18 May 2012).

Labadi, S. (2008) *Evaluating the Socio-economic Impacts of Selected Regenerated Heritage Sites in Europe*, Amsterdam: European Cultural Foundation.

Landau, M. (1993) *Narratives of Human Evolution*, New Haven: Yale University Press.

Lansing, P. and de Vries, P. (2006) 'Sustainable tourism: ethical alternative or marketing ploy?' *Journal of Business Ethics* 72(1): 77–85.

Larsen, K.E. (1994) *Nara Conference on Authenticity, Proceedings*. Paris: UNESCO.

Leighton, D. (2006) ' "Step back in time and live the legend": experiential marketing and the heritage sector', *International Journal of Nonprofit and Voluntary Sector Marketing* 12(2): 117–25.

Lichrou, M., O'Malley, L. and Patterson, M. (2010) 'Narratives of a tourism destination: local particularities and their implications for place marketing and branding', *Place Branding and Public Diplomacy* 6(2): 134–44.

Liss, A. (1993) 'Contours of naming: the identity card project and the Tower of Faces at the United States Holocaust Memorial Museum', *Public Art Culture Ideas* 8. Available online: http://pi.library.yorku.ca/ojs/index.php/public/issue/view/1737/showToc (accessed 19 May 2012).

Liu, Z. (2003) 'Sustainable tourism development: a critique', *Journal of Sustainable Tourism* 11: 459–75.

MacCannell, D. (1999) *The Tourist: A New Theory of the Leisure Class*, Berkeley and Los Angeles: University of California Press.

Macleod, N. (2006) 'Cultural tourism: aspects of authenticity and commodification', in M. Smith and M. Robinson (eds) *Cultural Tourism in a Changing World: Politics, Participation and (Re)Presentation*, Boulder: Channel View.

McCabe, S. and Foster C. (2006) 'The role and function of narrative in tourist interaction', *Journal of Tourism and Cultural Change* 4: 194–215.

McKercher, B. and du Cros, H. (2002) *Cultural Tourism: The Partnership between Tourism and Cultural Heritage Management*, New York: Haworth Hospitality Press.

Mitchell, T. (2002) *Rule of Experts: Egypt, Techno-Politics, Modernity*, Berkeley and Los Angeles: University of California Press.

Miura, K. (2005) 'Conservation of a "living heritage site" a contradiction in terms? A Case Study of Angkor World Heritage site', *Conservation and Management of Archaeological Sites* 7(1): 3–18.

Niles, J.D. (2010) *Homo Narrans: The Poetics and Anthropology of Oral Literature*, Philadelphia: University of Pennsylvania Press.

Noy, C. (2004) 'Performing identity: touristic narratives of self-change', *Text and Performance Quarterly* 24(2): 115–38.

Palumbo, G. (2006) 'Privatization of state-owned cultural heritage', in N. Agnew and J. Bridgland (eds) *Of the Past, for the Future: Integrating Archaeology and Conservation: Proceedings of the Conservation Theme at the 5th World Archaeological Congress, Washington, DC, 22–26 June 2003*, Los Angeles: Getty Conservation Institute.

Peacock, A.T. and Rizzo, I. (2008) *The Heritage Game: Economics, Policy, and Practice*, Oxford: Oxford University Press.

Petzet, M. (2009) *International Principles of Preservation*, ICOMOS, Berlin: Hendrik Bäßler Verlag.

Poria, Y., Reichel, A. and Biran, A. (2006) 'Heritage site perceptions and motivations to visit', *Journal of Travel Research* 44(3): 318–26.

Propp, V. (1968) *Morphology of the Folktale*, 2nd edn, Austin: University of Texas Press.

Russo, A. P. (2002) 'The "vicious circle" of tourism development in heritage cities', *Annals of Tourism Research* 29(1): 165–82.

Serageldin, I., and Martin-Brown, J. (1999) *Culture in Sustainable Development: Investing in Cultural and Natural Endowments: Proceedings of the Conference Held at the World Bank, Washington, DC, USA, 28–29 September, 1998.* Available online: www.cabdirect.org/abstracts/19991806852.html;jsessionid=5F7E7B4577E97113 0FF68EEDAE4CB4D9 (accessed 18 May 2012).

Sevcenko, L. (2010) 'Sites of conscience: new approaches to conflicted memory', *Museum International* 62 (1–2): 20–5.

Silberman, N.A. (1995) 'Promised lands and chosen peoples: the politics and poetics of archaeological narrative', in P.L. Kohl and C. Fawcett (eds) *Nationalism, Politics, and the Practice of Archaeology*, Cambridge: Cambridge University Press.

Silberman, N.A. (2004) 'Beyond theme parks and digitized data: what can cultural heritage technologies contribute to the public understanding of the past?' *Interdisciplinarity or the Best of Both Worlds: Selected Papers from VAST2004*, Budapest: Archaeolingua.

Silberman, N.A. (2007) 'Sustainable heritage? Public archaeological interpretation and the marketed past', in Y. Hamilakis and P. Duke (eds) *Archaeology and Capitalism: From Ethics to Politics*, Walnut Creek CA: Left Coast Press.

Slyomovics, S. (1995) 'Tourist Containment', *Middle East Report* Sept–Oct: 6.

Smith, N. (1979) 'Toward a theory of gentrification a back to the city movement by capital, not people', *Journal of the American Planning Association* 45(4): 538–48.

de la Torre, M. and Getty Conservation Institute (2002) *Assessing the Values of Cultural Heritage: Research Report*, Los Angeles: Getty Conservation Institute.

Tost, L.P. and Economou, M. (2009) 'Worth a thousand words? The usefulness of immersive virtual reality for learning in cultural heritage settings', *International Journal of Architectural Computing* 7(1): 157–76.

UNESCO (1972) *Convention Concerning the Protection of the World Cultural and Natural Heritage*, Paris: UNESCO. Available online: http://whc.unesco.org/en/conventiontext (accessed 18 May 2012).

UNESCO (2011) 'World Bank and UNESCO: Expanding opportunities for collaboration on culture and sustainable development, United Nations Educational, Scientific and Cultural Organization', *UNESCO Media Services* 1 July. Available online: www.unesco.org/new/en/media-services/single-view/news/world_bank_and_unesco_expanding_opportunities_for_collaboration_on_culture_and_sustainable_development/ (accessed 18 May 2012).

Weaver, A. (2005) 'Spaces of containment and revenue capture: "super-sized" cruise ships as mobile tourism enclaves', *Tourism Geographies* 7(2): 165–84.

White, H. (1990) *The Content of the Form: Narrative Discourse and Historical Representation*, Baltimore, MA: JHU Press.

Wilson, S. (2009) 'A city of brand names:(en)countering narratives of development in Qingdao, China tourism', *InTensions Journal* 2: 1–25.

World Bank (2012) 'Cultural heritage and sustainable tourism – overview', *World Bank Web*. Available online: http://web.worldbank.org/WBSITE/EXTERNAL/TOPICS/EXTURBANDEVELOPMENT/EXTCHD/0,,contentMDK:20204614~menuPK:430438~pagePK:210058~piPK:210062~theSitePK:430430,00.html (accessed 18 May 2012).

Yúdice, G. (2003) *The Expediency of Culture: Uses of Culture in the Global Era*, Durham, NC: Duke University Press.

Zan, L. and Lusiani, M. (2011) 'Managing change and master plans: Machu Picchu between conservation and exploitation', *Archaeologies* 7(2): 329–71.

Zimmerman, L.J. (2007) 'Plains Indians and resistance to "public" heritage commemoration of their pasts', in H. Silverman and D. Fairchild Ruggles (eds) *Cultural Heritage and Human Rights*, New York: Springer.

Part V

Managing the heritage-tourism engagement

Chapter 12

Cambodian experiences of the manifestation and management of intangible heritage and tourism at a World Heritage site

Georgina Lloyd and Im Sokrithy

Introduction

The role of intangible cultural heritage (ICH) within the cultural tourism experience of a heritage place is seldom a central focus of heritage conservation. Yet intangible heritage, or living culture, has a pivotal role to play in the tourist experience of a heritage place. Management of intangible heritage tourism – both the utilisation and presentation of forms of intangible heritage to tourists and the minimisation of impacts caused, directly or indirectly, by pressures of tourism on intangible heritage – are central aspects of heritage site conservation. At many heritage places, the management of intangible heritage is typically considered as an afterthought to the preservation and presentation of monumental remains or natural sites. There is, however, a growing understanding of the significance and interdependence of both tangible and intangible heritage. This general trend is consistent with the management of heritage at the Angkor World Heritage site (AWHS). While conservation of the monuments has been of primary importance, in recent years there has been considerable research on the significance of intangible heritage and focus placed on the management of this heritage.

At the intersection of intangible heritage and cultural tourism there are a number of matters that require consideration for the management of heritage places. These include the modification of intangible heritage forms for tourism consumption including standardisation, commodification, homogenisation and fossilisation of heritage and a consequent loss of authenticity of cultural performance and practice and the decontexualisation of intangible heritage for the tourism market. The other concern is a failure by the tourism industry to recognise the significance of ICH and the need to ensure that it is presented, marketed and utilised in a sensitive and appropriate manner. There is, therefore, a need to enhance the tourism value placed on ICH and educate the industry in the potential impacts to the continuation, transmission and presentation of ICH that result from its utilisation for tourism purposes.

The AWHS is a living cultural landscape with complex associated intangible heritage values (see Figure 12.1). While the Angkor temples continue to have considerable archaeological value, the contemporary AWHS represents a complex matrix of values. These values are present on many levels, from globally recognised outstanding artistic and architectural values, nationalistic values of symbolism and cultural identity, community Buddhist and spiritual values to localised animistic spirit associations. At Angkor there has been continuous animistic, spiritual and other religious links with the temple landscape from the pre-Angkorian period until the present day. Many of the religious links at Angkor are a unique representation of intermingled Hindu, Buddhist and Animist elements. Norindr (2006: 66) establishes that: 'Angkor remains a spiritual place of devotion, dynamic site of pilgrimage, teaching and reflection, and not simply an archaeological wonder for well-heeled tourists'.

Angkor designates not only a geographic region – one which is home to the magnificent Khmer temple ruins (including the legendary Angkor Wat, Bayon and dozens of other main temples), city walls, roads, water management systems and sites of local industry of the ancient Khmer Empire remaining in natural environments – it also designates a cultural landscape which includes a living cultural heritage of inestimable importance in anthropological and linguistic terms. The villagers of the Siem Reap Angkor Region are known to be particularly conservative with respect to ancestral traditions, and a great number of archaic cultural practices that have disappeared elsewhere continue to be performed in its villages. Angkor represents, then, a dynamic cultural complex reflecting all aspects of Khmer society. As such, Angkor reveals memories of the past and through them offers hope for the future. This chapter presents only an overview of the multitude of ICH representations at Angkor.

Villages within the Angkor World Heritage site

A growing sector of heritage tourism is the presentation to visitors of everyday landscapes that depict the lives of ordinary people (Dallen and Gyan 2009). Many of the village settlements within the AWHS are associated with ancient occupancies that date back to different periods of Cambodian history. Each village has accrued its own character and value. Some villages reflect the discernible ancient landscape along the historic arterial roads from Angkor (such as the road from Angkor to Pimai), and continue to use the roads as a central feature and communication artery (see Im 2008).

Village settlement and oral history

The settlement histories and stories of the villages are often reflected in their names. Several villages share a popular tale, which they consider to be

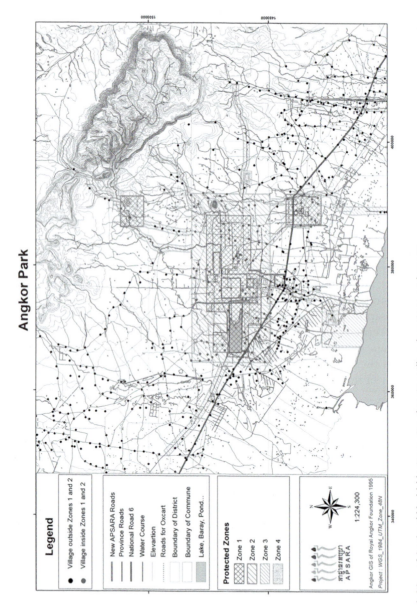

Figure 12.1 Map of Angkor World Heritage site showing village locations and zones

a common history that creates a linkage between their communities. Another historical theme relates to the first man who came and cleared land for developing that community. Other villages have histories relating to natural, cultural or historical events of the region. Most stories of this type relate to nature and are concerned with a specific plant grown in the area. Probably, these histories can be dated to after the fall of Angkor. They have been told from one generation to the next and exist primarily as oral traditions, although a few stories have been published (Im 2008).

Temples, ancient roads, bridges, forests and the rice fields, lakes and ponds, have the names of ancestors attached to them or are surrounded by legends remain as important landmarks for local people. The names of villages are similarly reflective of local and natural elements and markers, or of shared history with other villages.

Village landscape and traditional livelihoods

Village landscapes are constrained by settlement structure and the local environment. Many villages are situated on ancient infrastructure (for example, dikes, water structures or ancient roads). Other villages are found close to ancient temples or clustered around a temple, which gives a different character to the village landscape. Some villages have gradually developed in a cluster around a central Buddhist monastery, most of them built on an ancient temple or structure. The villages are surrounded by rice fields, vegetation or the forest of their communities. Some villages are isolated from others by rice fields.

The landscape reflects the different seasonal changes. Seasonal changes also influence traditional livelihood and ritual practices. The rainy season in particular can give much beauty to villages surrounded by rice paddy and seasonal vegetation. At this time of year the villagers are all busy with agricultural work, and their activities can be observed from dawn until night during half the year. Typically, a traditional rice paddy is grown, a variety adapted to this soil type and, particularly, water conditions. The second half year season comes next beginning with harvesting, new seasonal agriculture and the annual feast of agrarian rituals (see Figure 12.2). During this season handicraft construction, weaving, charcoal and blacksmith work are done along with the collection of medical plants and other natural forest products for trading with the citizen within Siem Reap. The residents of the Angkor area trade these products for fish and other commodities from the Tonle Sap area.

As the daily life of many Angkorian villages has not changed much, traditional crafts and weaving are still practised. These include roof thatch dressing, weaving cotton, making alcohol from rice and basket, mat and natural broom dressing (see Figure 12.3). These activities are performed under or near the house. These practices have unique cultural value and

Figure 12.2 Ritual at an Angkorian temple, Neak Pean, to ask for rain
Photo: APSARA 2009

Figure 12.3 Mat weaving at a village in the Angkor World Heritage site
Photo: APSARA 2007

should be the focus of sensitive management approaches as they may be utilised by the tourism industry.

There is a large diversity of traditional and ceremonial events performed within the Angkor region and in general communities within the Angkor landscape strongly preserve their cultural identity. There are two main categories of ceremony: the first is concerned with rites of passage, and with rituals associated with either the fixed ceremonial calendar or with special occasions (which can occur at any time); the second aspect is concerned with customs and performing arts, which are also considered to have a ritual component. While all of these traditions have significant cultural value they may also have tourism value and as such careful management is required to ensure that the practice, presentation and transmission of ICH is not compromised by its utilisation for the tourism industry.

Rites of passage

Rites of passage are a series of ritual practices performed throughout the lifecycle of an individual from the stage of new birth to death and can be measured in eight rituals. For some communities in Angkor many rituals are still commonly practised. Many of these practices are strong historical links. Those series of rituals can be summarised and literally translated into English as follows: 'a ritual concerning birth'; 'the keeping and cutting of the topknot'; 'the Buddhist monk ordination'; 'girls of this stage undertake another ritual called Chol Mlob'; 'Marriage'; 'a ritual concerning delivery'; 'the ceremony of prolongation of life'; 'the funerary rite'; and, 'the burying of the ashes from incineration'.

A ritual concerning birth is performed a few days after delivery, called in Khmer *Kat Sak Bankok Chmob*, whereby the community shows recognition of the newborn, the family demonstrates gratitude to the midwife and any misfortunes caused by the mother's blood during delivery (which is considered an unclean thing) are driven away. It is believed that the midwife has ritually shaped the newborn making the baby a new human being of our world. This ritual is largely performed throughout the villages in the AWHS.

The keeping and cutting of the topknot is called in Khmer, *Kor Chuk* and is a ceremony to mark human age entering into pre-adolescence. It is a very traditional ceremony which is rarely performed elsewhere in Cambodia (see Figure 12.4).

The Buddhist monk ordination is called in Khmer *Bous Neak* and marks for a man a new step of life to the age of religious study. Young adult men prepare for ordination as novices in the Buddhist order. These events are also observed commonly in the communities, but not for all young men (see Figure 12.5).

Girls of this stage undertake another ritual called Chol Mlob literally means 'entering to shadow'. The girl stays inside her room for a period of time

Figure 12.4 Topknot ceremony conducted at a village in the Angkor World Heritage site
  Photo: APSARA 2011

and is banned from talking with strangers and men. She learns from an old woman sage to be a good housewife. Very few communities still practise this but it still survives in few villages of the Siem Reap region.

Marriage, in Khmer, is called *Reap Kar* and is a conjugal step between a man and girl who have passed through the adolescent step of life. There is a diversity of rituals performed during marriage events in the Siem Reap region. In general, from village to another, the practise of the ritual is slightly different. The diversity of rituals is in some cases unique to villages in the AWHS.

A ritual concerning delivery marks the transition from housewife to a mother. This ritual can be seen across the whole AWHS.

The ceremony of prolongation of life has several names, as *Chansok Kiri Sout, Chhark Toch, Chhark Thom* or *Chhark Maha Bangsakol, Tor Ayuk*. This ritual practice is associated with the elderly. The ceremony aims to prolong the life of the person concerned by simulating a cycle of death–gestation–rebirth. Meditation is practised by the elderly, notably elderly women, and brings the mediator to envisage his or her self as a corpse, presumably in preparation for death. The ritual is widely practised in the Angkor region.

The funerary rite is known as *Bochea Sap*, and is composed of three major components of ceremony: first burial, exhumation and definitive burial.

Figure 12.5 Monk ordination ceremony at Angkor Wat
Photo: APSARA 2002

The two major ritual components are exhumation followed by cremation of the remains.

The burying of the ashes from incineration is known as *Banchus Theat*, and is the final stage of the human life circle. This is a testimony to the continuation of an ancient tradition in the Angkor region.

Ceremonies of fixed date

Some of the fixed-date ceremonies are agrarian rites which are part of the collective gathering of crops and other agricultural events; others are the traditional ceremonies of 12 months written in the traditional calendar such as *Tgnai Sel* (holy days), Khmer New Year or *Pchum Ben*, and last but not least, the practices of animism, a homage to *Neak Ta*, a spiritual village protector. The traditional ceremonies of 12 months are performed similarly elsewhere in the Kingdom. The difference is found in the way these ceremonies are practised from one place to another (Im 2008). Some of these ceremonies have particular meaning at Angkor such as *Visak Bochea* celebrations.

The ceremony of homage to Neak Ta is widely performed in every village within the AWHS. The most famous ceremony for the Siem Reap-Angkor region is the homage to *Ta Reach*, which is held within the monument of Angkor Wat. *Ta Reach* is one of the most prominent guardian spirits of the Angkor Site (see Figure 12.6). There are many *Neak Ta* spirits within the Angkor monuments and this form of intangible heritage shows the continuing spiritual beliefs linking the local community and the Angkorian monuments (Lloyd 2009).

The veneration of a god, Buddha or *Neak Ta* is a central element in the retention of village identity and memory of the Khmer people. Hindu gods and other elements of ancient structures also have spiritual power. Natural stones and Hindu or Buddhist icons have been appropriated as the embodiment of certain *Neak Ta* (Ang 2000; Im 2008).

Praying to the Hindu or Buddhist gods and the *Neak Ta*, and organising ceremonies and rituals is a continuing practice that reinforces both the sacred landscape and community identity. Within the landscape, certain 'special' places are commemorated through ritual, and their importance remembered and passed on within and between village communities (Im 2008).

Agrarian rites are commonly practised in the Angkor region and reflect the importance of agriculture as the main economic activity. A series of rituals concerning the rice paddy celebrates the beginning of the agricultural season through to the time the rice is stored. The agricultural season commences after the *Royal Ploughing Ceremony*, which is conducted by the King or his representative in late May.

Ceremonies of unfixed date

Ceremonies that are not tied into specific calendar events include those that are observed in the ritual of inauguration of a *Vihara*, or Buddhist monastery, or any public building: rituals related to the asking for rain; rituals to divert misfortune in a family or village or community; rituals at the beginning of house construction and house warming. This series of

Figure 12.6 Neak Ta Ceremony for *Ta Reach* in Angkor Wat
Photo: APSARA 2002

ceremonies is also widely performed throughout the region. Any ritual of this type can be performed on an auspicious date, determined by the traditional officiant or *achar* (Im 2008).

Customs

There are some performing arts which are considered to have a ritual gesture contributing to the collective events. These include dances, singing and music. Several popular dances are Indigenous to the Angkor region and relate to the chasing of evil, bad spirits or wild animals which provoke misfortune over the communities. *Trot* is a form of dance which is performed only during the New Year celebration for chasing bad luck and misfortune. Several traditional games such as tug-of-war are also played during the New Year days. The tug-of-war game is for getting rain for the coming agricultural season (Im 2008).

These descriptions of village life, traditions and beliefs illustrate that ICH is manifested in myriad ways at the AWHS in Cambodia. It can be seen through localised animistic and Brahmanic beliefs, continuing Buddhist practices and traditional livelihood activities. Research and documentation of ceremonies, livelihoods and customs has clearly shown that there is an organic and very spiritual link between Angkor and its people. The predominately rural World Heritage landscape of monuments and villages is steeped in rituals, ceremonies, orally transmitted knowledge and customary skills. Yet historically the management of this heritage site and the tourism industry has not reflected an awareness or appreciation of this living heritage.

Historical context

Until recently there has been little focus on the management of intangible heritage of Angkor. Since the late-19th century, stemming from the years of the French Protectorate, there has been a focus on monumental restoration and archaeological missions grounded in Western conservation theory. Early French laws outlined the role of the *École française d'Extrême-Orient* (EFEO) in the management of cultural property and the conservation and research of historical sites within the protectorate. To a large extent the French appropriated Cambodian heritage and managed sites and antiquities as French assets. In 1925 an area was officially delineated as the Parc d'Angkor and it is noteworthy that in 1929 there was acknowledgement that Indigenous peoples and other foreign Asians may visit the Park 'for a religious manner' and as such should be exempt from paying visitor fees. This acknowledgement, however, was relevant to the heritage value of the site and management was focused on the tangible heritage of Angkor. Even after Cambodia gained independence from France in 1953 a bilateral treaty was signed entrusting the EFEO with the management of the Angkor Conservation Office. The 1956 Treaty outlined that EFEO was responsible for supervising the work of the Angkor Conservation Office, pursuing archaeological research and maintaining the Angkor temples. This was again renewed in 1966. Following the period of independence and the period in the 1990s when heritage legislation was reintroduced, the French legal regime and conservation theory was strongly influential. In general, the system laid out by the French remained largely intact and applied to all moveable and immoveable objects of historic or artistic value in public or private possession (Royal Government of Cambodia 1998). The cultural heritage framework of Cambodia throughout the 20th century has been closely aligned to Western conservation ideals and monument focused conservation theories.

This historical focus on the tangible has meant that there has, in the past, been a failure to recognise the significance and meaning of intangible values and the protection of ICH has not been considered. Traditions, values and daily practices of local communities have often been overlooked. It is clear that the focus on tangible elements of Angkor, isolated from their spiritual context, has been the result of a process that began during the colonial period and was influenced by traditional Western conservation theory. The Authority for the Protection and Management of Angkor and the Region of Siem Reap (APSARA) has effectively managed Angkor in line with the laws and policies that make up the heritage framework (i.e. those governing the physical fabric of Angkor). They have addressed the management of activities within Angkor (such as the establishment of structures, organisation of tourist activities) and the restoration and safeguarding of the temples of Angkor.

As is illustrated above, in recent years there has been substantial research conducted by APSARA that has highlighted the significance and uniqueness forms of ICH at Angkor and this research is now in the process of being translated into policy for incorporation into site management.

A recent shift in the management of the WHS towards a holistic protection of natural, tangible and intangible heritage has been paralleled by a seemingly exponential growth in tourism. The safeguarding of intangible heritage requires an understanding of the tourism development and the interplay between tourism and the continuation of traditional practice.

Tourism trends at Angkor

Angkor is Cambodia's major tourist attraction and one of Asia's fastest growing tourism destinations (Winter 2003). In 2007 (Jan–Nov) Cambodia received 1.76 million international visitors (Ministry of Tourism 2007) and almost two million tourists (international and domestic) visited Angkor. In 2008, there were 2.1 million tourists (Ministry of Tourism 2009). Tourism is seen as a tool for economic development and poverty reduction (March 2001) and the continued rapid growth of this market is actively promoted to be a priority for the Cambodian government. There continues to be a growing tourism market being driven both by international and domestic visitors.

At Angkor there is a trend towards mass tourism with a large number of the visitors coming from countries within the Asian region. These tourists are classified as predominately 'leisure tourists' (Gonzáles 2008) who visit on package tours with an average stay in Siem Reap of two nights. In 2007, six of the top seven market arrivals were from Asian nations: South Korea, Japan, Vietnam, Taiwan, China and Thailand (Ministry of Tourism 2007). This trend is also visible in the first quarter of 2009 with 59.7 per cent of all international visitors to Cambodia (Jan–April 2009) arriving from Asian countries (Ministry of Tourism 2009). According to Tim Winter (2008, 2009) growth in tourism in Cambodia will likely continue this pattern, with increasing visitors coming from within the Asian region resulting in a parallel rise in mass leisure tourism.

Issues with intangible cultural heritage and tourism at the Angkor World Heritage site

Lack of awareness and respect for the contemporary spiritual aspects of the landscape

For a large sector of the current tourism market there is a general lack of awareness and respect for the contemporary values and spiritual aspects of the Angkor landscape. Most visitors to Angkor are not aware of the rich intangible heritage, contemporary culture and significance of Angkor (Lloyd 2009). This may be attributed to the fact that not all tourists that visit Angkor are actively participating in what Timothy and Nyaupane (2009) define as the commonly understood notion of 'cultural heritage tourism', nor seeking cultural experiences to reinvigorate their interest in culture and understanding of the cultural environment, values, traditions and lifestyles of the local population. Rather, as suggested previously, the majority of visitors to Angkor are dependant tourists or 'leisure tourists' (Gonzáles 2008), that is those travelling in large groups organised by travel agencies who are consumers of a heritage product sold by those agencies and tend to be simply visiting a prominent heritage site for its marketed aesthetic and archaeological value. Jonathan Wager (1995: 518) classifies these tourists as 'general interest sightseeing tourists who are attracted to Angkor because of its worldwide renown, including its World Heritage status, and travel in large groups, staying only one or two nights and making only a limited contribution to the local economy'. It has been recognised within recent studies on heritage tourism (e.g. Nyaupane, White and Budruk 2006) that there are different categories of visitors to heritage places depending on individual motivations. These can range from leisure tourists who wish to visit a place without engaging in any local cultural experiences to those who are seeking to immerse in or reconnect with the local culture or what Gonzáles (2008) differentiates as 'existential tourists' – those that are travelling for a deeper more spiritual understanding and connection with the intangible heritage of the place. At Angkor, however, there is a need to understand what Poria, Butler and Airey (2003: 249) refer to as the difference between '*heritage tourists* and *tourists at heritage places*'.

The preferences of tourists visiting the AWHS because of the status that Angkor embodies as an important global destination, has been geared towards the predominately marketed tourism experience of viewing monuments as relics of the past in a fabricated manner. As Winter (2009: 111) stipulates: 'the tourism industry that has evolved around Angkor has also thrived off the romantic, mysterious and adventurous tales of rediscovering lost antiquities'. At present, there is not the demand or the desire of tourism operators facilitating this segment of the tourism market to promote or explain the contemporary cultural significance of Angkor. After all, this is not part of the tourism product they are 'selling'. The tourism product of Angkor presented to most tourists follows a simplistic interpretation of the demise and abandonment of a glorious Khmer empire. Tourists are rarely presented with the modern significance of the Angkor monuments, their role in ceremonies both animistic and Buddhist, or the colloquial local legends and stories associated with them. Very little is presented of the recent history and cultural context of Angkor:

> In piecing together Angkor's history much less attention has been given to the Khmer inscriptions found among the temples or the evidence pertaining to the ongoing presence of animism. Indeed, within an account of architectural splendor and pristine glory, anthropological accounts that might reveal oral histories or the transmissions of cultural traditions across generations have been largely overlooked.
> (Winter 2009: 112)

In general the lack of awareness and understanding of the intangible heritage present at Angkor has resulted in a decrease in respect for the spiritual associations that continue to exist. Respect for the spiritual significance of Angkor is required to ensure that there is appropriate management and safeguarding of this heritage. Such respect may be generated through awareness-building measures and by encouraging respectful behaviour such as wearing appropriate clothing within the WHS. Awareness-raising measures may provide tourists with an enhanced experience of Angkor by developing a new appreciation for the spiritual value of the site.

Potential for commercialisation and commodification

Timothy and Nyaupane (2009: 62) state that one of the most 'often-cited side-effects of tourism is cultural commodification whereby culture becomes a product that is packaged and sold to tourists'. Tourism products performed and supplied in a commercial context have often lost the spiritual meanings or values that are present in their traditional cultural contexts. Ceremonies, performances, traditional healing or rituals conducted for economic benefit are often presented outside of the normal circumstances for that form of ICH as there is pressure to provide presentations to visitor on a regular basis rather than in the traditional context of, for example, the second full moon of the year or following the harvest season. Furthermore, often the commodification of culture involves privatisation by external stakeholders who utilise cultural elements for economic benefit without providing benefits to the local population. As George suggests, frequently there is:

> an inequity gap exists in benefits distributed to many rural communities whose cultural heritages are being appropriated and exploited by multiple commercial entities for tourism purposes and personal gain. Little, if any, of the profits realized benefit the local community – the actual creators and owners of the local culture.
>
> (2010: 376)

The commercialisation of cultural products by external stakeholders can lead to the perpetuation of false perceptions and stereotypes. This is present at Angkor with the perpetuation of the tale that the Frenchman Henri Mouhot was the lone explorer who discovered the abandoned city in a dense jungle. In reality there were many foreign visitors to Angkor before Mouhot – he was not even the first Frenchman, nor was the site completely abandoned although parts were heavily forested. Father Charles-Emile (Abbé C.) Bouillevaux visited Angkor and published his account in 1858, two years before Mouhot's arrival. It has been stated by Bouillevaux that the ruins of Angkor were not in fact found by Mouhot or any other Frenchman, for the reason that they were never forgotten or lost. Such stories, however, help to augment the commercialisation of the site, and Henderson (2009) argues that the Angkor Wat has been extensively commercialised by the tourism sector and multiple products created to maximise commercial opportunities.

Commercialisation and commodification has occurred for several forms of performing arts within Cambodia. Following the listing of *S'bek Thom* (Khmer shadow puppets) on the list of Masterpieces of the Oral and Intangible Heritage of Humanity in 2003 (now listed on under the Intangible Cultural Heritage Convention), the awareness and popularity of the artistic form within the tourism industry increased. A number of external stakeholders created commercial opportunities for the shadow puppet performance as the demand grew and there were increasingly more troupes performing without any formal training or reference to traditional presentation. Traditionally, *S'bek Thom* performances take place three or four times during the year as a call for rain or as part of other ceremonies undertaken for the good of the community' (Sisowath 2004: 96). Currently *S'bek Thom* performances are conducted several times a week for a purely touristic purpose and there is no portrayal of its intended function. Thus the performances are taken outside of their original context and performed by groups outside the community for reasons other than those intended. Similar concerns are found with the performance of Balinese dance (Barker, Putra and Wiranatha, 2006).

Potential for modification and simplification of traditions for tourism consumption

The motivations, circumstances and typology of visitors to heritage places influence the consumption and presentation of tourism products. For leisure tourists, those that make up a majority of tourists who travel to Angkor, there is a greater propensity to modify and/or simplify intangible heritage performances. These mass-market package tourists usually demand standardised services and goods (Bacuez 2009). Forms of intangible heritage performed to leisure tourists are thus more likely to be staged and adapted for tourist expectations. Bak argues that it is

> highly likely that the local communities may modify their heritage in the way they think will be more attractive to the tourists... [and] locally relevant and culturally genuine values of the heritage may be compromised in the process of making it more palatable to the tastes of the consumers of the cultures (the tourists who are cultural outsiders).
>
> (2007: 27)

For example, the dramatisation of an Indigenous oral tale may be simplified and shortened to fit a 30-minute window for tourist consumption (Greenwood 1989). Engelhardt (2007) refers to this as the 'dumbing down' of heritage interpretation whereas MacCannell (1973) suggests that this is 'staged authenticity', where forms of culture are performed to groups and are inauthentic, mass-produced misrepresentations of the local people. Gonzáles (2008: 809) stipulates that most leisure visitors have 'short contact with the intangible heritage element as spectators whilst travelling within the destination' and 'perceive the constructed authenticity... as being more authentic'.

With the growth of mass tourism at Angkor, the risk of simplification and modification of intangible heritage for tourism consumption may be greater. Engelhardt surmises:

> In the rush to provide expanded facilities for the rapid increase of mass-marketed tourism, the authenticity and integrity of Indigenous

traditional culture are all too frequently sacrificed. Likewise, typical tourism promotional activities take the form in which complex cultural heritage is simplified, homogenized, packaged and in the end, trivialized for the quick and easy consumption of the tourist. Ironically, it is precisely the authentic traditional culture and customs that tourists, both domestic and foreign, expect to experience when they visit a heritage site. But instead of getting rich and authentic cultural insights and experiences, tourists get staged authenticity; instead of getting culture, they get kitsch.

(2005: 3)

At Angkor and its nearby town of Siem Reap there are a number of examples of the modification and simplification of intangible heritage. Miura (2007) notes the standardisation of tourist experiences at Angkor and modification of the sacred space of Angkor. She uses the example of groups of people clad in theatrical and dance costumes within a number of the most popular temples as creating a standardised and altered experience or 'pseudo-event'. These experiences are not based on the traditional use of the temple space. In Siem Reap there is the Cambodian Cultural Village which presents performances on a regular basis of Khmer rituals such as wedding ceremonies. Winter (2009: 110) suggests that this cultural village and others like it in Asia are geared towards the mass market and present intangible heritage that is 'performed, modernized and aesthetically stylized for consumption as a tourist product'.

Freezing of culture and disassociation from the living landscape

A common factor associated with heritage sites is the disconnection of the tangible from the intangible (Engelhardt 2007). The perceived romantic notion of Angkor as a 'lost temple' landscape marketed by tourism companies has meant that the tourism industry has participated in the cultivation of a perception that Angkor is a select number of monuments that are relics of the past (Mar 2001), rather than a vast landscape comprising both tangible and intangible representations of heritage that have both historic and contemporary meaning. To a certain extent the monuments of Angkor have become a frozen landscape. At the very least tourism at Angkor is largely disassociated from the living aspect of the landscape. This follows a general theme of presenting a vision of the 'glorious past' in an unchanging or frozen environment (Winter 2006).

It is not only the tourism industry that has contributed to the process of secularisation of Angkor. For many years, following the French legacy of site management, Angkor was managed as an archaeological or historical park typically following the model outlined by Black and Wall (2001) where in general people have been removed from around the remains, the grounds have been landscaped and the historical remains are presented in a park-like setting. This stems from the historical focus on monumental restoration or, as Miura (2005: 3) states, an 'old conservation approach of freezing an idealized past for the interest of outsiders'. The result has been 'the museumification of the landscape via representations of the past as linear narratives' (Winter 2009: 113). While in recent years following the inclusion of Angkor on the World Heritage List, Angkor has been touted as a 'living heritage site'. The legitimacy of this phrase has been questioned as the living qualities of Angkor are frequently overlooked.

Recent developments in the management of intangible cultural heritage at Angkor

In the past, the management framework of Angkor has not effectively articulated the contemporary religious meaning of the AWHS to visitors (Baillie 2007). There remains further potential to develop appropriate presentation and interpretation of the intangible heritage within the AWHS, there are very few guides who can provide proper interpretation of ICH within the landscape and there is a general lack of knowledge and understanding of the meaning and significance of ICH.

Heritage managers at Angkor are left with a conundrum of how, if at all, to incorporate meaningful and appropriate contemporary intangible heritage (as a fundamental characteristic of the AWHS) within the tourism experience of the predominately regional, leisure mass tourists and how, if they wish to incorporate this heritage element, to ensure that tourism operators transmit such knowledge appropriately within their products. This is a demanding challenge as mass tourism has frequently been seen as the antithesis of meaningful appropriate tourism at heritage sites. The United Nations Educational, Scientific and Cultural Organization (UNESCO) even stipulated in the mid-1990s that tourism operators at Angkor should 'develop facilities for cultural tourism so as to prevent the onslaught of low quality mass tourism provoking irreversible destruction of Angkor's cultural and natural heritage' (UNESCO 1996). Since 2001 UNESCO has developed a specific World Heritage Tourism Program that recognises the importance of incorporating intangible heritage within WHS tourism-management policies (Pedersen 2004). These matters are being addressed by the APSARA Authority along with potential solutions such as introducing a professional course on ICH interpretation and raising public awareness.

In early 2000, APSARA created two main sections – the Social and Heritage Research Unit and the Pluridisciplinary Research Unit. The Pluridisciplinary Research Unit conducted predominantly archaeological research in partnership with international team. The Social Research Unit primarily worked with villagers within the WHS, engaging with an in-depth study of their way of life, their traditions and customs – all of which are significant components of the intangible heritage of Angkor. The project involved collecting cultural information from the villages. Unfortunately, the work of the unit was postponed due to an internal restructure of APSARA, but nevertheless the project was not fully abandoned. In 2006, the newly created APSARA Department of Demography and Development launched a new small project entitled 'Traditional Craft' of Angkor's villages. The project aimed to study socio-economic parameters of communities within the heritage area. The research was a component of the 'community development' section of APSARA.

The Living with Heritage (LWH) project, conducted by APSARA–UNESCO–University of Sydney in 2005 and 2006, identified that the values of Angkor cover a much wider spectrum than those previously assessed and acknowledged in the World Heritage citation which celebrates Angkor's unique artistic realisation, technical achievement and testament to a 'past civilisation' and which tended to concentrate on the larger and more obvious features such as the temples and their surrounding water-management systems. The LWH research helped to identify important significant scientific, symbolic and social values, in addition to the historic and aesthetic values that have previously been given prominence.

In recent years APSARA has also been part of a joint research project between Cambodian and Thai institutions. The collaborative work entitled Living Angkor Road Project (LARP) is a multidisciplinary research project. A socio-historic study has been conducted on communities living along the Royal Road in Cambodia and Thailand sides (LARP 2007, 2007–2008). The ethnographic survey has consisted of two sub-phases: location of all communities living along royal road and field survey to each community that has relation with the royal road (i.e. the community that has existed for long period of time, not newly established, with a buffer zone of two kilometres from each side of the predicted location of the royal road). The research has found that most of the village settlements are often associated with ancient occupancies. These villages have always been a spiritual landscape inhabited by protector spirits, *Neak Ta*, who live in temples and villages. Like many villages in the AWHS the royal road communities are continuing to live in the same spaces, within which there are inherited memories of ancestors' experiences and beliefs, overlain with the new generation's memories and experiences – and these all remain closely associated with particular places and localities within the wider landscape. Continuing practices also include storytelling, playing New Year games, dances, music and theatre.

The research conducted by APSARA has clarified the need to address intangible heritage within the management of the AWHS. In early 2010 H.E. Bun Narith, Director-General of APSARA, approved the creation of an intangible heritage project to examine the concept in Angkor and the creation of a policy for safeguarding ICH. An intangible heritage working group was created along with the appointment of an expert advisor (Professor Ang Choulean) and a consultant (Dr Georgina Lloyd).

The work of the intangible heritage project had the following principal objectives:

- Define the function of APSARA as the institution responsible for the safeguarding of intangible heritage at Angkor.
- Draft and put forward for adoption a policy for the safeguarding of intangible heritage and the recognition of, respect for and enhancement of intangible heritage in society particularly through education and awareness-raising.
- Increase the awareness and comprehension of the 1972 UNESCO Convention Concerning the Protection of the World Cultural and Natural Heritage (World Heritage Convention) and 2003 UNESCO Convention for the Safeguarding of the intangible cultural heritage (Intangible Cultural Heritage Convention) among APSARA staff.
- Assist APSARA departments to meet their tasks related to intangible heritage as established by the 2008 Sub decree regarding the Organisation and Functioning of the Office of the Director-General of APSARA (°50 ANK/BK).

The working group met on number of occasions throughout 2010 to examine the safeguarding of ICH and develop a draft policy for Angkor. On 20 September 2010, APSARA conducted a seminar to review the draft policy for protecting ICH. Several measures for managing intangible heritage were presented. For example, working with local communities to develop a calendar of traditional cultural events while ensuring that the community retains the ownership of the events and practises them within a traditional cultural context. Another action is the certification of holders of knowledge and local produce developed within the village context. H.E. Bun Narith established that APSARA will work towards raising awareness of intangible heritage among visitors, conduct further research on intangible heritage within the AWHS and undertake further training on intangible heritage for APSARA staff and guides.

In late 2010 the Angkor Heritage Management Framework (HMF) project started. This project was initiated by APSARA, in association with UNESCO and the Government of Australia. The HMF is being prepared by APSARA in collaboration with Godden Mackay Logan – an Australian heritage consulting firm. It will address heritage management concerns at Angkor, particularly tourism through the preparation of a Tourism Management Plan incorporating environmental and socio-cultural aspects of tourism including intangible heritage.

References

Ang, C. (2000) *People and Earth*, Exhibition catalogue, 7 March, Phnom Penh: Reyum Fallery.

Bacuez, P. (2009) *Intangible Heritage, Tourism and Raising Awareness on Kilwa Kisiwani and Songo Mnara: Findings and Recommendations*, Paris: UNESCO.

Baillie, B. (2007) 'Conservation of the sacred at Angkor Wat: further reflections on living heritage', *Conservation and Management of Archaeological Sites* 8: 123–31.

Bak, S. (2007) 'Domestic and international cultural tourism in the context of intangible heritage', Paper presented at UNESCO–EIIHCAP, Regional Meeting of Safeguarding Intangible Heritage and Sustainable Cultural Tourism: Opportunities and Challenges, Hue, Vietnam, December.

Barker, T., Putra, D. and Wiranatha, A. (2006) 'Authenticity and commodification of Balinese dance performances', in M.K. Smith and M. Robinson (eds) *Cultural Tourism in a Changing World: Politics, Participation and (Re)presentation*, Clevedon: Channel View Publications.

Black, H. and Wall, G. (2001) 'Global–local inter-relationships in UNESCO World Heritage sites', in P. Teo, T.C. Chang and K.C. Ho (eds) *Interconnected Worlds: Tourism in Southeast Asia*, Oxford: Pergamon.

Dallen, J.T. and Gyan, P.N (2009) *Cultural Heritage Tourism in the Developing World: A Regional Perspective*, New York: Taylor and Francis.

Engelhardt, R. (2005) 'Safeguarding intangible heritage: cultural industries and the cultural diversity lens', Paper presented at International Workshop of Local Government Administrators for Safekeeping of the Intangible Cultural Heritage, Gangneung, Republic of Korea, June.

Engelhardt, R. (2007) 'Safeguarding intangible heritage and sustainable cultural tourism: a conceptual framework', Paper presented at UNESCO-EIIHCAP, Regional Meeting of Safeguarding Intangible Heritage and Sustainable Cultural Tourism: Opportunities and Challenges, Hue, Vietnam, December.

George, W. (2010) 'Intangible cultural heritage, ownership, copyrights, and tourism', *International Journal of Culture, Tourism and Hospitality Research* 4(4): 376–88.

Gonzáles, M.V. (2008) 'Intangible heritage tourism and identity', *Tourism Management* 29: 807–10.

Greenwood, D.J. (1989) 'Culture by the pound: an anthropological perspective on tourism as cultural commoditization', in V.L. Smith (ed.) *Hosts and Guests: The Anthropology of Tourism*, Philadelphia: University of Pennsylvania Press.

Henderson, J. (2009) 'The meanings, marketing and management of heritage tourism in Southeast Asia', in D.J. Timothy & G.P. Nyaupane (eds) *Cultural Heritage and Tourism in the Developing World: A Regional Perspective*, London: Routledge.

Im, S. (2008) 'Social values and community context', in R. Mackay and S. Sullivan (eds) *Angkor: Heritage Values and Issues.* Available online: http://acl.arts.usyd.edu.au/angkor/lwh/images/stories/lwh/Documents/heritage%20values%20and%20issues%20report%20part%201.pdf (accessed 13 June 2012).

LARP (2007) 'Living Angkor Road report', in UNESCO, *16th Technical Committee Report*, Siem Reap, Sokha-Angkor Hotel, 5–7 July.

LARP (2007–2008) *Living Angkor Road: Technical Report.* Available online: http://larp.crma.ac.th (accessed 2 April 2011).

Lloyd, G. (2009) *The Safeguarding of Intangible Cultural Heritage: Law and Policy: A Case Study of Angkor,* Doctoral dissertation, University of Sydney, Australia. Available online: http://hdl.handle.net/2123/7027 (accessed 7 March 2011).

MacCannell, D. (1973) 'Staged authenticity: arrangements of social space in tourist settings', *American Journal of Sociology* 79(3): 589–603.

Mar, T. (2001) 'The reconstruction of Khmer culture for tourism: local implications', MA Thesis, The Netherlands: University of Amsterdam.

Ministry of Tourism, Kingdom of Cambodia (2007) *Tourism Statistical Report November 2007.* Available online: www.mot.gov.kh/ (accessed 19 March 2011).

Ministry of Tourism, Kingdom of Cambodia (2009) *Tourism Statistical Report April 2009.* Available online: www.mot.gov.kh/ (accessed 5 May 2011).

Miura, K. (2005) 'Conservation of a "living heritage site" a contradiction in terms? A case study of the Angkor World Heritage site', *Conservation and Management of Archaeological Sites* 7: 3–18.

Miura, K. (2007) 'A Note on the current impact of tourism on Angkor and its environs', *Conservation and Management of Archaeological Sites,* 8: 132–35.

Norindr, P. (2006) 'The fascination for Angkor Wat and the ideology of the visible', in L.C. Ollier and T. Winter (eds) *Expressions of Cambodia: The Politics of Tradition, Identity and Change,* New York: Routledge.

Nyaupane, G.P., White, D. and Budruk, M. (2006) 'Motive-based tourist market segmentation: an application to Native American cultural heritage sites in Arizona, USA', *Journal of Heritage Tourism* 1(2): 81–99.

Pedersen, A. (2004). 'The alliance between tourism and mankind's intangible heritage: the possible tangible benefits of working on intangible heritage issues at World Heritage sites', Paper presented at Conference Forum Barcelona, July. Available online: www.barcelona2004.org/www.barcelona2004.org/esp/banco_del_conocimiento/docs/PO_24_EN_PEDERSEN.pdf (accessed 25 August 2012).

Poria, Y., Butler, R. and Airey, D. (2003) 'The core of heritage tourism', *Annals of Tourism Research* 30(1): 238–54.

Royal Government of Cambodia (1998) *Request to the United States of America for Import Restrictions on Cambodian Cultural Objects and for Emergency Measures,* Cambodia: Royal Government of Cambodia.

Sisowath, K.C. (2004) 'Cambodian traditions at risk', Paper presented at Globalization and Intangible Cultural Heritage, Tokyo, Japan.

Timothy, D.J. and Nyaupane, G.P. (eds) (2009) *Cultural Heritage and Tourism in the Developing World: A Regional Perspective,* London: Routledge.

UNESCO (1996) *Angkor – Past, Present and Future,* Phnom Penh: APSARA.

Wager, J. (1995) 'Developing a strategy for the Angkor World Heritage site', *Tourism Management* 16(7): 515.

Winter, T. (2003) 'Tomb raiding Angkor: a clash of cultures', *Indonesia and the Malay World* 31(89): 58–68.

Winter, T. (2006) 'When ancient glory meets modern tragedy: Angkor and the Khmer Rouge in contemporary tourism', in L.C. Ollier and T. Winter (eds) *Expressions of Cambodia: The Politics of Tradition, Identity and Change,* New York: Routledge.

Winter, T. (2008) 'Asian destination: rethinking material culture', in T. Winter, P. Teo and T.C. Chang (eds) *Asia on Tour: Exploring the Rise of Asian Tourism*, London: Routledge.

Winter, T. (2009) 'The modernities of heritage and tourism: interpretations of an Asian future', *Journal of Heritage Tourism*, 4(2): 105–15.

Chapter 13

Heritage tourism in Africa

Anna Spenceley and Fred Nelson

Introduction

Africa is rich in natural and cultural heritage. Many of these destinations are recognised for their global importance and have been designated as World Heritage sites (WHS) by UNESCO. They include among the most iconic tourism destinations and experiences on the continent. They incorporate, for example, climbing Mount Kilimanjaro and viewing the diverse wildlife of the Serengeti in Tanzania, visiting the mountain gorillas of the Virunga National Park in the Democratic Republic of Congo (DRC), exploring cultural heritage and architecture of the Pays Dogon in Mali and experiencing the pyramids in Egypt. This chapter explores matters surrounding sustainable tourism at a selection of these and other sites.

Tourism can play a critical role in raising awareness of heritage and providing educational opportunities for both residents and international travellers. However, due to the sensitivity of the sites (e.g. fragile ecology, ancient monuments) it can be challenging to manage visitors so that a quality experience is balanced with conserving the site and with generating tangible economic benefits for local people. The cultural, environmental and economic lessons learned from tourism at a series of these sites are reviewed and discussed in this chapter.

Heritage in Africa

A central factor in the management of many WHSs in Africa is the contestation or conflict over rights to manage and benefit from tourism and the natural resources that tourism is based upon. Many WHSs are among the most valuable tourism attractions in African countries, and thus control over tourism businesses and revenues from such areas is often subject to fierce competition amongst local, national and transnational groups. Such conflicts are intensified by the reality that most WHSs are situated within landscapes that support local livelihoods in a range of different ways, and thus tourism is but one of a number of different social and economic values that these sites produce. At the same time, the long-term sustainability of many WHSs is contingent on support for conservation measures by these local communities, including their ability to establish and enforce resource-management practices that encourage sustainable use of natural resources. As such, matters surrounding land tenure, natural resource governance and control over tourism development and revenues are critical to the future of many WHSs and the tourism enterprises and industries that they support.

To be included on the World Heritage List, sites must be of outstanding universal value and meet at least one out of ten selection criteria (see Table 13.1).

Table 13.1 World Heritage site selection criteria

i.	to represent a masterpiece of human creative genius;
ii.	to exhibit an important interchange of human values, over a span of time or within a cultural area of the world, on developments in architecture or technology, monumental arts, town-planning or landscape design;
iii.	to bear a unique or at least exceptional testimony to a cultural tradition or to a civilization which is living or which has disappeared;
iv.	to be an outstanding example of a type of building, architectural or technological ensemble or landscape which illustrates (a) significant stage(s) in human history;
v.	to be an outstanding example of a traditional human settlement, land-use, or sea-use which is representative of a culture (or cultures), or human interaction with the environment especially when it has become vulnerable under the impact of irreversible change;
vi.	to be directly or tangibly associated with events or living traditions, with ideas, or with beliefs, with artistic and literary works of outstanding universal significance. (The Committee considers that this criterion should preferably be used in conjunction with other criteria);
vii.	to contain superlative natural phenomena or areas of exceptional natural beauty and aesthetic importance;
viii.	to be outstanding examples representing major stages of earth's history, including the record of life, significant on-going geological processes in the development of landforms, or significant geomorphic or physiographic features;
ix.	to be outstanding examples representing significant on-going ecological and biological processes in the evolution and development of terrestrial, fresh water, coastal and marine ecosystems and communities of plants and animals;
x.	to contain the most important and significant natural habitats for in-situ conservation of biological diversity, including those containing threatened species of outstanding universal value from the point of view of science or conservation.

The protection, management, authenticity and integrity of properties are also important considerations. Since 1992 significant interactions between people and the natural environment have been recognized as cultural landscapes.

Source: http://whc.unesco.org/en/criteria/ (accessed 26 February 2011)

Africa has 122 UNESCO WHSs; 37 have been designated as natural, 80 cultural and five are a mixture of natural and cultural heritage. In addition, three are trans-boundary, and shared by two countries (Mount Nimba Strict Nature Reserve, Stone Circles of Senegambia and Mosi-oa-Tunya/Victoria Falls). Twenty countries in Africa do not have any WHSs inscribed yet (namely Angola, Burundi, Chad, Comoros, DRC, Djibouti, Equatorial Guinea, Eritrea, Guinea-Bissau, Lesotho, Liberia, Mayotte, Reunion, Rwanda, Saint Helena, Sao Tome and Principe, Sierra Leone, Somalia, Swaziland and Western Sahara). This is not necessarily an indication that they do not have a rich heritage, but rather that they have not been through the inscription protocol required by UNESCO. For example, Rwanda shares the Virunga Volcano range with the DRC and Uganda, but it has not declared its share of the region a World Heritage site – though both DRC and Uganda have, in order to recognise the only remaining habitat of the mountain gorilla.

Several of Africa's WHSs are designated as 'in danger'. This designation is designed to inform the international community of conditions which threaten the very characteristics for which a property was inscribed on the World Heritage List and to encourage corrective action. For example, since 1994 all five WHSs of the DRC (The National Parks of Garamba, Kahuzi-Biega, Salonga, Virunga and the Okapi Wildlife Reserve) were inscribed on the List of World Heritage in Danger as a result of the impact of the war and civil conflicts in the Great Lakes region. In 1999, an international safeguarding campaign was launched by UNESCO (together with a number of international conservation non-governmental organisations [NGOs]) to protect the habitat of endangered species such as the mountain gorilla, the northern white rhino and the okapi. This resulted in a four-year US$3.5 million emergency programme to save the five sites, funded by the United Nations Foundation and the Government of Belgium. In 2004, international donors, NGOs and the governments of Belgium and Japan pledged an additional US$50 million to help the DRC rehabilitate these World Heritage parks (UNESCO 2011).

Tourism management at heritage sites

Managers of natural and cultural heritage sites carry a great responsibility when it comes to tourism management. They are empowered to share the destination with the world and encourage visitors to visit the site. Through tourism they can share understanding of the importance of the heritage, while also generating revenue that can support its conservation. The drawback of tourism is that, if poorly managed, it can adversely affect the aesthetic value of the site and may even lead to deterioration of the site itself. A number of agencies are providing support to improve the capacity of WHS managers to conserve these sites. These include the International

Union for Conservation of Nature (IUCN) World Commission on Protected Areas (WCPA) World Heritage Specialist Group, the Tourism and Protected Areas Specialist Group (TAPAS) all contributed to UNESCO's World Heritage Tourism Program and the African World Heritage Fund (WHF).

The IUCN WCPA Tourism and Protected Areas Specialist Group helped to devise a 'guide to good practice' for natural WHS (Stolton and Dudley 2010), with the collaboration of partners including the WCPA TAPAS group. Designed for the managers of WHS, this incorporates a chapter on the management of tourism. The guidelines incorporate advice on sustainable tourism policies and plans, zoning, community engagement, tourist perceptions, connections with wider landscapes and destinations, monitoring and research, visitor facilities and interpretation, concessions and, of course, links with the tourism industry.

UNESCO's World Heritage Tourism Program was established in 2001 in order to address growing threats on WHSs from tourism which, if sustainably managed, could offer socio-economic development opportunities. However, Africa's heritage sites were ignored by the programme, which focused on Europe, Asia and Central and Latin America (Jenkins 2010). The tourism programme was closed in 2010, and there are now plans to re-launch it with the overall objective of incorporating the principles of sustainable tourism into the management of WHSs (Jenkins 2010).

The Africa WHF is a NGO with a mission to support the implementation of the UNESCO World Heritage Convention. A WHF works on the conservation of Africa's natural and cultural heritage, and seeks to increase the presence of African sites on the UNESCO World Heritage List. They do this through investment and sustainable management of the sites and related activities. The African WHF's mission is to:

- Provide support to identify and list African heritage sites on the World Heritage List
- Provide support and assistance for the conservation and management of heritage sites in Africa, particularly those already inscribed on the World Heritage List
- Rehabilitate sites inscribed on the List of World Heritage in Danger
- Train heritage experts and site managers as ongoing capacity building
- Involve communities in decisions concerning their heritage and ensuring that tangible benefits accrue to them.

(African WHF n.d.: para. 2)

The programme aims to address conservation challenges as well as opportunities around WHSs through sustainable tourism, using situation analysis and pilot projects at selected sites. In 2011 they were working at Kilwa Kisiwani (Tanzania), Twyfelfontein (Namibia), Great Zimbabwe

(Zimbabwe), Forts and Castles (Ghana), Bwindi National Park (Uganda), Timbuktu (Mali), Island of Goree (Senegal), James Island and related sites (The Gambia), Tsodilo Hills (Botswana), Ngorongoro Conservation Area (NCA) (Tanzania) and Victoria Falls (Zambia and Zimbabwe).

Case study examples: tourism in African World Heritage sites

To illustrate the implications of tourism for sustainable development in Africa, three case studies of WHSs in Africa are described here. These are the Richtersveld National Park in South Africa, the Kilimanjaro National Park, NCA and Mount Kilimanjaro in Tanzania. The first, the Richtersveld, is a little-known tourism destination, with low levels of visitors and limited infrastructure. The second and third examples, the NCA and Mount Kilimanjaro, are iconic tourism destinations which are globally known. This contrast of emerging and well-established destinations is reflective of differences among many other heritage sites on the continent. Three key themes addressed here are: how to attract more visitors, how to manage the consequent number of visitors and how to ensure meaningful benefits to resident communities.

Case study 1: Richtersveld National Park: feasibility studies for natural and cultural tourism activities and attractions in an emerging destination

In June 2007 the Richtersveld World Heritage site was declared, covering 160,000 hectares of the Northern Cape in South Africa. A remote wilderness, with few passable roads and sparsely populated by sheep and goat herders, it was nominated as a natural site for its high plant diversity and as a cultural landscape shaped by the semi-nomadic Nama pastoralists – one of the last transhumance cultures in Southern Africa. Prior to the southern migration of Bantu peoples, the Indigenous Nama were more extensively spread across the sub-continent; now they live in the northern part of South Africa and Namibia, but only practice pastoral transhumance in and around the area (UNESCO 2007).

UNESCO states that the Richtersveld Cultural and Botanical Landscape demonstrates Outstanding Universal Value due to the extensive communal grazed lands as a testimony to land-management processes and which have ensured the protection of the succulent Karoo vegetation. They demonstrate a harmonious interaction between people and nature. The rich diverse botanical landscape of the Richtersveld, shaped by the pastoral grazing of the Nama (see Figures 13.1 and 13.2), supports a way of life that persisted for many millennia over a considerable part of Southern Africa and represents a significant stage in the history of this area. The seasonal

Figure 13.1 Landscape and flowers, Richtersveld National Park, South Africa
Photo: © Anna Spenceley

Figure 13.2 Stockfarming and nature, Richtersveld National Park, South Africa
Photo: © Anna Spenceley

migrations of grazers between stockposts with traditional demountable mat-roofed houses (*haru oms*) reflect a practice that was once much more widespread over Southern Africa, and which has persisted for at least two millennia. The Nama are now its last practitioners. Richtersveld is one of the few areas in Southern Africa where transhumance pastoralism is still practised; as a cultural landscape it reflects long-standing and persistent traditions of the Nama, the Indigenous community. Their seasonal pastoral grazing regimes, which sustain the extensive bio-diversity of the area, were once much more widespread and are now vulnerable (UNESCO 2007).

In principle, the World Heritage site is owned and managed by the people of the Richtersveld, through their Communal Property Association (CPA). The area is host to transhumant pastoralists who keep sheep and goats (RCC 2007). It also has a rich cultural heritage, including a number of petroglyphs or San rock carvings (although several have been damaged by graffiti), clusters of beacons and San burial sites (see Figures 13.3 and 13.4).

The World Heritage site contains all three biomes present in the Richtersveld: Desert, Succulent Karoo and a small area of Fynbos in the Stinkfonteinberge mountains. The area falls within the Gariep Centre, one of the five centres of endemism of the Succulent Karoo biome. The

Figure 13.3 Petroglyph by San people, Richtersveld National Park, South Africa
Photo: © Anna Spenceley

Figure 13.4 Cluster of beacons, Richtersveld National Park, South Africa
Photo: © Anna Spenceley

Succulent Karoo biome contains more than 5,000 plant species, of which over 40 per cent are endemic. It contains 33 species endemic to the protected area (RCC 2007). However, it is estimated that 18 per cent of Succulent Karoo plants (see Figure 13.5) are threatened by overgrazing, mining and illegal harvesting of plants. Of particular importance in the World Heritage site is the presence of one of the world's most endangered plants, the Giant Quiver Tree (see Figure 13.6) (RCC 2007).

The Richtersveld Community Conservancy, which manages the park on behalf of the CPA, identified a number of opportunities for tourism, but recognised that few benefits were realised for the local community. They also recognised tourism opportunities should not be in conflict with other activities in the conservation area (i.e. stockfarming). They appreciate that the nomadic culture of the Nama people is a potential attraction to tourists, in combination with the rich biodiversity of the mountain desert, with around 140 species of endemic succulent flowers. They appreciate that it is possible to combine traditional farming practices with tourism opportunities such as hiking, 4x4 trails, horse riding, canoeing on the Orange river and rock climbing, but do not know how to exploit them (Spenceley and Rylance 2008).

Figure 13.5 Karoo succulent plants, Richtersveld National Park, South Africa
Photo: © Anna Spenceley

Figure 13.6 Giant Quiver tree, Richtersveld National Park, South Africa
Photo: © Anna Spenceley

As part of a feasibility study for tourism in the Richtersveld in 2008, seven tourism accommodation enterprises were interviewed, which had collectively hosted 2,316 visitors. Given an average accommodation price of R 134 per person, per night, and an average length of stay of three nights, this implies turnover of R 1.1 million was generated by the Richtersveld World Heritage site area per year. This estimate, and the data provided in Table 13.2, demonstrates that the level of visitation to the park is very low (Spenceley and Rylance 2008).

Table 13.2 Visitation of the Richtersveld World Heritage site (2006–2008)

	2006	2007	2008 (January–May)
Visitation			
Day visitors	115	146	3
'Kom rus 'n bietjie' guesthouse	487	473	170
Rooiberg guesthouse	144	177	75
Camping in the World Heritage site	64	52	98
Total	*810*	*848*	*346*
Revenue generated			
Day visitors (R 30 per person)	R 3,450	R 4,380	R 90
'Kom rus 'n bietjie' guesthouse (R 150 per person)	R 73,050	R 70,950	R 25,500
Rooiberg guesthouse (R 150 per person)	R 21,600	R 26,550	R 11,250
Camping in the World Heritage site (R 20 per person)	R 1,280	R 1,040	R 1,960
Total	*R 99,380*	*R 102,920*	*R 38,800*

Source: Adapted from Eksteenfontien Tourism Information Centre data

Part of the problem faced by community members in planning and developing tourism in this park is their limited exposure to tourism destinations elsewhere. Staff members managing the area require more skills and expertise in financial planning and tourism management. Problems that have arisen include the vandalism of some culturally significant aspects of the site (e.g. petroglyphs) by visitors and poor control over waste management. Visitor management is itself constrained by the lack of control of access to the reserve. The roads within the World Heritage site are only accessible to 4x4 vehicles, which reduces the potential pool of visitors, and poor signage, inadequate maps and a lack of mobile phone reception in the area limit effective tourist negotiation of the site.

There has been limited promotion of the site to attract tourists and a marketing strategy and plan is needed. It does have two small Tourism Information Centres (see Figures 13.7 and 13.8), but they do not reach out to South African or international tour operators, or to the 4x4 market, to promote the destination (Spenceley and Rylance 2008). Developing partnerships with the private sector may provide an opportunity to diversify the tourism products and services offered in the Richtersveld, while drawing in marketing and promotion expertise.

Figure 13.7 Rooiberg Guest House, Richtersveld National Park, South Africa
Photo: © Anna Spenceley

In order to evaluate the tourism potential for the Richtersveld, a market-demand study was conducted. A sample of 48 tourists in the Richtersveld region were asked what activities they had undertaken, or would be undertaking, while in the Richtersveld area. Similarly, tourism accommodation enterprises were asked what their tourists do during their visit. Over half the tourists interviewed were visiting natural attractions and national parks in the area, while over a third were visiting villages and experiencing wildlife. More than 60 per cent of the sample rated guest houses, birding tours, research facilities, guided hiking trails, botanical tours and boat or

Figure 13.8 Tourism Office in Kuboes, Richtersveld National Park, South Africa
Photo: © Anna Spenceley

canoe trips on the Orange River as 'very important' or 'important'. In addition, over 85 per cent of the visitors rated wildlife re-introduction, medicinal plant tours, cultural attractions, information centres, research facilities, home stays with Nama communities, camping sites and guest houses as 'very important' or 'important'. Tourists were asked what activities they would like to undertake in future, as well as their willingness to pay for specified tourism products. This established that the majority of people desired camping sites, guest houses and opportunities to get more information about conservation, birding and cultural attractions (Spenceley and Rylance 2008).

The people of the Richtersveld recognise that the barriers they face in developing tourism, which include access to finance, limited skills in tourism, marketing and promotion and a lack of entrepreneurial spirit (Spenceley and Rylance 2008). To create a sustainable tourism destination where a balance between pastoral practices and sensitive visitation can be achieved, the people of the Richtersveld will need technical support from independent advisors and the commercial interest of the private sector. Making these links tangible proves to be an ongoing constraint for this World Heritage site.

Case study 2: Ngorongoro Conservation Area, Tanzania

Northern Tanzania is home to three WHS, which are among Africa's (and indeed the world's) most famous sites: Serengeti National Park, Mount Kilimanjaro and the NCA. These areas also comprise the main tourism attractions in Tanzania, underpinning a national tourism industry which now generates more than US$1 billion in annual revenues and has been a key driver of growth and economic recovery in Tanzania since the early 1990s. Of this amount, roughly US$600 million is derived from the northern circuit, and half of all visitors to Tanzania visit the NCA and its famous wildlife-filled volcanic caldera (the 'Ngorongoro Crater') (Mitchell and Keane 2008).

The NCA is the country's single most important tourism attraction, along with the Serengeti National Park which adjoins the NCA to the west, sharing the Serengeti plains between the two protected areas. The NCA was originally created out of the Serengeti National Park, which was re-gazetted with redrawn boundaries in 1959. That process involved evicting the Maasai residents from the Serengeti National Park in order to clear the park of human inhabitants (who at the time were considered an impediment to conservation). In exchange, the NCA was created as a multiple-use area with the explicit aim of managing the area primarily for its resident Maasai communities (Homewood and Rodgers 1991).

The original objectives of community development and multiple use have, however, never been effectively implemented, and the history of NCA is characterised by deep and enduring tensions surrounding local resource rights and livelihood interests, tourism development and wildlife conservation. NCA is managed by its own parastatal entity, the Ngorongoro Conservation Area Authority (NCAA) and its own governing legislation, the Ngorongoro Conservation Area Ordinance, originally passed in 1959 but revised various times since then. Documented repeatedly over the years, the overarching issue in the management of NCA is the general prioritisation of wildlife and tourism interests – and thus national and global interests – at the expense of the local development interests for which NCA was ostensibly originally created (Homewood and Rodgers 1991; Honey 2008; Shivji and Kapinga 1998). A range of fundamental management concerns and policy developments illustrate these enduring tensions and conflicts.

During the first three decades of Tanzanian independence – the 1960s, 1970s and 1980s – there was limited economic and infrastructural development in NCA, even while Maasai land and resource-use rights were progressively curtailed (Homewood and Rodgers 1991). NCA residents lost access to the Ngorongoro highland forest portion of NCA as well as the Ngorongoro Crater in the 1970s, with Maasai communities resident on the Crater floor being forcibly evicted in 1976. Investments in community development and service provision were limited, which partly reflected a general neglect of pastoralist livelihoods by the Tanzanian government during this period, with Maasai considered 'backwards' and primitive where modernisation framed the bureaucratic approach to pastoralism (Ole Parkipuny 1979). However, conservation interests – particularly the influence in the Serengeti and Ngorongoro of the Frankfurt Zoological Society – also played a role in generally discouraging human economic development in NCA out of concern for possible effects on wildlife or the 'wilderness' quality of the area (Homewood and Rodgers 1991).

During this period, tourism was relatively limited in NCA, and tourist arrivals in Tanzania collapsed completely following the 1977 closure of the border with Kenya – which lasted six years and set back development of the country's tourism industry until the 1990s (Honey 2008). By the late 1980s, however, Tanzania had formally abandoned socialism and a surge of private investment began, often linking transnational private investors with Tanzanian public officials who controlled access to land and resources (Kelsall 2002). Tourism investment picked up again in major destinations such as Serengeti National Park and NCA, with the construction of several lodges on the Ngorongoro Crater rim. While these properties offer stunning locations and are highly profitable, they have been controversial from the outset – for displacing local Massai people, for consuming locally critical resources such as water springs on the Crater rim and for their environmental effects on the forest around the Crater (Bonner 1993).

Since the early 1990s, the NCA has become the single most important attraction in Tanzania's tourism industry and the centrepiece of the northern tourism circuit (which includes the Serengeti as well as Lake Manyara and Tarangire National Parks and the climbing peaks of Mount Kilimanjaro and Mount Meru). This has not diminished, but rather continues to exacerbate, conflicts between tourism, the government and resident communities in NCA. Maasai communities have no role in planning or managing tourism developments in NCA and, unlike many villages elsewhere in northern Tanzania, have no rights to enter into joint venture agreements with private tourism operators. NCAA created their Pastoral Council in the 1990s to respond to criticisms of a lack of local participation in NCA management and to establish a mechanism for revenue sharing. While the Pastoral Council receives some proportion of NCA revenues for local development purposes, it has also evolved into a mechanism for NCA to mute the complaints of resident communities through the financial and political coercion of their elected representatives (Honey 2008). A number of new lodges in NCA have been approved in recent years, again without any formal local approval or participation. Maasai in NCA hold their land rights at the discretion of the NCAA, have no legal right to develop and enforce land use plans and other resource management regulations and no acknowledged claims over tourism revenue. The main mechanism for local participation in tourism is through the establishment of cultural *bomas*, which serve as a cultural attraction for tourists passing from NCA to Serengeti National Park.

In the past several years, tensions surrounding NCA have intensified. In 2006, the Tanzanian government carried out an exercise to identify 'immigrants' to NCA who it argued, unlike the 'traditional' resident Maasai, should not be allowed to reside in NCA. More than 2,000 people were relocated to Oldoinyo Sambu, near the Kenyan border above Lake Natron (Hammer 2010). Since then, some government leaders have suggested that the resident population in NCA (which today comprises over 60,000 people) should be relocated in order to safeguard the area's wildlife and tourism assets (*The Arusha Times* 2010). This follows a long-established (if generally unstated) government and ruling party policy which holds that the long-term solution to competition over land, resources and revenues in NCA is to 'persuade the Maasai to vacate the area' (see Honey 2008).

The government's generally stated position is that the Maasai cause environmental degradation in NCA and are incompatible with wildlife and nature tourism (Hammer 2010). Frequently cited is the reality that the Maasai population in NCA has increased sixfold since the 1960s, which creates food security challenges since livestock numbers have not increased and agriculture remains banned in NCA. Despite these demographic pressures, there is no evidence of negative impacts of Maasai communities on wildlife in NCA. Following the eradication of rinderpest (a zoonotic livestock disease), the Serengeti wildebeest population increased sixfold in the 1960s, and since the 1980s has been generally stable at around 1.2 million animals. In the Ngorongoro Crater there has been no general increase of wildlife since resident Maasai were evicted in the mid-1970s (Runyoro *et al.* 1995), and research elsewhere in NCA does not document any strong spatial disassociations between people and wildlife (Ellis *et al.* 2001).

If there is no evidence of negative impact by resident communities on natural assets in NCA, what accounts for the policy positions of the Tanzanian government concerning the site? A main factor is the resilience and durability of cultural and political bias against pastoralists in Tanzania. Narratives about overgrazing, the irrationality and 'backwardness' of pastoralists and the Maasai – and about the lack of pastoralist contributions to the national economy – persist, despite decades of research debunking these long-held assumptions (see Homewood and Rodgers 1987; Hesse and MacGregor 2006). A second factor is the increasing property value of NCA, driven by ever-growing tourism visitor and revenue volumes in northern Tanzania. A range of actors – from private investors to political elites – have growing interests in land and development in NCA, and in many respects the Maasai residents are perceived as a barrier to continued tourism development, particularly when new lodges or camps come into direct conflict with locals over use of land and water.

Notably, the NCA's status as a World Heritage site has itself recently contributed to growing tension and debate over the site's management. UNESCO carried out two monitoring missions to NCA in 2007 and 2008 in response to growing concerns since the late-1990s about human effects on NCA's 'Outstanding Universal Values' and its potential status as an endangered site. These missions recommended most urgently addressing the concomitant pressures of local population growth, agricultural expansion and overgrazing, as well as growing tourism congestion and development, particularly in Ngorongoro Crater (UNESCO 2007). Notably, both the government and the Tanzanian media have widely noted the importance of addressing these UNESCO concerns in order to maintain the NCA's World Heritage site status. However, public discussion in Tanzania has focused almost exclusively on the perceived problem of local communities' impacts through population growth, agricultural expansion and livestock grazing, with virtually no discussion of other prioritised recommendations such as tourism impacts, infrastructure development and financial management factors.

More recently a series of additional controversies around WHSs in Tanzania has emerged, highlighting the tensions between local, national and global interests in the management of tourism and wider natural resource use concerns in Tanzania. The greatest attention has been focused on the proposal by the government to build a major trunk road across the northern section of Serengeti National Park to connect Lake Victoria to Arusha. The road has received criticism from scientists as potentially endangering wildebeest migration and thus of the main natural spectacle that drives lucrative tourism earnings in Serengeti National Park and provides the basis for the World Heritage site designation. Opposition to the road has been spearheaded by international tourism interests (see Serengeti Watch n.d.) as well as ecologists and conservation organisations such as the Frankfurt Zoological Society.

The controversy over the Serengeti road, and perhaps the degree of criticism surrounding the proposal to build a road across one of the world's most famous natural reserves, has been accompanied by Tanzanian President Jakaya Kikwete's decision in early 2011 to have the country withdraw its application for World Heritage site status for the Eastern Arc Mountains, a range of exceptional biodiversity and species endemism. This application was in process for 14 years and perceptions are that it was withdrawn largely due to international controversy around the Serengeti road, as along with mining and hydroelectricity generation in the Selous Game Reserve (also a World Heritage site) and soda ash mining at the Lake Natron Ramsar Site (Hance 2011).

While in Ngorongoro, the main enduring conflict is between local development and economic interests and state control over tourism revenues derived from wildlife. In these other sites the emerging tensions all revolve primarily around Tanzania's ability to strike a balance between the global stewardship responsibilities of World Heritage site designations and around the economic values that World Heritage site status conveys through tourism promotion and marketing, with additional industrial development interests at these sites. Tanzania effectively wants to have its cake and eat it too, but it is not clear if the country's leadership is willing to enforce the rigorous environmental planning and mitigation tools that would be required to strike such a balance, or to firmly determine when certain industrial developments are incompatible with nature conservation, tourism and environmental stewardship. Tourism is a US$1 billion per year industry and one of the most important economic activities in the country, but it is also unclear if Tanzanian policymakers recognise the trade-offs involved with tourism in terms of needing to protect the natural assets that tourism relies upon, including the symbolic imagery of inviolate wilderness in areas such as Serengeti. The degree to which Tanzania is able to find more effective policy and administrative tools for balancing local, national and global (especially global touristic) interests in its unique natural heritage will determine the future course of its tourism industry and its global heritage in general.

Case study 3: Kilimanjaro National Park: local economic benefits but with environmental and social costs[1]

Mount Kilimanjaro is designated as a World Heritage site because of both its character as the highest free-standing mountain mass in the world and as a habitat for rare, endangered and endemic plants and animals (UNESCO 2000). Visitor numbers to the mountain has been increasing rapidly, and it is estimated that 35,000 to 40,000 tourists attempt to climb Mount Kilimanjaro each year (of whom 98 per cent are non-residents, see Mitchell, Keane and Laidlaw 2009: 4). Visitors also tend to stay in Kilimanjaro National Park for longer periods than other protected areas in the country because of the time it takes to acclimatise to and climb the mountain safely (five to ten days). This results in its position as the second-highest earner of all Tanzania's National Parks (Mitchell, Keane and Laidlaw 2009: 3) after the Serengeti. Climbing 'Kili' has become increasingly urgent for hikers who want to reach its peak before global climate change melts all of the permanent snow.

As a result of Kilimanjaro's growing popularity and visitor numbers, there have been a number of management problems on the mountain including:

- Congestion of people;
- Inadequate response to client rescue problems;
- Poor quality of food provided by some tour operators;

- Poor guiding and interpretation;
- Inadequate water supply at higher elevations;
- Use of undesignated trails and camp sites; and
- Litter.

(TANAPA 2006)

The park-management plan aims to address these problems and to maintain the routes in good condition for year-round visitor use and access. In relation to guides and porters, the Kilimanjaro Code of Conduct states that licensed guides must lead every climbing group and that porters are permitted to carry a maximum of 25 kilogrammes, including their own luggage (TANAPA 2006).

A typical climb package is sold by local tour operators for US$1,205. This is an all-inclusive arrangement and includes five days on the mountain with a night in a hotel before and after the climb (normally in the neighbouring towns of Moshi or Arusha). In addition to this package cost, tourists spend an average of US$171 of discretionary spending during the climb, which adds up to a total in-country spend of US$1,376 per tourist (Mitchell and Keane 2008).

Mount Kilimanjaro climbing staff receive an average annual income (including both wages and tips) of US$1,830 for guides, US$842 for porters, and US$771 for cooks. Porters' wages vary significantly between different tour operators and a survey of 2,507 interviews in 2009 by the Kilimanjaro Porters Assistance Project found very widespread abuses of porters' working conditions, with day rates varying from US$3.50 to $ 10.60 per day (KPAP n.d.; Mitchell, Keane and Laidlaw 2009).

There are two reasons that climbing staff capture such a large share of the benefits from tourism on Mount Kilimanjaro: visitor tips and the labour-intensive nature of climbing. First, tips from tourists to climbing staff are a very important supplement to the wages received from the tour operator, typically boosting climbing staff wages by over 50 per cent. Second, climbing Mount Kilimanjaro is extremely labour-intensive, with a typical group of 10 climbers supported by two guides, 40 porters and two cooks. It is estimated that 35,000 tourists each spending a week on the mountain generate jobs (albeit irregular and highly seasonal) for about 400 guides, 10,000 porters and 500 cooks. It is estimated that guides undertake 17 trips a year, and porters and cooks around 14 trips (Mitchell and Keane 2008).

The working conditions for porters can be arduous and dangerous. Up to 20 guides and porters die on Kilimanjaro every year – from altitude sickness, hypothermia and pneumonia brought on by inadequate equipment and the relentless, competitive pressure to keep working (Reid 2008). The Kilimanjaro Guides Association (KGA) and Kilimanjaro Porters Association (KPA) are 'home-grown' initiatives established as a form of self-regulation for porters. Currently around 7,000 porters are registered (out of an estimated total of 15,000), with most unregistered porters located in West Kilimanjaro (Mitchell and Keane 2008). One of the services offered by these associations is to represent aggrieved guides and porters who have been mistreated either by guides or tour operators (Mitchell and Keane 2008). Women find it difficult to work on the mountain (even if they are qualified guides) due to various reasons, including a sense of discomfort in the camps where there are no special provisions for women guides or porters. Despite this, there are some female porters (nine have registered with the KPA, of which two have subsequently become guides; see Mitchell and Keane 2008: 25).

There is a general management plan for the park, which includes zoning of developments and activities (e.g. from 'intensive use hiking zones' to 'wilderness zones'). The plan does not allow hikers to gather firewood on the mountain and requires that they remove all of their rubbish (UNESCO 2000). Seven major categories of environmental problems in the Kilimanjaro Region have nonetheless been identified. These problems include:

- Land degradation (including trail erosion);
- Inadequate water supply;
- Pollution;
- Habitat fragmentation and loss of biodiversity;
- Deforestation;
- Illegal grazing and poaching; and
- Frequent forest fires.

(KECMTF n.d.: para. 6; UNESCO 2000)

In 2001, trail erosion and firewood collection were the main negative environmental impacts of Kilimanjaro hiking trails (Newmark and Nguye 2001). At that time, trail erosion was most serious in areas of higher rainfall, where the slopes are steepest and where there are few water breaks. Firewood collection had also been problematic, with porters forced to collect wood up to four kilometres from the Horombo hut because of reduced local availability in that area. Now all firewood collection is prohibited in the park.

By contrast to the Richtersveld case, tourism in Kilimanjaro is struggling to manage the environmental impacts of large volumes of tourists in a sensitive ecosystem and to simultaneously provide a high quality of experience to visitors. They also require mechanisms to maximise the local economic impacts of hiking, in such a way that the working conditions for labourers can be safe and healthy.

Discussion

Africa is presently entering a period of intensifying pressures over land use which will shape its peoples and landscapes in fundamental and irreversible ways. In the past several years, surging demand for commodities, food and land itself has led to tens of millions of hectares of land being acquired for agriculture, forestry, biofuels and other land-based investments (*The Economist* 2011). The rapid growth of tourism during the past several decades in many African countries has also increased external interests in lands and resources and led to intensifying competition between local, national and global interests over local communities' resources.

Tourism thus plays a complex role in the future of African landscapes, national economies and local communities, including in particular at many iconic WHSs. For these areas to have their natural and cultural elements effectively conserved, tourism revenue is often the main actual or potential source required to sustain management. At emerging or relatively lesser-known WHSs, such as the Richtersveld, the development of environmentally and socially responsible tourism ventures will be vital to the long-term stewardship of the site and its resources. Across the continent, many examples exist where the recent growth of tourism has provided critical resources and incentives for effective conservation measures. Twenty years ago, Tanzania's Serengeti National Park depended heavily on the international community for its management, but today, after 20 years of tourism growth in Tanzania, the Serengeti earns more than US$25 million annually from tourism-derived fees and is amply able to fund its own management costs.

However, with growth in tourism comes environmental impact that is more challenging to manage, particularly in the relatively weak regulatory and institutional setting that characterises most African nations. Here also comes the potential for the types of conflicts over land rights, revenue capture and livelihoods that have long caused tensions in Ngorongoro.

Ultimately the future of Africa's WHSs will depend on the ability of stakeholders and interest groups to share benefits and costs, rights and responsibilities more equitably, and to devise creative ways of balancing environmental stewardship, tourism and wider economic development interests. In the African context, a major part of this will be vesting local people with more secure rights over lands and resources. Here locally owned WHSs such as the Richtersveld, or the Twyflfontein petroglyphs in neighbouring Namibia, provide a useful model of such 'decentralised' global heritage. In countries such as Tanzania, escalating tensions between local people and ruling regimes must be negotiated in ways that enhance local democracy and stakes in shared resources. International bodies such as UNESCO may need to strengthen their oversight and ability to assess underlying causes for management problems, to react quickly to proposed or actual changes in management at WHSs and to engage multiple stakeholders in brokering resolutions to conflicts.

This chapter demonstrates that communities face difficulties in the management of heritage and the tourism that is based on it. These difficulties include balancing the array of stakeholder interests and negotiating of power relations inherent in the making and management of any WHS. In new tourism destinations, such as the Richtersveld, people are attempting to balance the conservation of traditional pastoral practices, the conservation of rich biodiversity and the generation of income through the little-understood tourism sector. At Kilimanjaro the challenges relate to how to manage an increasing level of tourism visitation and to ensure that this does not undermine the ecological integrity of the mountain. For the Ngorongoro Crater, there are complexities relating to the power of and benefits generated by government and local communities.

The new 'guide to good practice' for natural WHSs recognises that 'at its best tourism can provide an outstanding opportunity to increase the understanding of natural and cultural heritage as envisaged by the World Heritage Convention, whilst providing long-term financial support to site management, local communities and tourism providers. But poorly managed tourism or excessive visitor numbers at a site can pose major threats to Outstanding Universal Value and degrade the quality of the visitor experience' (Stolton and Dudley 2010: 55). With technical support, political will and processes of tourism management that are inclusive of stakeholders, there is potential for destinations such as the Richtersveld, Ngorongoro Crater and Kilimanjaro to be sustainably managed heritage sites. Without such an approach it is unlikely that visitors will be able to engage effectively with these resources and in a way that satisfies the long-term economic interests of the communities concerned.

Note

1   This case study has been adapted from a World Bank Case Study by Anna Spenceley in the *Review of Nature-based and Cultural-Heritage Tourism Interventions and Best Practices in sub-Saharan Africa* series (2010)

References

African World Heritage Fund (n.d.) 'About us', *African World Heritage Fund Web.* Available online: www.awhf.net/index.php?option=com_content&view=article&id=19&Itemid=27&lang=en (accessed 13 June 2012).

Arusha Times, The (2010) 'MPs take issue with Maasai presence in NCA', 6 March. Available online: http://allafrica.com/stories/201003080846.html (accessed 6 March 2010).

Bonner, R. (1993) *At the Hand of Man: Peril and Hope for Africa's Wildlife*, London: Simon & Schuster.

Economist (2011) 'When others are grabbing their land', 5 May. Available online: www.economist.com/node/18648855 (accessed 13 June 2012).

Ellis, J., Lynn, S., Mworia, J., Kinyamario, J., Burn Silver, S., Maskini, M.S., Kidunda, R., Reid, R.S., Rainy, M., Mwilawa, A.J. and Runyoro, V.A. (2001) 'Ecosystem interactions: implications for human welfare and wildlife conservation', in R.B. Boone and M.B. Coughenour (eds) *A System for Integrated Management and Assessment of East African Pastoral Lands: Balancing Food Security, Wildlife Conservation, and Ecosystem Integrity*, Final report to the Global Livestock Collaborative Research Support Program, Fort Collins, CC: University of California, Davis.

Hammer, J. (2010) 'Last days of the Maasai?', *Condé Nast Traveler*, November. Available online: www.concierge.com/cntraveler/articles/503114 (accessed 13 June 2012).

Hance, J. (2011) 'Conservation issues in Tanzania', Mongabay.com, 9 June. Available online: http://news.mongabay.com/2011/0602-atbc_tanzania.html (accessed 9 June 2011).

Hesse, C. and MacGregor, J. (2006) *Pastoralism: Drylands' Invisible Asset? Developing a Framework for Assessing the Value of Pastoralism in East Africa*, Drylands Issue Paper No. 142, London: International Institute for Environment and Development.

Homewood, K. and Rogers W.A. (1987) 'Pastoralism, conservation and the overgrazing controversy', in D. Anderson and R. Grove (eds) *Conservation in Africa: People, Policies and Practice*, Cambridge: Cambridge University Press.

Homewood, K.M. and Rodgers, W.A. (1991) *Maasailand Ecology: Pastoralist Development and Wildlife Conservation in Ngorongoro, Tanzania*, Cambridge: Cambridge University Press.

Honey, M. (2008) *Ecotourism and Sustainable Development: Who Owns Paradise?* 2nd edn, Washington, DC: Island Press.

Jenkins, M. (2010) *The UNESCO World Heritage Tourism Program: Draft final report: Evaluation and Future Directions*. Brasilia: UNESCO. Available online: http://whc.unesco.org/archive/2010/whc10-34com-inf5F3.pdf (accessed 13 June 2012).

Kelsall, T. (2002) 'Shop windows and smoke-filled rooms: governance and the repoliticisation of Tanzania', *Journal of Modern African Studies* 40(4): 597–619.

Kilimanjaro Environmental Conservation Management Trust Fund (KECMTF) (n.d.) 'Introduction', KECMTF Web. Available online: www.kilimanjarotrust.org/ (accessed 19 October 2010).

Kilimanjaro Porters Assistance Project (KPAP) (n.d.) 'What we've found', KPAP Web. Available online: www.kiliporters.org/what_weve_found.php (accessed 19 October 2010).

Mitchell, J. and Keane, J. (2008) Tracing the tourism dollar in Northern Tanzania, Final report, Overseas Development Institute, 15 December 2009. Available online: www.odi.org.uk/work/projects/details.asp?id=901&title=tracing-tourism-dollar-northern-tanzania (accessed 13 June 2012).

Mitchell, J., Keane, J, and Laidlaw, J. (2009) *Making Success Work for the Poor: Package Tourism In Northern Tanzania*, Arusha and London: Overseas Development Institute and SNV. Available online: www.odi.org.uk/resources/docs/4203.pdf (accessed 13 June 2012).

Newmark, W.D. and Nguye, P.A. (2001) 'Recreational impacts of tourism along the

Marangu route in Kilimanjaro National Park', in W.D. Newmark (ed.) *The Conservation of Mount Kilimanjaro*, Gland and Cambridge: IUCN.

Ole Parkipuny, M.S. (1979) 'Some crucial aspects of the Maasai predicament', in A. Coulson (ed.) *African Socialism in Practice: The Tanzanian Experience*, Nottingham: Spokesman.

Reid, M. (2008) 'Scandal of the Kilimanjaro sherpas', *The Times* 26 May. Available online: www.almendron.com/tribuna/scandal-of-the-kilimanjaro-sherpas/ (accessed 19 October 2010).

Richtersveld Community Conservancy (RCC) (2007) *A Wanderer's Guide to the Richtersveld*, Cape Town, South Africa: RCC and EcoAfrica.

Runyoro, V.A., Hofer, H., Chausi, E.B. and Moehlman, P.D. (1995) 'Long-term trends in the herbivore populations of the Ngorongoro Crater, Tanzania', in A.R.E. Sinclair and P. Arcese (eds) *Serengeti II: Dynamics, Management, and Conservation of an Ecosystem*, Chicago, IL: University of Chicago Press.

Serengeti Watch (n.d.) *Serengeti Watch Web*. Available online: www.savethe-serengeti.org/#axzz1y3fU8g00 (accessed 13 June 2012).

Shivji, I.G. and Kapinga, W.B. (1998) *Maasai Rights in Ngorongoro, Tanzania*, London: IIED/HAKIARDHI.

Spenceley, A. and Rylance, A. (2008) *Feasibility of Conservation based Economic Opportunities in the Richtersveld World Heritage site: Including proposals for an Ecotourism Competitive Strategy, an Implementation Plan and a Performance Monitoring and Impact Assessment System*, South Africa: Richtersveld Company for Sustainable Development

Stolton, S. and Dudley, N. (2010) *Managing Natural World Heritage sites: A Guide to Good Practice*, Geneva, Swizerland: ICUN.

Tanzania National Parks (TANAPA) (2006) *Kilimanjaro National Park General Management Plan*, Arusha: Planning Unit, Tanzania National Park.

UNESCO (2000) *Convention Concerning the Protection of World Cultural and Natural Heritage: Periodic Reporting of the African Sites Inscribed on the World Heritage List*. Available online: http://whc.unesco.org/en/list/403/documents/ (accessed 19 October 2010).

UNESCO (2007) *Ngorongoro Conservation Area (United Republic of Tanzania): Report of the Reactive Monitoring Mission, 19 April to 5 May 2007*, Paris: UNESCO. Available online: http://whc.unesco.org/archive/2007/mis39-may2007.pdf (accessed 13 June 2012.

UNESCO (2011) 'World Heritage in Danger', *UNESCO Web*. Available online: http://whc.unesco.org/en/158/ (accessed 13 June 2012).

Chapter 14

Clustering industrial heritage tourists

Motivations for visiting a mining site

Alfonso Vargas-Sánchez, Nuria Porras-Bueno and María de los Ángeles Plaza-Mejía

Introduction

Heritage is, for many countries, a vital element and a major factor in attracting overseas visitors. Opportunities to develop heritage for tourism purposes have been enthusiastically embraced in recent years and heritage is increasingly recognised as a distinctive sector in the tourism industry (Cossons 1989). This chapter focuses on a particular kind of heritage, industrial (specifically, mining) heritage, which is viewed as having substantial weight in the construction and maintenance of a national or local identity (Palmer 1999; Ruiz-Ballesteros and Hernández-Ramírez 2007).

Relics of the past

Industrial heritage is a feature of the many regions of Europe that led the industrial revolution specialising in textile, iron and steel and other basic industries. Since the 1960s these regions have been in decline and have faced the need to restructure their economy. The relics of past activities – the industrial heritage remaining in place – have thus constituted, or may in the near future constitute, a resource for a very different kind of economic development: tourism. The preservation and opening up of all kinds of heritage resources for visitors also serves as a powerful force in the construction and maintenance of a national or local identity (Palmer 1999; Ruiz-Ballesteros and Hernández-Ramírez 2007). Industrial heritage tourism – and mining tourism in particular – is no exception.

Industrial heritage tourism does, however, face two main problems, each of which has claimed the attention of researchers in this field. The first is the relationship between tourism and heritage management. Several authors have published studies aimed at promoting the development of collaborative attitudes between the managers of heritage sites and tourism (Aas, Ladkin and Fletcher 2005; du Cros 2001; McKercher, Ho and du Cros 2005; Prideaux 2002; Prideaux and Kininmont 1999; Xie 2006). These studies have identified and confirmed the relevance of shifting the management focus away from merely conserving the heritage resources (although this task in itself is often complex and difficult) towards interpreting and presenting them, and actively exploiting them as tourist attractions (Cossons 1989; Moscardo 1996).

The second problem lies in the definition of the term 'heritage tourism'. The diversity of approaches has led to two lines of study. In one, the phenomenon of heritage tourism is considered from the perspective of the historical attributes of a site or attraction (Garrod and Fyall 2001). The other line focuses on the 'customers', the people who engage in this kind of tourist activity. Hence, heritage tourism can be studied as a phenomenon based on the motivations and perceptions of tourists, actual and potential. It is defined as a subgroup of tourism in which the main motivation for visiting a site is interest in the place's heritage and historical/cultural context and characteristics, according to the tourists' perceptions of the significance and value of that heritage (Poria, Butler and Airey 2001, 2003). Analysis of other variables – particularly the behaviour that follows the tourist's perception of this heritage (Poria, Butler and Airey 2003) – forms part of this approach. This chapter takes up this subject matter as its main point of interest.

As Poria, Butler and Airey (2003) point out, few studies have explored the relationship between the demand perspective and the core of site attributes. In this regard, the studies of Apostolakis (2003) and Beeho and Prentice (1997) are particularly relevant. Furthermore, already in 1996 the 'Future for Heritage Tourism' conference (organised by the Royal Geographical Society in London) emphasised the need for heritage providers to focus more directly on the consumer and, in particular, on understanding visitors' needs, motivations, experiences and benefits gained. This approach is stated to be the essential way forwards for heritage tourism (Frochot and Beeho 1997).

Given the importance to heritage tourism research of understanding the motivations for a tourist's visit (Poria, Reichel and Biran 2006), and given the lack of publications relating to motivational segmentation in industrial heritage tourism – and especially in mining sites – this study aims to delineate existing markets using a factor-cluster analysis. The research reported here consists of an analysis of heritage tourism from the demand viewpoint, using empirical research focused on the tourists visiting the mining attractions in Minas de Rio Tinto.

Minas de Rio Tinto is in a small locality in the province of Huelva, Spain, whose existence has for many centuries depended on mining activity, which is now in decline. Tourism is in the very early phase of development and this study forms part of wider research on industrial tourism in this province. The empirical research discussed in this chapter is centred on the locality of Minas de Rio Tinto specifically, and it takes into account the perspectives of tourists and residents, complemented with the views of a panel of experts constituted for this purpose. The research is primarily aimed at determining the characteristics of tourists to the area, and offers up analyses based on their motivations, socio-demographic profiles and levels of satisfaction with the visit. The focus of the work presented here is the segmentation of visitors based on motivation, and one object of this study is to establish possible differences between these segments based on demographic and psychographic variables and levels of satisfaction expressed by visitors. Several other research studies have focused on this specific segment of industrial tourism (Andreadakis and Davis 1998; Caravelis and Ivy 2001; Clarke *et al.* 2001; Conesa, Schulin and Nowack 2008; Pretes 2002; Ruiz-Ballesteros and Hernández-Ramírez 2007; Wanhill 2000), but the objectives of these studies differ from those proposed here. An added value of this study is its longitudinal character, involving visitor surveys conducted on two occasions in 2006 and 2008. It therefore offers an opportunity to monitor the evolution of the site as a tourist attraction and to provide a firm empirical foundation for its findings.

Propensity to visit heritage

Very little is known about individuals who visit heritage or cultural sites and the heritage tourist has been given a number of possibly more descriptive names: 'creative tourist' (Richards and Wilson 2006), 'legacy tourist' (McCain and Ray 2003) or 'authentic tourist' (Yeoman, Brass and McMahon-Beattie 2007). As such they have been characterised as better educated, with a higher average annual income; they travel more often in couples or large groups, are twice as likely to take group tours, but do not necessarily plan their trips in advance; they spend significantly more time on a visit than general travellers, tend to travel quite a distance to visit sites and spend almost three days in the area of the site; pleasure and fun are secondary to learning, since they travel to increase their knowledge of people, places and things, and to experience a sense of nostalgia for the past; they are motivated more by the desire for heritage experiences (to soak up the atmosphere and ambience of a site) than by interest in details of factual history (Confer and Kerstetter 2000; Wickens 2002).

Several authors have tried to classify or segment tourists of this type and attention has centred on the experiences and benefits obtained from the visit (Prentice, Witt and Hamer 1998), on the type of tourist attraction visited (Kerstetter, Confer and Bricker 1998) and on their degree of specialisation (Kerstetter, Confer and Graefe 2001), among other variables. Clearly, to be able to make realistic assessments of demand, attention must be given not only to the number of tourists but also to variations in their characteristics and perceptions (Glasson *et al.* 1994; Hernández López and Cáceres Hernández 2005).

Whilst there seems to be little evidence of major changes in heritage tourists' socio-demographic profiles, there do seem to be significant changes in travel behaviour and in the variables that predict the likelihood of an individual visiting heritage sites, suggesting that progress has been made in the notion of specialisation (Confer and Kerstetter 1996). Thus it may well be possible to associate the definition of the 'heritage tourist' (Poria, Butler and Airey 2003) with greater degrees of specialisation, as could be deduced from the motivations attributed to this type of tourist: they are more likely to be motivated to 'learn about historical periods or events', they want to 'experience authentic elements in a historic destination', they 'consider the site's historic character in their decision to visit', they 'visit because they have an interest in their own heritage, culture, and/or ethnicity' and they also 'visit other historic sites' (Kerstetter, Confer and Graefe 2001).

Who are heritage tourists?

The literature on tourist segmentation demonstrates the diverse criteria adopted by different authors. These include: the type of tourist (Carmichael and Smith 2004; Gallarza and Gil-Saura 2006; Keng and Cheng 1999; Shoemaker 1989; Weaver and Lawton 2002), typology of the tourism sector (Mooney and Penn 1985; Schroeder 1973; Swinyard and Struman 1986; Thomson and Pearce 1980), the benefits obtained (Calantone and Johar 1984), tourists' dining preferences (Yüksel and Yüksel 2002), motivation (Bieger and Laesser 2002), activity (Mehmetoglu 2007), value dimensions, perceived value, satisfaction and loyalty (Gallarza and Gil-Saura 2006), choice of holidays, types of activities and views of the host community (Wickens 2002), in-state residents, domestic and international (Bonn, Joseph and Dai 2005) and experiences and benefits (Prentice, Witt and Hamer 1998).

The consensus in these studies is that cultural tourists are identified as a minority segment that normally accounts for a very small proportion of the total number of visitors to cultural destinations. The cultural tourist proper is a visitor especially interested in the culture and heritage attributes of the destination, who has a high level of previous knowledge and who enjoys very rich experiences, thus responding to the image of the romantic visitor (Galí and Donaire 2006). Researchers on the sub-segment of heritage tourism have also shown an interest in determining the profile of these tourists. Heritage tourists are a heterogeneous group (Poria, Reichel and Biran 2006) and the typical visitor experience at the heritage site is complex and multifaceted, comprising many different elements, not only nostalgia (Caton and Almeida-Santos 2007). The Appendix offers a compilation of the main contributions in the literature, specifically focused on the type of segmentation applied to heritage tourists.

Motivations

The tourist's motivation or purpose is one of the variables that have attracted most interest among researchers on tourism (Snepenger *et al.* 2006). Motivational factors have been identified as more effective criteria for segmentation than, for example, the socio-demographic variables (Bieger and Laesser 2002; Chang 2006). Motivational factors best represent the personal psychological components that are likely to be satisfied through tourism activities (Formica and Uysal 1998). The most obvious classification of cultural tourists is made based on whether their cultural motivations are primary or secondary (McKercher 2002; Galí and Donaire 2006). When researchers rely only on demographic characteristics, the findings have proven to be so self-evident that the data are of little benefit for explaining or predicting behavioural tendencies (Chandler and Costello 2002; Johns and Gyimóthy 2002; Keng and Cheng 1999; Light 1996).

For Poria, Butler and Airey (2003), motivation is a critical variable when defining the concept of the heritage tourist. Those who perceive a site as a part of their own personal heritage are the basis of the phenomenon called 'heritage tourism' (group 4 in Table 14.1) and are distinguished from 'tourists at heritage places' (groups 1, 2 and 3 in Table 14.1) by their behaviour. Therefore, this type of tourism should not include those who are visiting a place just because it is there or those who are primarily motivated by a desire to learn (Poria, Butler and Airey 2003).

Table 14.1 Segmentation of tourists visiting a heritage site (Poria, Butler and Airey 2003)

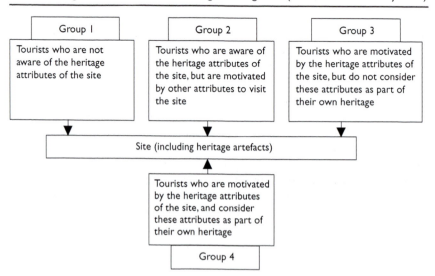

Poria, Butler and Airey (2004) classify the reasons for visiting heritage sites in three groups: 'heritage experience', 'learning experience' and 'recreational experience'. The segment called 'recreational experience' includes those reasons that do not relate to the content of the material presented, such as the desire to have a day out, the cost of entrance, the desire to be entertained, wanting to see a world-famous site and the desire to relax. The 'heritage experience' group is characterised by a *desire* to be involved in the heritage experience. The 'learning experience' segment is made up by those with reasons that are linked to the site being a historic one, which people are visiting to observe and learn about.

Poria, Reichel and Biran (2006) identify three specific categories of motivations: willingness to feel connected to the history presented, willingness to learn and motivations not linked with the historic attributes of the destination. Formica and Uysal (1998) identify six groups of motives: socialisation and entertainment, event attraction and excitement, group togetherness, cultural/historical, family togetherness and site novelty. McCain and Ray (2003) identify the following motivations: visiting historic sites; enjoying wilderness and undisturbed nature, being in the mountains and visiting friends and relatives, in addition to visiting the place where their family is from. Turning to more specific locales, Prentice and Andersen (2007) found four groups of motives in tourists visiting a pre-industrial urban heritage museum: for the enjoyment of being taken back in time and as somewhere to visit while in the area, for understanding how people used to live, for understanding better the country's heritage and for understanding more fully what it is to be from this country or for understanding better the visitor's family history.

Rio Tinto Mining Park, Huelva, Spain

Based on the discussion above, the objective of the present study was to gain a deeper understanding of the typology of visitors who consume tourism products associated with mining industry heritage and to define the profiles of these visitors in relation to the motivations they present. The Rio Tinto Mining Park (see Figure 14.1) offers a tourism package comprising several elements: the Mining Museum, a typical house ($N^{\underline{o}}$ 21) in the residential estate where the English mining engineers and managers formerly lived, the 'Peña del Hierro' and a trip on the mining railway. This latter item is the principal attraction for the tourists and, is generally the last point or activity on the 'circuit' of the visit.

The significance of this example of Huelva's industrial archaeology is demonstrated in its third placing in the national ranking of visitable places with a mining heritage. It is surpassed in the annual number of visits only by the caves of El Soplao in Cantabria and the Museum of Mining in Asturias, among the approximately 100 sites of this type that exist in Spain

Figure 14.1 The Rio Tinto Mining Park
    Photo: Emilio Romero

(*EuropaPress* n.d.). Another example of its relevance is the fact that the Rio
Tinto Mining Museum is the provincial museum that receives the most
visits each year. Specifically, according to data provided by the Rio Tinto
Foundation, the Rio Tinto Mining Park had 69,387 visits in 2010 (Zalamea
Noticias 2011) – a figure that is around ten times that recorded in 1992, the
year when it opened its doors. The trend of increasing numbers of visits
each year over this period has only slowed slightly in the past two years as a
consequence of the economic crisis and poor weather conditions (for the
complete evolution of visitor numbers see Cañizares Ruiz 2011). More than
half of the visitors to the Mining Park each year are individual tourists, not
organised groups. The more significant among the latter are school parties
(15 per cent) and groups organised by travel agencies (13 per cent; see
Zalamea Noticias 2011). Based on data for the year 2008, some 15 per cent
of visitors are foreigners (Huelva Información 2009). Considering the
temporal distribution of all tourists, the months of spring and summer are
when most visits are made, together with the main long holiday weekends
in autumn. Logically, the seasonality of demand means that most visits to
the Park are made at weekends rather than during the week.

In our case, the time periods selected for conducting the surveys were the months of March and April in 2006 (weekends and the Easter week) and the months of July and August in 2008. We believe that this difference in survey period between the two years does not introduce any significant distortion of results of the study, considering that, generally, the visits are distributed fairly homogeneously in these periods.

According to the totality of visitors that the Park received in both periods, the optimum size of the sample is slightly fewer than 400 persons. (More particularly, taking as the reference value the 78,683 visits of 2008, the optimum sampling size would be 383, for a level of confidence of 95 per cent, a margin of error of 5 per cent and population variance of 50 per cent.) However, the number of observations obtained exceeds that number (407 in 2006 and 400 in 2008), which reduces the respective margins of error. Random sampling was practised. The written questionnaire was provided to the tourist/visitor for completion during the Mining Railway trip and in all cases help was available from three survey personnel, previously trained to give assistance, support and clarification for understanding and answering the questions. The questionnaire was structured into sections:

- Socio-demographic profile (gender, age, occupational situation, final educational level reached);
- Type of tourist, according to the typology of Stanley Plog (1995);
- Interest in industrial tourism, with reference to a series of industrial activities present in the province of Huelva, available for tourists to visit;
- Knowledge of the destination/site (importance of the formal and informal channels of information about the locality of Minas de Rio Tinto and its Mining Park);
- Behavioural aspects, including: origin of the visitor; means of transport used to reach the site; the type of trip within which the visit is taking place; the type of establishment used for overnight accommodation; other persons with whom the trip is being made; other places included on the same trip; duration of the stay/trip; and average total daily expenditure and breakdown by item of this expenditure; and
- Motivational and attitudinal factors, such as: satisfaction with the Park and with the tourism offer of the locality (including whether or not the respondent would recommend the visit to others) and degree of loyalty (previous visits).

The 12 items outlined in Table 14.2 were used on both occasions to identify the extent to which the visitor to the Rio Tinto Mining Park appears to be motivated by emotion, by a desire to learn or by the search for entertainment, measured on a Likert scale of seven points.

Table 14.2 Questionnaire options regarding motivations for visits to Rio Tinto Mining
Park (March–April 2006; July–August 2008)

Motivation	Item
Emotional	Because I feel that I belong to this place
	Because it is part of my own heritage and history
	Because I want to feel emotionally involved
	Because I feel that I should visit the place
Learning	Because the site is a famous place
	Because I want to learn something about the world of mining
	Because of the historical context of the locality
	Because of the physical nature of the place
Entertainment	Because I feel like spending a day out
	Because I wanted some entertainment
	Because it would be relaxing
	Because it would be an experience of something different

The questionnaire was designed in accordance with the structure utilised in previous studies published by various authors. Data analysis provided reliability of scales, principal components analysis, cluster analysis, discriminant analysis and analysis of difference of means. Reliability of the scales was achieved through the Cronbach's alpha parameter and produced the values outlined in Table 14.3.

Table 14.3 Reliability of scales of analysis for motivations for visits to Rio Tinto Mining
Park (March–April 2006; July–August 2008)

Scale	2006	2008
Emotional reasons	0.825[a]	0.826[b]
Learning reasons	0.798[c]	0.864
Entertainment reasons	0.825	0.845

a 0.882 if the item 'Because I feel that I should visit the place' is eliminated.
b 0.860 if the item 'Because I feel that I should visit the place' is eliminated.
c 0.849 if the item 'Because the site is a famous place' is eliminated.

Although respective levels of internal consistency were acceptable, it was decided to eliminate the item 'Because I feel that I should visit the place', which in previous studies loaded on two components: 'Heritage/Emotional Experience' and 'Cultural/Educational Experience' (Poria, Butler and Airey 2004). This elimination left the scale corresponding to the emotional motivations reduced to three items.

The next step was to perform a principal components analysis with the items of the questionnaire (11 after the previous re-specification) utilised to measure the motivations of the visitors to the Mining Park. In this it was confirmed that the motivations were grouped correctly in three factors, corresponding to the three kinds of reason postulated (Kaiser method – eigenvalues larger than 1 – and Varimax rotation). Tables 14.4 and 14.5 demonstrate this conclusion.

Table 14.4 Test prior to performing the principal components analysis of motivations for visits to Rio Tinto Mining Park (March–April 2006; July–August 2008)

Test		2006	2008
Determining matrix of correlations		0.004	0.001
Kaiser-Meyer-Olkin measure of sampling adequacy		0.795	0.849
Bartlett sphericity test	approximate Chi-squared	1887.092	2134.532
	df	66	66
	Sig.	0.000	0.000

Table 14.5 Matrix of rotated components of analysis of motivations for visits to Rio Tinto Mining Park (March–April 2006; July–August 2008)

Item	2006*			2008**		
	F1	F2	F3	F1	F2	F3
Because I feel that I belong to this place	0.161	0.096	**0.873**	0.072	0.132	**0.896**
Because it is part of my own heritage and history	0.206	0.114	**0.851**	0.066	0.136	**0.912**
Because I want to feel emotionally involved	0.268	0.082	**0.859**	0.299	0.168	**0.790**
Because the site is a famous place	**0.563**	0.106	0.158	**0.755**	0.258	0.217
Because I want to learn something about the world of mining	**0.888**	0.045	0.194	**0.792**	0.130	0.112
Because of the historical context of the locality	**0.819**	0.024	0.220	**0.871**	0.214	0.148
Because of the physical characteristics of the place	**0.819**	0.060	0.103	**0.848**	0.107	0.027
Because I feel like spending a day out	−0.002	**0.738**	0.068	0.074	**0.747**	0.114
Because I wanted some entertainment	0.009	**0.890**	0.084	0.128	**0.880**	0.119
Because it would be relaxing	0.027	**0.880**	0.076	0.209	**0.831**	0.198
Because it would be an experience of something different	0.276	**0.705**	0.086	0.327	**0.758**	0.081

F1: Learning. F2: Entertainment. F3: Emotional.
*Total variance explained: 69.895%;
**Total variance explained: 74.207%

The mean values obtained for each indicator are outlined in Table 14.6.

Table 14.6 Mean values of the indicators of motivations for visits to Rio Tinto Mining Park (March–April 2006; July–August 2008)

Motivation	Item	Mean 2006	Mean 2008
Emotional	Because I feel that I belong to this place	2.71	1.71
	Because it is part of my own heritage and history	3.45	1.89
	Because I want to feel emotionally involved	3.17	2.12
	Mean	3.11	1.91
Learning	Because the site is a famous place	4.08	3.44
	Because I want to learn something about the world of mining	5.26	4.08
	Because of the historical context of the locality	5.12	3.99
	Because of the physical characteristics of the place	5.52	4.32
	Mean	4.99	3.96
Entertainment	Because I feel like spending a day out	3.41	3.15
	Because I wanted some entertainment	3.38	2.81
	Because it would be relaxing	3.55	2.74
	Because it would be an experience of something different	4.60	3.44
	Mean	3.73	3.03

The analysis suggests, therefore, that the desire to learn is, in general, the predominant motivation, with the physical nature of the place being the most attractive attribute, followed by the desire to know more about the world of mining. In all cases, this interest in learning appears to result from the curiosity of the layman rather than from any desire for deeper knowledge by the more erudite visitor, a finding that is corroborated by the low degree of existing personal knowledge about the world of mining and its history reported by the average visitor. We can, therefore, identify two principal motivational factors of different kinds: a 'push' factor or motive associated with culture or learning, of intrinsic character, that would arouse in the individual visitor the desire to make the trip in order to satisfy this kind of need, and, secondly; a 'pull', factor or motive, extrinsic and related to the attributes of the site, that strongly conditions the choice of the specific site to visit (Dann 1977; Gnoth 1997; Jang and Wu 2006; Pearce 1996).

Another striking aspect is the decrease apparent between 2006 and 2008 in the intensity with which every one of the motivations proffered in the survey is recognised by respondents (i.e. each of the motivations is given a notably lower average score). We believe that this is not a true fall-off in interest or enthusiasm over this period, rather it seems to be a reflection of differences in the types of tourist who visit the Park in spring and in summer – a difference that is revealed in Table 14.7.

Table 14.7 Profiles of visitors to Rio Tinto Mining Park (March–April 2006; July–August 2008)

Characteristics	March–April 2006	July–August 2008
University-level education	54%	37%
Originating from Andalusia	70%	50%
Day-trippers	66%	35%
Average duration of the trip	3.1 days	9.7 days
Average daily expenditure	€64	€42
Visit made on the recommendation of friends and family	60%	30%

In effect, the profile of the person who visited the Mining Park in the spring of 2006 matches that of a cultural tourist (Richards 2004) – with higher educational levels, who lives fairly locally or within the same region as the site, staying for a short period of time, with a high average daily expenditure and influenced by the recommendation of friends and family who are the principal source of knowledge of the site. However, the person who visited in the summer of 2008 matches more closely the profile of the 'beach and sunshine' tourist, but one who wishes to experience the Mining Park as a complement to their stay on the coast – a person of average educational level, more likely to live further afield in other parts of Spain, staying for a longer period of time and with a lower average daily expenditure.

However, having performed a hierarchical cluster analysis (using the method of Ward and the Euclidean distance squared as measure of dissimilarity), four clusters were identified from the three blocks of motivations expressed, each cluster having the average values displayed in Table 14.8.

On the basis of this analysis, we can state that the motivational pattern of those who visit the Mining Park is fairly consistent, as is demonstrated in Table 14.9.

The first group is that of the visitors who come motivated purely by a desire for learning, the second is that of the visitors who come seeking both learning and entertainment and the third is that of those who come

Table 14.8 Profile of visitors to Rio Tinto Mining Park (March–April 2006; July–August 2008), according to cluster analysis

2006 Motivation (means)	Cluster 1	Cluster 2	Cluster 3	Cluster 4
Emotional	1.7063	1.9780	4.7486	2.5484
Learning	5.5893	4.8297	5.8955	3.6048
Entertainment	5.3452	1.9808	4.3545	3.9570

2008 Motivation (means)	Cluster 1	Cluster 2	Cluster 3	Cluster 4
Emotional	3.8590	1.5706	1.2985	1.7892
Learning	4.3413	5.4322	2.3619	5.1912
Entertainment	3.9615	4.7966	2.2780	2.1654

Table 14.9 Predominant motivations for visitors to Rio Tinto Mining Park (March–April 2006; July–August 2008)

Predominant motivation	2006* % of valid cases	2008** % of valid cases
Learning	26.1	21.7
Learning plus Entertainment	12.1	18.8
Learning plus Emotional	**35.1**	16.6
No clearly defined motivation	26.7	**42.8**

* After performing the corresponding discriminant analysis, 86.5% of the original grouped cases are found to be correctly classified.

** After performing the corresponding discriminant analysis, 92.3% of the original grouped cases are found to be correctly classified.

motivated mainly by a desire for learning, combined with an emotional motivation (but also with the desire for entertainment). This last cluster was found to be the most numerous in the research conducted in 2006, whereas in 2008 the most numerous cluster was that which expressed no clearly defined motivation.

The result that particularly draws the attention is the decline of the emotional component in favour of the circumstantial – that is, the absence of a clearly defined motivation. The explanation for this may again be found in the differences in socio-demographic and behaviour profiles between the tourists who visit the Park in spring and summer. This would therefore seem to be an aspect that merits more detailed investigation, although logically one would expect that on average the strength of a visitor's previous emotional link would be diluted to the extent that more of the visitors come from more distant places. Clearly the management of the site needs to devote efforts towards generating that emotion through the experiences offered during the visit.

To appreciate the existence of statistically significant differences between the clusters, the variables 'gender', 'age', 'final educational level reached' and the rating given to the experience (the visit to the Mining Park) have been analysed. Having used the Kolmogorov-Smirnov test to confirm that these variables are not distributed according to the normal law, the non-parametric test of Kruskal Wallis was applied for four independent samples. The following results were obtained, for a level of significance of 0.05. In both cases there are significant differences only in respect of the variable of the rating given to the experience (measured on a scale from 1 to 10), as reflected in Table 14.10.

Table 14.10 Levels of satisfaction of visitors to Rio Tinto Mining Park (March–April 2006; July–August 2008), by clusters

2006 Experience	Cluster 1	Cluster 2	Cluster 3	Cluster 4
Behaviour	**Learning plus Entertainment**	**Learning**	Learning plus Emotion	Not clearly defined
Mean	**8.32**	**7.65**	8.12	7.78

2008 Experience	Cluster 1	Cluster 2	Cluster 3	Cluster 4
Behaviour	Learning plus Emotion	**Learning plus Entertainment**	**Not clearly defined**	Learning only
Mean	8.13	**8.19**	**7.20**	8.07

In 2006, it can be seen that those stating that their motivation is purely that of learning show the lowest levels of satisfaction. By contrast, those seeking a combination of learning and entertainment are the most satisfied with the experience, although this group is the least numerous. In 2008 the highest satisfaction rating is again given by those seeking both learning and entertainment. By contrast, the cluster of visitors with no clearly defined motivation (the most numerous) is the group that on average rates their visit to the Mining Park with the lowest satisfaction score.

These results give support to the hypothesis that the motivation of the visitor conditions their degree of satisfaction with the visit. In future research it would be interesting to break down that rating of the trip by items, with the object of analysing whether the motivation of the visitor can condition the assessment of those aspects of the visit or destination most intimately associated with the motive for the trip, as suggested by studies made in other segments such as rural tourism (Devesa, Laguna and Palacios 2010).

Conclusion

The existence has been verified of three kinds of motivation (emotional, desire for learning and desire for entertainment); however, these can form various combinations to give rise to archetypes of behaviour in visitors, since 'the same individual may be interested in several simultaneous experiences' (Poria, Biran and Reichel 2009; Poria, Butler and Airey 2004). Those archetypes have been found to be the same in the two periods of time analysed (spring 2006 and summer 2008), which confirms their consistency. Specifically, these motivations are: learning, learning plus entertainment, learning plus emotion and those with no well-defined motivation. The strongest motivations are, in general, those of learning – in particular, about the physical nature of the site and about the world of mining. This finding corroborates the result studies of previous centred on heritage tourism (Poria, Reichel and Biran 2006) and on cultural tourism in general (Falk and Dierking 2000). In its current configuration, the Rio Tinto Mining Park satisfies, above all, those who are seeking a combination of learning and entertainment in their visit. This is a group that, although not the most numerous, has increased its relative weight over this period of time.

The emotional reasons seem to have become weaker, on average, whereas the proportion of visitors without a well-defined motivation has increased. From the detailed analysis of this phenomenon, these findings present a new challenge that the managers of the Park should recognise and accept. As suggested in the literature, particularly when the object is to attract more visitors and increase revenue, it is necessary to customise the experience provided to visitors of heritage sites, rather than to provide only one predictable and standardised experience because visitors to heritage sites are now active and curious and expect the interpretation to provide specific knowledge and to reinforce their own cultural identity (Poria, Biran and Reichel 2009).

References

Aas, C., Ladkin, A. and Fletcher, J. (2005) 'Stakeholder collaboration and heritage management', *Annals of Tourism Research* 32(1): 28–48.

Andreadakis, M. and Davis, J.A. (1998) 'Industrial heritage tourism at the Bingham Canyon copper mine', *Journal of Travel Research* 36(3): 85–9.

Apostolakis, A. (2003) 'The convergence process in heritage tourism', *Annals of Tourism Research* 30(4): 795–812.

Beeho, A. and Prentice, R. (1997) 'Conceptualizing the experiences of heritage tourists: a case study of New Lanark World Heritage village', *Tourism Management* 8(2): 75–87.

Bieger, T. and Laesser, C. (2002) 'Market segmentation by motivation: the case of Switzerland', *Journal of Travel Research* 41(1): 68–76.

Bonn, M.A., Joseph, S.M. and Dai, M. (2005) 'International versus domestic visitors: an examination of destination image perceptions' *Journal of Travel Research* 43(3): 294–301.

Brown, T.J. (1999) 'Antecedents of culturally significant tourist behaviour', *Annals of Tourism Research* 26(3): 676–700.

Calantone, R. and Johar, J. (1984) 'Seasonal segmentation of the tourism market using a benefit segmentation framework', *Journal of Travel Research* 23(2): 14–24.

Cañizares Ruiz, M.C. (2011) 'Protección y Defensa del Patrimonio Minero en España', *Scripta Nova (Revista electrónica de Geografía y Ciencias Sociales) XV (361)*. Available online: www.ub.edu/geocrit/sn/sn-361.htm (accessed 13 June 2012).

Caravelis, M. and Ivy, R. (2001) 'From mining community to seasonal visitor destination: the transformation of Sotiras, Thasos, Greece', *European Planning Studies* 9(2): 187–199.

Carmichael, B. and Smith, W. (2004) 'Canadian domestic travel behavior: a market segmentation of rural shoppers', *Journal of Vacation Marketing* 10(4): 333–47.

Caton, K. and Almeida-Santos, C. (2007) 'Heritage tourism on Route 66: deconstructing nostalgia', *Journal of Travel Research* 45(4): 371–86.

Chandler, J.A. and Costello, C.A. (2002) 'A profile of visitors at heritage tourism destinations in East Tennessee according to Plog's Lifestyle and Activity Level Preferences Model', *Journal of Travel Research* 41(2): 161–66.

Chang, J. (2006) 'Segmenting tourists to Aboriginal cultural festivals: an example in the Rukai Tribal Area, Taiwan', *Tourism Management* 27(6): 1224–34.

Clarke, J., Denman, R., Hickman, G. and Slovak, J. (2001) 'Rural tourism in Roznava Okres: a Slovak case study', *Tourism Management* 22(2): 193–202.

Conesa, H.M., Schulin, R. and Nowack, B. (2008) 'Mining landscape: a cultural tourist opportunity or an environmental problem? The case of the Cartagena-La Unión Mining District', *Ecological Economics* 64(4): 690–700.

Confer, J. and Kerstetter, D. (1996) *Pennsylvania's Path of Progress Heritage Route 1995. Visitor Profile Study Follow-up Report: Determining Target Markets for the Path of Progress Heritage Route*, University Park, PA: Pennsylvania State University, School of Hotel, Restaurant and Recreation Management.

Confer, J. and Kerstetter, D. (2000) 'Past perfect: explorations of heritage tourism', *Parks & Recreation* 35(2): 28–33.

Cossons, N. (1989) 'Heritage tourism: trends and tribulations', *Tourism Management* 10(3): 192–4.

Dann, G.M.S. (1977) 'Anomie, ego-enhancement and tourism', *Annals of Tourism Research* 4(4): 184–94.

Devesa, M., Laguna, M. and Palacios, A. (2010) 'The role of motivation in visitor satisfaction: empirical evidence in rural tourism', *Tourism Management* 31(4): 547–52.

du Cros, H. (2001) 'A new model to assist in planning for sustainable cultural heritage tourism', *International Journal of Tourism Research* 3(2): 165–70.

EuropaPress (n.d.) 'El Parque Minero de Riotinto bate su récord histórico y recibe

73.900 visitas en 2007', Huelva. Available online: www.europapress.es/00354/
20080111141403/huelva-parque-minero-riotinto-bate-record-historico-recibe-
73900-visitas-2007.html (accessed 11 January 2008).

Falk, J. and Dierking, L. (2000) *Learning from Museums*, Walnut Creek CA: Altamira.

Formica, S. and Uysal, M. (1998) 'Market segmentation of an international-cultural
historical event in Italy', *Journal of Travel Research* 36(4): 16–24.

Frochot, I. and Beeho, A. (1997) 'Conference report: the future for heritage
tourism', *Progress in Tourism and Hospitality Research* 3(3): 271–2.

Galí, N. and Donaire, J.A. (2006) 'Visitors' behaviour in heritage cities: the case of
Girona', *Journal of Travel Research* 44(4): 442–8.

Gallarza, M. and Gil-Saura, I. (2006) 'Value dimensions, perceived value, satisfaction and loyalty: an investigation of university students' travel behaviour', *Tourism
Management* 27(3): 437–52.

Garrod, B. and Fyall, A. (2001) 'Heritage tourism: a question of definition', *Annals
of Tourism Research* 28(4): 1049–52.

Glasson, J., Godfrey, K. and Goodall, B., van der Borg, J. and Absalom, H. (1994)
'Visitor management in heritage cities', *Tourism Management* 15(5): 388–9.

Gnoth, J. (1997) 'Tourism motivation and expectations formation', *Annals of
Tourism Research* 21(2): 283–304.

Hernández López, M. and Cáceres Hernández, J.J. (2005) 'Forecasting tourists'
characteristics by a generic algorithm with a transition matrix', *Tourism
Management* 28(1): 290–7.

Huelva Información (2009) *El Parque Minero De Riotinto Recibió el Pasado Año Casi
80.000 Visitas*, 10 January, Huelva.

Jang, S. and Wu, C.M.E. (2006) 'Seniors' travel motivation and the influential
factors: an examination of Taiwanese seniors', *Tourism Management* 27(2):
306–16.

Johns, N. and Gyimóthy, S. (2002) 'Market segmentation and the prediction of
tourist behaviour: the case of Bornholm, Denmark', *Journal of Travel Research*
40(3): 316–27.

Keng, K. and Cheng, J. (1999) 'Determining tourist role typologies: an exploratory
study of Singapore vacationers', *Journal of Travel Research* 37(4): 382–90.

Kerstetter, D., Confer, J. and Bricker, K. (1998) 'Industrial heritage attractions: types
and tourists', *Journal of Travel and Tourism Marketing* 7(2): 91–104.

Kerstetter, D., Confer, J. and Graefe, A. (2001) 'An exploration of the specialization
concept within the context of heritage tourism', *Journal of Travel Research* 39(3):
267–74.

Kim, H., Cheng, C. and O'Leary J.T. (2007) 'Understanding participation patterns
and trends in tourism cultural attractions', *Tourism Management* 28(5): 1366–71.

Light, D. (1996) 'Characteristics of the audience for 'festivals' at a heritage sites',
Tourism Management 17(3): 183–90.

McCain, G. and Ray, N.M. (2003) 'Legacy tourism: the search for personal meaning
in heritage travel', *Tourism Management* 24(6): 713–17.

McKercher, B. (2002) 'Toward a classification of cultural tourists', *International
Journal of Tourism Research* 4(1): 29–38.

McKercher, B., Ho, P. and du Cros, H. (2005) 'Relationship between tourism and
cultural heritage management: evidence from Hong Kong', *Tourism Management*
26(4): 539–48.

Mehmetoglu, M. and Olsen, K. (2007) 'From cultural consumer at home to heritage tourist away', *Advances in Hospitality and Leisure*, 3: 19–37.

Mooney, S. and Penn, J. (1986) 'Market segmentation in hotels: a move up-market with the 'club' concept', *International Journal of Hospitality Management* 4(2): 63–4.

Moscardo, G. (1996) 'Mindful visitors: heritage and tourism', *Annals of Tourism Research* 23(2): 376–97.

Palmer, C. (1999) 'Tourism and the symbols of identity', *Tourism Management* 20(3): 313–21.

Pearce, P.L. (1996) 'Recent research in tourists' behaviour', *Asia Pacific Journal of Tourism Research* 1(1): 7–17.

Plog, C.S. (1995) *Vacation Places Rated*, Redondo Beach CA: Fielding Worldwide.

Poria, Y., Biran, A. and Reichel, A. (2009) 'Visitors' preferences for interpretation at heritage sites', *Journal of Travel Research* 48(1): 92–105.

Poria, Y., Butler, R. and Airey, D. (2001) 'Clarifying heritage tourism', *Annals of Tourism Research* 28(4): 1047–9.

Poria, Y., Butler, R. and Airey, D. (2003) 'The core of heritage tourism', *Annals of Tourism Research* 30(1): 238–54.

Poria, Y., Butler, R. and Airey, D. (2004) 'Links between tourists, heritage and reasons for visiting heritage sites', *Journal of Travel Research* 43(1): 19–28.

Poria, Y., Reichel, A. and Biran, A. (2006) 'Heritage site management: motivations and expectations', *Annals of Tourism Research* 33(1): 162–78.

Prentice, R. and Andersen, V. (2007) 'Interpreting heritage essentialisms: familiarity and felt history', *Tourism Management* 28(3): 661–76.

Prentice, R.C., Witt, S.F. and Hamer, C. (1998) 'Tourism as experience: the case of heritage parks', *Annals of Tourism Research* 25(1): 1–24.

Pretes, M. (2002) 'Touring mines and mining tourists', *Annals of Tourism Research* 29(2): 439–56.

Prideaux, B. (2002) 'Creating rural heritage visitor attractions – The Queensland Heritage Trails Project', *International Journal of Tourism Research* 4(4): 313–23.

Prideaux, B. and Kininmont, L. (1999) 'Tourism and heritage are not strangers: a study of opportunities for rural heritage museums to maximize tourism visitation', *Journal of Travel Research* 37(3): 299–303.

Richards, G. (2004) *¿Nuevos Caminos para el Turismo Cultural?*, Barcelona: Association for Tourism and Leisure Education (ATLAS), Observatorio Interarts.

Richards, G. and Wilson, J. (2006) 'Developing creativity in tourist experiences: a solution to the serial reproduction of culture?', *Tourism Management* 27(6): 1209–23.

Ruiz-Ballesteros, E. and Hernández-Ramírez, M. (2007) 'Identity and community: reflections on the development of mining heritage tourism in southern Spain', *Tourism Management* 28(3): 677–87.

Schroeder, D. (1973) 'Usable market segmentation for recreation businesses', *Journal of Travel Research* 12(1): 15.

Shoemaker, S. (1989) 'Segmentation of the senior pleasure travel market', *Journal of Travel Research* 27(3): 14–21.

Snepenger, D., King, J., Marshall, E. and Uysal, M. (2006) 'Modeling Iso-Ahola's Motivation Theory in the tourism context', *Journal of Travel Research* 45(2): 140–9.

Swinyard, R.W. and Struman, D.K. (1986) 'Market segmentation, finding the heart of your restaurant's market', *The Cornell Hotel and Restaurant Administration Quarterly* 27(1): 89–96.

Taylor, D., Fletcher, R. and Clabaugh, T. (1993) 'A comparison of characteristics, regional expenditures, and economic impact of visitors to historical sites with other recreational visitors', *Journal of Travel Research* 32(1): 30–5.

Thomson, C. and Pearce, D. (1980) 'Market segmentation of New Zealand package tours', *Journal of Travel Research* 19(2): 3–6.

Timothy, D.J. (1997) 'Tourism and the personal heritage experience', *Annals of Tourism Research* 24(3): 751–4.

Wanhill, S. (2000) 'A tourist attraction: coal mining in industrial South Wales', *Journal of Travel Research* 39(1): 60–9.

Weaver, D. and Lawton, L. (2002) 'Overnight ecotourist market segmentation in the Gold Coast Hinterland of Australia', *Journal of Travel Research* 40(3): 270–80.

Wickens, E. (2002) 'The sacred and the profane: a tourist typology', *Annals of Tourism Research* 29(3): 834–51.

Xie, P.F. (2006) 'Developing industrial heritage tourism: a case study of the proposed jeep museum in Toledo (Ohio)', *Tourism Management* 27(6): 1321–30.

Yeoman, I., Brass, D. and McMahon-Beattie, U. (2007) 'Current issue in tourism: the authentic tourist', *Tourism Management* 28: 1128–38.

Yüksel, A. and Yüksel F. (2002) 'Market segmentation based on tourists' dining preferences', *Journal of Hospitality & Tourism Research* 26(4): 315–31.

Zalamea Noticias (2011) 'El Parque Minero de Riotinto Recibe 69.387 Visitantes en 2010', *Redacción ZN*. Available online: http://zalameanoticias.wordpress.com/2011/01/15/el-parque-minero-de-riotinto-recibe-69-387-visitantes-en-2010/ (accessed 21 January 2011).

Appendix

Table 14.11 Academic literature specifically focused on the type of segmentation applied to heritage tourists

Publication	Place	Resource	Focus	Segmentation variables	Other variables	Segments identified
Timothy (1997)	n/a	n/a	n/a	Tourism experience or degree of personal attachment to the site visited	n/a	4 segments: world heritage experience; national heritage experience; local heritage experience; personal heritage experience
Taylor, Fletcher and Clabaugh (1993)	4 counties in north-central Wyoming (US)	Bighorn National Forest, Bozeman Trail and others	Natural and historic sites	Visit or not to historical sites	Trip and demographic characteristics	2 segments: visitor to historical sites; other recreational visitors
Light (1996)	South Wales (UK)	Caerphilly Castle	Special event (historical re-enactments)	Visit on the day of a specific event, or on a non-event day	Socio-demographic, characteristics of the visit (including reasons for the visit), visitor 'behaviour, benefits and satisfaction with the visit experience	2 segments: visitors on event days; visitors on non-event days
Formica and Uysal (1998)	Italy	Spoleto Festival	Musical-cultural international events	Motivations and preferences	Demographic characteristics	2 clusters: moderates; enthusiasts
Prentice, Witt and Hamer (1998)	South Wales (UK)	Ronda Heritage Park	Mining attractions	Experiences and benefits gained	Socio-economic profile, motivations	5 clusters

Table 14.11 continued

Publication	Place	Resource	Focus	Segmentation variables	Other variables	Segments identified
Brown (1999)	Central Australia	Uluru (Ayers Rock)	Indigenous heritage site	Gender and climbing behaviour	Climbing belief strength, evaluation of outcomes, attitude (expectancy–value formulation)	2 segments: climbers; non-climbers
Kersetter, Confer and Graefe (2001)	Pennsylvania (US)	500-mile Path Of Progress National Heritage Tour Route	Industrial places	Specialisation index	Socio-demographic characteristics, visitation behaviour, motivations and/or perceptions	3 segments: high specialists; medium specialists; low specialists
Chandler and Costello (2002)	East Tennessee (US)	Sequoyah Birthplace Museum, Historic Rugby, Blount Mansion, Rocky Mount Living History Museum, Andrew Johnson National Historic Site, Historic Jonesborough	Significance of historic places	Lifestyle preferences and activity level preferences (Plog's model)	Demographic characteristics	6 segments: active venturers; active centrics; active dependables; mellow venturers; mellow centrics; mellow dependables

Table 14.11 continued

Table 14.11 continued

Table 14.11 continued

Table 14.11 continued

Table 14.11 continued

Table 14.11 continued

Table 14.11 continued

Table 14.11 continued

Table 14.11 continued

Table 14.11 continued

Table 14.11 continued

Table 14.11 continued

Table 14.11 continued

Table 14.11 continued

Table 14.11 continued

Table 14.11 continued

Table 14.11 continued

Table 14.11 continued

Table 14.11 continued

Table 14.11 continued

Table 14.11 continued

Table 14.11 continued

Table 14.11 continued

Table 14.11 continued

Table 14.11 continued

Table 14.11 continued

Table 14.11 continued

Table 14.11 continued

Table 14.11 continued

Table 14.11 continued

Table 14.11 continued

Table 14.11 continued

Table 14.11 continued

Table 14.11 continued

Table 14.11 continued

Table 14.11 continued

Publication	Place	Resource	Focus	Segmentation variables	Other variables	Segments identified
Johns and Gyimóthy (2002)	Denmark	Danish Island of Bornholm	Cultural/ historic attractions and unique local arts and crafts	Total amenity, activity and attractions scores	Country of origin, age, gender, planning, autonomy, activity importance, amenity usage, attraction visits	2 segments: 'active' vacationers; 'inactive' vacationers
Poria, Butler and Airey (2003)	Israel	The Wailing Wall	Religious and historic places	Perception of the site in relation to their own heritage	Motivations, behaviour during the visit, perception of the visit, potential behaviour (satisfaction)	2 segments: the site is part of their own heritage; the site is not part of their own heritage
Poria, Butler and Airey (2004)	Israel	The Wailing Wall and Masada	Religious and historic places	Motivations	Perceptions of the sites in relation to their own heritage and their willingness to be exposed to an emotional experience	3 segments: heritage/emotional experience; learning history; recreational experience
Chang (2006)	Taiwan	Rukai Cultural Festival	Aboriginal cultural Festival	Motivations	Demographics	3 segments: aboriginal cultural learner; change routine life travellers; active culture explores
Galí and Donaire (2006)	Girona (Spain)	Old quarter in the city of Girona	Urban space	Behaviour	Socio-demographic, characteristics of the visit itself, environmental factors	4 segments: non-cultural tourists; ritual tourists; interested tourists; erudite tourists

Table 14.11 continued

Publication	Place	Resource	Focus	Segmentation variables	Other variables	Segments identified
Poria, Reichel and Biran (2006)	Amsterdam (Holland)	Anne Frank House	Historic place	Perceptions of the site in relation to tourists' own heritage	Motivations before the visit take place, expected effects on the experience, onsite interpretation expectations	3 segments: the site is part of their own heritage; the site is not part of their own heritage; those who are in the middle
Kim, Cheng and O'Leary (2007)	United States	29 cultural attractions	Festival and musical attractions, commercial recreation parks, local festival and fairs, knowledge/aesthetic-seeking attractions	Type of cultural attractions	Socio-economic variables and the number of trips on cultural attraction participation	4 segments: visitors to festival and musical attractions; commercial recreation parks; local festival and fairs; knowledge/aesthetic-seeking attractions
Mehmetoglu and Olsen (2007)	Alta (Norway)	Alta Museum	Museum	Frequency of visitation	Reasons for visitation, leisure activities of the respondents, educational level, annual household, satisfaction level with the entrance fee to the museum, frequency of visit to museums when they are on holiday	3 segments: infrequent visitor; medium frequency visitor; frequent visitor
Prentice and Andersen (2007)	Denmark	Den Gamle By (The Old Town)	Pre-industrial museum	Motivations, experiences	Familiarity, nationality, heritage enthusiasm	2 segments: reiteratives; make-believers

Index

Adorno, Theodor 128
Adur district 120
affect 75–8, 158–9
Africa, heritage tourism in 251–71
African World Heritage Fund 254–5
agrarian rites 236
Ahmed, Sara 76
Aida 17
Airey, D. 241, 275, 278–9
Aitchison, C.C. 74
Alfriston 120
Aliens 90
Allcock, J.B. 74
Amoamo, M. 69
ancient Rome 85–7, 90–9, 109
Anderson, Benedict 67–8, 116
Anderson, V. 279
Ang Choulean 247
Angkor 17, 19, 176–81, 228–9;
    ceremonies at *fixed* and *unfixed* dates
    236–7, 242–3; Heritage
    Management Framework for 247;
    recent developments at 245–7; ritual
    practices at 233–5; tourism trends at
    239–40; villages within the World
    Heritage site 229–33
Aparicio Vega, M.J. 130
Apostolakis, A. 275
Ashfield district 121
Asian tourism 175–6, 179–84
Askins, K. 76, 108
Atacameño people, culture and
    'brand' 187–91, 199, 202–9
'attractor' concept in chaos theory
    56–7
Auerhahn, Annette 167
Aung-Thwin, Michael 179
'authenticity' 176, 181, 215, 217, 243–4

authorised heritage discourse (AHD)
    67–72, 76, 103, 105, 110–12, 116,
    122–3
authorised and *unauthorised*
    interpretations of heritage objects
    46–51, 55–7
Authority for the Protection and
    Management of Angkor and the
    Region of Siem Reap (APSARA)
    239, 245–7
Avatar 93
awareness-raising for tourists 241
Ayutthaya 17

Bærenholdt, J. 6, 9
Bak, S. 243
Bali 26–41, 182; massacre (1965–66)
    26–7
Balinese dance 243
Barthes, Roland 91
Bascopé, J. 202
Bateson, Gregory 38
Bauman, Zygmunt 49, 57
Beeho, A. 275
Beijing 17, 183
Belo, Jane 38
belonging, sense of 75–8
Ben Hur 90, 94
Bender, B. 143
Benjamin, Walter 92
Bennett, Jane 47–8, 51
Berlin *see* Memorial for the Murdered
    Jews of Europe
Bingham, Hiram 130
Biran, A. 279
Black, H. 244–5
Blade Runner 90
Blanco, H. 205